DATE DUE

APR 1 6 1978	
MAY 9 1983	
APR 2 9 1985	

{93D CONGRESS, 1ST SESSION . . HOUSE DOCUMENT NO. 93–131}

MEMORIAL SERVICES IN THE

CONGRESS OF THE UNITED STATES

AND TRIBUTES IN EULOGY OF

Harry S Truman

LATE A PRESIDENT OF THE

UNITED STATES

Compiled Under the Direction of the
Joint Committee on Printing

UNITED STATES GOVERNMENT PRINTING OFFICE

WASHINGTON : 1973

House Concurrent Resolution No. 110

(Mr. RANDALL submitted the following concurrent resolution)

IN THE HOUSE OF REPRESENTATIVES,
February 6, 1973.

Resolved by the House of Representatives (the Senate concurring), That there be printed with illustrations as a House document the eulogies and encomiums of the late President of the United States, Harry S Truman, as expressed in the House of Representatives and the Senate. Such publication to include the text of the funeral service held in Independence, Missouri, as well as the prayers and scriptural selections delivered at the memorial service on January 5, 1973, at the Washington Cathedral; and that thirty-two thousand five hundred additional copies shall be printed, of which twenty-two thousand one hundred and fifty shall be for the use of the House of Representatives and ten thousand three hundred and fifty shall be for the use of the Senate.

SEC. 2. The copy shall be prepared and bound in such style as the Joint Committee on Printing may direct.

A compilation of addresses and tributes as given in the United States Senate and House of Representatives plus such additional materials, including the texts of eulogies, messages, prayers, and scriptural selections delivered at the funeral services held in Independence, Mo., and in Washington, D.C., on the life, character, and public service of the late President Harry S Truman.

Harry S Truman

1884–1972

HARRY S TRUMAN, thirty-third President of the United States, was born in Lamar, Missouri, on May 8, 1884, the son of John Anderson and Martha Ellen (Young) Truman. In 1887 the Truman family moved to a farm near the present site of Grandview, Missouri, and in 1890 to Independence, Missouri, the county seat of Jackson County. He attended the Independence public schools, graduating from high school in 1901. After serving briefly as timekeeper for a railroad construction contractor, he obtained employment in nearby Kansas City, to which his family, including a younger brother and sister, had moved in 1902. He worked as a clerk at the National Bank of Commerce, and later as a bookkeeper at the Union National Bank. In 1906, at the age of 22, he returned to Grandview, where he spent the next ten years assisting his father in operating the family farm.

Mr. Truman joined the Missouri National Guard in 1905 and was discharged as a corporal in 1911. At the outbreak of World War I he helped organize the 2d Regiment of Missouri Field Artillery which was called into Federal service as the 129th Field Artillery. In France he was promoted to captain and given command of Battery D of that regiment, participating in the Vosges, Saint-Mihiel, and Meuse-Argonne campaigns. After the war he joined the reserves and was commissioned a major. He was promoted to colonel June 17, 1932.

On his return from overseas he married Bess Wallace, whom he had known since childhood, on June 28, 1919. Their only child, Mary Margaret, was born February 17, 1924. From 1919 to 1922 he ran a haberdashery shop in Kansas City with a war-time associate Eddie Jacobson. The firm failed as a result of the depression of 1921, but Mr. Truman refused to file a petition for bankruptcy and paid off his share of the firm's debts during the following 15 years.

In 1922, Mr. Truman, a Democrat, was elected one of the three judges of the Jackson County Court (an administrative rather than a judicial body), representing the eastern part of the county. He was defeated for reelection in 1924, but was elected presiding judge of the court in 1926, and reelected in 1930. In that position he had the chief responsibility for expending sixty million dollars in tax funds and bond issues in Jackson County, including Kansas City.

In 1934, Mr. Truman was elected to the United States Senate with a plurality of 262,000 votes. During his first term in the Senate he was chairman of a Senate subcommittee which wrote the Civil Aeronautics Act of 1938 and was one of the sponsors of the Transportation Act of 1940 (Wheeler-Lea-Truman Act). He was reelected to the Senate in 1940. In 1941 the Senate Special Committee to Investigate the National Defense Program (the Truman committee) was established at his suggestion. With him as chairman, it revealed waste and extravagance in the World War II defense program, saving the American taxpayers inestimable sums in defense production costs.

In July 1944, Mr. Truman was nominated as the vice-presidential candidate at the Democratic National Convention to run with Franklin D. Roosevelt. Elected in November, he served as Vice President only 83 days, succeeding to the Presidency April 12, 1945, on Roosevelt's death. His first year as President was marked by the dropping of the first atomic bomb and the end of World War II. Beginning in 1946 his administration was beset by reconversion problems at home and increasing difficulties with the Communist nations abroad. The 1946 victory of the Republicans in both Houses of Congress was interpreted as a repudiation of his policies, but after a hard-fought "whistle-stop" campaign, he was reelected to office on November 2, 1948. At the beginning of his second term he announced his "Fair Deal" program for promoting the general welfare of the people of the country and the "Point Four" program for technical assistance to underdeveloped nations abroad. When Communist forces invaded South Korea in June 1950, he ordered United States troops to resist the invaders in behalf of the United Nations. Two Puerto Rican Nationalists tried unsuccessfully to assassinate him in November 1950. In the fall of 1952 he gave full support to Governor Adlai Stevenson of Illinois, the Democratic Presidential Candidate.

After leaving the White House, the former President returned to Independence to devote his time to writing and lecturing. On July 6, 1957, the Harry S Truman Library in Independence, built with his encouragement and collaboration, was presented to the Federal Government, along with his personal papers and mementos. The Library is operated by the National Archives and Records Service of the General Services Administration as a research center and museum.

Mr. Truman died on December 26, 1972. He was buried in the courtyard of the Truman Library.

STATEMENT OF MILITARY SERVICE OF HARRY S TRUMAN, O 129 869

APPOINTMENTS AND PROMOTIONS

Grade	Appointment	Date of rank	Acceptance
Private, Missouri National Guard	June 14, 1905		
Honorably discharged June 13, 1911.			
First Lieutenant, Field Artillery, Missouri National Guard	June 17, 1917		June 22, 1917
Captain, Field Artillery, National Guard in the service of the United States	May 2, 1918	Apr. 23, 1918	May 2, 1918
Honorably discharged, May 6, 1919.			
Major, Field Artillery, Officers' Reserve Corps	Jan. 24, 1920	Jan. 10, 1920	Feb. 10, 1920
Reappointed	Jan. 10, 1925		Jan. 10, 1925
Lieutenant colonel, Field Artillery, Officers' Reserve Corps	May 27, 1925		June 6, 1925
Reappointed	May 27, 1930		May 27, 1930
Colonel, Field Artillery, Officers' Reserve Corps.	June 17, 1932		June 27, 1932
Reappointed	June 17, 1937		June 17, 1937
Transferred to Honorary Reserve and placed on the honorary retired list, Nov. 5, 1951.			
Colonel, Honorary, U.S. Army Reserve (indefinite term)	Sept. 29, 1952		Oct. 10, 1952
Placed on the Army of the United States retired list, Jan. 31, 1953.			

DUTY ASSIGNMENTS

He served as a Battery Officer with Battery "F", later Battery "D", 129th Field Artillery, at Camp Doniphan, Oklahoma, from August 1917 to March 1918 when he was placed on detached service with the Overseas Detachment, 35th Division. He attended a course of instruction at the Second Corps School, Montigny sur Aub, France, from April 20, 1918, to June 10, 1918, when he rejoined the 129th Field Artillery, 35th Division, American Expeditionary Forces in France. He was Adjutant, 129th Field Artillery, later Commanding Officer, Battery "D", 129th Field Artillery, American Expeditionary Forces in France from June 1918 to April 1919 when he returned to the United States and was honorably discharged on May 6, 1919. While a member of the Organized Reserve Corps he had ten (10) periods of active duty for training from July 1923 to August 1933. He was placed on the Army of the United States Retired List on January 31, 1953, under the provisions of Title III, Public Law 810, 80th Congress.

DECORATIONS AND AWARDS

He was authorized the World War I Victory Medal with two battle clasps for participation in the St. Mihiel and Meuse-Argonne Campaigns and the Armed Forces Reserve Medal with two 10-year devices:

ACTIVE SERVICE

Commissioned Officer:

From:

Aug. 5, 1917, to May 6, 1919.
July 16, 1923, to July 30, 1923.
July 5, 1925, to July 19, 1925.
July 5, 1926, to July 19, 1926.
July 10, 1927, to July 23, 1927.
July 9, 1928, to July 22, 1928.
July 7, 1929, to July 20, 1929.
July 20, 1930, to Aug. 2, 1930.
July 26, 1931, to Aug. 8, 1931.
July 10, 1932, to July 23, 1932.
Aug. 17, 1933, to Aug. 30, 1933.

By Authority of Wilber M. Brucker, Secretary of the Army:

HERBERT M. JONES,
Major General, USA,
The Adjutant General.

FUNERAL SERVICES FOR

Harry S Truman

1884–1972

FUNERAL SERVICES FOR
THE HONORABLE

HARRY S TRUMAN

1884–1972

THIRTY-THIRD PRESIDENT OF THE UNITED STATES OF AMERICA

THE HARRY S TRUMAN LIBRARY
INDEPENDENCE, MISSOURI

THURSDAY, DECEMBER 28, 1972
2:00 P.M.

THE MASONIC RITE
Grand Lodge of Missouri, A.F. & A.M.

THE ORDER FOR
THE BURIAL OF THE DEAD
Adapted from the Book of Common Prayer

IN THE AUDITORIUM

MASONIC SERVICE BY

W. HUGH McLAUGHLIN

GRAND MASTER OF THE LODGE

A.F. & A.M. OF MISSOURI

The Grand Lodge of Ancient, Free and Accepted Masons of the State of Missouri shares the grief and sorrow of Mrs. Truman, Mrs. Daniel and her family, Miss Mary Jane Truman and other family members in the loss of our beloved and cherished native son. This expression comes from the Grand Lodge offices and from more than 108,000 of his Masonic brothers in Missouri.

We express our gratitude to the family, to Father Lembcke, and to all other participants for the privilege of sharing in this service. We join, humbly and reverently, in paying lasting tribute to a great American and a renowned world statesman.

Masons are taught never to engage in any solemn, great or important undertaking without first invoking the aid and blessing of Diety. Shall we pray?

We hail you, Supreme Architect of the Universe. We come to you with spirits bowed low and ask the bounty of Thy Grace and mercy in our bereavement. May our deeds be such as to prepare us for entry into Your spiritual kingdom, that house not made with hands, eternal in the heavens. Amen!

President TRUMAN distinguished himself in many Masonic services, the most laudable of which was that of Grand Master of Masons of this State in 1940 and 1941. At that time he was also a member of the United States Senate. We express our gratitude to Mrs. Truman and Mrs. Daniel for sharing a portion of his exciting, magnificent life with us. He was our brother by adoption. He was our companion by choice.

The tenets of a Mason's profession are Brotherly Love, Relief and Truth. There abide with us Faith, Hope and Charity. The greatest of these is Charity for it extends through the boundless realms of eternity. Our notable brother exemplified Charity in a universal way when he directed relief to be administered, on an unprecedented scale, to alleviate human degradation in the aftermath of World War II.

The lambskin or white leathern apron is the badge of a Mason, more ancient than the Golden Fleece or Roman Eagle. It is white to admonish us to keep our personal lives pure. Our exalted brother wore it proudly and worthily.

The evergreen symbolizes a Mason's belief in immortality of the soul. It represents that vital spark of our spiritual life which shall never be quenched. President TRUMAN expressed that belief.

The Beehive is an emblem of a Mason's industry. By it we are taught to be workers in the great hive of nature. Even in his later years our distinguished and beloved citizen practiced that teaching. No more striking example than this great edifice, named for him, in which he performed his last labors, could conceivably be demonstrated to us today.

It is, therefore, fitting that we should assemble here to pay this deserved tribute. We, as Masons, extol his many virtues, not the least of which was his recognition of the high level of individual dignity. May we emulate him in his simple, sincere, sturdy and forthright conduct. May all our good intentions be crowned with success. May Brotherly Love prevail in all the earth and every moral and social virtue cement us.

SERVICE CONDUCTED BY

THE REVEREND CANON

JOHN H. LEMBCKE, JR.

RECTOR, TRINITY EPISCOPAL CHURCH

INDEPENDENCE, MISSOURI

The People rising, the Minister shall say,

I AM the resurrection and the life, saith the Lord; he that believeth in me, though he were dead, yet shall he live: and whosoever liveth and believeth in me, shall never die.

I know that my redeemer liveth, and that he shall stand at the latter day upon the earth: and though this body be destroyed, yet shall I see God: whom I shall see for myself, and mine eyes shall behold, and not as a stranger.

We brought nothing into this world, and it is certain we can carry nothing out. The Lord gave, and the Lord hath taken away; blessed be the name of the Lord.

Then shall the People say together with the Minister the Psalms following.

PSALM XXVII

THE Lord is my light and my salvation; whom then shall I fear? the Lord is the strength of my life; of whom then shall I be afraid?

One thing have I desired of the Lord, which I will require; even that I may dwell in the house of the Lord all the days of my life, to behold the fair beauty of the Lord, and to visit his temple.

For in the time of trouble he shall hide me in his tabernacle; yea, in the secret place of his dwelling shall he hide me, and set me up upon a rock of stone.

And now shall he lift up mine head above mine enemies round about me.

Therefore will I offer in his dwelling an oblation, with great gladness: I will sing and speak praises unto the Lord.

Hearken unto my voice, O Lord, when I cry unto thee; have mercy upon me, and hear me.

My heart hath talked of thee, seek ye my face; thy face, Lord, will I seek.

O hide not thou thy face from me, nor cast thy servant away in displeasure.

Thou hast been my succour; leave me not, neither forsake me, O God of my salvation.

I should utterly have fainted, but that I believe verily to see the goodness of the Lord in the land of the living.

O tarry thou the Lord's leisure; be strong, and he shall comfort thine heart; and put thou thy trust in the Lord.

PSALM XLVI

GOD IS our hope and strength, a very present help in trouble.

Therefore will we not fear, though the earth be moved, and though the hills be carried into the midst of the sea;

Though the waters thereof rage and swell, and though the mountains shake at the tempest of the same.

There is a river, the streams whereof make glad the city of God; the holy place of the tabernacle of the Most Highest.

God is in the midst of her, therefore shall she not be removed; God shall help her, and that right early.

Be still then, and know that I am God: I will be exalted among the nations, and I will be exalted in the earth.

The Lord of hosts is with us; the God of Jacob is our refuge.

Glory be to the Father, and to the Son, and to the Holy Ghost;

As it was in the beginning, is now, and ever shall be, world without end. *Amen.*

The People being seated, the Minister shall read the Lesson following.

I CORINTHIANS XV. 20

NOW IS Christ risen from the dead, and become the firstfruits of them that slept. For since by man came death, by man came also

xix

the resurrection of the dead. For as in Adam all die, even so in Christ shall all be made alive. But every man in his own order: Christ the firstfruits; afterward they that are Christ's at his coming. Then cometh the end, when he shall have delivered up the kingdom to God, even the Father; when he shall have put down all rule and all authority and power. For he must reign, till he hath put all enemies under his feet. The last enemy that shall be destroyed is death. For he hath put all things under his feet. But when he saith all things are put under him, it is manifest that he is excepted which did put all things under him. And when all things shall be subdued unto him, then shall the Son also himself be subject unto him that put all things under him, that God may be all in all.

But some man will say, How are the dead raised up? and with what body do they come? Thou foolish one, that which thou sowest is not quickened, except it die: and that which thou sowest, thou sowest not that body that shall be, but bare grain, it may chance of wheat, or of some other grain: but God giveth it a body as it hath pleased him, and to every seed its own body. All flesh is not the same flesh: but there is one kind of flesh of men, another flesh of beasts, another of fishes, and another of birds. There are also celestial bodies, and bodies terrestrial: but the glory of the celestial is one, and the glory of the terrestrial is another. There is one glory of the sun, and another glory of the moon, and another glory of the stars: for one star differeth from another star in glory. So also is the resurrection of the dead. It is sown in corruption; it is raised in incorruption: it is sown in dishonour; it is raised in glory: it is sown in weakness, it is raised in power: it is sown a natural body; it is raised a spiritual body. There is a natural body, and there is a spiritual body. And so it is written, The first man Adam was made a living soul; the last Adam was made a quickening spirit. Howbeit that was not first which is spiritual, but that which is natural; and afterward that which is spiritual. The first man is of the earth, earthy: the second man is the Lord from heaven. As is the earthy, such are they also that are earthy: and as is the heavenly, such are they also that are heavenly. And as we have borne the image of the earthy, we shall also bear the image of the heavenly.

Now this I say, brethren, that flesh and blood cannot inherit the kingdom of God; neither doth corruption inherit incorruption. Behold, I shew you a mystery; We shall not all sleep, but we shall all be changed, in a moment, in the twinkling of an eye, at the last trump: for the trumpet shall sound, and the dead shall be raised incorruptible, and we shall be changed. For this corruptible must put on incorruption, and this mortal must put on immortality. So when this corruptible shall have put on incorruption, and this mortal shall have put on immortality, then shall be brought to pass the saying that is written. Death is swallowed up in victory. O death, where is thy sting? O grave, where is thy victory? The sting of death is sin; and the strength of sin is the law. But thanks be to God, which giveth us the victory through our Lord Jesus Christ. Therefore, my beloved brethren, be ye stedfast, unmoveable, always abounding in the work of the Lord, forasmuch as ye know that your labour is not in vain in the Lord.

Then shall the Minister and the People together say the Apostles' Creed, all standing.

I BELIEVE in God the Father Almighty; Maker of heaven and earth:

And in Jesus Christ his only Son our Lord: Who was conceived by the Holy Ghost, Born of the Virgin Mary: Suffered under Pontius Pilate, Was crucified, dead, and buried: He descended into hell; The third day he rose again from the dead: He ascended into heaven, And sitteth on the right hand of God the Father Almighty: From thence he shall come to judge the quick and the dead.

I believe in the Holy Ghost: The holy Catholic Church: The Communion of Saints: The Forgiveness of sins: The Resurrection of the body: And the Life everlasting. *Amen.*

The People still standing, the Minister appointed shall say the prayers following, first pronouncing,

The Lord be with you.
Answer. And with thy spirit.
Let us pray.

O GOD, whose mercies cannot be numbered; Accept our prayers on behalf of the soul of thy servant departed, and grant him an entrance into the land of light and joy, in the fellowship of thy saints; through Jesus Christ our Lord. *Amen.*

ALMIGHTY GOD, with whom do live the spirits of those who depart hence in the Lord, and with whom the souls of the faithful, after they are delivered from the burden of the flesh, are in joy and felicity; We give thee hearty thanks for the good examples of all those thy servants, who, having finished their course in faith, do now rest from their labours. And we beseech thee, that we, with all those who are departed in the true faith of thy holy Name, may have our perfect consummation and bliss, both in body and soul, in thy eternal and everlasting glory; through Jesus Christ our Lord. *Amen.*

REMEMBER, O LORD, thy servant Harry, according to the favour which thou bearest unto thy people, and grant that, increasing in knowledge and love of thee, he may go from strength to strength, in the life of perfect service, in thy heavenly kingdom; through Jesus Christ our Lord, who liveth and reigneth with thee and the Holy Ghost ever, one God, world without end. *Amen.*

A Prayer for The President of the United States, and all in Civil Authority

ALMIGHTY GOD, whose kingdom is everlasting and power infinite; Have mercy upon this whole land; and so rule the hearts of thy servants THE PRESIDENT OF THE UNITED STATES, *The Governor of this State,* and all others in authority, that they, knowing whose ministers they are, may above all things seek thy honour and glory; and that we and all the People, duly considering whose authority they bear, may faithfully and obediently honour them, according to thy blessed Word and ordinance; through Jesus Christ our Lord, who with thee and the Holy Ghost liveth and reigneth ever, one God, world without end. *Amen.*

Then the Priest shall let the people depart with this Blessing.

UNTO GOD'S gracious mercy and protection we commit you. The Lord bless you and keep you. The Lord make his face to shine upon you, and be gracious unto you. The Lord lift up his countenance upon you, and give you peace, both now and evermore. *Amen.*

Reverend HAROLD M. HUNT
Pastor, First Baptist Church
Independence, Missouri

Eternal God, Our Father, we come to Thee because Thou has been our habitation in all generations.

During this time of loss and grief, may we find renewed in the hopes we cherish, the faith to which we desperately cling, love that will not let us go.

We lift our thanks to Thee for the inspiring light in national leadership President Truman furnished all of us in the time of trouble and crises during and after World War II.

We are grateful that with foresight and faith in a period fraught with danger to our Nation and the world, his decisions were courageous and wise.

Establish Thou the work, his hands, yea the work of his hands, establish Thou it.

He truly served his generation and now belongs to the ages.

As Thy children, we all pray for Thy comfort, but especially we would pray that Thou would be near his wife and daughter, sister and grandchildren.

Come now, Dear Lord, to chase away the shadows and light anew our walk with Thee. Come, and bear us up with healing on Thy wings.

AT THE GRAVE

When they come to the Grave, while the body is made ready to be laid into the earth, the Minister shall say,

MAN, that is born of a woman, hath but a short time to live, and is full of misery. He cometh up, and is cut down, like a flower; he fleeth as it were a shadow, and never continueth in one stay.

In the midst of life we are in death; of whom may we seek for succour, but of thee, O Lord, who for our sins art justly displeased?

Yet, O Lord God most holy, O Lord most mighty, O holy and most merciful Saviour, deliver us not into the bitter pains of eternal death.

Thou knowest, Lord, the secrets of our hearts; shut not thy merciful ears to our prayer; but spare us, Lord most holy, O God most mighty, O holy and merciful Saviour, thou most worthy Judge eternal, suffer us not, at our last hour, for any pains of death, to fall from thee.

Then shall the Minister say.

Let us pray.

O LORD Jesus Christ, who wast laid in the new tomb of Joseph, and do thereby sanctify the grave to be a bed of hope for thy people: Vouchsafe, we beseech thee, to bless, hallow, consecrate this grave, that it may be a resting place, peaceful and secure, for the body of thy servant which we are about to commit to thy gracious keeping; who are the resurrection and the life, and who livest and reignest with the Father and the Holy Ghost, one God, world without end. *Amen.*

Then, while casting earth upon the Body, the Minister shall say,

UNTO Almighty God we commend the soul of our brother departed, and we commit his body to the ground; earth to earth, ashes to ashes, dust to dust; in sure and certain hope of the Resurrection unto eternal life, through our Lord Jesus Christ; at whose coming in glorious majesty to judge the world, the earth and the sea shall give up their dead; and the corruptible bodies of those who sleep in him shall be changed, and made like unto his own glorious body; according to the mighty working whereby he is able to subdue all things unto himself.

I HEARD a voice from heaven, saying unto me, Write, From henceforth blessed are the dead who die in the Lord; even so saith the Spirit; for they rest from their labours.

Then the Minister shall say,

The Lord be with you.
Answer. And with thy spirit.

Let us pray.

Lord, have mercy upon us.
Answer. Christ, have mercy upon us.
Lord, have mercy upon us.

Then shall the people say together with the Minister.

OUR Father, who art in heaven, Hallowed be thy Name. Thy kingdom come. Thy will be done, On earth as it is in heaven. Give us this day our daily bread. And forgive us our trespasses, As we forgive those who trespass against us. And lead us not into temptation, But deliver us from evil. *Amen.*

Then the Minister shall say the following Prayers.

O MERCIFUL God, the Father of our Lord Jesus Christ, who is the Resurrection and the Life; in whom whosoever believeth, shall live, though he die; and whosoever liveth, and believeth in him, shall not die eternally; who also hath taught us, by his holy Apostle Saint Paul, not to be sorry, as men without hope, for those who sleep in him; We humbly beseech thee, O Father, to raise us from the death of sin unto the life of righteousness; that, when we shall depart this life, we may rest in him; and that, at the general Resurrection in the last day, we may be found acceptable in thy sight; and receive that blessing, which thy well-beloved Son shall then pronounce to all who love and fear thee, saying, Come, ye blessed children of my Father, receive the kingdom prepared for you from the beginning of the world. Grant this, we beseech thee, O merciful Father, through Jesus Christ, our Mediator and Redeemer. *Amen.*

MOST merciful Father, who hast been pleased to take unto thyself the soul of thy servant Harry; Grant to us who are still in our pilgrimage, and who walk as yet by faith, that having served thee with constancy on earth, we may be joined hereafter with thy blessed saints in glory everlasting; through Jesus Christ our Lord. *Amen.*

Then shall follow the Military Honours, after which the Priest shall pronounce the blessing.

THE GOD of peace, who brought again from the dead our Lord Jesus Christ, the great Shepherd of the sheep, through the blood of the everlasting covenant; Make you perfect in every good work to do his will, working in you that which is well pleasing in his sight; through Jesus Christ, to whom be glory for ever and ever. *Amen.*

Then the flag covering the casket shall be removed, folded, and presented to the next of kin.

After which the Minister and next of kin shall leave the grave, the people following.

MEMORIAL SERVICE FOR
THE HONORABLE

HARRY S TRUMAN

1884–1972

THIRTY-THIRD PRESIDENT OF THE UNITED STATES

Friday, January Fifth, A.D. 1973

Eleven o'clock in the morning

WASHINGTON CATHEDRAL, WASHINGTON, D.C.

THE ORDER OF SERVICE

CHORALE PRELUDE

"Wenn wir in höchsten Röten sein" *Johann Sebastian Bach*

OPENING SENTENCES *Dr. Howell*

I am the resurrection and the life, saith the Lord: he that believeth in me, though he were dead, yet shall he live: and whosoever liveth and believeth in me, shall never die.

I know that my redeemer liveth, and that he shall stand at the latter day upon the earth: and though this body be destroyed, yet shall I see God: whom I see for myself, and mine eyes shall behold, and not as a stranger.

We brought nothing into this world, and it is certain we can carry nothing out. The Lord gave, and the Lord hath taken away; blessed be the name of the Lord.

PSALM 23 (*sung by Cathedral Choir*) *Chant: H. Wolford Davies*

PSALM 46 (*read responsively*) *Dr. Howell*

God is our hope and strength, a very present help in trouble.

Therefore will we not fear, though the earth be moved, and though the hills be carried into the midst of the sea;

Though the waters thereof rage and swell, and though the mountains shake at the tempest of the same.

There is a river, the streams whereof make glad the city of God; the holy place of the tabernacle of the Most Highest.

God is in the midst of her, therefore shall she not be removed; God shall help her, and that right early.

The nations make much ado, and the kingdoms are moved; but God hath showed his voice, and the earth shall melt away.

The Lord of hosts is with us; the God of Jacob is our refuge.

O Come hither, and behold the works of the Lord, what destruction he hath brought upon the earth.

He maketh wars to cease in all the world; he breaketh the bow, and knappeth the spear in sunder, and burneth the chariots in the fire.

Be still then, and know that I am God: I will be exalted among the nations, and I will be exalted in the earth.

The Lord of hosts is with us; the God of Jacob is our refuge. Glory be to the Father, and to the Son, and to the Holy Ghost;

As it was in the beginning, is now, and ever shall be, world without end. Amen.

ANTHEM   *T. Tertius Noble*

> Souls of the righteous in the hand of God,
> Nor hurt nor torment cometh them anigh;
> O holy hope of immortality!
>   To eyes of men unwise they seemed to die:
> They are at peace. O fairest liberty!
> On earth as children chastened by love's rod,
> As gold in furnace tried;
> So now on high they shine like stars,
>   A golden galaxy.

Wisdom 3:1–8

READING OF THE SCRIPTURES AND EULOGY   *Dean Sayre*

Like a great chain are the generations of man, linked across the endless span of Time:
—Beginning long before us at the deep well where God imprinted His image upon our ken,
—and stretching after us to successions of children in whose lives the hopes we have cherished shall be fulfilled.

xxvii

Blessed is the Creator Majesty who in loving Providence forges such a chain, made of spirit and flesh, and history—all marvelously put together.

Blessed too is that man who is *ready:* of sturdy soul and tempered true: whose life is bowed to the summons that would lay on him the mantle of destiny.

In the eyes of his countrymen, Harry Truman was found to be such a man.

   —earthy plain, there were no wrinkles in his honesty;
   —when the time came, he stepped to the anvil humble but not afraid, relying always in his independent way upon the goodness of the Lord, in whose hand is the hammer of our fate.

By the instinct of his straightforward faith, Harry Truman knew that God does not leave his people comfortless, no matter what may happen on the crowded stage of this world.

   —He was ready.
   —So was Elisha long ago.
   —Listen to that ancient tale:

   And it came to pass, when the Lord would take up Elijah into heaven by a whirlwind, that Elijah went with Elisha from Gilgal. And Elijah said unto Elisha, Tarry here, I pray thee; for the Lord hath sent me to Bethel. And Elisha said unto him, As the Lord liveth, and as thy soul liveth, I will not leave thee. So they went down to Bethel.

   And the sons of the prophets that were at Jericho came to Elisha, and said unto him, Knowest thou that the Lord will take away thy master from thy head today? And he answered, Yea, I know it; hold ye your peace.

   And Elijah said unto him, Tarry, I pray thee, here; for the Lord hath sent me to Jordan. And he said, as the Lord liveth, and as thy soul liveth, I will not leave thee. And they went on.

   And fifty men of the sons of the prophets went, and stood to view afar off: and they two stood by Jordan.

   And Elijah took his mantle, and wrapped it together, and smote the waters, and they were divided hither and thither, so that they two went over on dry ground.

   And it came to pass, when they were gone over, that Elijah said unto Elisha, Ask what I shall do for thee, before I be taken away from thee. And Elisha said, I pray thee, let a double portion of thy spirit be upon me.

And he said, Thou hast asked a hard thing; nevertheless, if thou see me when I am taken from thee, it shall be so unto thee; but if not, it shall not be so.

And it came to pass, as they still went on, and talked, that, behold, there appeared a chariot of fire, and horses of fire, and parted them both asunder; and Elijah went up by a whirlwind into heaven.

And Elisha saw it, and he cried, My father, my father, the chariot of Israel, and the horsemen thereof. And he saw him no more; and he took hold of his own clothes, and rent them in two pieces.

He took up also the mantle of Elijah that fell from him, and went back, and stood by the bank of Jordan;

And he took the mantle of Elijah that fell from him, and smote the waters, and said, Where is the Lord God of Elijah? and when he also had smitten the waters, they parted hither and thither: and Elisha went over.

II Kings 2: 1–2, 5–14

Sometimes it must seem to every President as if the path ahead is blocked by an impenetrable wall,
  —a river impassable.
  —the mendaciousness of man in all his affairs makes prisoner of that
    leader who must see beyond.
  —who may not allow the world to quench the spark of truth God
    has given to his keeping.
Many of us remember still the dark days that Harry Truman faced—
  —the loneliness of his responsibility
  —and the generous impulse he ever brought to it.
His buoyancy was surely born of the vision to which he was so deeply loyal:
  —a vision he would certainly have expressed in other words than
    those of Isaiah, though I think he must have loved these old sayings
    of the prophet:
      Who hath measured the waters in the hollow of his hand, and
      meted out heaven with the span, and comprehended the dust of
      the earth in a measure, and weighed the mountains in scales, and
      the hills in a balance?

      Who hath directed the spirit of the Lord, or being his counsellor
      hath taught him?

      With whom took he counsel, and who instructed him, and taught him in the path of judgment, and taught him knowledge, and shewed to him the way of understanding?

Behold, the nations are as a drop of a bucket, and are counted as the small dust of the balance: behold, he taketh up the isles as a very little thing.

Why sayest thou, O Jacob, and speakest, O Israel, My way is hid from the Lord, and my judgment is passed over from my God?

Hast thou not known? hast thou not heard, that the everlasting God, the Lord, the Creator of the ends of the earth, fainteth not, neither is weary? there is no searching of his understanding.

He giveth power to the faint; and to them that have no might he increaseth strength.

Even the youths shall faint and be weary, and the young men shall utterly fall:

But they that wait upon the Lord shall renew their strength; and they shall mount up with wings as eagles; they shall run, and not be weary; and they shall walk, and not faint.

Isaiah 40: 12–15, 27–31

Time after time did the Lord renew the strength of this man whose absence from our midst we mourn this day, but in whose faith we may still rejoice.

Now we must pray that God shall renew the strength of the people whom Mr. Truman served:
  —giving them singleness of heart
  —and grace to lay aside the things that divide them;
  —the vision of peace and a fresh resolve to achieve it.
We pray too for the family of our erstwhile President; his wife and daughter; all who loved him and all whom he loved in that garden God puts about each man.
  —for as St. John wrote:

Let not your heart be troubled: ye believe in God, believe also in me.

In my Father's house are many mansions: if it were not so, I would have told you. I go to prepare a place for you.

And if I go and prepare a place for you, I will come again, and receive you unto myself; that where I am, there ye may be also.

And whither I go ye know, and the way ye know.

Thomas saith unto him, Lord, we know not whither thou goest; and how can we know the way?

Jesus saith unto him, I am the way, the truth, and the life: no man cometh unto the Father, but by me.

John 14: 1–6

HYMN (*Sung by all, standing*)   *St. Dunstan's*

He who would valiant be
    'Gainst all disaster,
Let him in constancy
    Follow the Master.
There's no discouragement
Shall make him once relent
His first avowed intent
    To be a pilgrim.

Who so beset him round
    With dismal stories,
Do but themselves confound,
    His strength the more is.
No foes shall stay his might,
Though he with giants fight;
He will make good his right
    To be a pilgrim.

Since, Lord, thou dost defend
    Us with thy Spirit,
We know we at the end
    Shall life inherit.
Then fancies flee away!
I'll fear not what men say,
I'll labor night and day
    To be a pilgrim. *Amen.*

John Bunyan, 1684

APOSTLE'S CREED (*people standing*)

I BELIEVE in God the Father Almighty, Maker of heaven and earth: And in Jesus Christ his only Son our Lord: Who was conceived by the Holy Ghost, Born of the Virgin Mary: Suffered under Pontius Pilate, Was crucified, dead, and buried: He descended into hell; The third day he arose again from the dead: He ascended into heaven, And sitteth on the right hand of God the Father Almighty: From thence he shall come to judge the quick and the dead.

I believe in the Holy Ghost: The Holy Catholic Church: The Communion of Saints: The Forgiveness of sins: The Resurrection of the body: And the Life everlasting. *Amen.*

PRAYERS (*people kneeling or sitting*)

The Lord's Prayer

Our Father, who art in heaven, Hallowed be thy name. Thy kingdom come, Thy will be done, On earth as it is in heaven. Give us this day our daily bread. And forgive us our trespasses, as we forgive those who trespass against us. And lead us not into temptation, but deliver us from evil. For thine is the kingdom, and the power, and the glory for ever and ever. *Amen.*

For Mr. Truman

We Thy people, Lord, do praise Thee for a fearless son of simple soil, our brother Harry. By what good Providence Thou didst raise him to be our leader in time of peril and of peace; by what plain and honest grace did he respond. Steady was his hand to Thine annealing fire; open his heart to Thy healing provision for all mankind. He wore the mantle of our trust with truth; and bore his solitary power with humility, following in this the silent steps of Him whom Thou didst long ago give to be our Saviour, even Jesus Christ our Lord. *Amen.*

For Missouri

Great God whose plough is weather and whose season is Time itself, we thank Thee for the Earth Thou hast fashioned in Missouri:

smoothing the glacial plain with great blades of ice;
irrigating the land with burnished streams and
bounding it with Ozark beauty.

When Thou wast ready, Thy spirit stood by the Gate, inviting all mankind to the heart of Thy goodly continent.

Bless us now as we seek to retrace the mighty sweep of Thy making;

possessing our inheritance to the little step of mules,
or the roar of city wheels;
by the flutter of a steamer upon the river,
by the sound of sweet blues upon the lips of a trumpet,
or the cry of some distant train across the night.

At every turn may we find the door; beyond learning to wisdom; beyond living to Life; beyond receiving to the happier joy of giving. And so, as river threads the prairie, may our hearts be open to Thy truth and blessed independence; through Jesus Christ our Lord. *Amen.*

For the Nation

Keep bright in our hearts, O Lord, the openness which Thou didst spread before our forebears upon this Continent. In the wideness of Thy glory let freedom be fresh kindled, and courage given for the new day.

So may Thy blessing rest upon the children as upon their fathers, that we may ever dwell in Thine abiding; through Jesus Christ our Lord. *Amen.*

For Those Who Mourn

O Merciful God, and heavenly Father, who hast taught us in Thy Holy Word that Thou dost not willingly afflict or grieve the children of men; Look with pity, we beseech thee, upon the sorrows of Thy servants. Remember them, O Lord, in mercy; endue them with patience; comfort them with a sense of Thy goodness; lift up Thy countenance upon us all, and give us peace; through Jesus Christ our Lord. *Amen.*

Lord, now lettest thou thy servant depart in peace, according to thy
    word
For mine eyes have seen thy salvation,
Which thou hast prepared before the face of all people;
To be a light to lighten the Gentiles, and to be the glory of thy people Israel. *Amen.*

HYMN (*sung by Cathedral Choir*)   *H. Wolford Davies*

God be in my head, And in my understanding;
God be in mine eyes, And in my looking;
God be in my mouth, And in my speaking;
God be at mine end, And at my departing. *Amen.*

Sarum Primer, 1558

BLESSING   *Bishop Creighton*

Unto God's gracious mercy and protection we commit Harry; the Lord bless him and keep him. The Lord make his face to shine upon him, and be gracious unto him. The Lord lift up his countenance upon him, and give him peace, both now and evermore. *Amen.*
The Lord lift up his countenance upon him, and give him peace, both now and evermore. *Amen.*

And now may the God of peace, who brought again from the dead our Lord Jesus Christ, the great Shepherd of the sheep, through the blood of the everlasting covenant; Make you perfect in every good work to do his will, working in you that which is well pleasing in his sight; through Jesus Christ, to whom be glory for ever and ever.

Amen.

RECESSIONAL   *St. Anne*

O God, our help in ages past,
   Our hope for years to come,
Our shelter from the stormy blast,
   And our eternal home:

Under the shadow of thy throne
   Thy saints have dwelt secure;
Sufficient is thine arm alone,
   And our defense is sure.

Before the hills in order stood,
   Or earth received her frame,
From everlasting thou art God,
   To endless years the same.

A thousand ages in thy sight
   Are like an evening gone;
Short as the watch that ends the night
   Before the rising sun.

Time, like an ever-rolling stream,
   Bears all its sons away;
They fly, forgotten, as a dream
   Dies at the opening day.

O God, our help in ages past,
   Our hope for years to come,
Be thou our guide while life shall last,
   And our eternal home. *Amen.*

                                       Issac Watts, 1719; based on Psalm 90

POSTLUDE

       Grove (Fantasia in G Major)   *Johann Sebastian Bach*

OFFICIATING CLERGY

The Very Reverend Francis B. Sayre, Jr.   The Reverend John E. Howell
Dean of Washington Cathedral   *Pastor of the First Baptist Church*
                                          Washington, D.C.

The Right Reverend William F. Creighton
Bishop of Washington

Choir of the Washington Cathedral
Paul Callaway (*Organist*)

Memorial Tributes

IN THE

House of Representatives of the United States

IN EULOGY OF

Harry S Truman

In the House of Representatives
of the United States

JANUARY 3, 1973

This being the day fixed by the 20th amendment of the Constitution for the annual meeting of the Congress of the United States, the Members-elect of the House of Representatives of the 93d Congress met in their Hall, and at 12 o'clock noon were called to order by the Clerk of the House of Representatives, Hon. W. Pat Jennings.

The Chaplain, Rev. Edward G. Latch, D.D., prefaced his prayer with these words of Scripture:

Be strong and of good courage; be not afraid, neither be thou dismayed; for the Lord thy God is with thee whithersoever thou goest.—Joshua 1: 9.

Eternal God and Father of us all, make us aware of Thy presence as we prepare ourselves for a new year together in the service of our beloved country. Bless these Representatives of our people with Thy most gracious favor and so move within their hearts that they may look to Thee for guidance and from Thee receive wisdom to walk in Thy ways, strength to stand steadfastly for the common good, and confidence to labor courageously for peace, justice, and freedom in our world. Support them all the day long as they face the responsibilities entrusted to them.

Before Thee we remember with affection and with sorrow Hale Boggs, Frank Bow, Nick Begich, George Collins, and HARRY S TRUMAN. May these beloved colleagues and our former President find favor in Thy sight and receive the reward of work well done for our Republic. Comfort their families with the strength of Thy spirit.

Now let us unite in praying together:

Our Father, who art in heaven, hallowed be Thy name. Thy kingdom come. Thy will be done in earth as it is in heaven. Give us this day our daily bread. And forgive us our trespasses, as we forgive those who trespass against us. And lead us not into temptation, but deliver us from evil. For Thine is the kingdom, and the power, and the glory, forever. Amen.

The Speaker laid before the House the following communication from the President of the National Assembly of Turkey:

TURKISH EMBASSY,
Washington, D.C., December 28, 1972.
Hon. CARL ALBERT,
Speaker of the House of Representatives,
Washington, D.C.
DEAR MR. SPEAKER: I have the honor to enclose herewith the message of His Excellency Sabit Osman Avci, the President of the National Assembly of Turkey, to Your Excellency, on the occasion of the death of His Excellency HARRY S TRUMAN, former President of the United States.
In sharing the sentiments expressed in the message, please accept, Mr. Speaker, in behalf of my wife and myself, our heartfelt condolences.
MELIH ESENBEL,
Ambassador of Turkey.

⚓

The Honorable CARL ALBERT,
The Speaker of the House of Representatives,
Washington, D.C.
DEAR MR. SPEAKER: I am deeply grieved by the passing away of H. E. HARRY S TRUMAN, the former President of the U.S.A.
His efforts directed towards the establishment of a sound universal peace gained him admiration all over the world and his name went in history as one of the unforgettable statesmen of all times. By means of the Truman

1

Doctrine he pioneered a new era of friendship and alliance between Turkey and the U.S.A., and gained a special place in the minds and hearts of the Turkish people.

On this sad occasion I convey, on behalf of the members of the National Assembly of Turkey and on my own behalf, our sincere condolences to you, Mr. Speaker, and to the Members of the U.S. House of Representatives.

SABIT OSMAN AVCI,
President of the National Assembly of Turkey.

The Speaker laid before the House the following communication from the Acting Secretary of the Department of State:

DEPARTMENT OF STATE,
Washington, December 27, 1972.
Hon. CARL ALBERT,
Speaker of the House of Representatives.

DEAR MR. SPEAKER: I enclose herewith a copy of the Proclamation by President Nixon officially announcing the death of HARRY S TRUMAN, former President of the United States, which occurred in Kansas City, Missouri, on Tuesday morning, December 26, 1972, at 7:50 o'clock.

Sincerely,
U. ALEXIS JOHNSON,
Acting Secretary.

ANNOUNCING THE DEATH OF HARRY S TRUMAN BY THE PRESIDENT OF THE UNITED STATES OF AMERICA

A PROCLAMATION

To the People of the United States:

It is my sad duty to announce officially the death of HARRY S TRUMAN, thirty-third President of the United States, on December 26, 1972.

Throughout his long career in public service, HARRY S TRUMAN was known as a man of forthrightness and integrity. He served with distinction in the United States Senate; and when the death of President Franklin Delano Roosevelt thrust him suddenly into the Presidency in April of 1945 at one of the most critical moments of our history, he met that moment with courage and vision. His far-sighted leadership in the postwar era has helped ever since to preserve peace and freedom in the world.

Confronted during his Presidency with a momentous series of challenges, his strength and spirit proved equal to them all. His fortitude never wavered, and his faith in America never flagged.

President TRUMAN had a deep respect for the office he held and for the people he served. He gave himself unstintingly to the duties of the Presidency while he held it, and in the years afterward he honorably supported and wisely counseled each of his successors.

The Nation to which he gave so much will honor his memory in admiration and respect, and the other countries for which he helped keep freedom alive will remember his name with gratitude.

Now, therefore, I, Richard Nixon, President of the United States of America, in tribute to the memory of President TRUMAN, and as an expression of public sorrow, do hereby direct that the flag of the United States be displayed at half-staff at the White House and all buildings, grounds, and Naval vessels of the United States for a period of thirty days from the day of his death. I also direct that for the same length of time the representatives of the United States in foreign countries shall make similar arrangements for the display of the flag at half-staff over their Embassies, Legations, and other facilities abroad, including all military facilities and stations.

I hereby order that suitable honors be rendered by units of the Armed Forces under orders of the Secretary of Defense on the day of the funeral.

I do further appoint December 28, 1972 to be a National Day of Mourning throughout the United States. I recommend that the people assemble on that day in their respective places of worship, there to pay homage to the memory of President TRUMAN and to seek God's continued blessing on our land and on His servant. I invite the people of the world who share our grief to join us in this solemn observance.

In witness whereof, I have hereunto set my hand this 26th day of December, in the year of our Lord nineteen hundred seventy-two, and of the Independence of the United States of America the one hundred ninety-seventh.

Richard Nixon.

Mr. Randall. Mr. Speaker, I offer a resolution (H. Res. 14) and ask for its immediate consideration.

The Clerk read the resolution as follows:

HOUSE RESOLUTION 14

Resolved, That the House has learned with regret and profound sorrow of the death of HARRY S TRUMAN, former President of the United States, who as an illustrious Member of the Senate of the United States, Vice President, and President gave so generously of his energy and wisdom and contributed so greatly to the cause of freedom.

Resolved, That the Clerk communicate these resolutions to the Senate and transmit a copy of the same to the family of the deceased.

The resolution was agreed to.

A motion to reconsider was laid on the table.

Mr. Randall. Mr. Speaker, at an appropriate time in the very near future we will ask for some time here on the floor to pay our respects to our former President. An announcement will be made to all Members at that time.

Mr. Speaker, it has been my honor and privilege for the past 14 years to represent the district of former President HARRY S TRUMAN. At this time I wish to announce there will be time for the purpose of paying tribute to this great man on Tuesday next.

SPECIAL ORDER

Mr. Speaker, at this time I ask unanimous consent that at the conclusion of the legislative business on Tuesday next that 1 hour be set aside so that all Members may have the opportunity to pay tribute to this great American.

The Speaker. Without objection, it is so ordered.

Hon. Robert L. F. Sikes

OF FLORIDA

Mr. Speaker, the death of HARRY S TRUMAN saddened America as few events have done. He was given universal acclaim for his courageous administration as President. This is a very different story from the one which generally prevailed when he was President. I recall very well that he left office widely condemned by the news media for having been a poor President. Now 20 years later they say he was one of America's 10 best Presidents. I think the latter assessment is the correct one.

Here was a most interesting individual. HARRY S TRUMAN was a man who did not want to be Vice President. The Nation viewed him with concern and apprehension when he succeeded to the Presidency. He had been very much in FDR's shadow and there was little understanding nationwide of his ability or his determination.

The public gained an awareness of his qualities of leadership just in time for him to be elected over Tom Dewey. The experts had not given him a chance. Here again, courage and determination saw him through.

He was destined to continue to grow in public esteem with each passing year particularly after he left office. Now the history books properly record him as a strong and courageous and yet a humble President who did not duck the issues—and they were heavy. Few national leaders in our time now are held in higher regard. Here was a man—a great man.

Hon. Jonathan B. Bingham

OF NEW YORK

Mr. Speaker, some Presidents seem to shrink in stature as the years pass following their term in office.

With others it is to the contrary. From the vantage point of a few years' perspective, they loom much larger than they did while in office. HARRY S TRUMAN belongs in this category.

Of all the many thousands of words that have been uttered and written since Mr. TRUMAN's death, I have seen none more apt than those of Mary McGrory in the following column, which appeared in the New York Post of December 29, 1972:

THE LESSON OF HIS LIFE

(By Mary McGrory)

WASHINGTON.—In death, as in life, HARRY TRUMAN did not impose.

His funeral, like himself, was plain, prayerful and to the point.

He had planned it that way.

Except for the gold braid and the ceremonial firings, it could have been the funeral of any man from Missouri who had been a war veteran and a Mason.

Only family and old friends were invited.

There was no eulogy. He was not one to stain rhetoric or extort emotion. Besides, history, always his guide, had become a friend. He had never needed anyone to tell him who he was. The library was there to remind the world of what he had done.

The funeral repeated the lesson of his life—that any American can get to be President, and get over it.

He had assumed office amid universal lamentations, in which he humbly joined. He was patronized as "a little guy." But by the time he left the White House, the country and the world thought he had been big enough for the job.

What he brought to the White House was a quality sadly lacking in his two most recent successors, that is a sense of perspective. He was the only President of this generation who had an eye-level relationship with the country. Eisenhower was the revered patriarch who could do no wrong; Kennedy was the idolized prince. Lyndon Johnson, a Gargantuan figure, demanded to be loved, and was not. The present occupant is an emperor, vindictive secretive, mirthless.

TRUMAN was a man without pretense, who happened to be President. Neither he nor the country ever seemed to lose sight of the fact. He was not a hero or a magician or a chess player, or an obsession. He was a certifiable member of the human race, direct, fallible and unexpectedly wise when it counted.

He did not require to be loved. He did not expect to be followed blindly. Congressional opposition never struck him as subversive, nor did he regard his critics as traitors. He never whined.

He walked around Washington every morning—it was safe then. He met reporters frequently as a matter of course, and did not blame them for his failures. He did not use the office as a club or a shield, or a hiding place. He worked at it.

He had a sense of what was due the presidency if not to himself. People were so unawed by him that they considered him insubordinate when he fired General MacArthur. It was not personal pique. He understood the Constitution, he understood the principle of civilian control of the military. He never said war was peace.

He dropped the atomic bomb, a fact much recalled this week when American power is being used savagely over another Asian country. The decision is still disputed, but at least he gave the country plausible military reasons for what he did. His present successor has dropped the equivalent of two Hiroshima bombs and has yet to give the public the first syllable of explanation. HARRY TRUMAN believed the public business was the public's business.

All week, the television has been bringing him back as he was, the twanging voice, the forthrightness, the humor. Was it only twenty years ago that we had a President who explained his actions, who admitted his mistakes and could imitate a commentator?

TRUMAN was not a "splendid misery" sort. Since his time—it began with the Cuban missile crisis—we have been given hour-by-hour accounts of Presidential agonies.

Nothing to it, according to the man from Independence. "You get all the facts and you make up your mind," he explained briskly to an audience.

He brought to his retirement the same unwavering perspective that had marked his presidency. He actually went home to his old house in Independence. He came to the door for his morning paper.

He took, as long as he was able, his daily walk, and zestfully built his library. He sounded off a time or two but as reluctantly as he had taken power, as readily he relinquished it.

"Three things ruin a man," he told a reporter on the occasion of his seventy-fifth birthday. "Power, money and women."

"I never wanted power," he said. "I never had any money, and the only woman in my life is up at the house right now."

He is buried in the countyard of his library. He said he lived by the Bible and history. So armed, he proved that the ordinary American is capable of grandeur. And that a President can be a human being. At the present grim moment, there is some doubt on both points. We mourn for him as we mourn for lost certainties.

I cannot improve on what Mary McGrory said, but I should like to add a few words about two of HARRY TRUMAN's great qualities.

One was his honesty. He was forthright with the American people, and they trusted him when he said something, we knew he was telling the truth. The contrast these days is obvious and painful.

The other quality I want to single out was his understanding of the tripartite nature of the American Government. An avid student of American history, Mr. TRUMAN had just as much respect for the legislative and judicial branches as he did for the Presidency. He fought with the Congress, but he never ignored it or downgraded it.

I am intensely proud of the fact that I was appointed to office by President TRUMAN. History will rank him, I believe, among the top 10 of our Presidents.

Hon. Peter W. Rodino, Jr.
OF NEW JERSEY

Mr. Speaker—

I want you to succeed in whatever you undertake. To do that you must give it all you have. . . . Right must always prevail. Do not let glamor get you. There are decent, honorable people among the very rich, just as there are among the very poor. Honor knows no class. . . . Remember always to keep your balance no matter how great you may become in your own time. Your Dad will never be reckoned among the great but you can be sure he did his level best and gave all he had to his country.

The above counsel has been extracted from a letter HARRY TRUMAN wrote to his daughter, Margaret. The statement reveals the words of a man who had the courage, the spirit, and the tenacity to stick to his convictions, to carry forward the strength of his decisions and to uphold, always, the principles of his family code:

To do the right thing, to do the best we could, never complain, never take advantage, don't give up, don't be afraid.

Simple words—but words forceful and dynamic in their simplicity.

President HARRY TRUMAN possessed an immense capacity for making up his mind to do what had to be done. He welcomed and encouraged the views of others, no matter how far they differed from his own initial impressions. Yet, he never forgot that the final responsibility for all decisions rested solely on his shoulders. When the "buck stopped," he answered and he acted with a full and biting awareness of his accountability to the American people. Gen. George C. Marshall, looking back upon the 33d Presidency stated—

There never has been a decision made under this man's Administration that has not been made in the best interest of his country. It is not only the courage of these decisions that will live, but the integrity of them.

Mr. TRUMAN, himself, addressing a crowd of workers in Grand Rapids, Mich., explained:

I don't want you to vote for me, I want you to get out on election day and vote for yourselves—for your interests.

On his return to Independence at the close of his arduous campaign, he concluded:

We have told the people the truth and the people are with us. The people are going to win this election.

HARRY TRUMAN remained a man of the people. To his countrymen and to the world, he came to symbolize the potential, when history demands it, of the common man. Neither as a public nor private figure did he ever pretend to be anything but what he was. As a farmer, his resourcefulness, his independent spirit, his ability to solve the everyday practical problems served him well. As a timekeeper, bank clerk, and bookkeeper, his thorough and meticulous approach became a most valuable resource. And, as a Senator, his inquisitive and retentive mind, his dedicated and conscientious manner were known to all. Mr. TRUMAN's successful efforts as chairman of the Special Committee To Investigate the National Defense Program remain as an example for all of us in this body of the importance of our ideas, programs, and actions in directing and influencing governmental policy and in serving the men and women of this Nation.

Courage, compassion, concern, strength, self-lessness, honesty, and a dedication to get the job done and to accomplish this task the best he could—these are the qualities HARRY TRUMAN brought with him to serve as F. D. R.'s Vice President and these are the qualities with which, on April 12, 1945, less than 3 months later, he faced the American people as their leader.

We remember well the European recovery program, the Truman doctrine, the creation of NATO, the birth of the U.N., the impact of the atomic bomb, the Korean intervention, the point 4 plan. All, when judged in the context of their times, stand as a symbol of the commitment of America and of the West to the cause of freedom. TRUMAN refused to compromise with injustice. From his insistence that all captured Nazis be given a fair trial, to his unprecedented order to desegregate the Armed Forces, HARRY TRUMAN firmly believed that—

Each man should be free to live his life as he wishes. He should be limited only by his responsibility to his fellow countrymen. The only limit to an individual's achievement should be his ability, his industry, and his character.

Meeting with opposition in every quarter, TRUMAN recognized the State of Israel 11 minutes after she declared her independence. He told Chaim Weizman:

You more than made the most of what you received and I admire you for it.

HARRY TRUMAN believed there was no limit to man's ability to learn. He once stated—

A person learns as long as he lives.

And, HARRY TRUMAN worked, questioned, studied, investigated, discovered, and grew. In later years he loved to speak with schoolchildren on the meaning of democracy and was looked upon by many of us as a kind of roving teacher.

The years I served under his administration as Congressman and the meetings and discussions I held with Mr. TRUMAN remain most special for me. It is not enough for us to remember and honor his memory and to speak in eloquent words of his deeds and his service to the American people and to the world. For HARRY TRUMAN struggled to insure that the principles and precepts of America's ideals be preserved and carried forward. We must, therefore, continue this struggle and this dream for peace, justice, and freedom for this generation and for all generations to come.

Hon. Bertram L. Podell
OF NEW YORK

Mr. Speaker, the years following the end of World War II were bleak ones for the remnants of European Jewry. After being almost totally wiped out in the German death camps, they were herded into displaced person camps. When they sought to escape to Palestine, to start life over again and forget the horrors of the holocaust, they were turned back by the British. It seemed that there was no one who cared whether they perished or survived.

No one, that is, except HARRY S TRUMAN, the brash, forthright man from Missouri, who almost reluctantly found himself in the White House. From 1945 on, HARRY TRUMAN pressed the British to open the gates to the Holy Land, and to honor the promise they made in the Balfour Declaration. At first, he sought 100,000 immigrant visas. When this failed, he became the foremost supporter of the partition plan in the

United Nations. He fought and won against the members of the State Department who would rather cater to the Arabs than save Jewish lives. In his support of the concept of a Jewish homeland, he demonstrated the heights to which the Presidency could rise.

It has often been said, that if it were not for HARRY S TRUMAN, Israel would not exist. He was the first to recognize the new nation, and he lived up to his commitment by providing loans and other forms of aid so that Israel would have a chance to survive.

TRUMAN had a particular vision of the role Israel would play in the future. He saw it as a source for the rebirth of the entire Middle East. It would be a highly developed land, from which the benefits of modern technology would spread throughout the region. Israel would be the fountain from which all the Middle East would take nourishment and flower. It was only in this way, TRUMAN felt, that peace would come.

The years have unfortunately not seen HARRY TRUMAN's dream come true. The gulf between the Arabs and Israelis has widened. But HARRY TRUMAN's hope for Israel will live on. Through his eyes we can see a land where all the residents live together in peace, all sharing in each other's successes. President TRUMAN's memory should inspire us to remain steadfast in our support for Israel, in the hope that one day soon we will see with our eyes what he only saw with his heart.

Hon. Wm. J. Randall

OF MISSOURI

Mr. Speaker, on December 26, 2 weeks ago today, my neighbor in Independence, the people of Missouri, all Americans, as well as all the people in the free world, were bowed in sorrow and grief when they heard the sad news of the passing of former President HARRY S TRUMAN.

Today, here in the great hall of the House of Representatives, we have an opportunity to pause once again to pay tribute to this great American. Many Members who are here in the House served in Congress when Mr. TRUMAN was President.

For some of the other Members he will be remembered as one, who in 1948 as he traveled across America, took time from his own desperate campaign to help by saying a good word for fellow candidates running for office.

Some of those who are here as Members today were then running for either State senate, State representative, or even county office.

My own close and pleasant association with Mr. TRUMAN goes back to 1932, the year I cast my first vote. I was ushered into his personal and political fellowship and association by a close mutual friend, the late Judge E. I. "Buck" Purcell. Later I had the opportunity to hold the same seat on the Jackson County Court which he occupied. Now, for the past 14 years, it has been my privilege and high honor to be his Congressman, and with great pride I acknowledged him as my No. 1 constituent.

My purpose today is not to repeat what every American—from the most advanced student of the Presidency to the youngest reader of a third grade history book—knows well. I shall not be concerned with dates or historical facts, but with the man himself. I do not wish to repeat what this outstanding leader did, or how or even why he did it, but rather to look beyond the deed at the doer.

HARRY TRUMAN exemplified the American ideal of success. He worked his way up from railroad timekeeper, to bank bookkeeper to farmer, to postmaster, to road overseer, to soldier, to haberdasher, and finally to public servant. The trial was not easy as he met failures in both private and public life. Still in the face of adversity he continued to strive for success.

His humility, boldness, doughtiness, and yes, also his unpretentiousness contributed to his integrity which always endeared him to the American public. In keeping with his adolescent talent of plowing the straightest furrow in Jackson County, the then Missouri Senator actually fought against accepting the 1944 Vice-Presidential nomination because, as he put it, he did not want to enter the White House through the back door. He practically had to be ordered by President Roosevelt to accept the bid. After Mr. TRUMAN became President, he proved he was strong enough to fire an American military hero who was responsible for some of our greatest and most brilliant victories. It was this same President who displayed his humility by stating doubts that his signature would ever be wanted as a souvenir. But he was tough whether in withstanding the German artillery as a soldier, in deciding to drop the atomic bomb, or in defending against the critics, that is, the musical critics, about the musical talents of his daughter.

Even as the occupant of the second highest office in our Nation, he demonstrated his unpretentiousness. The then Vice President TRUMAN personally journeyed back to Missouri to pay his final respect to an important western Missouri political leader, even though this man had experienced some difficulties with the law. Mr. TRUMAN was a man with whom almost everyone could identify.

In April 1965 on the 20th anniversary of his assumption to the Presidency, Mr. TRUMAN received the coveted Freedom Award, presented annually since 1943 for outstanding contributions to the cause of freedom. In explaining the selection of President TRUMAN to receive the year's award, the judges said:

> President TRUMAN's leadership—particularly in initiating the Marshall Plan, the Truman Doctrine and the defense of South Korea—set the pattern for America's worldwide activities in behalf of freedom.

The plaque presented to President TRUMAN summed up this courageous man's place in history more succinctly, but no less meaningfully:

> Wise in Policy
> Valiant in Action
> Decisive in Leadership
> You Gave a Battered World New Hope

But perhaps the most eloquent and meaningful tribute to our former President was delivered by one who served with him as he took upon his shoulders the problems of our country and the world, and who therefore knew him best. Dean Acheson, in the major address at the Freedom Award ceremony, reminded us that the policies of the Truman administration in foreign affairs showed a sweep, a breadth of conception and boldness of action which were new in this country's history.

"Many of President TRUMAN's decisions," the former Secretary of State said, "constituted expanding action in truly heroic mold."

All of them were dangerous; all of them required the rare capacity first to decide and then not simply decide, but to act. All of them were decided rightly and they were vigorously followed through.

When they appraise Mr. TRUMAN, most persons will invariably say he grew in office. Of course, this has become one of the moldier cliches about many U.S. Presidents, but no one seemed more deserving of these words than HARRY S TRUMAN, who died 2 weeks ago today at the age of 88.

Remember, he was propelled, shall we say, stammering to himself, into the White House by F.D.R.'s death on that day in April 1945, when the word came from Warm Springs.

It was not long until this little Missourian took firm command, mapped the postwar recovery in the United States and Europe, won an astounding election victory and laid the foundations of a foreign policy that led Churchill to declare, "You, more than any other man, have saved Western civilization."

He believed in simplicity, and just as he wished it his memorial services were without fanfare as he was put to rest in the courtyard of his cherished Truman Library in Independence, Mo., in a ceremony of austere simplicity.

I think one of the myths of modern American folklore is that our 33d President, HARRY S TRUMAN—you may recall many times he said he should have been described as the 32d President—was an average man, or sometimes called a common man. HARRY TRUMAN certainly seemed average but he was not average, and he was a most uncommon man. True, he had never gone to college. He had been a dirt farmer and a clothing salesman, but to compound his image, HARRY S TRUMAN sounded like an average man as well. Never in his life did he ever have to make anything "perfectly clear," because people knew what he meant. His language was simple, direct and often earthy, as political opponents and, yes, you recall those music critics, could attest. HARRY TRUMAN could, as he said, "give 'em hell" just like the common man.

He was above all a man of the people. He understood them. More importantly, they understood him. They trusted him maybe because he considered himself, as he once put it, "a lobbyist for the people."

But, can we say that it was an average man or a common man who had to make that momentous decision to order that the atomic bomb be dropped on Japan; brought the United States into the U.N.; raised Europe out of the ashes of World War II with the Marshall plan; the man who established NATO? Can you call average a man who first developed technical assistance programs for the poorer nations of the world; who introduced the first sweeping civil rights legislation in this country; who helped bring to life the State of Israel; who decided to send American troops to fight in Korea? Could it have been an average man who had the courage to remove General MacArthur? Could it have been an average man who came from behind against all the great odds to win the election in 1948? And what kind of an average man would it be who could go to sleep election night before the returns were in?

No, for all of these things it had to be a most uncommon man. Now, Mr. TRUMAN may have seemed like every man, but he was in fact tougher, more decisive, more courageous and more independent than most men.

I am sure scholars will disagree with some of his policies and question some of his judgments.

But one thing is quite clear. This man from Independence, Mo., was no average man, or even an average President. Rather, he was a great man and a great President.

I think an interesting insight into the man's inner beliefs will be found in a note in his own handwriting saying how long and how often he said his favorite prayer. This is quoted both in the book "Good Old Harry" compiled by George S. Caldwell and also in the book "Mr. President" by William Hillman. Reference in those sources is made to a note written in Mr. TRUMAN's handwriting on White House stationery and dated August 15, 1950, about the prayer he used so often, like writing to himself, this note said:

> This prayer has been said by me—HARRY S TRUMAN—from high school days, as a window washer, bottle duster, floor scrubber in an Independence, Missouri, drugstore, as a timekeeper on a railroad contract gang, as an employee of a newspaper, as a bank clerk, as a farmer riding a gang plow behind four horses and mules, as a fraternity official learning to say nothing at all if good could not be said of a man, as a public official judging the weaknesses and shortcomings of constituents, and as President of the United States of America.

That note was found attached to his favorite prayer in his own handwriting on his desk in 1950 at the White House, and the prayer he carried with him and referred to as his favorite prayer reads as follows:

> Oh, Almighty and Everlasting God. Creator of heaven and earth and the universe: Help me to be, to think, to act what is right, because it is right: Make me truthful, honest and honorable in all things: Make me intellectually honest for the sake of right and honor and without thought of reward to me. Give me the ability to be charitable, forgiving and patient with my fellow men—Help me to understand their motives and their shortcomings—even as thou understandest mine: Amen.

It is my judgment that one of the shortest and best appraisals of the Truman years is by Cabell Phillips, who for a long time was the New York Times Washington Bureau representative; for some 20 years, I think. He knew intimately many of the key people of the period. He had a trusted reporter's grasp of the Truman administration from its beginning to the end. In his book, "The Truman Presidency," which he calls the history of a triumphant succession, he points out the problems that confronted TRUMAN were enormous in their scope. But with his rocklike character he faced up to them unflinchingly, through the Potsdam Conference, the terrible decision to drop the atom bomb, the onset of the cold war, and even the attempts of his own party to dump him in 1948.

Then there was the grim campaign of that year, and its glorious upset.

As I mentioned, he had to confront the insubordinate MacArthur and even the insolent McCarthy. But probably some of his greatest achievements, if we limit them to three, were the Marshall plan, the formation and establishment of NATO, and the Korean intervention.

He set a course for this Nation's foreign policy which endures to this very day.

He was a sentimental man, admittedly a stubborn man, often impetuous, but he was unwavering in his determination to do what he thought was right, and he was temperamentally incapable of walking away from a fight.

But he was a man who admitted his mistakes. He did have flashes of temper, but he also had a sense of humor. He had strong loyalties, and he had unabashed affection for his mother, his wife, and his daughter. And all these blend with his stern sense of duty to make HARRY TRUMAN one of the warmest and most believable figures in all American history.

Hon. Richard Bolling
OF MISSOURI

Mr. Speaker, I would like to have included in the Record at this point the statement that I issued on the death of Mr. TRUMAN. I think it says quickly and as well as I can say it what I think of Mr. TRUMAN's place in history.

> HARRY S TRUMAN now belongs to the ages. He has long since joined the list of great American Presidents for his foresight, courage and determination in the field of foreign and defense policy. More and more people are coming to realize that had the people of the United States been wise enough to support his domestic programs they would have saved themselves many agonies and many

tragedies. His foresight on civil rights and health care, on housing and education, matches his leadership of the Marshall Plan and the defense of Korea from aggression.

Mr. Speaker, I would like to take a minute at this point to add to the remarks that have been made and will be made, with this thought: That too ofen we neglect to note those who live after the person that we eulogize.

This is particularly true in the case of a lady who, I think, contributed enormously to Mr. TRUMAN himself personally and to his Presidency. She, I believe it is safe to say, was as popular a First Lady as there ever was in the history of our land. She was and is a distinguished citizen of Independence. She has always conducted herself with infinite kindness, patience, and sweetness.

Mr. Speaker, I think Mrs. Bess Truman is one of the more remarkable people whom I have ever had the privilege of meeting, and, of course, all of us feel very strongly her bereavement and extend to her our condolences, but I think that this occasion would not be fully met if some mention were not made of this quite extraordinary woman, the woman who was such an extraordinarily fine companion and loving mate of the remarkable President we are eulogizing today.

Hon. Wm. J. Randall

OF MISSOURI

Mr. Speaker, I thank the gentleman from Missouri (Mr. Bolling) for his contribution.

Of course, our prayers and deepest sympathy go to this beloved lady and the daughter whom our former President loved so much.

Hon. Leonor K. Sullivan

OF MISSOURI

Mr. Speaker, the Nation and the world have joined the people of Missouri in mourning the passing, on December 26, of one of the great Americans of our era—a man who rose from farm lad to President and who, nearly 20 years after leaving office, was honored and respected and loved even more than while he served in the most powerful elective office in the world.

At the time of his Presidency, HARRY S TRUMAN was bitterly attacked from all sides for the actions he took as President. He lived long enough to have history not only set the record

straight, but also to elevate him to a place among our greatest Presidents.

It was as a great human being, however, that he captured the love of the American people. What he did for humanity in a world in turmoil and chaos made him a statesman of the foremost rank. What he was as a person—fiercely loyal to friends and completely devoted to family and unashamedly patriotic—earned him a place in the hearts of Americans which few Presidents managed to achieve or maintain after the glamor of holding our highest office had ended.

We in Missouri regarded HARRY TRUMAN as a man of such complete personal integrity and honor that he became a symbol of the best in political service. He was a good politician in every sense of the word, and he made politics a respectable profession in our State.

Although he had been out of the political battles for most of the past 20 years, devoting his time to the Truman Library of which he was so deeply proud, he was always willing to share his wisdom and political experience with those who sought out his views, and he never pulled his punches.

His gracious and courageous wife, one of the finest First Ladies to have served in the White House, his sweetheart through a long, long life together, has our deepest sympathy and great affection as she faces the lonely days and years ahead. We all realize the tremendous loss she has suffered. And to Margaret Truman Daniel, in whom HARRY TRUMAN took such fatherly pride, we express our profound sympathy and also our joy that she was so successful in so many ways in honoring her father through her love and devotion.

Hon. William L. Hungate

OF MISSOURI

Mr. Speaker, I am pleased to join in the tribute to our great President, Mr. HARRY S TRUMAN.

One of Mr. TRUMAN's statements was that "If you do your best, history will do the rest." I think his life has certainly demonstrated that fact.

One of the things I liked about Mr. TRUMAN and one of the stories that followed him was about the time he faced the problem that we all face in politics when people would run up and say, "Do you know who I am? Can you tell me my name?"

Someone is alleged to have run up to Mr. TRU-MAN when he was running for the Senate and said, "I bet you do not know who I am," to which Mr. TRUMAN said, "No, and I don't give a damn."

Well, a lot of us wish we could have that courage, but few of us could be elected doing that, except a man like HARRY TRUMAN.

Another story in Mr. TRUMAN's memoirs relates to an incident in Wellsville, Mo., in my district, when he was running for the Senate at the time of his second term. There was a Republican meeting over there, Mr. TRUMAN relates in his memoirs, and the man running against him, I believe, was named Davis, in the year of 1940. According to Mr. TRUMAN's story, he said that there had been some lies printed about him in the St. Louis Post Dispatch and the Kansas City Star and Mr. Davis was repeating them and apparently having a grand time doing it. When he got done a man from that community, Jim Wade, went up to Forrest Donnell, who was the elected Governor in that year, a Republican, campaigning with Davis on the Republican ticket, and Wade said, "Could those stories about Mr. TRU-MAN be true, and if it is true, could he still be Grand Master of the Masonic Lodge," to which he was elected. To his great credit, Forrest Donnell said, "No," whereupon Mr. Wade repeated that story around, and according to Mr. TRUMAN that was good for many votes.

They also report that in Mr. TRUMAN's career he first learned that you must be faithful to your friends, although they may sometimes fall on bad times. This was certainly demonstrated in the Pendergast affair with Mr. TRUMAN. It was, indeed, they say, a semi-falling out between Mr. Pendergast and Bennett Clark over the patronage through Franklin Delano Roosevelt that led Mr. Pendergast to look for someone to take the other Senate seat and Pendergast sought someone who was opposing Clark's candidate for the Senate. Of course, Mr. TRUMAN came to be that man after being turned down earlier in his desire to run for Congress. They had a Senate opening, and it was offered to him, and he was successful in it. Of course, it became the privilege then of Senator Bennett Clark, then senior Senator from Missouri, to present Mr. TRUMAN to the Senate when he took his oath.

Later on it was Bennett Clark, the son of Speaker Champ Clark of Missouri, who made the nominating speech for Mr. TRUMAN when he became Vice President in 1944. Senator TRU-MAN was opposed, as I have mentioned, in 1940 by then Gov. Lloyd C. Stark. TRUMAN was seeking his second term in the Senate, and as one who lived in Governor Stark's home county in those days I can attest to Mr. TRUMAN's popularity. As fast as you took down his posters, someone else put them up. He was recognized across the State as a champion of the people.

He had a certain grandness of character, and again he relates in his memoirs how in World War II he appointed Paul Stark, who was the brother of his old senatorial opponent Gov. Lloyd Stark, to conduct a victory garden campaign throughout the country.

Mr. TRUMAN drew valuably on his Army experience. He knew what that meant in the service of his country. He relates, in fact, that it was through that experience it made him such a great friend of the State of Israel, that is, in recognizing Israel's independence only minutes after it had been declared.

He related the story of how his old haberdashery partner, Mr. Jacobson, a Jewish friend, came to the White House. One of the great rabbis had come to Washington, but Mr. TRU-MAN repeatedly refused to see either him or anyone from either side in the controversy. However, this Jewish buddy of his from his Army days came to him and said he had never asked him for anything but this was a great religious leader and that he should see him. He did, and this led to historic action from which the world profits today.

It has been written that Mr. TRUMAN was wrong in most of his small decisions, but right on all of the big ones. I think that we all join in that commendation, and hope that other leaders of our national life can have a similar success.

Hon. Wm. J. Randall

OF MISSOURI

Mr. Speaker, I might interject at this point that the gentlemen to which he was referring were Eddie Jacobson and also Eddie Meisberger. But while HARRY S TRUMAN was very close to those men he was also close to each of those whom he regarded as his buddies in Battery D.

Mr. Speaker, I could not conclude these observations made in the memory of this great President without calling your attention to two of his famous sayings that describe the man perhaps better than anything else.

As you know, on President TRUMAN's desk were the words, "The buck stops here." That should show his forthrightness and his straightforwardness as well as his courage.

Then again there were the words that he used so many times, "If you can't stand the heat, get out of the kitchen."

Well, Mr. Speaker, this man from Missouri proved again and again that he could thrive on the heat of the kitchen, and he had the courage and the grit to take heat from any source once he was convinced that he was right.

I said in the beginning of these comments that rather than reciting events which are a matter of history, or particular official enactments, I would try to say something about the doer of those deeds. It seems to me that we should take a moment to look back on some of his personal characteristics. And if I may be pardoned I know firsthand of some of those from my personal experience.

I would first consider the matter of the personal honesty of this man, which was also mentioned by the gentleman from Missouri (Mr. Hungate) in his remarks. He referred to his membership in what was then called the Pendergast organization—and it is true there had been some local scandals—but one evening in August of 1934 Mr. TRUMAN came to me and asked me if I would journey south about 90 miles to the city of Nevada, Mo., in Vernon County, which is now in our congressional district.

He said, "I heard those people down there say that because I am a part of the Pendergast organization there must be guilt by association. Will you go down there to speak for me?" I said, "Why, of course." He was then serving as judge of the county court. I went that night because I was personally convinced of his honesty. I went down there because I knew that. Here was a man who was a presiding judge, and chief administrative officer of a large metropolitan county who was spending, even in those days, between $15 and $20 million a year without ever a hint of any sort of scandal of any kind. And he served for two full terms in that capacity. The man was completely honest.

Then we hear it so often said that he was a man who had lots of other good characteristics and personal traits of character of a very high order. And when it comes right down to it these characteristics were ingrained in him. Once again I go back to a comment made by the gentleman from Missouri (Mr. Hungate) when he was referring to the campaign in 1940. At that time it was my lot to be driving and working in the campaign with the candidate for Governor, the late Larry McDaniels, and the late Hunter Allen was Mr. TRUMAN's driver. And one day in the early part of September Mr. Allen became ill, and Mr. McDaniel offered to loan me as a driver to Mr. TRUMAN, who was then a candidate in his second term. And he said to Mr. McDaniel, "That is a generous offer, and I am grateful."

One night about 5:30 or a quarter of 6 we were together, the candidate for Governor and the candidate for Senate, Mr. TRUMAN in a motel out west of Columbia, Mo., known as the Pierce Pennant Motel, and which was run by the Sinclair Oil people. That night, Mr. TRUMAN discovered that he had used his last clean shirt.

I recall I stepped up and said, "Well," referring to my own shirt, I said, "I do not know whether this is much better, but you are certainly welcome to it." Actually another aide ran downtown and bought one just before the stores closed.

From then on, again and again, he expressed his gratitude to me many times. He said, in my presence to others, "Here is a man who is such a good friend that he would take the shirt off his back and give to a friend in need."

He was a man who believed that gratitude was one of the most important traits of character that a man can have.

Finally, there was one other trait that he demonstrated so many times—his humility. It was in early 1971 when there was a movement by several Members to introduce legislation to award to our former President the Congressional Medal of Honor. I, as his Congressman, knowing of the man's reluctance to have so many edifices and stadiums and highways and airports named after him, thought it was best that I be certain of his wishes in this matter.

So it was that I had one of the last and one of the longest and one of the most pleasant conversations with Mr. TRUMAN in April of 1971 at their home and in the presence of Mrs. Truman, in which we asked him about his wishes in this matter.

I think the whole thing was summed up by The New York Times in their story following that occasion. The headline of the story was "Thanks, But No Thanks."

He made it so plain to me that even if the President of the United States came out to present him with that Medal of Honor, he would decline to accept it because of his humbleness and his humility—he said he did not deserve it and that it should be reserved only for those who earned it in combat.

Here is a letter which I shall always treasure and which I will read into the Record at this time, from HARRY S TRUMAN, Independence, Mo., on April 8, 1971:

> INDEPENDENCE, Mo.,
> *April 8, 1971.*
>
> Hon. WM. J. RANDALL,
> *House of Representatives, Washington, D.C.*
>
> DEAR BILL: Your visit with me about the proposed award of the Congressional Medal of Honor was most pleasant and I greatly appreciate your interest in this matter. I am writing this to confirm my views and reasons and my unwillingness to accept one.
>
> In the first place, I do not consider that I have done anything which should be the reason for any award, Congressional or otherwise.
>
> Next, the Congressional Medal of Honor was instituted for combat service. This is as it should be and to deviate by giving it for any other reason lessens and dilutes its true significance. Also, it would detract from those who have received the award because of their combat service.
>
> Therefore, I again confirm what I told you—I would not accept it.
>
> This does not mean I do not appreciate what you and others have done, because I do appreciate the kind things that have been said and the proposal to have the award offered to me.
>
> Therefore, I close by saying thanks, but I will not accept a Congressional Medal of Honor.
>
> Sincerely yours,
>
> (S) HARRY S TRUMAN.

"Thanks, but no thanks"—that was proof once again of that trait of character of a man who was a great man but also a humble man.

Mr. Speaker, all of us will mourn his passing in the days which lie ahead. We will all miss this great American who was loved by everyone.

Hon. Carl Albert

OF OKLAHOMA

Mr. Speaker, I wish to join with my colleagues who have expressed tributes to HARRY S TRUMAN.

The passing of the former President brought a special loss to the American people and to me personally. HARRY TRUMAN was President when I came to Congress, and I will be eternally grateful for his thoughtfulness and wise counsel. He was one of the finest men I have ever known.

HARRY TRUMAN was loved and respected by millions of people he never had a chance to meet. He was a people's President, a man who always was himself and a man with whom every citizen could identify. As President he displayed an unequaled courage and determination in his selfless service to our Nation. A fighter who vigorously entered many battles, HARRY TRUMAN weathered every storm. Only after an insurmountable weariness of body did his fighting heart lay down to rest.

No one could deny that HARRY TRUMAN lived every minute of his life to the fullest. Even his 20 years of retirement were filled with productivity and service to others. Memories of HARRY TRUMAN will live forever in the hearts of all Americans. He made too great a mark to ever be forgotten. He has made his place not only as a great human being but as one of the extraordinary Presidents in our Nation's history.

Hon. Richard H. Ichord

OF MISSOURI

Mr. Speaker, one of the thrilling aspects of American history is that we so often see ordinary men accomplishing extraordinary things in this country. Some of our great leaders have been men of noble birth and wealth as George Washington. Others have been men of common birth and poor childhoods as Abraham Lincoln. HARRY S TRUMAN, who is undoubtedly the most famous son of the great State of Missouri, was an ordinary man in every respect, but few men in the history of this proud Republic will be remembered for more extraordinary accomplishments.

Each time a great leader passes away, Mr. Speaker, we talk of the great loss our country has suffered. Yet in the case of former President HARRY S TRUMAN I somehow feel that we have lost more than a great man, a great leader, and a true statesman. I feel that the death of Mr. TRUMAN may symbolize the loss of a great spirit in this Nation. There was a spirit which prevailed in the early days of this country enabling the pilgrims to endure the hard winters and the attacks by unfriendly Indians and allowing Washington's men to survive the impossible winter at Valley Forge. This spirit guided our forefathers as they took this vast uncharted wilderness and turned it into the greatest, most advanced and most powerful nation in the history of man in a few short years.

Mr. TRUMAN had this spirit which enabled him to make the big decisions without taking a poll to determine the public reaction or worrying about the political risks involved. HARRY S TRUMAN was a rugged individualist who did not start out to be President, but was not afraid to take a stand and stick it out. He was a common man—a man of the people—and his only concern during the 7 years he held the most important office in the world was to do what was best for the Nation and her people. He was a decisive man and a true politician with great love for and dedication to his political party, but he was statesman enough to know where partisan politics must cease and the country must come first.

HARRY TRUMAN, the simple haberdasher from a small town in Missouri, was called upon to make some of the most difficult and momentous decisions in the history of our country, ranging from the dropping of the atomic bomb on Hiroshima to the institution of the Marshall plan. The use of the atomic bomb against the Japanese was particularly a difficult decision for a gentle kindhearted man to make, yet it undoubtedly saved the lives of thousands of my own generation of Americans in an invasion of the Japanese islands. To paraphrase one of his own favorite sayings, "he could stand the heat and stay in the kitchen."

HARRY TRUMAN was indeed a man who could make a decision and stand by it without weakening. The buck always stopped with HARRY TRUMAN. His courage and decisive action saved Iran, Greece, Turkey, South Korea and all of Western Europe from falling into the Communist camp. The Truman doctrine was responsible for containing the runaway spread of communism. He loved freedom and felt that the right to be free could not be limited only to our own shores. Sir Winston Churchill quite frankly confessed that though he dreaded to see HARRY TRUMAN become President of the United States, the unimposing Missourian had done more to contain communism than any man in the world.

On the occasion of the burial of Julius Caesar, Mark Antony stated his concern that:

The evil that men do lives after them, the good is oft interred with their bones.

This I do not believe is the case with HARRY TRUMAN. History has already been much kinder to him than his contemporaries were. His term of office has been marked as a period of one of America's strongest, most courageous and greatest Presidents. It is my opinion that future historians will recognize this fact even stronger.

As I said, Mr. Speaker, HARRY TRUMAN's death may signify the end of a great era in our history when leaders knew the real meaning of courage, loyalty, statesmanship, and dedication. It is entirely possible that President TRUMAN will be the last man of modest means who rose from the ranks of the common people to become President. I believe that our Nation is stronger and our lives richer because this man of the people served in the highest office in our land. I also strongly believe that if we will all remember his dedication in serving the people that our roles in government will be more meaningful and productive.

Hon. William A. Barrett
OF PENNSYLVANIA

Mr. Speaker, on December 26, 1972, the distinguished 33d President of the United States, HARRY S TRUMAN, died at the age of 88 years. As one of the few remaining Members of this body who served here during the Presidency of HARRY S TRUMAN, I can recall that my service in those years from 1945 to 1953 under his leadership as one of the great experiences of my political career. I have always said, even in those lean, post-war years when everyone was condemning President TRUMAN, that he would be recorded in history as one of our greatest Presidents. History is beginning at this time to so record him.

The man from Independence succeeded to the Great Office of the Presidency at one of the most difficult times in our history. It was his duty to end World War II, to preside over the reconstruction of Europe, and the reordering of our domestic affairs following the war. Few people in 1945 knew or expected HARRY TRUMAN to be able to handle this impossible task. His first decisive actions were of the caliber that led me to believe early that HARRY TRUMAN had the makings of a great President. He was one of those rare Presidents who understood and respected the Congress, but more importantly, who understood the American people. It was his grasp of the issues that affected the American people that led him to believe all the time that he would win the 1948 presidential election. I can recall in 1948 myself the doubts that most people in my own city of Philadelphia had as to whether President Truman would carry Philadelphia. Early in the campaign, I was one of those who felt that he would not be able to win in Philadelphia, but as the campaign wore on, as I spoke to more and more of my constituents, they told me that Truman was their choice. It was the little man, the workingman, who gave Harry Truman the support.

We have all read and heard of the great accomplishments of Harry S Truman during his presidential career, but I think one of the truly great attributes of this man was this dignity and independence that he retained as an ex-President from 1953 till his death on December 26. President Truman's career has been heralded for the great accomplishments in presiding over the ending of the war, the reconstruction of Europe and the containment of communism in both Europe and Asia. His accomplishments on the domestic scene, in my opinion, were as extraordinary as his accomplishments in foreign affairs. He did not succeed in enacting many of his domestic proposals such as Federal aid to education, federally assisted medical care for the aged, and greatly expanded Federal assistance to housing and urban development. He provided the leadership and initiative in these domestic areas for succeeding Presidents and Congresses to enact into law. In the field of which I am particularly interested, housing and community development, President Truman's 4-year battle to establish major new initiatives in housing and urban development came to fruition in the historic Housing Act of 1949. Without his leadership and patient negotiations this historic act would have never been enacted in its existing form. He was the first President to stand up and assert the rights of all Americans. He boldly desegregated the Armed Forces and sent the first civil rights message to the Congress. He always held firmly to his convictions and never wavered even when the political odds were against him. Harry S Truman was a great and humble man, a friend and truly one of the great Presidents of this country.

Hon. Joe L. Evins
OF TENNESSEE

Mr. Speaker, I want to take this means of paying a brief but sincere tribute to the late President Harry S Truman.

Harry Truman was an outstanding Senator, a great President, and an American in the truest sense of the word. History has already judged this unassuming President from Missouri as one of our great Presidents.

It so happened that when I first came to the Congress, the Members of our "freshman class" in the 80th Congress were invited to meet with President Truman. Our "class" included our distinguished colleagues, Speaker Carl Albert and former President John F. Kennedy, and we all enjoyed the cordial get-together with President Truman, which was arranged by the late Speaker Sam Rayburn.

Years later on the occasion of President Truman's 70th birthday, Dean Acheson, who served as Secretary of State in his administration, discussed the life and career of this outstanding leader. Secretary Acheson pointed out that Harry Truman had a rare quality—a quality few people possess—the ability to make decisions and to make up one's mind on public issues—and, more than that, the ability to make right decisions.

Many Presidents appoint commissions and committees to study matters that are brought before them for action. Not Harry Truman—he refused to pass the buck. He accepted the responsibility of the Presidency and he acted with courage and decisiveness.

Some of the major decisions—right decisions—which President Truman made include his orders to resist Communist aggression in Korea; drop the atomic bomb on Japan, to end the war and which saved thousands of American lives; to strengthen Greece and Turkey against the threat of communism through a program of assistance known as the Truman doctrine; and his support of the establishment of the United Nations as an instrument to promote peace.

At the Democratic National Convention when he was nominated for the Presidency in 1948, the banners pin-pointed another of President Truman's great qualities with the words: "Truman is Human."

Indeed he was, in the tradition of Andrew

Jackson. He was truly a man of the people, plain, outspoken, shunning pomp and ceremony.

As a result of the hard and difficult decisions which he made unhesitatingly, HARRY TRUMAN attracted some criticism during his years in office. But the criticisms are now forgotten and even though he has been out of office only 20 years, his place in history as one of our greatest Presidents is assured.

Certainly I want to extend my deepest sympathies to Mrs. Bess Truman and daughter Margaret and other members of the family in their loss and bereavement.

Hon. Frank Annunzio
OF ILLINOIS

Mr. Speaker, our Nation is now in a period of mourning for the passing of a great man, HARRY TRUMAN, 33d President of the United States.

I was privileged to have the opportunity during the historic election campaign of 1948 to be the regional director of the Truman campaign in the States of Illinois, Indiana, and Wisconsin for the United Steelworkers of America. In 1948, I had the pleasure of meeting with President TRUMAN in the Blackstone Hotel in Chicago where we discussed the various phases of his campaign affecting the Midwest section of our country.

I was also the labor chairman of one of the greatest labor parades held in the history of our country for any presidential candidate. The parade assembled on Michigan Avenue and proceeded down Madison Street where 1 million people cheered this great and humble man who symbolized to them such human qualities as honesty and integrity, for Mr. TRUMAN did not indulge in the kind of political rhetoric that spells out demagogue. He was blessed with humility, compassion and understanding of the common man because he was one of them. People were inspired by his leadership because they knew instinctly that he gave of himself.

The TRUMAN style of leadership was a style of tough compassion in those crucial post-war years. It took toughness to stand up to the challenges of that era and deal decisively with the various economic and military threats poised by the Nation's antagonists. Yet, through it all, President TRUMAN was also able to establish the

Nation he loved as a model of compassion—a model of selfless concern the likes of which the world had never seen.

President TRUMAN will never be forgotten by Americans or by people around the world. His personal example of integrity in the face of difficulties and detractors will endure as an inspiration to all of us who must carry on. He did his best and that is all any of us can ask of our fellow human beings or of ourselves.

Mrs. Annunzio and I extend our deepest sympathy to President TRUMAN's devoted wife, Bess, and daughter, Margaret. We are proud to have been associated with this great man.

Hon. Clement J. Zablocki
OF WISCONSIN

Mr. Speaker, I am proud to join my colleagues in paying tribute to the late President HARRY S TRUMAN. As President TRUMAN was the first President under whom I had the privilege to serve as a Member of the House of Representatives, I feel a special sense of loss at his passing.

While he was President, Mr. TRUMAN was called upon to make some of the most difficult decisions ever required of a President, and for his courageous and firm convictions he has rightly been called one of our Nation's truly great Presidents.

What is equally important is that while Mr. TRUMAN was a great President of and for the people of this Nation, he was essentially a humble man who saw his first duty to his wife and daughter. His retirement years were quitely spent with his wife in Independence, at the same time he continued his contributions of public service through the Truman Library. The sad news of his passing grieved his friends and acquaintances. The world's great leaders remembered him and sent tributes to his widow. Although they all would have been privileged to pay their respects in person, typical of his life, President TRUMAN requested a simple service. Only close friends and neighbors were honored to be participants in the funeral rites, although thousands throughout the Nation were in attendance in spirit, paying homage to a great humanitarian leader.

Mr. TRUMAN will be remembered for his contribution to the welfare of his fellowman, his firm determination to prevent aggression and oppression. Most of all, he will be remembered for his sincerity, honesty, humility, and devotion to his friends and countrymen.

President TRUMAN never forgot his friends or a favor—although he forgave his adversaries, he apparently never forgot their deeds.

My wife Blanche joins me in expressing deep sympathy to Mrs. Truman, her daughter, Mrs. Daniel, and to all of the Truman family. We hope they derive consolation from the knowledge that his loss is shared by his many friends.

Hon. Henry B. Gonzalez

OF TEXAS

Mr. Speaker, if there is any one word to describe HARRY S TRUMAN, that word is "courage."

HARRY S TRUMAN probably never thought of himself as a great man. If we are to believe his own words, he never wanted to be Vice President, let alone President. He did want to be a Senator, and accepted higher office only on the insistence of President Roosevelt. We are fortunate that Roosevelt made this choice, and even more fortunate that TRUMAN accepted Roosevelt's invitation to become Vice President. For if TRUMAN never thought himself a great man, his stature has surely grown in our eyes, and it is plain that the 33d President of the United States was among the very great ones.

TRUMAN never accomplished all he set out to do—but most of the ideas he espoused have since been adopted, and it is to his great credit that he advanced proposals that where bold enough to encompass the real needs of this Nation—even though there were not enough people of courage here on the Hill to make those ideas into law. TRUMAN's failures were only temporary; his successes were on the other hand hardly temporary at all, but lasting victories for us, for humanity, for the causes of right and justice.

TRUMAN understood the nature of his job—to make hard decisions. He never shrank from that. He did not equivocate and he did not hide. He did not resist a fight, and did not attempt to hide hard truths in glittering language. He did not want to change his image, but only to be himself. It did not matter to him that he would be criticized as uncouth or unstylish, because that did not make any difference to the job he wanted to do.

Who can imagine the shock that TRUMAN must have felt when he was told on April 12,

1945, that he was President? He had only been Vice President for 3 months. The war was raging toward its conclusion; he knew little about the great and secret issues of the time; he had had no time to learn, and less opportunity. But beginning at that moment, he had to make decisions affecting all mankind, possibly for generations to come. TRUMAN did not shrink from it. He did what he had to do—and most of it turned out to be right.

It was up to TRUMAN to make the terrible decision on whether to use the atomic bomb against Japan. Such a decision no man should have to make, but he decided, and never looked back. We may now disagree, but we never had the responsibility, and can never know exactly what TRUMAN's reasons were—only that he thought he had taken the best available course of action to end the bitterest and most costly struggle in history.

Having ended the war, TRUMAN carried on bravely the efforts to construct a lasting and universal peace. It was he who got the United Nations charter approved, and he who appointed Roosevelt's widow to represent the United States in the organization—perhaps our most effective representative ever.

It was TRUMAN who decided that the development of atomic energy should take place under civilian auspices, and who successfully sponsored the creation of the Atomic Energy Commission for that purpose. This decision made it possible for us to begin at the earliest possible date a program to make atomic energy more than a tool of war, but a source of power for peace.

It was TRUMAN who saw and met the danger of Communist expansion in Greece and Turkey, and who created a doctrine to meet and resist that danger—successfully. From that came the Marshall plan, which TRUMAN supported and fought for, and which made possible the postwar reconstruction of Europe. Later, this same program gave birth to the World Bank and its affiliates, which today include 116 or more member nations, and which provides billions in loans for development programs. More than any other action, these programs made it possible for the world to regain the lost productivity and prosperity destroyed by the world war; these programs enabled our postwar generation to avoid the bitter depression, and the war-seeding frustrations that followed World War I.

But TRUMAN was not only a great decisionmaker in the foreign field.

TRUMAN proposed what he called the Fair Deal—plain language for a plain purpose. Not much of this program became law, not because it was wrong, but because Congress was hostile to him and his program. Years later, virtually every part of the Fair Deal became law— though it then was called the New Frontier and the Great Society. TRUMAN wanted universal, compulsory medical insurance. He never got it. More than a dozen years after he retired, Congress approved medicare. This program aroused the most bitter and fanatic kind of opposition—but after its enactment, no one questioned its wisdom or the need for it. TRUMAN had been right.

It was TRUMAN who desegregated the military services and went as far as he could to get fair employment practices required in defense contracts. But it was years later before he saw the poll tax outlawed, saw the courts strike down legalized segregation, and saw Congress enact laws requiring desegregation of public facilities, all goals he had set in early 1948.

TRUMAN raised the minimum wage, expanded its coverage, strengthened the social security program, worked for an adequate housing program, bitterly fought against programs he saw as being against the public interest, and stood firm for what he saw as the right—and always with plain and straightforward talk.

TRUMAN won the most remarkable election contest in history, in 1948. All of us then, and all of us now, admire the courage and resolution he showed in running a hard contest at a time when everybody said he would lose, and when he could not raise enough money to carry on a decent campaign. TRUMAN's famous train would be stalled in one place or another, because he could not raise the money to pay for moving it further; but somehow he carried on. He could not raise adequate money for radio time, and more than once was cut off the air for failure to pay. But he fought on, and he won. Those who wondered at his courage did not know that in 1940 President Roosevelt had asked TRUMAN not to run for reelection to the Senate, but TRUMAN insisted anyway. It was a formidable decision—the kind of decision that showed the strength of the man who later carried off his miracle in 1948.

TRUMAN's enemies were on top of the world by 1951. They had Communists to hunt—mostly phantoms. They roared about corruption. They decried the tragedy of Korea. But time passed those men by—McCarthy died a disgrace, corruption under TRUMAN was nothing like it later was under the administrations of his severest critics and staunchest enemies; and Korea ended in a stalemate that to this day requires U.S. troops and lives to maintain—more men than we have even in Vietnam. And where an obscure man named Nixon could attack TRUMAN on Korea, that same man today has a much greater tragedy in Vietnam, but where TRUMAN spelled out the situation honestly, today we meet only silence from a mostly empty White House.

TRUMAN was a simple man. He did not want to put up a fence around his house. He did not want to discourage people from knowing him. He did not want empty honor.

Most of all, TRUMAN was an honest man. He did his best, never shirked, and never looked back. He had no image makers, wanted none, and needed none. He knew what his job was, and he did it. A simple, honest, brave man, HARRY S TRUMAN. We were lucky to have him serve this great country, and I am sorry to see him gone.

Hon. Charles E. Chamberlain
OF MICHIGAN

Mr. Speaker, in reflecting on the service of former President HARRY S TRUMAN to our country I want to call the attention of my colleagues to two editorials appearing in the Citizen Patriot of Jackson, Mich., December 17, 1972, and December 27, 1972. The first one is entitled "HARRY S TRUMAN Improved World" and the second, "A Bit of History Lost in HST's Death." They both call attention to the fact that President TRUMAN was a man who did what had to be done.

The editorials follow:

[From the Jackson (Mich.) Citizen Patriot, Dec. 17, 1972]

HARRY S TRUMAN IMPROVED WORLD

The life and times of HARRY S TRUMAN are Horatio Alger carried to heights that make the author pale in comparison:

A Missouri farm boy who ascended to the presidency of the world's most powerful nation;

A politician schooled and aided by a corrupt political machine who forced his detractors to admit he had outgrown that influence;

A man who ordered the first use of the atomic bomb, but who also pioneered in the civil rights movement;

A statesman who engaged in international politics as Bobby Fischer handles chess, who blocked the advance of communism around the world with bold moves;

A commander-in-chief who, when challenged by one of the nation's most popular generals, summarily fired him for refusing to carry out orders;

A compassionate leader of a victorious nation who implemented the Marshall Plan for rebuilding devastated Europe;

The list is tremendously long, including such things as the Truman Doctrine, the North Atlantic Treaty, Point Four program for underdeveloped nations, to add but a few.

Yet two things stand out formidably in President Truman's journey through life: courage and humbleness.

He proved he had the courage to do what he felt needed doing, often in the face of challenge that would make other, more ordinary mortals pale.

As inheritor of the presidency when Franklin Delano Roosevelt died on April 12, 1945, Truman also inherited World War II and the climactic work of the Manhattan Project which culminated in the first successful explosion of an atomic bomb on July 16 of the same year. Truman accepted control of the awesome device and used it to end the war in the Pacific within weeks. That momentous decision which ushered in the age of atomic jitters, was closely followed by approval of plans to move ahead with the more formidable hydrogen bomb.

In a manner of speaking he set the tone of international politics for decades, and the name of the game became raw power.

Then he turned his talents to peaceful goals and led the nation to new heights in helping others, not just other nations, but people.

He implemented the civil rights of Roosevelt, both with legislation pressed through Congress and by example in his executive orders and appointments.

Thus a man, at times derisively referred to as a "Missouri cracker," again proved his humanity, leadership and courage.

When he finally retired from office, President Truman set about proving he also had a sense of history, establishing the $1,750,000 Harry S Truman Library with private contributions paying the cost.

In it is displayed a tremendous array of material relating to the war years and his presidency. It was his stated wish at the time that the library should be a repository for both scholars and the general public, and to help it come true, he worked there daily from 1952 until 1966. Today the repository is valued at $21 million and is open to the public as well as scholars.

He also established a little-known activity called the Truman Institute, which provides grants-in-aid to students, again demonstrating his consuming interest in people.

His years in office were often marked with controversy, but he thrived on it. He made no bones about liking a drink and a hand of poker, and often entertained visitors by playing the piano.

Unpredictability and an outspokenness that often startled people were trademarks, as were the "press conferences" held as he strode on his long walks until arthritis slowed him down.

Harry S Truman became a legend in his own time, a man of small stature who nonetheless will always be regarded as a giant.

Cast for a time in the legendary role of Atlas, he responded to the demands of history-in-the-making in the best tradition of a Horatio Alger hero, and then improved the model.

It can truly be said that the world is a better place because Harry S Truman chose to leave the Missouri farm of his parents and enter the world of statesmanship.

❧

[From the Jackson (Mich.) Citizen Patriot, Dec. 27, 1972]

A BIT OF HISTORY LOST IN HST'S DEATH

Harry S Truman's political friends and foes agree that America lost a bit of its history in the death yesterday of the 33rd president of the United States.

A colorful but humble man who left his Missouri farm home to enter politics, Mr. Truman had the responsibility of the White House thrust on him overnight with the death of President Franklin D. Roosevelt on April 12, 1945. The fiery man from Independence was pushed onto the stage of world statesmanship at a time when America, at the time the mightiest nation in the world, needed his courage and fearless leadership to guide it through a critical period of world history.

His great and difficult decisions always were made in the interest of the United States and its place in the community of world nations. And his actions and his policies laid the foundation for world peace.

As was noted in this column on December 17 when Mr. Truman was tenaciously struggling for life, he "had the courage to do what he felt needed doing, often in the face of challenge that would make other, more ordinary mortals pale."

His career in the White House was marked by unprecedented decisions—the atomic bombing of Japan, the Marshall Plan, the Berlin blockade airlift, the go-ahead for the development of the hydrogen bomb—and many more.

His most difficult decision? The dispatch of U.S. troops to Korea in a "police action" that kept Communist troops from advancing past the 38th parallel.

Harry Truman was the last of the great leaders of World War II—Stalin, Churchill, deGaulle, MacArthur and Eisenhower—all of whom preceded him in death.

World leaders in paying tribute to this typical and extraordinary American, mentioned his lack of fear. This was Mr. Truman's greatest quality as a president and world leader. His disdain of fear contributed to the building of a proud America. Regretfully, it is a trait that seems to be fading from our society.

The free world grieves the passing of the fiery Man from Independence, but it regards him as a man whose life was complete. He made it that way.

Mr. Truman's courage, decisiveness, integrity and judgment secure his place in history. He was a man who "did what had to be done."

Mr. Speaker, as we pay tribute to former President Harry S Truman, I would like to take this opportunity to call attention to an editorial in The State Journal of Lansing, Mich., of December 29, 1972, entitled "Truman Won Place in History." This particularly emphasizes the fact that President Truman was a man destined by fate to become Chief Executive of the most powerful Nation in the world at one of its most crucial periods in history. The editorial points out that he moved swiftly to marshal national unity as World War II drew to its conclusion. I commend this editorial to the attention of my colleagues.

TRUMAN WON PLACE IN HISTORY

Former President HARRY S TRUMAN was a man destined by fate to become chief executive of the most powerful nation in the world at one of its most crucial periods in history.

The burden that fell on his shoulders in April of 1945 was greater than that faced by any president in this century. He went on to become one of the most respected world leaders of our times. Now he is dead at age 88, and the nation mourns a truly outstanding American.

Mr. TRUMAN stepped into the shoes of Franklin D. Roosevelt at a time when a whole generation had grown up never having known or remembered a previous president. There were many wisecracks about "whatshisname" in the White House and real concern about how he would do.

From his very first day in office Mr. TRUMAN demonstrated that he was a leader and not just a little-known man from Missouri who would be overwhelmed in the great Washington mansion on Pennsylvania Ave.

He moved swiftly to marshal national unity as World War II drew to its fiery conclusion. At the Potsdam Conference, following the end of the war in Europe, he put Soviet leaders on quick and blunt notice that he was no political novice.

The President made it clear to Joseph Stalin that he would not tolerate any Communist military ventures or expansion ambitions. He backed it all up with the Marshall Plan and a head-on confrontation in the Berlin Blockade.

When North Korea Communist armies, goaded by Stalin, invaded South Korea in 1950, President TRUMAN startled the Communist world when he ordered immediate retaliation by U.S. armed forces. Stalin never tested Mr. TRUMAN's willpower again.

Mr. TRUMAN was also a man who believed that his title of Commander in Chief of the armed forces meant exactly that. He risked political disaster by dismissing the revered and powerful Gen. Douglas MacArthur from his command in the feud over Korean War policy—and he made it stick.

In his campaign for re-election in 1948, HARRY TRUMAN was labeled a sure loser. Characteristically, he charged out on the campaign trail to tell his story to the people. Everybody knows the results.

President TRUMAN is remembered more than anything else for his down-to-earth, blunt confrontation with the people and issues he faced. He tackled the mighty and joked with people on the streets, and provided the best description of his own job and philosophy when he said, "the buck stops here!"

HARRY TRUMAN made that remark the trademark of his career. Millions of Americans and other people the world over mourn him. History will not forget him.

Hon. Bill Nichols

OF ALABAMA

Mr. Speaker, the flags in our Nation remain at half-staff today as we continue to mourn the death of HARRY S TRUMAN, the 33d President of the United States.

It is extremely difficult, if not impossible, for us to evaluate the Presidency of HARRY TRUMAN; that will be up to the historians of tomorrow. But during that period from 1945 to 1952 when he served his country in that high office, HARRY TRUMAN gave our war-weary Nation a leader— a plain but outspoken man that almost every citizen of this country could identify with.

Mr. Speaker, in recent days, we have read many tributes to President TRUMAN. One of the finest I have read was written by Charles Greer, the editor and publisher of the Sylacauga, Ala., News. I would like to submit Mr. Greer's editorial for my colleagues reading and evaluation:

THE NATION MOURNS

"When President Roosevelt died, I thought there must be a million men better qualified than I to take up the presidential task, but the work was mine to do and I had to do it and I tried to give it everything that is in me."—HARRY S TRUMAN.

So spoke the man who was destined to become the 33rd President of the United States, and who history will prove to have been one of the most qualified and consequential presidents chronicled.

He is dead now, this incorruptible man who was only the tenth vice-president of our country to be elevated to the position of president. And during the almost eight full years from 1945 to 1953 his actions changed the face of history.

The rise of HARRY TRUMAN from farm boy to President of the United States is a tribute to the country which he served with such fervor and dedication. Armed with only a high school education (he failed to enter West Point because of poor eyesight), he worked as a time-keeper for a railroad, wrapped papers for the Kansas City Star, clerked in a bank and finally worked the family farm in Missouri after his father's death.

World War I saw this young man rise to the rank of artillery captain because of outstanding leadership under the stress of battle. Then after this war, in partnership with a fellow veteran, he again showed his abilities by completely paying off debts incurred by business failure at the age of 37—though it took some ten years to pay off a $20,000 debt.

It was then that HARRY TRUMAN turned to "Big Tom" Pendergast and his powerful Missouri political machine. Impressed with his background, the "machine" backed TRUMAN from county judge to presiding judge and finally United States Senator.

It is interesting to note that during his tenure as judge, HARRY TRUMAN attended law school that he might be more qualified for this position and also, the fact he was never involved in a political scandal—even when Boss Pendergast was sent to the penitentiary. He was, in fact, reelected to the Senate as the famous political machine was toppling.

HARRY TRUMAN first gained national attention when, as chairman of the now famous Truman Committee he saved the country literally billions of dollars with his committee's investigation of the National Defense Program.

Then, in 1944, when it was generally conceded by the well informed that Franklin Roosevelt might not live out a fourth term in the office of president, his nomination (on the second ballot) to the vice-presidency was tantamount to that of the presidency. It was the first result of the national prominence he had attained through his investigating committee.

Though it was only some 83 days later that he was to become President of these United States, in that short span of time he proved as vice president his ability as presiding officer over the Senate. He even voted (breaking the tie) to continue lend-lease aid to America's allies.

Now, in fact President, he was totally unprepared for the post. The war in Europe was ending and he had little (if any) knowledge of the late president's agreements at Yalta. Yet he must go to Potsdam and attend a conference that ended with an agreement among allies that Japan must submit to unconditional surrender.

Indeed it did. But only after President TRUMAN made the momentous decision to drop the atomic bomb (which he only learned about after Roosevelt's death) first on Hiroshima and then Nagasaki.

It was following these war years that "give 'em hell HARRY" became the man of the hour—the man who destiny called to reshape in part the world. The Truman Doctrine, which called for United States resistance to international aggression wherever it appeared, was born. It guaranteed U.S. intervention against the more insidious forms of Communist attack—propaganda, infiltration and sabotage. And it came at a time when Great Britain had reached the point it could no longer be the prime defender against the Soviet aggressor in the Near East.

Next came the Marshall Plan, probably the most noteworthy of the late president's accomplishments. For the formula of this plan called for the economic recovery (at the cost of billions of dollars to the United States) of all war-injured nations. Accepted by 16 nations (excluding the Communist bloc), it worked.

His administration also helped draft the North Atlantic Treaty Organization (NATO), lent its support to Latin America, called for the unification of the armed forces and created the Department of Defense. His defeat of the Berlin Blockade through the use of the U.S. Air Force airlift was phenomenal as the entire world watched the Soviet Union finally back down in its efforts to close off the German city.

Of course Mr. TRUMAN suffered setbacks. He witnessed the collapse of the Chinese Nationalist Government and the escape of Chiang Kai-shek to Formosa. And his own popularity waned with the firing of General Douglas MacArthur over disagreement between the two men on how best to wage the Korean War. Yet through all of this, the sign on his desk remained—"The buck stops here."

HARRY TRUMAN wanted to be elected President of these United States on his own—and he was. True he received the nomination by his party at his own insistence, but he won—when every available poll said it was impossible. And though he was not invective, he did have some fun as he mimicked his severest critic H. V. Kaltenborn, who when radio was in its heyday, predicted TRUMAN's defeat right up to the finish.

And the president was relected against overwhelming odds because he threw away the scripts—toured the country making speeches at railroad stations and meetings in the only language he knew, homespun language. When he said, "the next four years there will be a Democrat in the White House and you're looking at him," he meant it . . . sure did.

Many, many of HARRY TRUMAN's sayings have been quoted over the years, but one that will stay with us the longest, and one that symbolizes the man, as far as we are concerned is: "If you can't stand the heat, stay out of the kitchen." HARRY TRUMAN could stand the heat. And the country is better off for having him pass our way.

Hon. Wm. Jennings Bryan Dorn
OF SOUTH CAROLINA

Mr. Speaker, we first came to the Congress during the administration of President TRUMAN; we knew him and served under him. He was the embodiment of some of our Nation's highest traditions. He came from a family of pioneers who had moved to Missouri from Kentucky, and he always represented the hopes and ideals of the American Heartland. HARRY TRUMAN knew what it was like to plow the fields, and he possessed in full measure the traditional rural American virtues of self reliance, honesty, dependability and self-respect.

Mr. Speaker, one cannot make a decision about the future unless he knows the past. Like Washington and Lincoln, what TRUMAN may have lacked in formal higher education was more than made up by his self-education in the university of hard work and experience. TRUMAN had a strong sense of American history and he studied it all his life. He read a great deal, and mastered the story of man down through the corridors of time.

His two great heroes were Andrew Jackson and Robert E. Lee, and it has rightly been said that he combined the qualities of both of them. It was his commonsense grasp of history and current events that enabled him immediately to take control of the situation when the Presidency was thrust upon him.

He barely knew where our armies were when he took office, yet in spite of these very difficult circumstances he became one of our greatest Presidents. TRUMAN had been Vice President for only

83 days when President Roosevelt died, and had not been completely briefed on many crucial developments, including the development of the atomic bomb. Once in office, he took command. His actions were momentous and historic, including crushing Japanese resistance and countering Communist aggression in Europe through the Marshall plan, aid to Greece and Turkey and the Berlin airlift. His decisions were characteristic of a man who understood history and human nature and who knew when it was the time to act. He had a grasp of what the various agencies of Government were doing that few other Presidents have possessed.

HARRY TRUMAN was a master politician. The rough and tumble of Missouri politics had equipped and trained him to handle the Nation's most demanding position. He understood that politics is basically shoe leather, hard work, and handshakes.

No combination of slick public relations and barrels of money could prevent him from successfully taking his case to the people. Through hard work and shoe leather, he won the most astounding upset in American history.

He fought hard in a partisan way, but once in office he put the country first and cooperated fully with the other party. TRUMAN entered public life relatively late in life, after distinguished World War I service in Europe. Because of his reputation for honesty and reliability he was endorsed by the Kansas City political organization, which needed a man of unquestioned integrity to lead the ticket. In his entry into politics he was strongly supported by the men of his World War I local regiment. His word was his bond. It was characteristic of HARRY TRUMAN that after an earlier business reverse he had refused to claim bankruptcy, but insisted on paying all his debts, even though it took him years to do so.

President TRUMAN was one of the great men of our time. He was dedicated to the Presidency. He exalted the office, and would do nothing that would demean it. He zealously guarded the prerogatives of the Chief Executive's office.

His honesty and integrity, sense of history, and the traditional virtues of rural America never left HARRY TRUMAN. He did his duty to the Nation and while President made some of the most far-reaching and momentous decisions ever made affecting the Nation's future. History will rank HARRY S TRUMAN among the great Presidents of all time.

To Mrs. Truman, who has been by his side through the years of public service, and to Mrs. Margaret Truman Daniel, we extend our deepest respect.

Hon. John C. Kluczynski
OF ILLINOIS

Mr. Speaker, the passing of HARRY S TRUMAN, 33d President of the United States, is an occurrence saddening to everyone familiar with the extraordinary political career of that most remarkable man.

It is no exaggeration to say that HARRY TRUMAN earned for himself a place among the elite guard of our Presidential greats. In every area he was knowledgeable; in every act he was swift and sure. No more can be asked of a President of the United States, except victory—and HARRY TRUMAN provided victory, as well.

Moreover, HARRY TRUMAN was capable of learning, in the midst of political turmoil. Elevated to the Presidency in the final stages of World War II, he took to the job in the manner of a man who had been preparing for the experience all his life.

Never before a diplomat, he joined in inaugurating the United Nations, with notable success; never before in a position to implement his reform ideas on a grand scale, he quickly assumed leadership of several major reform movements; never before a farmer, in the literal sense, he took on the task of sustaining wartime agricultural prosperity in the postwar world, and confronted for the first time by the tidal wave of world communism, he met the challenge in the manner of a champion.

No person with interest either in domestic or foreign affairs can easily forget the work of HARRY TRUMAN, with respect to the rescue of postwar Western Europe. In no time at all, following the war, Poland went Communist; then Rumania, Czechoslovakia, Albania, Latvia, Estonia—meanwhile, the Communists were also winning votes in France and Italy, while England, crippled by the rigors of war, stood by helplessly, unable to intervene.

At this point, President TRUMAN, with the guidance of George C. Marshall and the heartfelt support of the American people, came forward with the famed Marshall plan. This was enough to close the floodgates in the face of the

Communist wave and sustain the cause of democracy in the West.

Starving Europe became the recipient of American food and other goods; the French and German economies revived; also those of Italy, the low countries, and Scandinavia. In short time, communism was checked and held fast. Never before was so monumental a victory, affecting the entire world, attributable to the iron will of one leader and the immediate response to one community. The leader, of course, was HARRY S TRUMAN; the community: the great mass of the American people. They made a great and mighty team of which America could well be proud.

I take this occasion to express my admiration for the late HARRY S TRUMAN, one of the outstanding Presidents of our national career.

Hon. Charles E. Bennett

OF FLORIDA

Mr. Speaker, our country and the future of mankind were greatly assisted by the excellent leadership of the late and much beloved President HARRY S TRUMAN.

It was my good fortune to know our late President well. I came to Congress at the time when he was inaugurated in 1949. While he was President, and afterward, we frequently corresponded and met together in the friendly and vigorous exchange for which he was so famous. This will always be a thing for which I will be grateful to him. I join my colleagues here today in sending our deepest sympathy to his beloved wife and daughter and others of their family.

Hon. Thomas P. O'Neill, Jr.

OF MASSACHUSETTS

Mr. Speaker, I join my colleagues today in rising to pay tribute to a distinguished President and an outstanding American, HARRY S TRUMAN.

One of the most conscientious and dynamic President, HARRY S TRUMAN exhibited a pugnacious spirit that not only characterized his tenure in the White House, but indeed, exemplified his whole life. As a young Senator from Missouri, as Vice President, and later as President, HARRY TRUMAN consistently fought for the ideals which this Nation holds dear.

To chronicle all his important achievements as President would still not do him the honor and justice he deserves. HARRY TRUMAN had to assume the mantle of the Presidency during one of the difficult periods in our Nation's history. The United States was in the middle of the most devastating and horrifying wars of all time. Yet, President TRUMAN always kept the interests of our Nation uppermost in mind when he sat down with other eminent leaders of his day at Potsdam or when he made that difficult decision to drop the atom bomb. His personal courage and integrity in fulfilling the duties of the great Office of President are unparalleled.

The Truman doctrine, which bears his name, served to inform our allies all over the world that America would stand by them in defense of freedom and self-determination, and made emphatically clear to our enemies that the United States would never tolerate the unwarranted and insidious spread of communism. The Marshall plan of economic assistance to rebuild an impoverished Europe following the holocaust of World War II was inaugurated during his administration and enabled the nations of Europe to live in dignity and peaceful coexistence.

To those of us in this Chamber who knew and admired him, HARRY S TRUMAN, the 33d President of the United States, will continue to be remembered as the beloved President he was, and as an American who represented the values of courage and decency by which he lived, both in his family and public life.

We all mourn the passing of this great leader, and Mrs. O'Neill joins me in expressing heartfelt sympathy to members of the late President HARRY S TRUMAN's family.

Hon. Walter Flowers

OF ALABAMA

Mr. Speaker, today we in the House of Representatives pay tribute to a man whom history is destined to record as one of the truly courageous Americans of all time, our late President HARRY S TRUMAN.

President TRUMAN will be remembered as the champion of the underdog and the downtrodden. His place in history is assured by the momentous and often difficult decisions he had to make during his administration. But, perhaps he will best be remembered for his fighting spirit. For in this attribute, which he possessed so fully, he was probably of all of our Presidents the most exemplary of the great American people that he led. In this great trait of his individual character, we could all find identity of national purpose so needed at the particular time.

A short time after he was sworn in following the death of President Roosevelt, he gave this insight into the Presidency:

Within the first few months I discovered that being a President is like riding a tiger. A man has to keep on riding or be swallowed.

President TRUMAN definitely was not swallowed by the job. He rode whatever tiger came along.

Thanks be to God that such a man was there to succeed to the job when fate called upon him to do so. Let us hope and pray that our country will continue to produce men like HARRY TRUMAN to lead us in future times of crisis.

Hon. Joseph P. Addabbo

OF NEW YORK

Mr. Speaker, the passing of former President HARRY TRUMAN was a loss to all Americans. I join my colleagues in the House of Representatives in this eulogy to a man who was not only a great President, but a very real person. Perhaps his outstanding attribute as President was his ability to reach the people, to communicate his thoughts, and to make the average American understand his motives and believe in his sincerity.

President TRUMAN led our Nation in a time when awesome decisions needed to be made and implemented. He rose to that task with conviction and determination. President TRUMAN led our Nation in a period of war and he brought us to peace. He compiled a record which historians will undoubtedly judge to be most successful and admirable.

As we mourn the passing of this great leader, let us remember that ability to communicate and . reach the people which was President TRUMAN's special quality. It is imperative that we who are elected public officials understand the importance of that special quality for that is what seems to be missing in the political world of today. We have lost that ability to reach the people, to

instill confidence, to make them believe us and trust in our motives.

As we mourn his passing, let the memory of this great American, President HARRY S TRUMAN, help us to regain that faith in America's new generation of political leaders.

Hon. Glenn M. Anderson

OF CALIFORNIA

Mr. Speaker, the Honorable HARRY S TRUMAN, the 33d President of the United States, will be remembered by all of us as a man of forthrightness and integrity—a man of vision and action.

When in April 1945, the death of President Franklin Roosevelt thrust him into the Presidency, he met the challenges of some of the most critical moments in our history with courageous and inspired leadership. He will be remembered for his histroic role in the restoration and reconstruction of the war-shattered Europe, the development of the Marshall plan and NATO, the Truman doctrine in Greece and Turkey, the Berlin airlift, and his support for the United Nations.

In addition, President TRUMAN's great sense of justice led to his momentous decision at 6:11 p.m. on May 14, 1948, to declare:

The White House announced de facto recognition of the provisional government of Israel.

Later, on January 31, 1949, after Israel repelled the attacks of the Arab states and had elected Dr. Chaim Weizman President, President TRUMAN recognized the Israel nation de jure.

Truly a "man of the people," President TRUMAN was humble, yet proud, and he held a deep respect for the office he held and for the people he served.

I first got to know President TRUMAN well during the 1948 campaign. Being Democratic chairman of Los Angeles County that year, I was automatically made chairman of the Truman campaign since there was not very much competition for the spot anyway.

I raised the finance for a million mailout, and was later told it was the largest single TRUMAN-Barkley mailing piece west of the Mississippi.

Whenever President TRUMAN would come to the west coast, he would try to see as many of the grassroots people as his schedule would allow.

I remember one time in San Francisco at the Fairmont Hotel, he had two of us brought into his room, and for 45 minutes we talked. He asked questions—and seemed appreciative of our ideas—and I know that I for one went away with the feeling that here was a man who had the world's problems on his shoulders as a President, yet worked to maintain both of his feet on the ground.

Mr. Speaker, because of the leadership, vision, and courage of President TRUMAN, the world today is a better and safer place—and future generations will be in his debt.

With great affection and respect, Mrs. Anderson joins me in paying homage to the memory of President TRUMAN and in sending our sympathies to his beloved wife and daughter.

He was indeed a good man who became a great President.

Hon. Dominick V. Daniels

OF NEW JERSEY

Mr. Speaker, the December 27 edition of the Jersey Journal carried an exemplary editorial memorializing the great career of President HARRY S TRUMAN. The editorial, written by Jersey Journal executive editor Eugene Farrell, eloquently eulogizes our late President.

Mr. Speaker, I am pleased to associate myself with the Jersey Journal's editorial and insert it into the Congressional Record. The editorial follows:

HARRY S TRUMAN

When HARRY TRUMAN moved into the presidency the whole country was sorry for him and worried about itself. We were at war. We had had a brilliant leader for 13 years in Franklin Roosevelt. He had fought a depression which crushed all the country. He had forseen the evil represented by Adolf Hitler and Nazism. He had rallied the country from the terrible sneak blow at Pearl Harbor. He was our nearest thing to an indispensable man since Washington and Lincoln. In an instant his place was to be taken by a man projected into the vice presidency via the Senate by a boss-ridden Missouri political machine not unlike our own Frank Hague's. Neither HARRY TRUMAN's nor the country's prospects looked good on April 12, 1945.

But HST made good by growing quickly into the world's biggest job. He just applied some country-boy common sense and a Middle American rectitude.

He ended the Pacific war with the atom bomb, convinced that otherwise only an invasion of the main Japanese islands could end that war at a cost of thousands of American lives. The atom's scourge was visited upon Japan in accordance with the accepted military rule that to save one life on our side is worth sacrificing any number of lives on the other side. In spite of the moralizing that has gone on since, HST never backed down from that.

His other major decision was to fight a half-war in Korea, firing Gen. MacArthur to do so. Like the first, it was highly controversial. TRUMAN, a mere artillery captain in World War I, overruled the greatest American military mind since Robert E. Lee. The controversy was heightened by an element of personal pique. MacArthur could not disguise his contempt for HARRY TRUMAN and so he decided to make national policy. But HST was the President of the United States, the commander-in-chief all generals must obey. MacArthur stayed fired and HST never backed down from that decision, either.

Whether TRUMAN was right about fighting half-wars never will be known. It is hard to believe there would have been a Vietnam without his precedent in Korea. Yet, only history can decide whether all-out war, half-war or no war would have been best.

Unhesitatingly, HARRY S TRUMAN stood up against Communist grabbing in every corner of the world. He helped the Greeks and Turks beat off communism and broke the Berlin blockade. He also presided at the foundation of the United Nations and he launched the Marshall foreign aid plan to lift up the countries broken by World War II.

All in all, it was quite a performance for a peppery little man catapulted into one of history's greatest crises in a job for which there can be no preparation.

A characteristic of HARRY TRUMAN's years in the White House was his reverence for the office of the presidency. He never confused the man HARRY TRUMAN with the President HARRY TRUMAN. In this respect he was quite unlike either his predecessor or his successor. Franklin Roosevelt accepted the presidency as a necessary tool to fashion the things FDR, the man, thought the country needed. Dwight D. Eisenhower accepted the presidency almost as a kind of semiretirement job for one who had done greater things; there was no height in his administration to compare with D-Day.

But to TRUMAN, the presidency was a great office to which the man, who happened to be in it, must subordinate himself. He exercised the powers of the presidency decisively, yet with humility—less interested in HARRY TRUMAN's place in history than in the 33d president's carrying forward the work started by the first.

When historians have finished arguing over the correctness of his vision as he looked into terribly complex and obscured problems, the last memory of HST will be that of a courageous man, ill-prepared for formidable difficulties, bravely tackling what had to be done and bringing off success by clinging to the homely virtues.

Hon. Henry Helstoski

OF NEW JERSEY

Mr. Speaker, a truly fine and great statesman has been taken from us. A man who exemplified the better qualities of the American way of life as few others have is gone.

I speak of HARRY S TRUMAN, undoubtedly one of the most outstanding Presidents ever to serve this Nation. Just as surely, he was one of the most outstanding leaders the world has ever known.

He guided the United States with exceptional adroitness in the difficult transition from war to peace in the late 1940's. His accomplishments throughout his time in office are many and one could spend endless hours enumerating them and praising them and still not do this man justice.

Even as a Senator, he was invaluable to his country. The Senate committee which he chaired was instrumental in coordinating the war effort. His work on that committee convinced President Roosevelt that this was the man to be his running mate in 1944, a position coveted in the Democratic Party because Mr. Roosevelt was visibly aging and many feared he would not live out his fourth term.

Yet HARRY TRUMAN only reluctantly accepted the position, exemplifying the humility of this great man. He was even willing to nominate another man for the job.

And humility was not his only virtue. His integrity was impeccable and his courage extraordinary. Often he made unpopular decisions which he knew to be best for the country, thus putting the needs of the world and the Nation above his own political survival.

Once he made a decision, he backed it all the way. When he determined to keep the world "safe for democracy" through the Truman doctrine, he saved Greece, Turkey, and Korea from impending aggression. He gave life to the state of Israel.

Through the Marshall plan, he stymied Communist designs on Western Europe as well as standing that war-torn and poverty-stricken continent back up on its feet. Thus he established the basis which has kept the world as a whole relatively at peace and prevented nuclear holocaust.

Honest and straightforward, President TRUMAN never deceived the American people. He told it like it was, even though it may have been politically hazardous. Pollsters predicted that this forthrightness would bring about his demise in 1948, implying that honesty in politics was archaic and foolhardy. But Mr. TRUMAN had tremendous faith in the American people and he stumped the experts by winning reelection in a valiant campaign.

And though the polls still insisted he was unpopular when he left the White House in 1952, Presidents and other statemen continued to turn to him for advice and assistance. The public, too, grew to reflect upon him fondly and with admiration. When the wailings of a hostile press were finally overshadowed by the more accurate judgments of history, HARRY TRUMAN began to assume his proper position in the annals of mankind.

We will sorely miss him.

Hon. John M. Slack
OF WEST VIRGINIA

Mr. Speaker, around our Capital City and our country the flags are flying at half-mast. Those of us who remember the years just after World War II are sadly reminded that former President HARRY TRUMAN has passed on.

TRUMAN was an American of unique capability. He laid no claim to intellectual superiority. He had no special training for the Presidency. He was not even among the best informed about current events at home or aboard when he was called to assume the responsibility of the White House.

He asked for the people's prayers. He took the oath of office. He listened to the problems described by his subordinates. And, he made decisions. TRUMAN will go down in history primarily because he made decisions, and he made them stick.

He shouldered the responsibility for the results of his decisions. History has already written that, on balance, the vast majority of his decisions were proper. They strengthened the United States and the cause of peace everywhere in the world.

They were the decisions of a human being devoted to the Christian ethic and the old-fashioned style American patriotism who had been entrusted to a job of maximum power. He knew his own shortcomings and never assumed he was infallible. But, he knew final decisions affecting the whole world must be made at his desk, and nowhere else. So he faced what must be done and proceeded to do it.

With his passing we have lost a brand of leadership of which there is no present equal on the horizon. But, he served us while he could, and future American Presidents in time of crisis will be measured against the memories of his courage and determination.

TRUMAN pledged to the American people when he took the oath of office that he would give it "everything that's in me." And that he did. When we see those flags at half-mast today and remember his years in office, it is difficult to understand how many Americans can justify any lesser commitment to his heritage.

Hon. Harold T. Johnson

OF CALIFORNIA

Mr. Speaker, I joined with all Americans in grieving over the passing of President HARRY S TRUMAN, our 33d President, who fought the good fight until the very end. Today I join my colleagues in paying tribute to a great American, one who loved his country and served it so well.

As all of us know he became President while we were engaged in World War II. Many, including the President himself, felt that there were others who might be better qualified to be President. However, he took command of this high office, as he had taken command of other offices, and guided us to an end of World War II, the establishment of the United Nations, the reconversion from a wartime to a peacetime economy, and providing assistance to the war-torn lands.

President TRUMAN served as a world leader, a great modern-day President, and continued until his death to serve as an inspiring genius for the American people whom he loved and who loved him.

In describing his activities I intentionally used the term "command" because that was what HARRY S TRUMAN did in his own words "the buck stops here" on the desk of the President. His forceful and inspired leadership was augmented by his great courage, his loyalty, and his integrity. At the same time he was a man with great affection for his family, for his Nation and the people who made this Nation great. He was a man of compassion. Along with the courageous actions which he undertook to bring to an end World War II and to stop the aggressive spread of communism, HARRY S TRUMAN never forgot the individual citizen—the working man, who found in HARRY S TRUMAN a President who was one of their own.

His dedication to the rights of the individual can best be demonstrated by the proposals which he first advocated as President. He called for a national health insurance plan for all citizens. He advocated the concept that the Federal Government has a responsibility to act to halt any subsequent rise in unemployment, and should come to the aid of the less fortunate. His administration led the effort to enact the National Housing Act in 1949, and President TRUMAN became the first President since Abraham Lincoln to make civil rights a truly national issue.

To pay tribute to this great American is an honor. He established himself among the list of the truly great American Presidents, and a grieving nation extends deepest sympathy to his beloved wife Bess, his daughter Margaret and her family, and his sister.

Hon. Wright Patman

OF TEXAS

Mr. Speaker, over 27 years ago—April 12, 1945, to be exact—in a small private room in the Capitol, Speaker Sam Rayburn and Vice President HARRY TRUMAN were talking things over as was their custom when a telephone call came through for Mr. TRUMAN summoning him to the White House. It was learned later on that historic day that President Roosevelt had passed away in Warm Springs, Ga., and that HARRY S TRUMAN, of Missouri, was now President of the United States. No other man in our history has been thrust into the position of ultimate national responsibility at so critical and difficult a period. President TRUMAN himself realized this full well when, in all humility, he said to the press the following day:

When they told me yesterday what had happened, I felt like the moon, the stars, and the planets had fallen on me.

The sterling quality of our 33d President was quickly revealed, however, as he promptly shouldered the heavy burden of war-time President, displaying the strength, courage, and tenacity for which he later became world famous. Great office has a way of taking its toll, but HARRY TRUMAN, perhaps more than any of his predecessors, remained the same tough, independent, intensely human individual that his associates had known so well through all his years in public office. What is truly remarkable is the fact that HARRY TRUMAN's hard shell of political sagacity concealed a compassion that was world-wide and encompassed the entire human race.

The man that made the heartbreaking decision to bomb Hiroshima also conceived the Marshall plan that rebuilt the war-torn nations of Europe. His Americanism was intense; he made the decision to prevent Communist aggressors from overrunning South Korea, Greece, and Turkey—wherever the spark of democratic liberty offered hope for the future against totalitarian encroachment. In keeping with the sign on his desk, "The buck stops here," he made decisions and his Marshall plan did rebuild Europe; his policy of containment was successful in drawing a circle around communism and keeping it from achieving world supremacy; and his point 4 program strengthened underdeveloped nations and enabled them to resist the forces of aggression.

Throughout his career, HARRY TRUMAN served the people with courage and candor. He was frank and straightforward; his honesty had no taint of diplomatic guile; and Americans came to regard the man from Independence with deep and abiding respect, a wonderful tribute indeed. The statement he made some years after leaving office—"I never did give anybody hell. I just told the truth and they thought it was hell," in retrospect, says again, that HARRY TRUMAN was really above the arena of partisan politics. There was no credibility gap; people knew where he stood, and they knew he had their interests at heart.

Like our greatest Presidents, HARRY TRUMAN was a man of the people. He was not afraid of work and he knew from personal experience what it was like to meet a payroll; he knew the day-to-day struggles of our farmers; he knew, from combat in World War I, the terrors and the tragedy of war; he knew, from his 12 years as a county court judge, the problems and difficulties that people must cope with to keep going. His career of public service at the highest levels of National Government, had a core of tough but malleable humanism forged in the actual give and take of American society. His close identification with the average man was typified in a statement he made as a Senator in 1944:

> Of course I believe in free enterprise but in my system of free enterprise, the democratic principle is that there never was, never has been, never will be room for the ruthless exploitation of the many for the benefit of the few.

It is impossible to overemphasize the enormous contribution which HARRY TRUMAN made to his Nation and the world. He himself, properly sized up the importance of strong leadership:

> Men make history and not the other way 'round. In periods where there is no leadership, society stands still. Progress occurs when courageous, skillful leaders seize the opportunity to change things for the better.

HARRY TRUMAN proved the truth of this statement—he got things done, and he brought in the Truman era of progressive Americanism.

The thoughts we express today, in all probability, do not properly evaluate the historic stature of HARRY TRUMAN, for only in recent years have historians and political commentators recognized the debt we all owe to the strong-minded and dedicated man from Missouri, and I am confident that his bulldog determination, his total commitment to the public interest, and his selfless dedication to peace and prosperity for all the people will be even more greatly respected with the passing of time.

In 1945, HARRY TRUMAN presented a scroll rewarding a "good public servant" and said at that time:

> I hope that will be my epitaph.

It is indeed his epitaph for it is the sum of this philosophy in the contex of an active working life, and the scholarship which gave depth to his extraordinarily perceptive comments. The Truman Library is a further dimension of this great President—it is a splendid and important historical center, but it is also a symbol of HARRY S TRUMAN's lifelong devotion the ideals of American democracy. HARRY TRUMAN was a great man because he was an indomitable human being with profound faith in humanity, which is to say he was of the people and for the people.

Hon. Edward R. Roybal
OF CALIFORNIA

Mr. Speaker, the passing of former President HARRY S TRUMAN was truly a great loss to all Americans, and I join my colleagues in the House of Representatives in paying tribute to his memory.

He was one of those public figures whose reputations flourish only after many years of retirement. All the things that, at first, made him seem too small for the office he held dwindled in importance with the passing of decades. What loomed larger than these relative trivialities was a sense of the man's courage—a realization that he faced and made more great decisions than most other American Presidents before and after him.

When catapulted into the White House by the death of Franklin Roosevelt in 1945, he was challenged by some of the most critical moments in our history. He responded to them with conviction and determination, aften making awesome decisions that aroused the ire of the American press and public. But, driven by an inner sense of confidence that was neither proud nor ashamed, he acted resolutely and irrevocably. When confronted by the great issues, HARRY TRUMAN never flinched. And right or wrong, he never made a decision that he did not feel was in the best interests of the country.

It was his wish that there would be no hymns or eulogies at his funeral, but I think that TRUMAN himself made the best assessment of his life and career. When asked to select one statement to sum up his life in politics, he chose a speech he had made in North Carolina during the 1948 campaign. Its moral is typical of him.

In that speech he discussed three southerners who became Presidents of the United States—Andrew Jackson, James Polk, and Andrew Johnson. All of them, he said:

Lived through days when reason was overcome by emotion and because of this their actions were misunderstood and misinterpreted. So it is not surprising that the estimates of these men made by their contemporaries have been almost completely discarded by later generations.

Of these estimations, he added:

A President may dismiss the abuse of scoundrels, but to be denounced by honest men honestly outraged is a test of greatness that none but the strongest men can survive.

There was, he concluded, only one lesson to be drawn from the story of these three Presidents:

Do your duty and history will do you justice.

His assertion is true.

Hon. Charles H. Wilson

OF CALIFORNIA

Mr. Speaker—

Some are born great . . . some achieve greatness, and some have greatness thrust upon them.

William Shakespeare's insight had a perfect embodiment in HARRY S TRUMAN, whose greatness was thrust upon him suddenly with the death of Franklin D. Roosevelt. Few at the time thought him equal to the task. Even Mr. TRUMAN, ever a humble and forthright man, held no exaggerated opinion of himself.

But HARRY TRUMAN was the sort of man who, equipped with a sharp sense of history and a respect for decisive leadership, rose to the challenge of leading a troubled nation at a very critical time in American history. His philosophy was simple: That one has a moral duty not to shirk one's obligations, that government is an instrument of the people, not a special privilege, and that we must "repay our debts to God, to our dead, and to our children" by working at our fullest capacities.

Yet this man of high principle was also a direct and salty character who had an easy philosophical attitude toward the capriciousness of life. After the abortive assassination attempt at Blair House in 1950, he shrugged:

A President has to expect these things. The only thing you have to worry about is bad luck. I never have bad luck.

The milestones of the Truman era are justly celebrated. The Marshall and point 4 plans are surely two of America's greatest contributions to the peace of the world; for, by "building up rapidly the combined political, economic, and military strength of the free world," they formed the cornerstone of President TRUMAN's enlightened foreign policy: That American generosity could enable Western Europe to repel the tyranny of communism.

The dropping of the bomb on Hiroshima to bring a swift end to World War II was, of course, a controversial decision then and now. But President TRUMAN took sole responsibility for this momentous action—"The buck stops here" philosophy was never more apparent—which was made in calculation that a half million lives would be lost were the ground war to continue. His dismissal of General MacArthur was similarly controversial, characterizing TRUMAN's decisiveness in implementing an unwavering belief in civilian control of the military.

The TRUMAN wartime maneuvers are well known. Less acclaimed, but equally important, were his great efforts on the domestic front; he himself voiced an overriding concern with "balancing the human budget," and his "Fair Deal" program contained the seeds of today's civil rights, housing, and social welfare programs. Believing that "man has the moral and the intellectual capacity, as well as the inalienable right, to govern himself with reason and justice," President TRUMAN's faith in the spirit of the American people was unceasing.

When we remember President TRUMAN, we think primarily of his great individuality and tough decisionmaking. His lack of egotism and courage to do the unpopular thing are rare in history. Popularity and polls were discounted as he said that Presidents who allowed themselves to be led by the press and pollsters were "complete washouts." "The President hears a hundred voices telling him that he is the greatest man in the world. He must listen carefully indeed to hear the one voice that tells him he is not."

HARRY TRUMAN listened to one voice: his conscience. His actions were rooted in the solemn belief that no single problem was insurmountable "if approached in the spirit of the Sermon on the Mount." Indeed, he could have been speaking of himself when he said that what counts "is right and wrong, and leadership—man with fortitude, honesty, and a belief in the right that make epochs in the history of the world."

President TRUMAN was an example of what a basically earthy and simple man with old-fashioned values can do if he sets his mind, heart, and energy to it. Perhaps that is his great legacy to us all.

My deepest condolences go to Bess Truman, a gallant lady who, like her husband, was unimpressed by the trappings of power and served her country proudly as a First Lady of great dignity, and to Margaret Truman whose devotion to her father is evident in her recent memoir as she writes that—

A strong man, whom I happen to love very much, did his duty. I am confident that history will do him justice.

Perhaps, if it were possible to sum up HARRY TRUMAN, one might say that he was, first and last, a family man—to his mother and sister, his wife and daughter, and to the people of his country.

Hon. William L. Hungate

OF MISSOURI

Mr. Speaker, the following is an account of President TRUMAN's visits to Fulton, Mo., as recorded by the Honorable Hugh P. Williamson, judge of the probate and magistrate courts, Calla-

way County, Fulton, Mo., in "Memories of Friendships," from the Fulton Sun-Gazette, on December 26, 1972:

MEMORIES OF FRIENDSHIPS, POLITICAL TIES IN CALLAWAY

(By Hugh P. Williamson)

Margaret Truman Daniel, in her book "HARRY S TRUMAN," is reported by the press to have stated that her father did not want to become President "by the back door." By this she meant that he did not want to move into the Presidency from the position of Vice-President by the death of the incumbent, which of course is exactly what he did. An experience that I had with Mr. TRUMAN provides some interesting information on this matter. I was a delegate from Missouri to the 1944 Democratic National Convention in Chicago. There was before the convention only one question to be resolved and that was the candidate for Vice-President, since it was assumed that Mr. Roosevelt would be renominated. For a number of days following the convening of the convention very little was done. Tiring of this inactivity I went one morning to Mr. TRUMAN's suite in the old Stephens Hotel. He was alone except for a political hanger-on of no importance. I motioned for TRUMAN to come out into the hall, which he did. These halls were very wide and very high and on this morning were completely deserted. Mr. TRUMAN leaned up against the wall, stuck out his right leg, and, with the foot resting on the heel, began to rotate the toes of the shoe from right to left and left to right at a fairly moderate rate, somewhat like the pendulum of a clock upside down. I stated the obvious, which was that there was a vast amount of inaction and asked him if it would be agreeable to him if a committee from the Missouri Delegation visited other state delegations in an attempt to get them to endorse him. At this suggestion the toe of the shoe rapidly increased in motion, he remained silent for as much as half a minute, and then said, in a very low voice, "I am not sure that I want it." My reply was, "You have no doubt seen Mr. Roosevelt recently and you must surely realize that whoever gets the nomination for Vice-President here will be President sometime within the next four years." At this point the toe of the shoe accelerated to very rapid motion indeed, and after perhaps a full minute had passed he straightened up, put his mouth practically inside my ear, and in a low whisper said, "Well, go ahead." While all of this was going on the hall continued to be completely deserted!

I did "go ahead," the result of my efforts were completely nil, I have no illusion that I was in any sense a President maker, but I believe that this incident throws an interesting light upon Mr. TRUMAN's attitude toward going into the Presidency "by the back door."

I also have reason to believe that Mr. TRUMAN never did like his role as Vice-President or consider that it was very important. My reason for so believing is a letter in my possession from TRUMAN dated April 6, 1945. This letter reads:

"OFFICE OF THE VICE PRESIDENT,
Washington, D.C., April 6, 1945.

Mr. HUGH P. WILLIAMSON,
*Prosecuting Attorney, Callaway County,
Fulton, Mo.*

DEAR HUGH: Thanks a lot for your good letter of the third.

I am certainly glad to have the reactions which you gave me on the various phases of the State administration.
Sincerely yours,

HARRY S TRUMAN.

Keep sending 'em. Tell Tom VanSant that just because I've become a political eunuch he needn't strike me from his list."

Six days after writing this letter, in which he refers to himself as "a political eunuch," as President of the United States he occupied the most powerful position of any man in the world! On August 6th following, he ordered an atomic bomb to be dropped on Hiroshima and three days later another on Nagasaki. The combined mortality of these bombs was somewhere between four and five hundred thousand people. The "political eunuch" had indeed become a man of vast power.

Where and when I first met HARRY TRUMAN I do not remember, but it was doubtless at some of the many Democratic meetings which we both attended. By the time he made his first race for the United States Senate we were rather well acquainted. During the early summer of that year, which was 1934, I met TRUMAN and his close friend, Major Harry Vaughan, on the street in Fulton. This was about 10 o'clock in the morning, and after discussing the local political situation, TRUMAN said that he and Vaughan were about to leave for Excelsior Springs, where they had a political meeting scheduled for two o'clock that afternoon. TRUMAN then said in a jocular but unfortunately truthful manner, "You do not have any law business, I imagine, so if you want to come with me and Harry we would be glad to have you, and after the meeting you can hitch-hike back to Fulton." We proceeded to the Elms Hotel in Excelsior, washed up, ate a light lunch, and about 1:30 went to the meeting place in a small park back of the hotel. There was nobody present, time went on, two o'clock came, 2:15, and still nobody! My embarrassment for Mr. TRUMAN increased in proportion to the passage of time, but it was not shared by him. Finally, at about a quarter of three, I expressed rather strongly my feeling about the Democrats in Clay County for not coming to the meeting. Mr. TRUMAN blandly said that he guessed that they had something better to do! He and Vaughan drove me out to the highway, they wheeled off in the direction of Kansas City, and in the early hours of the next morning I reached Fulton. I was astonished at his apparent unconcern, his acceptance of what I considered to be a treasonable action on the part of the local Democrats, and his calm acceptance of human nature being what it was. I think that this attitude may have been one of the main-springs that propelled him to prominence and that enabled him, in later years, to pursue a calm and steady course while the political and social seas raged furiously and unceasingly about him.

I may here note that while TRUMAN did have the endorsement of Tom Pendergast, the political boss of Missouri, I did not believe that Pendergast furnished him with any financial assistance because surely no man ever made the race for the United States Senate in Missouri on a more scanty campaign budget. On several occasions of which I knew, his campaign was sharply curtailed by this lack. On one such occasion a large amount of mail which had been prepared could not be sent because there was no money to buy stamps! I heard of numerous other such situations. I may also add that for many years TRUMAN walked somewhat under the shadow of his association with Pendergast. In 1943 the Republican National Committee sent an investigative team to Kansas City in an attempt to find evidences of corruption in the public career of TRUMAN, which included being Road Overseer of Jackson County and judge of the Jackson County court. After about five months of intensive work they came up with absolutely nothing. And to me this has always been another amazing facet of this amazing man: that he could live with the Pendergast corruption and not be corrupted. But he very clearly did.

Sometime during TRUMAN's tenure as Senator an important Democratic meeting was scheduled to be held at Convention Hall in Kansas City. I went up for the meeting and stayed at the Muehlbach Hotel. The morning of the meeting—dressed immaculately—I left the hotel with TRUMAN and some men whom I have forgotten, to go to the meeting. As we started up the street I was a short distance ahead of the other two, and met, coming down the street, a little eight or nine year old boy, ragged, extremely dirty, forlorn looking indeed! His nose was very badly in need of being blown, the lace of one of his tattered shoes had come undone, and at every other step he tripped on it. I made a wide detour around him because I did not want my immense cleanliness and impeccable appearance to be contaminated by any near approach to him. When TRUMAN came up he did not detour around this pitiful small object but went directly up to him, knelt on one knee on the dirty sidewalk, jerked a white handkerchief out of his pocket, blew the nose, tied the shoe lace, gave the little fellow a friendly pat on the behind, pressed a handful of change into his grimy hand, and smiling broadly came on up the street.

A few years later I had what has always seemed to me to be a very amusing incident with relation to TRUMAN. In Kansas City, for many years, there lived a distant relative of mine named John T. Barker. Barker had been Attorney General of Missouri, Speaker of the Missouri House, and almost got the Democratic nomination for Governor. He had been a Chautauqua lecturer, and was one of the most prominent lawyers in Missouri. His life had been highly active and quite colorful. In his later years, he and I became quite intimate. In the late summer of 1943 he sent me, literally, nearly a bushel of notes, some typewritten, some written in longhand, regarding his life and many experiences. They were accompanied by a letter with the request to "make these into a book when you get time." The thought appeared to be that this could be done on some not very busy weekend. In fact I spent almost a year in my spare time, on this very interesting project. In September of 1948, preceding the TRUMAN-Dewey election, I finished work on this manuscript after considerable revision and numerous conferences with Barker. One of the chapters was entitled, "A New Client Named TRUMAN." I sent the book to an Eastern publisher and about a week before the election I received a letter from the publisher stating that they would accept the book, but adding that the chapter on TRUMAN must come out because, "after the election nobody will be interested in TRUMAN." Obviously they not only took the chapter out but threw it away because a few days after the election I received a wire from the publishers with the terse request, "Please send us the chapter on TRUMAN." I sent the chapter which appears as Chapter Twenty-One in the book, "A Missouri Lawyer."

I wish to quote to some extent from a portion of this chapter for a number of reasons. One is that it gives Barker's evaluation of TRUMAN. This evaluation I believe is one which would have been generally shared by people who knew TRUMAN intimately, as Barker did. Another feature of TRUMAN, which Barker speaks of, was his very great, almost childish it seemed to me, admiration of lawyers and his deep regret that he was not one of that controversial brotherhood. The other incident related by Barker is illustrative of the perfect and rock-life integrity of TRUMAN. Barker writes:

"More than intellectual brilliance, more than cleverness, more than education, Americans appreciate basic honesty. Certainly this country and no country in all recorded time has ever had a chief executive who possesses this fine quality of greater degree than HARRY S TRUMAN. This fact is illustrated by many incidents in his career, only two of which I will mention.

"In the early '20's he was studying in the Kansas City Night School of Law. He carried on these studies for nearly three years. In those times examination for a license to practice law in Missouri was lax and nearly anyone could be admitted even without examination. He had a very great desire to become a lawyer and could very easily have received his license, as he well knew, but since he did not have all of the technical requirements provided by law, he did not apply for and receive something which he prized and coveted very much, although it could have been his for the asking.

"Another instance which is even more illustrative of this point is furnished by the old family farm in Jackson County. Prior to the depression his mother owned a splendid farm of 360 acres about ten miles from Kansas City. His father was dead and his mother an aged woman. In the early '30's she mortgaged this farm for $30,000 at which time it was well worth the amount of the mortgage. As is too well known the depression ruined farm values, and the TRUMAN mortgage, as a result of this depression, could not be paid. While a Senator of the United States, TRUMAN saw his farm, the home of his aged mother, put up at auction and sold for the price of the mortgage. A hundred banks in Missouri would have renewed the loan for him if he had asked them to do so. Thousands of people would have carried such a mortgage for a United States Senator. He did not ask any of them to do this because he did not want to be under any obligation to anybody while he was occupying the responsible position of a Senator of the United States. I wonder how many men prominent in American public life today and in the years that are passed, would have been possessed of the integrity of TRUMAN under these circumstances? I wonder how many of them would have seen the family farm sold at a public foreclosure sale, have seen his aged mother evicted, when by a mere gesture of his hand he could have prevented it? A happy conclusion of this matter is that since the time of the foreclosure sale, a portion of this farm has been repurchased by President TRUMAN and his mother has returned to her old home."

During the many years that I knew TRUMAN I received many letters from him, only three of which I have preserved. The one written on April 6, 1945, has been noted.

One of the remaining two is dated August 29, 1958, and was written from Independence. The letter follows:

HARRY S TRUMAN,
Independence, Mo., August 29, 1958.
Hon. HUGH P. WILLIAMSON,
Office of the Attorney General,
Jefferson City, Mo.

DEAR HUGH: Thank you very much for your letter of the 27th.

After I had read Jerome Walsh's article in the Journal of the Missouri Bar, I wrote him a letter on the subject. Most of us in Independence thought Dr. Hyde was guilty, but, of course, I cannot blame Jerome for protecting his father in the matter. His article is a good one.

I am glad that you told me about Mrs. VanSant, and I am sorry that she is not in good health.

That book of yours is sure to be a good one, and I would like very much to have a copy for the Library.

Sincerely yours,

HARRY S TRUMAN.
I wrote Mrs. VanSant.

The reference to Dr. Hyde was in regard to one of the most celebrated murder trials ever held in Missouri. Dr. Ben C. Hyde lived and practiced in Independence, and was married to one of the Swope girls, of the family that gave Swope Park to Kansas City. One fall Colonel Swope, an uncle, Chrisman Swope, a brother, and two sisters became ill with typhoid fever and died. Dr. Hyde was charged with innoculating these people with typhoid germs in order to inherit the Swope fortune. Jerome Walsh was the son of the man that prosecuted Hyde, without success, due to a sequence of bizarre circumstances. The Mrs. VanSant referred to was the widow of that Tom VanSant referred to in the letter of April 6, 1945.

HARRY S TRUMAN,
Independence, Mo., July 16, 1958.
Hon. HUGH P. WILLIAMSON,
Assistant Attorney General,
State of Missouri.

DEAR HUGH: I was happy to receive the brochure about your new book, The Overland Diary of James A Pritchard from Kentucky to California in 1849, and I know that it will be a very interesting publication.

If you will let me know when it comes out, I'll invest in a copy.

Sincerely yours,

HARRY S TRUMAN.

The book to which TRUMAN refers was one which I had written and was soon to be published.

While I was writing the Barker story, in the comparative quiet of my study, and reliving with him the interesting events of his career, TRUMAN was engaged in a life-or-death political struggle with Governor Thomas E. Dewey of New York, for the election to the Presidency. All opinion polls and large segments of the press predicted a Dewey victory. TRUMAN, characteristically, and again putting principle above politics, had previously taken a very strong stand in favor of Civil Rights Legislation, indifferent to political consequences, and against the urgings of his political advisors. The consequences were that this had lost him the support of a large group of Southern Democrats. TRUMAN, almost alone, never seemed to doubt that he would win. He did, and carried with him a Democratic majority in both the House and Senate. The Literary Digest, whose poll showed a Dewey victory by a wide margin was so discredited by the election of TRUMAN that it ceased publication soon afterward.

That there have been many men in American public life who had more mental power, scope, and brilliance than TRUMAN would not, I believe, be questioned. That there have been many who were far better educated is plain. That there were many who had a far greater knowledge and understanding of affairs, both domestic and foreign, but especially foreign, is true. But that there are any who possessed his perfect and rock-like integrity; his understanding of the heart and soul of his country and countrymen; his identification with the masses of our people; his total courage, both physical and moral; his knowledge of men; his vast and encompassing common sense, I very much doubt. And in a highly difficult and critical period in the history of our country, these qualities proved to be sufficient.

Hon. L. H. Fountain

OF NORTH CAROLINA

Mr. Speaker, I would like to take this opportunity to pay humble tribute to our great 33d President, HARRY S TRUMAN.

HARRY S TRUMAN, more than any other President since Andrew Jackson, was a man of the people, a man who epitomized the very essence of the American spirit. He stood for a sense of dogged determination, dedication to duty, and devotion to the bedrock principles of high courage, common intelligence, and individual integrity—principles on which this Nation was built.

President HARRY S TRUMAN spoke often of freedom and challenged all freedom-loving people the world over to protect and preserve that freedom from the insidious encroachment of totalitarianism. All of mankind—the free and those who hope to be free—in this generation and for generations yet unborn—stand in debt to our great 33d President.

There can be no doubt that President TRUMAN occupied a unique place in the hearts of the American people, and, in my estimation, he stands shoulder to shoulder with such great American Presidents as Jackson and Lincoln— men who left their own distinctive marks on the American Presidency.

The resemblance to Jackson is apparent in personality, in thinking, and in tactics. Both men fought hard and both men "gave 'em hell" out of a sublime dedication to the public interest. Jackson's struggle with predatory wealth and privilege, foreshadowed the dynamic TRUMAN and the broad concepts of his Fair Deal.

The TRUMAN likeness to Lincoln is for me the most arresting, because it is a likeness in depth. Both men had an extraordinary impact on history, despite the fact that nothing in the past of either indicated the singular greatness they were to achieve. Both gave to the Presidency a special dimension of their own, a decisiveness and a dignity, and in turn, the Presidency made them great. Both exercised an unerring and brilliant instinct for command. This was complete and unwavering, whether it involved giving drive and force to a nation at war or cutting a great popular general down to size.

Yet, there is still a greater point of mutual identity—courage and a deep sense of devotion to the American democratic tradition. Lincoln and TRUMAN have, as figures in history, what I can only describe as distinctly American personalities. This made them, even in their speech and manner, the very symbols of America, the embodiment of freedom and free men. Each was supreme in his hour on the stage of history. They breathed the will and the power, the conscience and the tradition of the American people, and spoke again and again as the American instruments of freedom.

I mourn and the Nation mourns this man of the people—this man from Independence, Mo., who spoke and gave international meaning and substance to this country's love of freedom and individual liberty. President HARRY S TRUMAN walked with steady tread, and firm resolve. It is to his work as Chief Executive that the entire free world owes a profound debt of gratitude.

When HARRY S TRUMAN was summoned to the White House from Capitol Hill on the night of Franklin D. Roosevelt's death, the Nation and the world wondered what type of man had suddenly assumed the regions of Government. Although TRUMAN was no novice in the political arena, having served as a judge and a distinguished investigative Senator from Missouri, the Nation knew little about its new President. Consequently, the American people anxiously awaited the administration of their new Chief Executive, shocked at the death of Franklin D. Roosevelt, and uncertain as to the future.

However, President HARRY S TRUMAN seized the reigns of government with decisiveness and firm resolve. Relying upon the basic American attributes of courage, commonsense, and steadfastness, President TRUMAN brought the American people through the last tumultuous months of the Second World War and launched the world on its infinitely long and hard march toward self-determination and freedom.

It was President TRUMAN who decided to drop the atomic bomb, thus obviating the need for an American invasion of the Japanese mainland and thereby saving 500,000 American lives, and just as many, if not more, Japanese lives.

It was the Truman doctrine which shattered the long U.S. tradition of peacetime isolation by supporting Greece and Turkey against the Communist threat.

It was the Marshall plan, instituted by President TRUMAN, which committed U.S. resources to the extremely successful rebuilding of Europe, thereby saving Western civilization from communism.

Later President TRUMAN defied the Soviet blockade of Berlin and risked war by authorizing the most massive airlift in history. The United States fed, fueled, and supplied a beleaguered city of 2.4 million by air for nearly a year.

Still later, it was President TRUMAN who met the Communist invasion of South Korea by ordering U.S. Forces into the field and obtaining the help and support of the United States.

What looms large about these tough decisions, all made amidst bitter debate and uncertainty, was HARRY TRUMAN's courage—the courage to make tough decisions and to stand firm behind those decisions—a courage made even more impressive by the realization that the crucial problems and decisions he faced were perhaps more awesome than those hitherto faced by any other American President.

The American people could have chosen no greater leader in those harrowing years of international crisis than its humble, but decisive, servant from Missouri, HARRY S TRUMAN.

Indeed, the death of our 33d President is more than just a national loss, for his death was profoundly noted by the entire free world.

No greater tribute could be recalled than that given by one of the world's giants, Winston Churchill.

It was in the closing months of HARRY S TRUMAN's Presidency that Churchill said the following, with blunt honesty:

The last time you and I sat across a conference table in Potsdam, I must confess Sir, I held you in very low regard. I loathed your taking the place of Franklin Roosevelt. I misjudged you badly. Since that time, you more than any other man have saved Western Civilization.

Few will ever again doubt HARRY S TRUMAN's greatness. Those who knew him and treasured his friendship will miss him, but his work and deeds will live for so long as our great American democracy shall stand.

President TRUMAN's epitaph does not, I understand, include a favorite quote of his, but that quote sums up the essential greatness of the man. In his presidential press conference of April 1952, he said:

I'll always quote an epitaph on a tombstone in a cemetery in Arizona: "There lies Jack Williams. He done his damndest."

Hon. Chet Holifield
OF CALIFORNIA

Mr. Speaker, I rise to pay tribute to a great and good President of the United States, the late HARRY S TRUMAN of Missouri.

I have had the privilege to serve under six Presidents. Each of our Presidents have had their own personalities and capabilities, and each will be accorded his respective place in the annals of history.

On April 12, 1945, President Roosevelt died. On that same day, Vice President HARRY S TRUMAN took the oath of office as President of the United States. That was in my third year as Representative in the U.S. Congress.

During the ensuing 7 years, I worked closely with the President in achieving many of his legislative goals. I processed 41 Truman Presidential Reorganization Plans, as well as the bill which consolidated the Army, Navy, and Air Force Departments into the one Department of Defense.

In August of 1949, the Soviet Union tested successfully their first atomic weapon. As chairman of an atomic energy subcommittee, I directed a study of the feasibility of developing a far more powerful weapon, the hydrogen bomb. A national controversy arose, much of it directed against the development of the hydrogen weapon. The scientists were split on the issue.

Notwithstanding this opposition, the subcommittee and the full committee decided that we must protect the national securiy by developing this new weapon. Chairman Brian McMahon and I presented our affirmative recommendations to President TRUMAN at the White House.

After less than 30 days of consideration between President TRUMAN and his military advisers, the President accepted our recommendations and initiated the hydrogen bomb project. Its goal was successfully achieved some 20 months later. President TRUMAN's decision was proven wise, for within a period of 9 months thereafter, the Soviet Union tested successfully their hydrogen bomb. This decision was one among many decisions that President TRUMAN made. I believe it was one of the most important because it assured the balance of military power between the free world and the Communist world.

HARRY TRUMAN's background was similar to millions of his fellow Americans. During the closing years of World War II and most of the years of that decade, time and events elevated him to the most important office in the world.

President TRUMAN's ability to make important decisions when our Nation's values were challenged was based on his inherent commonsense, his courage, and his deep belief in our Constitution and the responsibilities of the office of the Presidency.

In my humble opinion, President HARRY S TRUMAN's name will be inscribed on any list of the five greatest American Presidents and certainly he will be remembered with warm affection in the hearts of his countrymen.

Hon. J. Herbert Burke
OF FLORIDA

Mr. Speaker, I rise to add my voice to those paying tribute to our 33d U.S. President—HARRY S TRUMAN. The facts of Mr. TRUMAN's life are well known to most of the Nation. Television, newspapers, and radio have related how his life was shaped and how he shaped world history. He is frequently touted as a simple man in a simplier era. However, I would not agree with this assessment. Hindsight always make situations and problems seem simple. Life is different today than it was in the Truman era, but, it is no more complex.

Mr. TRUMAN was a moral giant. A man fashioned from the humblest clay with the highest spiritual values. History shows that there are different periods of stress for nations. There are quiet periods when everything goes along smoothly no matter who is running the country, and then there are times when the survival of the nation is called into question. The way a man meets this challenge is the proof of his mettle, and the stuff of history.

The experiment in democracy in a republican form of government that is the United States of America has always been fortunate to have leaders who during times of stress met the challenge. We are just beginning to realize the tests which he was called upon to surmount and the courage and strength he showed in guiding our country as its President. Thank God for the example HARRY TRUMAN set for us all to follow with his simple and pure love for his country and his unswerving belief in the correctness of its principles.

Hon. Wm. J. Randall
OF MISSOURI

Mr. Speaker, with 3 days yet remaining of the period proclaimed to mourn our former President HARRY S TRUMAN, the country is saddened again by the loss of a great and honored leader, Lyndon B. Johnson.

The reason I have asked for this time today is to announce that a resolution will soon be offered to authorize the Joint Committee on Printing to prepare a book containing tributes to Mr. TRUMAN. The immediate purpose of my special order today is to request unanimous consent to include in the Congressional Record certain editorials written on the life and times of Mr. TRUMAN from the Examiner, published in his home city of Independence, Mo.; the Kansas City Star of Kansas City, Mo.; the two St. Louis papers, being the St. Louis Globe Democrat and the St. Louis Post Dispatch; the St. Joseph News Press and the Springfield Leader Press. All of these are major publications with wide circulation in their respective areas of Missouri.

In each instance I have selected for inclusion only the principal or lead editorial in tribute to Mr. TRUMAN.

Now, Mr. Speaker, as we come within 3 days of the end of the mourning period for Mr. TRUMAN, I ask unanimous consent that all Members may have 5 legislative days from today to revise and extend their own remarks and to include excerpts from any editorials from districts they represent written in memory of HARRY S TRUMAN.

Mr. Speaker, during all of my years as a Member of Congress, our residence in my home city of Independence, Mo., has been located only four short city blocks distant from that of our former President, HARRY S TRUMAN. When Mr. TRUMAN served as a member of the Jackson County Court, on which body I was later elected to serve, and during his years in the Senate and in the Presidency, I know Mr. TRUMAN was a regular reader of our hometown newspaper, the Independence Examiner.

I mention this fact only to emphasize that I know that our former President read, admired, and respected not only the paper's journalistic excellence, but also its editorial policy. It is for these reasons that I am sure Mr. TRUMAN would have approved his editorial written and appearing in the edition of the Independence Examiner on December 26.

While the editor's comments devotes some of its space to the importance of the Truman Library to Independence, Mo., his hometown paper goes on to quote our former President to the effect that while the Library happened to be located in Independence, Mo., it belonged to all the people in the United States.

The important fact about the editorial published by Mr. TRUMAN's home newspaper is that it completely demolishes the sometimes expressed belief that a great man may not enjoy honor in his own country. The key content of the editorial, in my judgment, is that portion which states:

TRUMAN, who set out to be a good president, became a great president by doing a good job.

The editorial follows:

[Editorial from the Independence (Mo.) Examiner, Dec. 26, 1972]

HARRY S TRUMAN

The whole world joins us in our sorrow.

Independence was HARRY TRUMAN's home town and a city never had a more loyal citizen. We naturally feel his loss more acutely than any other place could.

But through the years we have shared him with others. First, with Missourians when we sent him to the Senate, and then the nation when he became the 33rd President. And finally with the world as he provided leadership in the post-war years.

And now HARRY TRUMAN is dead at 88.

The Examiner extends its sympathy to his wife and his daughter and to his sister, hospitalized herself.

HARRY TRUMAN wasn't the kind of president who was forgotten when he left the White House. He wasn't the kind of man who felt his work was done when he retired from the presidency although he was already a senior citizen.

TRUMAN made the presidential library which he chose to locate in his home city, his personal project and he working untiringly, traveled hundreds of miles, and made dozens of speeches in its behalf.

The flag is now at half mast at the beautiful structure on the crown of the hill where TRUMAN spent eight busy, happy years involved in a maze of activities.

"The library will belong to the people of the United States," he said in the legend for one of the cornerstones. "My papers will be the property of the people and will be accessible to them. The papers of the president are among the most valuable sources of material for history. They ought to be preserved and they ought to be used."

TRUMAN wanted his papers available for "furthering the study of free government and of the participation of the United States in world affairs."

And as TRUMAN wished and dreamed, his library has been used by researchers who wrote books, and has been visited by more than two-million history-loving Americans. His beliefs and philosophy are perpetuated there.

And students fortunate enough to visit the library in educational groups in the years when the former president kept office hours will never forget his folksy history lessons.

He told them that their government is the greatest in the history of the world and urged them to study their history and "learn what we have."

TRUMAN made more major decisions in his nearly eight years as chief executive than any other president. Reading, particularly history, a lifelong hobby, gave him invaluable background for his role.

TRUMAN, as no other American president, told it like it was—he said what was on his mind. He was willing to speak up if he felt the occasion justified it, a trait which endeared him to the common man.

TRUMAN, who set out to be a good president, became a great president by doing a good job.

He was willing to fight for what he thought was right. He fought a good fight all of his life, even to the end.

HARRY TRUMAN now belongs to immortality.

Mr. Speaker, the Kansas City Times is a paper which is the morning edition of the Kansas City Star, both of which are owned by the Star Co. Thus there is really only one paper in Kansas City, Mo., with both a morning and an evening edition. Most of us in the metropolitan area believe it is a good paper. It has achieved nationwide recognition as a great paper.

This is the paper whose reporters covered Mr. TRUMAN when he was a member of the Jackson County Court. This paper has maintained a Washington bureau during all the years when Mr. TRUMAN was in the Senate and in the Presidency. The Star has long maintained a bureau in Independence, Mo., and covered Mr. TRUMAN's years in his home city after he left the White House. It is for the foregoing reasons that the editorial in the Kansas City Times of December

27, 1972, should and must be made a part of the permanent record of the life of Mr. TRUMAN.

The following editorial sets the theme for several others written throughout Missouri as well as throughout the Nation when it points out that this supposedly common man from Independence became a most uncommon leader of the world.

While the editorial speaks for itself, it closes on the note that while Mr. TRUMAN seemed to be an ordinary man, in the best sense of the phrase, because he was without vanity or pretention, his qualities of intellect and character made him a most unusual man. The editorial follows:

[From the Kansas City (Mo.) Times, Dec. 27, 1972]

HARRY TRUMAN, MISSOURIAN AND PRESIDENT

HARRY S TRUMAN was the supposedly common man from Independence who became a most uncommon leader of the world.

The long-range successes and failures of the Truman years cannot be finally assessed, for the era has not played out its theme. But HARRY TRUMAN, the man and President, can be gauged. He lived among us in our own time: More than that, he was one of us; an apparently ordinary sort of person with the farm background and upbringing that were much the same as for millions of Middle Westerners.

Yet when events took him to the American presidency at a crucial turning point in the history of the world, the ordinary man became an extraordinary strong and decisive leader. He acted with what must have been an innate wisdom and ability to clarify issues based on a lifetime of self-education and reading in history. Whether HARRY TRUMAN would have been on anybody's list in 1943 as a potential occupant of the White House is doubtful; the fact is, however, that in 1945—with almost no tutoring from his predecessor—HARRY TRUMAN was in the White House and facing decisions as momentous as any ever thrust on a man.

He rose to the challenges prayerfully but with not a quaking humility. There was a degree of self-assurance that carried no hint of arrogance. He became President when Hitler's cruel reign was dissolving in Europe and the Empire of Japan was under siege. Within weeks he would be sitting at a conference table with Winston Churchill and Josef Stalin. Within months he would make the fateful decision to drop the first and only atomic bombs used in war.

A GENEROUS MIND

Dean Acheson many years later, wrote of his chief as having a "truly hospitable and generous mind, that is, a mind warm and welcoming in its reception of other people's ideas. Not in any sense self-deprecating, his approach was sturdy and self-confident, but without any trace of pretentiousness. He held his own ideas in abeyance until he had heard the ideas of others . . . alert and eager to gain additional knowledge and new insights. He was not afraid of the competition of others' ideas; he welcomed it".

This is a picture, not of a man who thought he was born to rule, as did Churchill, nor of a tyrant in the Stalin mold, who sought power as naturally as other men breathed. It is, instead, the description of a quick, intelligent and compassionate man who knew the gravity of his responsibility and who wanted to do the right thing. And who knew that whatever had to be done, it was HARRY TRUMAN who would have to do it.

The United States, surely, and the world were fortunate that such a man was ready to step on the global stage at just such a juncture in history. The American processes of politics and government seem to have an uncanny way of producing a Jackson, a Lincoln or a Truman when such an individual is needed. The consequences of a weak presidency in 1945–1953, or of a blustering, aggressive individual would have made for a very different world today. In the perspective of less than three decades, HARRY TRUMAN seems to have been the right man for the right time.

That time, now receding past the terms of four subsequent Presidents, was a period unparalleled in the history of the United States or any other nation. The fall of Nazi Germany and expansionist Japan had left a vacuum into which the old Russian imperialism with an even more dangerous face of international communism was rushing. The United States, with its nuclear monopoly, industrial power, and limited conventional forces, was the only challenger.

HIS DELICATE DECISIONS

The decisions in those days of HARRY TRUMAN's presidency were delicate in the extreme. All of the old rules were off. Europe was a ruin of bomb craters and dead cities. Asia was a ferment of confusion in the wake of the Japanese defeat. There were no blueprints to guide a future in the midst of the convulsions that ended World War II and the beginning of the nuclear age.

Mr. TRUMAN acted with caution and deliberate decision. From the very beginning he was steadfastly loyal to the ideal of the United Nations. His support in this area was crucial, both in giving the organization an early status and in placing it at the center of American foreign policy. He tried to head off an atomic arms race—and failed—but he tried, and that will always be to the credit of the United States and HARRY TRUMAN. At a time when the U.S. was the sole possessor of the bomb, this country did not and would not coerce the rest of the world with the ultimate threat. Other nations might not have been so generous.

Very quickly HARRY TRUMAN perceived that the Stalinist government of the Soviet Union based its policy on diplomatic duplicity and coercion. Out of this observation came the Truman Doctrine—the response to Russian intimidation in the region of Greece and Turkey. He proclaimed a policy of aid to all free people who would resist aggression or absorption.

The best example of a positive and creative foreign policy was the Marshall Plan that rebuilt postwar Europe. It was called the Marshall Plan because Mr. TRUMAN's hero, George C. Marshall, was the secretary of state when it was implemented. It might more accurately have been called the Truman-Clifford-Acheson plan after the President and his lieutenants, Clark Clifford and Dean Acheson. Before that, while the Russians were dismantling German industry in their zone, Mr. TRUMAN was moving to rehabilitate the smashed land. He firmly rejected the Morgenthau plan of a pastoral Germany. Later, he stood up to the Russian challenge and provided a classic example of the use of power with restraint in the Berlin airlift. He used the best American resource—airpower—and avoided the ground action that could have led to general combat.

At the same time the Truman administration was pushing the Point Four program of technical assistance that became a model for the best kind of aid to underdeveloped countries. And as Europe emerged from the ruins, TRUMAN and his advisers restored national pride with the formation of the North Atlantic Treaty Organization. The modern state of Israel was born under his auspices. The prompt recognition of the new nation by the United States helped make an ancient dream become reality.

Mr. TRUMAN said more than once that his most difficult decision was to order American arms against the Communist North Korean aggression in South Korea in 1950.

Out of that period came the firing of Gen. Douglas MacArthur, a genuine American folk hero. Mr. TRUMAN did it because the general was defying the elected authority of the American people. Mr. TRUMAN was right on this issue and most of the American people sensed it.

His action in Korea might be seen in contrast to the timidity of the Allies when Hitler was marching into the Rhineland and ushering in the age of Munich. His caution in restraining MacArthur and his refusal to put ground troops on the road to Berlin can be compared to the unhappy involvement of more than a half-million American troops in Southeast Asia.

The 1948 election, of course, was not only one of the great chapters in American politics, but pure HARRY S TRUMAN as well. Nobody, outside the Truman family, gave him the slightest chance.

With the defection of the Dixiecrats, led by Strom Thurmond, and the Progressives, led by Henry A. Wallace (TRUMAN had had to fire him, too), ignominious defeat seemed certain. But TRUMAN was drawing the crowds on his whistle-stop campaign. He denounced the "Do-Nothing 80th Republican Congress" with splendid contempt and great effect. And when the nation woke up after the election, HARRY TRUMAN had 303 electoral votes; Thomas Dewey had 189 and Strom Thurmond had 38, Wallace got none. Only TRUMAN and his family were truly unsurprised, although a great many Democrats had begun to hedge as they watched the crowds swell.

THE POLITICAL LEGACY

The 1948 election also was a Truman legacy. Even in this day of the most scientific polls and the fanciest electronic computation on election night, something in the back of the American political mind always says: "Remember 1948".

The association of Mr. TRUMAN in the 1920's and 1930's with the Pendergast machine of Jackson County is a fact of history although it can be seen now in the perspective of the rough politics of those days. Mr. TRUMAN, of course, would not apologize for that association and would resent excuses offered by others. His loyalty to Pendergast long after he had any necessity to depend on him politically was a measure of the Truman allegiance to friends.

If that fidelity sometimes was misplaced in trust of weaker men, it nevertheless was a Truman trait. He

was intensely loyal, not only to the people who had helped him in the early days of politics but to the associates of a lifetime. The men of Battery D, 129th Field Artillery, 35th Division, who served with Captain HARRY in World War I, were special favorites.

TRUMAN was a combat soldier; he saw men die under his command. He had been to Europe before he met Stalin and Churchill at Potsdam, although neither of those two might have appreciated it. No scandal that came out of the years of machine rule touched him. He was, in fact, a progressive and far-seeing judge of the Jackson County Court who paved roads and planned parks.

International issues were in the forefront of the Truman years but he left a mark on the domestic scene. His Fair Deal laid the groundwork for Medicare and possibly for a national health insurance. He put through the rudiments of federal aid to education and equal employment opportunity. Federal housing was a germ of his administration. The armed forces were unified in his days of power and racial segregation in the military came to an end.

He could bear grudges. People accustomed to the suavity of a Roosevelt sometimes found TRUMAN's style not easy to take. He was a fierce partisan whose opinions were expressed in a way to leave no doubt in the mind of listeners. He was a fond father and husband, a President out of the mold that began to change the spirit of the presidency with Andrew Jackson. TRUMAN was a Middle Westerner with Southern overtone, a product of the American movement westward across the continent. But no politician who played Chopin on the piano could be classified as a routine politician.

HOME TO INDEPENDENCE

In 1953 when he left the White House he returned easily to his home in Independence. Churchill once wrote of the pain a statesman feels when the mantle of power suddenly drops; when one whose favor meant everything one day meant nothing the next. HARRY TRUMAN apparently felt no such twinges. He returned home as naturally as the day he left it. He busied himself with the magnificent Truman Library (which he saw as a memorial to the presidency, not to himself) and sometimes would answer the phone there at 7:30 a.m. before the staff had arrived. He dropped garcefully from the pinnacle of power to the pleasant life around the square in Independence, writing, speaking, traveling, while he could, and enjoying the family.

In the last analysis, HARRY TRUMAN did seem to be an ordinary man in the best sense of the phrase: Without vanity, pretension or vainglorious ambition. But his qualities of intellect and character were most unusual. He was a man who suddenly found himself in the mainstream of human events and whose special gift was to act decisively and with courage to change the course of history.

Mr. Speaker, the State of Missouri boasts two metropolitan areas—one in the heartland of America on the western edge of the State, being Kansas City, Mo., and the other the great metropolitan area on the east side of the State at the confluence of the Mississippi and Missouri Rivers, being St. Louis, Mo. St. Louis has long enjoyed the benefits of two great metropolitan papers, the

St. Louis Globe-Democrat and the St. Louis Post-Dispatch. At this point, Mr. Speaker, I offer for inclusion in the Record an editorial from the St. Louis Globe-Democrat entitled "HARRY S TRUMAN—A Good President." For my part, I appreciate so very much the opening sentence which points out that the perspective of time has made it clear that HARRY S TRUMAN was an able President. In my judgment, history will say that he was a great President. I relish, particularly, the comment in the editorial which says that—

When the chips were down Mr. TRUMAN could be counted upon to do what was right—for he had the rarest of gifts—the ability to know exactly what he had to do and the courage to do it.

The editorial follows:

[From the St. Louis (Mo.) Globe-Democrat, Dec. 27, 1972]

HARRY S TRUMAN—A GOOD PRESIDENT

The perspective of time has made it clear that HARRY S TRUMAN was an able President.

This was not readily apparent when he left office. His opponents at that time dwelled on some of Mr. TRUMAN's unsuccessful domestic programs and his involvement with such cronies as poker-playing friend Gen. Harry Vaughan.

But when his record in the White House was dispassionately examined, in the years that followed, it became apparent the farm boy from Missouri had indeed risen to the heights of White House competence.

He had been President only a short time when he had to make the awesome decision to proceed with the atom bomb over the objections of the nation's top nuclear scientist, and then a few months later to issue the orders to drop atomic bombs on Hiroshima and Nagasaki.

After making these decisions, TRUMAN said he lost no sleep because he was certain the bombings would end the war and make the invasion of Japan unnecessary, thereby saving at least 250,000 American lives.

In 1949 he was instrumental in forming the North Atlantic Treaty Organization, the military alliance that prevented an aggressive, expansionist Soviet Union from moving against the West.

He will be remembered, too, for the massive economic aid that rescued a war-weary Europe and spared a threatened Greece from Communist takeover.

In 1950 Mr. TRUMAN again had an historic decision to make when North Korea invaded South Korea. He unflinchingly sent American troops to Korea, saving not only Korea but the fledgling United Nations.

These are only some of the decisions that will give Mr. TRUMAN high marks in history. But, to those who knew him, the thing they liked best about HARRY TRUMAN was his rare ability to "give 'em hell." They like it because they saw the plain-spoken Missourian as a wry, flinty champion of the underdog.

Their eyes popped and their ears tingled as HARRY tore into "the Wall Street gluttons of privilege" who were trying to "stick a pitchfork in the farmer's back." And they laughed sympathetically when the President flew into

a rage because a music critic wrote that Margaret Truman's voice was flat.

Mr. TRUMAN called the review "lousy" and added, "I've never met you, but if I do you'll need a new nose and plenty of beefsteak and perhaps a supporter below."

Perhaps this fascination with the immensely human and likeable President tended to obscure some of his other accomplishments. It isn't well known, for example, that he campaigned hard for civil rights and asked for laws against racial discrimination in voting and employment, and other legislation to stop lynchings.

But he was ahead of his time and southern Democrats blocked most of the reforms that were later enacted by Congress.

When the chips were down Mr. TRUMAN could be counted upon to do what was right.

Even though he had fought enactment of the Taft-Hartley Act, he didn't hesitate to use its authority when the nation's welfare was threatened by several national strikes.

The people of Missouri and the nation mourn the death of HARRY S TRUMAN, who not only became a good President but a beloved champion of his fellow man.

For he had the rarest of gifts—the ability to know exactly what he had to do and the courage to do it.

Mr. Speaker, as I mentioned earlier, the Kansas City Star for many years has maintained an Independence, Mo., bureau for its paper. While James W. Porter, commonly known as "Bud," was the head of that bureau, another native son of Independence—Fred Schulenberg—also worked in the Independence office of the Kansas City Star. Like most native sons of Independence, he knew Mr. TRUMAN well and even intimately. His story written for the St. Louis Globe-Democrat, "TRUMAN Always Could Be Counted on for a Story," underscores a fact that had never before been given proper perspective, and that is that while Mr. TRUMAN may not have been much of a cheerleader for the printed media because he sometimes felt that it was not completely fair and impartial, he nonetheless had great respect for what we could call the working press. He recognized that these men had no voice or control of editorial policy and were only trying to do their best job as reporters.

The story told by Fred Schulenberg in the St. Louis Globe-Democrat about the famous Harpie Club was until this publication almost unknown except to the closest friends of Mr. TRUMAN. In my judgment, Fred has not only made a contribution to Truman memorabilia but also added another interesting sidelight to the life of Mr. TRUMAN when he tells of the time the President was able to evade the Washington press corps to visit his mother. Fred also does a good job as he describes Mr. TRUMAN's personal enthusiasm for the Truman Library at Independence, Mo. The editorial follows:

[From the St. Louis (Mo.) Globe-Democrat, Dec. 27, 1972]

TRUMAN "ALWAYS COULD BE COUNTED ON FOR A STORY"

(By Fred Schulenberg)

(For almost 12 years the author, now editing a magazine in St. Louis, was night manager of the Independence bureau of the Kansas City Star. The period covered a portion of the time Mr. TRUMAN was President and the years from 1953, when his second term expired, to April 1957, when the author changed jobs and moved here. These are the author's recollections of some of his contacts with the former president.)

President HARRY S TRUMAN was a man reporters liked to cover—not so much because he was easy to cover, which he wasn't, but because he always could be counted on for a story. Although he held newspaper management in contempt during much of his time in public life, he had a warm regard for the working newspaperman.

My recollections are of President TRUMAN at Independence. Many of the most vivid stem from the firm belief that in his home town he was entitled to privacy. If he had difficulties in Washington with newsmen—and a certain music critic—he also had a few in Independence, some of which have never been reported.

The former President never quite got used to the tight security imposed on him by the importance of his office. It was the veil which reporters sought to penetrate and, for many, Independence seemed a good place to do it.

The Truman temper probably was most sharply displayed on a cold December morning during his annual Christmas visit home while he was President.

An Independence newsman from the Kansas City Star, James W. Porter, was subjected to one of the most caustic dressing downs a reporter could have received. The pity was that Porter was not responsible for the reporting incident which triggered the criticism.

As was his custom, Mr. TRUMAN took his early morning walk from his home to the Independence square six blocks away, followed by an entourage of Secret Service men, local newsmen and members of the Washington press corps, and Independence citizens.

He stopped, as he frequently did, at the grocery store owned by the late Roger T. Sermon, mayor of Independence. Only Mr. TRUMAN and Secret Service men entered the store, but one of the agents soon came out and told Porter that "the chief" wanted to see him.

What happened in the store, which the Star did not print, was that the President proceeded to tell Porter everything Mr. TRUMAN had done since he got up before 6 a.m. According to Porter, who filed a complete report of the incident with his paper, Mr. TRUMAN spared no details, even reciting particulars on his morning preparations and dressing techniques.

Then, Porter said, the President specifically criticized him and the Star for the "invasion of his privacy," on the previous night, when it had been reported that the President had played poker with friends.

I have to assume part of the blame for the incident, because it was I who had been the only reporter waiting outside the Truman home the previous evening who knew all the members of the Harpie Club, the chief executive's long-time poker group. By process of elimination, I had located the Truman car and that of his Secret Service escort at a club member's home, and had learned from children who went in and got his autograph that "there were poker chips and cards around."

No one could know the former President without admiring him for his strong belief in the strength of the family unit.

I had just returned to the Star after serving in World War II when on Mother's Day I called the President's mother's home to see if he had called from Washington or sent flowers.

After one ring of the phone, Mr. TRUMAN answered. After I had gotten over my surprise and we had exchanged brief pleasantries I asked how long he would be at Grandview. He said he would be leaving within the hour, because hardly anyone in Washington knew he had gone.

Among those who did not know were the Washington newspaper reporters. This was probably the only time the President did leave Washington without a second plane loaded with reporters accompanying him.

He told me he thought it was something of a trick to slip away without them knowing. It was a pleasure for us to file a story on his leaving Washington, using the dateline, "Grandview, Mo."

No memorial was ever built to a man that had more of that man's architectural touch than does the Truman Library at Independence. ("For gosh sakes," he told me, "don't call it a memorial library until I'm dead.")

When the library was about half completed I asked Mr. TRUMAN if he would let me do a feature story for the Star, centering it on his attachment to the project.

"Could you meet me at the building in the morning at 6:30," Mr. TRUMAN said. "We can take a tour and you can get what you want."

Next morning it was five degrees above zero and he was waiting when I arrived. There was no heat in the building, but we made a two-hour inspection of the progress being made and he was still full of enthusiasm when I was virtually frozen. My fingers would no longer operate properly to use the camera I was carrying.

Mr. Speaker, while the St. Louis Post-Dispatch entitled its editorial, "The President From Missouri," the writer of that editorial goes on to make it plain that Mr. TRUMAN rose from a lowly farmboy to the Presidency and met on equal footing with the other great and powerful men of the world.

The concluding paragraph of this editorial contains some well-expressed thoughts when it points out that Mr. TRUMAN was a man of the people, earthy, honest, with a mixture of pride and humility. It concludes with the comment that he gave each day's responsibilities the best he had and slept at night in the comfort of knowing that no man can do more. The editorial follows:

[From the St. Louis (Mo.) Post-Dispatch, Dec. 26, 1972]

THE PRESIDENT FROM MISSOURI

HARRY TRUMAN's place in history may safely be left to historians who will in time evaluate the Truman Doctrine, the containment of Communism and the Cold War within the context of this turbulent century. For Missourians he will remain their first President, a decent man of modest attainments thrust suddenly upon the world stage, possessed of the frailties and the nobility of anyone's next door neighbor.

Mr. TRUMAN had character, and it saw him through many a crisis in his official life. He knew where he stood, and so did his friends and his enemies. If he was cranky and contentious at times, he could be magnanimous and conciliatory, too. He believed in the dignity of human beings, and he was not afraid to take political risks in pursuit of what he considered to be right.

It was typical of Mr. TRUMAN that when Tom Pendergast, the discredited Democratic boss of Kansas City, died six days after Mr. TRUMAN became vice president in 1945, Mr. TRUMAN disregarded advice that it would be politically smart to ignore the event. He boarded a plane for Kansas City, telling reporters, "I'm as sorry as I can be; he was always my friend and I have always been his."

The nation's shock over the death of President Roosevelt on April 12, 1945, was exceeded only by its questions as to the capacity of the former Senator who succeeded him. Mr. TRUMAN had received much favorable attention for his exposures of graft and waste in the defense establishment—in 1942 Marquis Childs referred to him as "one of the most useful and at the same time one of the most forthright and fearless of the ninety-six"—but as an executive he was unknown.

Mr. TRUMAN quickly reassured the country, with a fine address to a joint session of Congress and in a press conference that revealed decisiveness and understanding. Few Presidents have assumed office in a period of greater crisis, and Mr. TRUMAN had the added handicap of following the monumental and popular FDR. He never really felt secure until he won the presidency in his own right in 1948, defeating Gov. Dewey of New York in a legendary give-'em-hell campaign.

Looking back on the Truman years, some of our younger writers are inclined to fault the President for politics that in perspective appear to have been misguided. Should he have dropped atomic bombs on Hiroshima and Nagasaki? Should he have promulgated the Truman Doctrine (sparked by Greece and Turkey) of supporting "free people who are resisting attempted subjugation by armed minorities or by outside pressure?" Should he have prosecuted the Cold War by attempting to prevent the expansion of Communism? Should he have fired Gen. MacArthur for insurbordination; and what about Korea?

It should be remembered that when Mr. TRUMAN entered the White House the world was falling apart. Colonialism was on its last legs; big powers and little powers alike were scrambling to fill vacuums. The aims and capabilities of the Communists were not fully understood. A generation has passed since the Truman years and some of the problems the Missourian faced have not yet been solved: Germany remains divided, Korea is divided, the U.S. is engaged in paracolonialism in Vietnam,

One can well afford to look back with a measure of charity.

Mr. TRUMAN was overwhelmingly a man of the people—earthy, gregarious, stubborn, courageous, honest, a mixture of pride and humility. He had small preparation for high office, but he gave the day's responsibilities the best he had and slept at night in the comfort of knowing that no man can do more. He was not only a native of this State, in many ways he was typical of its citizenry. We can be thankful that Mr. TRUMAN walked among us.

Hon. Wayne Owens
OF UTAH

Mr. Speaker, in 1948 when I was 11 years old I found my first national hero in the form of the tough-minded, fighting man from Missouri then facing an apparently impossible campaign. It was in that year that I made my first political commitment by writing on the sidewalks in chalk in my hometown of Panguitch, Utah, "Vote for HARRY TRUMAN."

In 1952 I traveled 250 miles for the opportunity for an introduction and brief conversation with President TRUMAN. I found him gracious, yet awesome, and it has been my opportunity over the years to meet him on two other occasions and in that way, to touch as it were, contemporary world history.

He taught that politics was an honorable profession. He proved that a politician could be independent, strong, personally straightforward, yet also win high office. I believe that history will judge him, after the 50 years' interim period he requested, as one of the greatest and strongest leaders of our time. At this point, 20 years past his departure from office, as a very amateur American politician, I place him among the all-time great American Presidents.

President TRUMAN refused to be bullied about by political opponents at home or abroad and effected more than any other person, the reconstruction of Europe and saved them from external domination.

The name of HARRY TRUMAN will not be forgotten in the Owens household, just as it will live on in millions of homes where stories of unusual men are retold. My repertory of HARRY TRUMAN stories is extensive and illustrative of all that is good about the American political system. I am proud, indeed, of having been alive to watch the formation of the Truman heritage.

Hon. Edwin D. Eshleman

OF PENNSYLVANIA

Mr. Speaker, for the benefit of my colleagues and others who read the Congressional Record, I wish to include in the Record the remarks of Dr. Wallace E. Fisher, senior pastor of Trinity Lutheran Church, Lancaster, Pa., when the citizens of our community paid tribute to the life and service of the late President HARRY S TRUMAN at a memorial service held on December 28, 1972.

Dr. Fisher's remarks follow:

MEMORIAL ADDRESS FOR HARRY S TRUMAN

Dean Acheson in his enlightening volume of memoirs, "Present At The Creation," wrote of the seven years from 1945 to 1952 (the years of Mr. TRUMAN's Presidency): "Only slowly did it dawn on us that the whole world structure and order that we had inherited was gone . . ." And it was. It had begun to crumble in 1914.

For the first time in *America's national history* the British Empire fell apart; Stalinist Russia emerged as one of the two competitive power centers in the world; the birth of Communist China was imminent; nuclear weapons were first used and then developed competitively to frightful potential; the speed and load of fighter planes and bombers increased radically; the Third World took shape; the dispossessed in America and throughout the world began to demand their place in the sun. In that chaotic decade after World War II, HARRY S TRUMAN served as the thirty-third President of the United States.

Never in the history of American government had any president, more untrained and inexperienced, faced so many awesome changes on so many domestic and international fronts. George Washington presided over the establishment of our national government, but *that* government embraced only several millions of people and the geographic isolation of the new nation was almost absolute. Abraham Lincoln came to office as eleven Southern states seceded and formed a rival government. But states' rights and secession had been debated philosophically and probed pragmatically in the North and South for fifty years. And the explosive socio-economic issue—slavery—had been argued pro and con in households North and South since 1787. Franklin Roosevelt came to office when the economy and spirit of America had dropped to its bootstraps. But Mr. Roosevelt was relatively free to concentrate on domestic issues until 1938.

HARRY S TRUMAN—untrained for the President's office, lacking any first-hand knowledge of secret international agreements, and unaware until he took office that the atomic bomb was almost operable—was called to guide the nation in a period of cataclysmic political, economic, technological, and social change.

Those unprecedented changes required President TRUMAN to make a series of far-reaching decisions that ranged from using the atomic bomb to the firing of a military leader who had become a legend in his own time. Mr. TRUMAN, during his almost eight years in office, was criticized, caricatured, ridiculed, vilified. He was also respected, appreciated, trusted, and followed, first by ordinary citizens and then by urbane intellectuals like Dean Acheson who called him, "the captain with the mighty heart."

Mr. TRUMAN, stepping down from the Presidency in January, 1953, declared that he would like the epitaph he had found on a particular grave marker in Tombstone, Arizona, to be applied descriptively to his administration: "Here lies Jack Williams. He done his damndest." Millions of Americans agreed to that epitaph the day HARRY TRUMAN left office. Twenty years later, knowledgeable students of American government were suggesting that Mr. TRUMAN would win a place alongside Washington, Jefferson, Lincoln, Wilson, and Franklin D. Roosevelt; some, without equivocation, had already given him that place.

What sort of person and president was this man who, entering office so humbly, carved so boldly such a distinguished niche in American history?

HARRY S TRUMAN was a gentle family man. Unlike Franklin Roosevelt who first broke his marital vow when he was Assistant Secretary of the Navy and apparently cherished that relationship to the day he died, HARRY TRUMAN was devoted to the childhood sweetheart who eventually became his wife. His meanest critics never intimated that he was untrue to the woman he married. The worst they suggested was that he was gauche in speaking publicly of Mrs. Truman as his "Sweetheart" and as "The Boss."

Mr. TRUMAN's life-long devotion to his daughter, Mary Margaret, flashed into world view when he wrote a petty letter to a music critic who had suggested that Mary Margaret was not overly talented musically! Margaret Truman's recent book about her father is not especially helpful to the critical historian when she talks about him as a public figure. It is invaluable to the historian, however, when she writes insightfully about the father she loved and who loved her.

From first to last, HARRY TRUMAN—in spite of heavy public responsibilities—enjoyed a meaningful relationship with his wife, daughter, sister, and mother. When he retired from office twenty years ago, HARRY and Bess Truman went eagerly to their unpretentious home in Independence, Missouri. After her marriage to Clifton Daniel, Margaret and her family visited Independence regularly and happily. Her father's relationship with his grandchildren was proud and warm. HARRY S TRUMAN was a gentle, responsible family man.

HARRY S TRUMAN was a tough-minded, stout-hearted politician. When he came to the Senate at fifty-one, he was referred to disdainfully as "the man from Pendergast." Indeed, without that particular political boss, Mr. TRUMAN would not have gained a place in the United States Senate. He never pretended otherwise. Refreshingly, he acknowledged his personal debt. Boss Tom Pendergast, imprisoned for graft during Truman's first term as a Senator, came home to Missouri to die. Senator TRUMAN was the only national figure present at Pendergast's funeral. The Hagues, the Pendergasts, the Daleys, and other political bosses have had a large hand in bringing hundreds of effective politicians to state and national power in our American system, but I can recall no national figure who was more candid about his political origins than HARRY S TRUMAN.

When Senator TRUMAN ran for reelection to the United States Senate, President Roosevelt endorsed TRUMAN's opposition in the primaries. But Senator TRUMAN, a rugged political in-fighter, slugged it out in a mean campaign in the primaries, winning the state election with the slim majority of eight thousand votes.

During Mr. TRUMAN's second term in the Senate, he served as the Chairman of the committee appointed to investigate war contracts. He proceeded without regard for party or person, saving the United States thousands of lives and millions of dollars by keeping government contractors reasonably reliable and honest.

Everyone remembers Mr. TRUMAN's courageous uphill fight for the Presidency in his own right. Certain members in his own party, most Republicans, the political opinion polls, and the majority of newspapers named Thomas Dewey a hands-down winner. But all these had underestimated HARRY S TRUMAN *and* the rank and file voter. TRUMAN whistle-stopped thirty thousand miles around the country, speaking extemporaneously. When the ballots were tallied, he had over-matched the platitudinous Thomas Dewey, the reactionary Strom Thurmond, and the starry-eyed Henry Wallace.

That same politican's skill served Mr. TRUMAN and the nation well during his years at Blair House and in the White House. In the American political system, a president without political know-how is severely handicapped. HARRY TRUMAN—like Abraham Lincoln and Franklin Roosevelt—was a master politician. He also loved rough-and-tumble politics, stating bluntly that public figures "who couldn't stand the heat should get out of the kitchen."

HARRY S TRUMAN was a stout-hearted, tough-minded politician.

HARRY S TRUMAN was a bold, imaginative, decisive statesman. Ethicists will debate for centuries the rightness of his decision to drop two atomic bombs on Japan. But judging President TRUMAN's decision in historical context—the evident possibility of saving several million American and Japanese lives; his newly gained knowledge of the weapon; the uncertainty of its potential; and the national psychological conditioning effected by the Allies' insistence on unconditional surrender—one accepts that he did his duty as President.

Nonetheless, I have wished since August, 1945—and expressed that wish publicly on occasion—that the American government had first demonstrated the effectiveness of its new weapon to Japanese observers before dropping it on Hiroshima and Nagasaki. I have also said publicly that one bomb was certainly enough; Nagasaki need not have been hit. But neither then nor since have I been a self-righteous critic of Mr. TRUMAN on this issue. My remembrance of the historical situation in 1945 has restrained me. And from that day to this, I have admired Mr. TRUMAN for not shifting the responsibility for that decision on other members of his government.

But that was only his first unprecedented decision! History asked HARRY S TRUMAN to make scores of other far-reaching decisions. He made them with caution, insight, and boldness: support for the United Nations, aid to Greece and Turkey, the rebuilding of Western Europe, the fashioning of NATO, a firm but reasoned resistance to Communism, the Korean War, the firing of Douglas MacArthur, a firm if modest fight for civil rights legislation, a continuing plea for Medicare—and more.

Decisions—Decisions—Decisions. The farmer from Missouri, the politician from Pendergast, the ordinary citizen from Independence, "the captain with the mighty heart"—HARRY S TRUMAN, thirty-third President of the United States—decided so boldly and so wisely that before he died this week at eighty-eight, he knew that most of his fellow-citizens had rated him a near-great President and that some had rated him a great President.

HARRY S TRUMAN, the ordinary citizen from Independence, Missouri, was an extraordinary President of the United States.

Hon. Garner E. Shriver
OF KANSAS

Mr. Speaker, I join with my colleagues in the House of Representatives to pay tribute to the memory of former President HARRY S TRUMAN. His passing is truly a great loss to all Americans. HARRY TRUMAN was a man who assumed the responsibilities of the Presidency in a difficult and critical time in our history, and went on to prove that he was a man who could act decisively and shoulder the responsibility for the decisions he made.

HARRY TRUMAN brought World War II to an end with the decision to bomb Hiroshima. He set up the Marshall plan to assist war-torn nations abroad, and gave vital support during the establishment of the United Nations. He fought Communist takeover wherever it threatened, with such actions as the Truman doctrine in Turkey and Greece, and the Berlin airlift. HARRY S TRUMAN gave our Nation courageous leadership in a time when such leadership was essential.

He was also a man who was not self-impressed with his role as President. He knew his shortcomings and never thought of himself as infallible. He always considered himself "just a simple man from Missouri." His courage and integrity, his compassion and commonsense, and his ability to reach the people of this Nation and gain their trust, should stand as shining examples to all of us in government today.

Mrs. Shriver joins with me in extending deepest sympathy to Mr. TRUMAN's family.

Hon. Edward J. Derwinski
OF ILLINOIS

Mr. Speaker, when the history books are finally closed on America's great experiment in democracy, the name HARRY TRUMAN will occupy a cherished position among this country's great leaders. It does not take much of a prophet to make that statement: historians have already rated him as one of the five best Presidents to serve in the White House.

Mr. TRUMAN was never called an intellectual and rightly so. But while his formal education was merely normal, this great country of ours has never, and probably will never, be led by a man with more backbone. In the face of history's most challenging problems, Mr. TRUMAN never lost his native knack of seeing things in their proper prospective and explaining them simply to all of us.

In addition to a special kind of courage, President TRUMAN possessed another gift—humility. The day after the Presidency was thrust unto him, TRUMAN told a group of reporters:

Last night the whole weight of the moon and stars and all the planets fell on me. Please pray for me.

Apparently, the prayers were answered as he completed Franklin Roosevelt's term and his own 4-year administration with honor. Never a man to back away from a fight, Mr. TRUMAN faced each crisis with the best interest of the Nation at heart.

Probably the best example of the former President's courage is his decision to use the atom bomb on the Japanese. While experts still argue over the wisdom of his action, there can be little doubt that TRUMAN put the interests of America above his own place in history. An image-minded President-politician would have hesitated while thousands more Americans died in needless battle.

HARRY TRUMAN had a straightforward way of saying things. About the Presidency he said: "The buck stops here." When a reporter blasted his daughter's singing, TRUMAN called him an s.o.b. and wrote him a letter on White House stationery offering to punch his face in. Faced with "certain defeat" at the hands of Thomas Dewey in the 1948 election, Truman defied the "experts" by predicting victory, "I'll give 'em hell," HARRY said. And hell is just what he gave them.

They learned not all Chief Executives have the sound of a public relations man with a Harvard law degree. If TRUMAN was President in this era, people would say he tells it like it is, but in those days the phrase had not been invented. In those days there was no need for such an expression.

TRUMAN was once asked what he thought of the chances of a woman being President. TRUMAN replied:

I've said for a long time that women have everything else, they might as well have the Presidency.

I am not sure how women's liberation people would react today, but I kind of like that answer.

Mr. Speaker, as a Member of Congress who respects all Presidents regardless of the political controversy which may swirl about them, I pay tribute today to a great President and great American, HARRY TRUMAN.

Hon. Wm. J. Randall
OF MISSOURI

Mr. Speaker, in remarks previously made on the floor of the House referring to newspaper comments on the life of Mr. TRUMAN, I have heretofore included editorials by the newspaper of his home city, the Independence Examiner of Independence, Mo., the large neighboring metropolitan paper to the west, the Kansas City Star, and the two metropolitan dailies from the St. Louis area, the St. Louis Globe-Democrat and the St. Louis Post-Dispatch.

At this time it is my privilege to preserve for the record the comments of two other leading newspapers in our State, a great newspaper in Northwest Missouri, the St. Joseph, Mo., News-Press, and an excellent newspaper which serves what we in Missouri call the Ozark Empire, the Springfield, Mo., Leader-Press.

Mr. Speaker, each editor has contributed his own special treatment or viewpoint on the traits of character and personal qualities of our first citizen of Missouri, former President TRUMAN. In many instances, the same conclusion is reached but by using different language. In some instances, there is included the recollection of an incident of personal association with Mr. TRUMAN.

The editor of the St. Joseph, Mo., News-Press, headlines his comments, "HARRY S TRUMAN, Man of the People." In this particular appraisal, the writer points out that Mr. TRUMAN never lost the common touch because he was always able to relate himself to the little man. To the man in the street, HARRY S TRUMAN became almost an idol. Another facet of his character which this writer dwells upon has never been so well expressed as when it is said, "rule 1, page 1, in his book of politics was 'loyalty.'" He lived up to that rule himself and expected others to do the same. The editorial follows:

[From the St. Joseph (Mo.) News-Press, Dec. 27, 1972]

HARRY S TRUMAN, MAN OF THE PEOPLE

He met on equal footing with the other great and powerful men of the world. He rose from a Missouri farm to the Presidency of the United States where he made some of the most important decisions in history.

Yet he never lost the common touch.

That was HARRY S TRUMAN, 33rd President of the United States, who died Tuesday, nearly 20 years after he had left the White House.

First, last and always he was a man of the people. The greatness of the office he held, the power he wielded never went to his head. The friends he had in the days when he was a county judge in Jackson County were still his friends when he was President.

To the little man, to the man in the street, HARRY TRUMAN was an idol. They related him to themselves, impressed by his courage, sincerity, boldness in action, and willingness to tread on important toes when he thought the situation justified it.

Some men, given great power, swell. Others grow. HARRY TRUMAN grew.

Probably no President in the history of this nation made as many great and fateful decisions as fell to his lot. He made them after due thought, but, once he made them, he did not look back. He knew that would do no good. He knew that he had acted always in what he believed were the best interests of his fellow countrymen.

It fell to his lot to succeed President Franklin D. Roosevelt as Chief Executive in the waning days of World War II in Europe. He was to preside less than a month later—on May 8, 1945—when the surrender of the Nazi forces of Germany came. Four months later it was President TRUMAN who announced the surrender of Japan, the end of World War II.

It was his role in history to bring the United Nations actively into being, to aid the battered and bruised nations with the Marshall Plan. He directed the airlift that saved Berlin during its beleaguered days. Too, it became his duty to fire General Douglas MacArthur when he decided the popular general was overstepping his authority, disobeying orders from the President.

He was a man who could stand up against political heat, and who frequently did. No one bluffed him. In 1948 he pulled off the greatest political upset in history when he won election to the Presidency in his own right when all the cards seemed so thoroughly stacked against him. The little man, the people he had so long befriended, came to the fore to give him that victory.

He clashed with powerful John L. Lewis, the miner's head, and John L. Lewis lost. "Give 'em hell, HARRY" became part of the political language due to the manner in which he went after his political enemies from the rostrum.

Rule one, page one, in his book of politics was "Loyalty." He lived up to that rule himself and expected others to do the same.

No one who ever knew HARRY TRUMAN ever will forget him. He was a man who made deep and lasting impressions.

And now he is gone. A great patriot, a great American, a great United States Senator, and a great President whose stature mounted and mounted and mounted after he departed the White House. He belongs now only to history, which will give him the justice he so greatly earned.

Peace to his fighting yet always friendly spirit!

Southwest Missouri never returned large majorities for Mr. TRUMAN in either of his two races for the U.S. Senate. However, when he ran for the presidency in 1948, he carried most of the counties of the Ozark area which traditionally are never very enthusiastic for a democratic candidate. In that year most of them voted for him because they recognized that a Missourian was in the race for the presidency, and when it became a match between Mr. TRUMAN and the little man from New York, the choice to vote for a Democrat became much more palatable.

In my judgment, the editor from the Springfield, Mo., Leader-Press reflects some of that feeling in the Ozark area when he writes his story on the subject of, "As We Remember HARRY S TRUMAN." The writer quite frankly admits that his newspaper voiced vehement disagreement with Mr. TRUMAN as U.S. Senator and as President, but that his home State nearly always was friendly to him even though all of its citizens did not completely agree with his programs or his proposals.

The editor also quite appropriately takes the space to emphasize that one of the personal characteristics of Mr. TRUMAN which guided his entire life was the trait of personal honesty which served as a foundation for his belief that public office is a public trust. It is quite appropriate to note that, although he remained loyal to Tom Pendergast, never in any single instance did the Kansas City machine's corruption rub off on its member, HARRY S TRUMAN. The editorial follows:

[From the Springfield (Mo.) Leader-Press, Dec. 27, 1972]

AS WE REMEMBER HARRY TRUMAN

HARRY TRUMAN, incorruptible, loyal, tough-minded, blunt-spoken former President of the United States, has lost his typically valiant fight against the ravages of heart, lung and kidney ailments.

Despite his 88 years, Mr. TRUMAN had twice fought his way off the critical list during this final illness in a Kansas City hospital. But the third time, it was too much for him, and now he has gone.

He will be sorely missed. During his years as a U.S. Senator and as President, he had made some enemies. At times, this newspaper voiced vehement disagreement with him. But few men who reached a position of prominence have ever enjoyed more friends than HARRY TRUMAN did, and the fact that a host of them were residents of his home town of Independence, Mo., and his home state generally says a great deal.

A considerable number of those friends were here in Springfield at one time, though most of them have long since left us. As a judge of the Jackson County court and as senator, he was a frequent visitor here, counseling and socializing with colleagues who were leaders of the Democratic party in these parts.

During World War I, he commanded Battery D, 129th Field Artillery, of the 35th Division, in which he served as father-confessor as well as leader to his men. As long as his health permitted, he never failed to attend the spring reunions of the dwindling roster of Battery D, including one in Springfield while he was President. Several of his former battery mates kept a steady vigil at the hospital where he waged his last fight.

After the war, he ran a small haberdashery in downtown Kansas City. It failed in 1921 under the burden of a heavy debt. It took Mr. TRUMAN about nine years after that, but he paid off every dollar of that debt.

While Mr. TRUMAN was serving as a county judge, Tom Pendergast, notorious Missouri Democratic boss, picked him to run for the Senate and saw him elected. By the time his first term expired six years later, Pendergast was in jail, his machine discredited. Mr. TRUMAN ran for re-election without his help, and with very little money, and barely won renomination. And he remained loyal to Tom Pendergast through it all, and through it all none of the machine's alleged corruption rubbed off on him.

The rest of his political history is well-known to Americans who can remember as far back as the 1930's—his genuinely reluctant acceptance of the vice presidential nomination at the insistence of President Franklin D. Roosevelt; his anguished accession to the presidency after Mr. Roosevelt's death; the awesome and world-shaking decision he had to make to drop the atomic bomb on Japan; his stubborn and victorious battle for re-election against Thomas E. Dewey in 1948.

Just before his 80th birthday, he surveyed the collection of memorabilia of his historic administrations in the Truman Library in Independence and announced his intention of living to be 90 because "there's at least 10 more years of work to be done around here." But he didn't make it—quite. His failing health prevented him from keeping a regular schedule at the library some months ago. But he still worked at his home with his secretary, Miss Rose Conway, and he still spent some time studying history, his favorite subject, until his final illness.

Goodbye, Captain HARRY, President HARRY, Friend HARRY. It probably would be inappropriate to remind you just now, as your supporters often did in former years, to "give 'em hell." But you'll know what we mean.

Mr. Speaker, as we near the end of the officially proclaimed 30-day period of mourning of that great American, HARRY S TRUMAN, it is again my privilege to help preserve in the Congressional Record, as reference for future students of his-tory, the comments made by several editors and publishers whose newspapers circulate within the congressional district that it has been my honor to represent and which is also the home district of our late beloved President.

Nearly every one of the great papers in the four corners of this land have taken the time to reflect upon the rare characteristics and sterling personal qualities of the Man from Independence. They have all written with great journalistic ability. Just about everything that has been written has been most impressive. However, Mr. Speaker, it seems to me that our historians of the future should not be denied the benefit of the appraisal of those who knew him best and that means to preserve the special analysis of his life and times by those neighbors who lived close to him in west central Missouri.

Few Members of Congress have had the good fortune to be the recipient of so much reflected glory from such a great man as has been mine. It has been my honor the past 14 years to represent in Congress not only his home city of Independence, Mo., but also to represent Barton County, Mo. Its county seat, the city of Lamar, Mo., was the birthplace of Mr. TRUMAN. On the day after his passing, the new publisher of the Lamar Democrat, James C. Kirkpatrick, a distinguished Missourian, who has served for many years as secretary of state for the State of Missouri, wrote a column under the headline, "HARRY S TRUMAN Was a Traditional American."

Most appropriately, Secretary Kirkpatrick characterizes Mr. TRUMAN as being one who proved the adage that in America every boy has a chance to grow up to be President. He outlines his early setbacks by setting out the fact that he was defeated for a second term on the county court. He suggests that any temporary setback only intensified his future efforts.

Yes, Secretary Kirkpatrick—writing from the city of the birthplace of HARRY TRUMAN—provides for us two separate threads of thought: first, that Mr. TRUMAN was a traditional American—as much so as apple pie, turkey on Thanksgiving, and Santa Claus on Christmas.

Then he departs on another thread, equally important, to survey the happenings in the life of HARRY TRUMAN to show that he was a self-made man, a Horatio Alger, and a perfect example for a parent to tell to his son that by hard work, study, application, and perseverance that son can become a President of the United States.

When I said there were two threads of thought in this editorial worthy of emphasis, I neglected to mention how good it is that Secretary Kirkpatrick recalls the time when Mr. TRUMAN, as Vice President, was criticized for attending the funeral services of Tom Pendergast. He responded with the words:

Only rats desert a sinking ship.

This most excellent editorial follows:

[From the Lamar (Mo.) Democrat, Dec. 28, 1972]

HARRY S TRUMAN WAS A TRADITIONAL AMERICAN

(By James C. Kirkpatrick, Democrat copublisher)

HARRY S TRUMAN was as traditionally American as pumpkin pie and turkey on Thanksgiving and Santa Claus on Christmas.

He proved the age old adage that in America every boy has a chance to grow up to be president.

HARRY TRUMAN was a college drop-out. He started to law school but quit. In his early life he changed jobs several times. He was railroad worker, newspaperman, banker, farmer and merchant. His first venture in business failed. Finally he drifted into politics.

He was an organization politician in the Tom Pendergast era. Honesty and integrity were trademarks with the Jackson County Court judge, the first position to which he won election.

Defeat in his campaign for a second term on the court only intensified his efforts. Two years later he won the presiding judge's seat on the court.

In later years there was a tendency on the part of big-time politicians to look down their nose at TRUMAN because of that humble beginning on the county court. He was criticized for his association with Pendergast, the machine political boss.

Judge TRUMAN was the underdog in his 1934 race for the Senate against such a well-known Missourian and governor, Lloyd C. Stark. That didn't bother him. Instead he worked all the harder shaking hands and winning votes. Many who did not support him in his statewide and presidential campaigns found out to their sorrow that he also had a long memory of those who opposed him.

During those campaigns we were editing the Daily Star-Journal at Warrensburg. Mr. TRUMAN never carried Johnson County in any of his primary campaigns. Though county Democrats rallied to his support in the general election he never forgave them for their failure to support him in the primaries. There are people in Lamar now that can testify to that. Johnson County never benefited from senatorial or presidential favors from Mr. TRUMAN.

It was Mr. TRUMAN's intense loyalty and his ability to cut through red tape that endeared him to friends and associates. The former president worked hard to inform himself on matters of importance. He expected others to get to the point quickly and not waste his time on chit-chat.

Old-timers will recall the newspaper criticism directed at President TRUMAN when he returned to Kansas City to attend funeral services for Tom Pendergast. His curt reply was, "Only rats desert a sinking ship".

Today the entire nation mourns a humble man, born in Lamar, a Jackson County politician, an intensely loyal American and former U.S. senator who ferreted out waste and wrong-doing in the nation's defense program, a common man who became president and then returned to his native Missouri to follow a normal life as neighbor and friend.

HARRY TRUMAN grew in whatever job he undertook. He worked hard to carry out every responsibility. And above all else, he kept the common touch.

Kings or the man on the street made no difference.

HARRY TRUMAN, a self-made man, a Horatio Alger, will always remain as the symbol to which every proud parent can point as an example to a son and claim—work hard, study and apply yourself and you can become president of the United States.

Mr. Speaker, Belton, Mo., is situated in the northwest corner of Cass County, Mo., which is very near, geographically, to the southwest corner of Jackson County, Mo., wherein is located the city of Grandview, Mo. This city has always proudly proclaimed itself as the boyhood home of Mr. TRUMAN.

At the memorial services for Mr. TRUMAN in the auditorium of the Truman Library in Independence, Mo., one of the participants was the grand master of the Grand Lodge of Missouri. Mr. TRUMAN, during his entire lifetime, was an active Mason—one who had learned to apply the principles of Masonry to his daily life. He had risen to the highest ranks of the Masonic Lodge.

The Belton Star-Herald, in its editorial comments, provides valuable background material when it recites that Mr. TRUMAN's years as a youth were spent in and around the Grandview-Belton area. It was at Belton on March 18, 1909, that he became a member of the Masonic Lodge. There he was raised to the sublime degree of Master Mason. Moreover, it was Mr. TRUMAN, along with several other Master Masons from Belton, Mo., who were given permission to organize the Grandview, Mo., lodge on April 4, 1911. In 1940 Mr. TRUMAN became Grand Master of the Grand Lodge of Missouri. That year he had the pleasure to revisit both the Belton and the Grandview Masonic Lodges. This most interesting and informative editorial follows:

[The Belton (Mo.) Star-Herald, Dec. 28, 1972]

HARRY S TRUMAN WAS LINKED WITH BELTON; THE BOND REMAINED UNBROKEN UNTIL HIS DEATH TUESDAY

The fabric of our lives is woven with threads that bind us to many localities, persons and events. One of the threads of former president HARRY S TRUMAN's life was his connection with Belton. To the end of his life the thread remained unbroken.

One of his special duty nurses during his last illness which began when he was admitted to Research Hospital in Kansas City on December 5 was a Beltonite. Mrs. Walter Killilae, 218 Park Drive, is a general staff duty nurse at Research Hospital and except for three nights, she was Mr. TRUMAN's night nurse. She was assigned to him two years ago February and in July of this year when he also was a patient at Research Hospital.

"He was a warm, sweet, witty individual, who was most appreciative of anything you did for him," Mrs. Killilae said of the former president. She said this last illness had taken its toll on Mr. TRUMAN but that it was her personal feeling that until a day or so before his death on Tuesday, he was still aware even though he was in a semi-conscious state.

Mrs. Killilae was on duty Saturday night. When she left him Sunday morning, she leaned over to tell him she was to have the next evening off (Christmas Eve) and asked him if he would be here when she got back. "He squeezed my hand, which leads me to believe his mind was still responsive until he slipped into the final coma."

The 110th Engineer Battalion, Missouri National Guard, was assigned security duty at the Carson Funeral Home two hours after Mr. TRUMAN's death. Several area men are members of the battalion and were on duty.

TRUMAN's early life was spent in and around the Belton-Grandview area.

TRUMAN's ties with Belton surfaced early in the century when he became a member of the Masonic Lodge in Belton. He was raised to the Sublime Degree of Master Mason on March 18, 1909 as a member of the local lodge. He and several Master Masons were granted permission to organize the Grandview Lodge on April 4, 1911 and the Belton Lodge gave them their old jewels. He later became Grand Master of Missouri and, in that office, visited the Belton Lodge on Nov. 21, 1940.

He presided at the ground-breaking ceremonies for the new building of the Belton Lodge on April 20, 1963. He donated $1,000 to the building fund and also was present at the laying of the cornerstone on Dec. 7, 1963. He was proud of his membership in the Masons as evidenced by his signature on that day. Asked to autograph a book on presidents of the United States, under his picture he signed, "HARRY S TRUMAN, 33rd Degree, P.G.M., Mo."

He was a personal friend to many in the area. Mrs. L. T. Brown, 5 Belmo Dr., remembers vividly a day in the early fifties when he stopped by the Cleveland farm home of her stepfather, Bruce Shubert, who had met him in his early political life. "I was in the kitchen making pie dough when my mother (Mrs. Dean Shubert, 100 Circle Dr.) called me into the living room," according to Mrs. Brown. "There stood Mr. TRUMAN in yellow trousers and a cream-colored jacket. When mother introduced me, he shook my hand as if it were covered with a white glove rather than flour. Bruce never got over the fact he wasn't home that day!"

People from all walks of life in Belton have a memory of TRUMAN at different points in his career. Mrs. Joe Bill Looney, 609 Minnie Avenue, remembers that as a student at UMKC she was a member of the university choir and sang at the ceremonies held when TRUMAN received an honorary Doctor of Laws degree from that institution. "I remember that the gentleman who introduced him

spoke 45 minutes but Mr. TRUMAN's acceptance speech was no longer than five minutes," said Mrs. Looney.

At least one Beltonite had visions of great things for TRUMAN while he was still a young man. Mrs. Grace Van Brunt of Kansas City, founder of the Grace Company and granddaughter of George Scott the founder of Belton, recalls an introduction to TRUMAN which took place prior to 1920. She stopped in the Bank of Belton one day and James Franklin Blair, president of the bank and father of Frank Blair, Jr., who is now president, said to her, "Grace, come over here, I want you to meet a young man who is going places in this world." The man of course was HARRY TRUMAN.

Another former Beltonite, Sammie Feeback of Kansas City, recorded in pictures some of the former president's life after he retired from the presidency to that of "citizen" of Independence.

Earlier this year Mr. TRUMAN took notice of Belton's Centennial year in a letter written to Mrs. Everett Wade, Route 1, when he wrote, "On the occasion of the observance of Belton, Missouri, Centennial Celebration, I am happy to extend congratulations for the progress and advancement that has been made in the past, and I send you my best wishes for continued progress." The letter was made a part of the Belton Centennial book published in June.

TRUMAN's refusal to succumb to the perils of power is legend. His attitudes, his demeanor and his habits remained very much like the "common man". J. Weldon Jackson, president of Citizens Bank of Belton, recalled that several years ago he attended a bankers convention in Washington, D.C. His badge indicating he was from Missouri, caused hotel employees, waitresses and others to ask, "You live near HARRY?"

Perhaps the greatness of the man lies in those words. Millions identified with him and the 1948 campaign slogan, "Give 'em hell, HARRY," was fondly the wish of many during his last illness. His death on Tuesday leaves a void in the hearts of many, not only in Belton, but throughout the nation and the world.

One of the better editorials on Mr. TRUMAN, produced within our congressional distict, comes from the pen of Ben Weir of the Nevada Daily Mail. Nevada is the county seat of Vernon County, which is the first county in the so-called stateline tier of counties immediately and directly north of Barton County, Mo., the birthplace of Mr. TRUMAN. Mr. Weir not only enjoys long residence as a geographical neighbor to the birthplace of Mr. TRUMAN but also for many years was the editor and publisher of the Independence Examiner. For such reasons he enjoyed the enviable opportunity to report on many of the happenings during the erroneously described retirement years of Mr. TRUMAN. In fact, Mr. TRUMAN never retired.

Because of these two reasons, Ben Weir is eminently qualified to express himself as he proceeds to review the life of Mr. TRUMAN. In his editorial Mr. Weir addresses himself to a facet of the life of Mr. TRUMAN that we should all take note of with approval. He points out that President TRUMAN was not the product of a prestigious Eastern college nor a member of a wealthy family. He went to work straight from high school and even suffered the loss of some jobs which hurt so much that he had to go back to the farm to earn a living. The important point, however, made by the writer is that never once during his serious troubles did Mr. TRUMAN hide behind the excuse of his inexperience or lack of knowledge, but rather displayed the unusual ability to make up his mind, always in command of himself, keeping his own counsel but doing what he thought was right.

His admonition that a man in public life should not be influenced by the polls or afraid to make a decision which might be unpopular should remind each of us that every person in public office should first do what he thinks is right and then try to persuade the people that he is right and thus hopefully win the peoples' support.

Finally, Mr. Speaker, the Nevada, Mo., editorial adds a kind of postscript which is the only explanation that I have read which reveals the reason for the missing period after the letter "S" in Mr. TRUMAN's name. For my part, I am so glad that Mr. Weir was thoughtful enough to add this comment beneath his well-written editorial.

The editorial follows:

[From the Nevada (Mo.) Daily Mail, Dec. 29, 1972]

AN UNCOMMON MAN

The death of former President HARRY TRUMAN touches us all more intimately, probably, than that of any other great figure in recent history.

Not because he was a fellow Missourian, an outstanding U.S. Senator and one of our more illustrious Presidents, which he was, he was like our own father unexpectedly thrust into an international role, which he then handled forcefully and effectively, exposing in the process hidden talents we didn't know he possessed.

Unlike so many of the Presidents who preceded and followed him, he was not the product of a prestigious eastern college and a wealthy family. His background was pure midwest: Raised on a farm and in a small town, went to work straight from high school, quit that to farm on his own, joined the National Guard, served as an artillery officer during World War I, came home to work briefly for Nevada's own Farm & Home in Kansas City, went into business for himself, became bankrupt, then entered politics by running for county judge.

And even in politics, he wasn't ambitious. In his "Memoirs," he wrote:

"I never wanted to fight for myself or to oppose others just for the sake of elevating myself to a higher office. I would have been happy to continue serving my community as a county judge. I would have been even happier as a senator, and would have been content to stay entirely clear of the White House. I had accepted the nomination as Vice President not with a sense of triumph but with a feeling of regret at having to give up an active role in the Senate."

Mr. TRUMAN didn't seek the vice presidential nomination at the 1944 Democratic convention. Although he had been widely touted for the job, he was maneuvered into agreeing to nominate Jimmy Byrnes for vice president—and held to his commitment until President Roosevelt himself said that he wanted him on the ticket.

The rest, of course, is history: President Roosevelt's re-election to a fourth term, his death three months after his inauguration, and Mr. TRUMAN's succession to the presidency; and that poignant scene when Mrs. Roosevelt told Mr. TRUMAN of her husband's death.

"Is there anything I can do for you?" Mr. TRUMAN asked Mrs. Roosevelt.

"Is there anything we can do for you?" she asked. "For you are the one in trouble now."

And Mr. TRUMAN did have his troubles, but never once did he hide behind the excuse of inexperience, ignorance or inability to make up his mind. Throughout his almost eight years in office, he was in command; and he let the world know it by the motto he kept on his desk, "The buck stops here."

Unfailingly, he kept his own counsel and did what he thought was right.

"Throughout history," he wrote in his memoirs, "those who have tried hardest to do the right thing have often been persecuted, misrepresented, or even assassinated, but eventually what they stood for has come to the top and been adopted by the people.

"A man who is influenced by the polls or is afraid to make decisions which may make him unpopular is not a man to represent the welfare of the country. If he is right, it makes no difference whether the press and the special interests like what he does, or what they have to say about him. I have always believed that the vast majority of people want to do what is right and if the President is right and can get through to the people he can always persuade them.

"A President cannot always be popular. He has to be able to say 'yes', and 'no', and more often 'no' to most of the propositions that are put up to him by partisan groups and special interests who are always pulling at the White House for one thing or another. If a President is easily influenced and interested in keeping in line with the press and the polls, he is a complete washout. Every great President in our history had a policy of his own, which eventually won the people's support."

Mr. TRUMAN, of course, did have a policy of his own and it did, eventually, win the people's support. And he stands now in the Pantheon of America's heroes, an uncommon man who brought his country through a period of great and unusual trials.

Yet as we respect him for his heroic stature, we remember him for his many human and warm foibles:

His fierce defense of his daughter Margaret's vocal abilities which had been demeaned by a Washington music critic;

His morning walks, during which he spoke to all he met;

His loud shirts when he vacationed at Key West;

His poker parties and affection for bourbon; and
His strong loyalties to all old friends.

HARRY TRUMAN was, indeed, a likable man.

(Incidentally, in reviewing several books for this tribute, we noticed that in his own writings, Mr. TRUMAN always showed his name as HARRY S. TRUMAN—with a period after the "S." An apparent fable has contended that the "S" stood for nothing and was invented by Mr. TRUMAN sometime during his life as a substitute for the letters "NMI" (no middle initial); hence the "S" required no period. Other books about his life, however, carefully avoided the period.)

Mr. Speaker, in our congressional district, there are four counties lying just east of the Kansas line which we call our State-line counties. These all lie south of Mr. TRUMAN's home in Independence and north of his birthplace at Lamar. From these counties come four editorial comments as found in the Drexel Star, published in southwestern Cass County, Mo.; the Butler Headliner, published in the county seat of Bates County, Mo.; the Rich Hill Mining Review; and the Liberal News, published in western Barton County not very far away from Mr. TRUMAN's birthplace.

The editorials follows:

[From the Drexel (Mo.) Star, Dec. 28, 1972]

Death claimed, in our opinion, one of the five top American Presidents, HARRY S TRUMAN, Tuesday morning. We believe that history will prove our statement. Since we lived most of our life, to date anyway, in the Independence area, President TRUMAN was a familiar figure, even before he became the top executive of this nation. His record as a county judge, as a Senator for the people is outstanding. Certainly, he made history with his decisions as Senator and President. Missouri and the nation benefited by this man's wisdom.

[From the Butler (Mo.) Headliner, Dec. 28, 1972]

Fellow Missourians of HARRY S TRUMAN, along with the nation and the world, share in the grief and loss of our 33rd President of the United States, who died early Tuesday morning.

Our heartfelt condolences go to Mr. TRUMAN's wife, Bess, and their daughter, Margaret Daniel.

One of the many attributes to Mr. TRUMAN's career in public life was his directness. There was never any doubt how he felt and he seldom held back in expressing himself.

Like any national figure, HARRY TRUMAN had his enemies. Often accused of cronyism, described as the plain little man from Independence, he rose above his critics to deliberate and take decisive action on some of the country's most crucial problems, and history will no doubt install Mr. TRUMAN as one of America's outstanding leaders.

Mr. TRUMAN, like Lyndon Johnson, was plunged into the Presidency upon the death of the President. But also, like Mr. Johnson, HARRY TRUMAN won it big—on his own—when he sought election in 1948 against Thomas E. Dewey.

Thursday, the day of Mr. TRUMAN's funeral, has been proclaimed as a day of national mourning. It should perhaps also be a day of national reflection upon the war and post war years of HARRY S TRUMAN, a period of time which he devoted to much to this country and to the free world.

[From the Rich Hill (Mo.) Mining Review, Jan. 11, 1973]

A VISIT WITH HARRY S TRUMAN

During the years from 1932 to 1944, my late husband (Clyde Merchant) and myself operated the Highway Cafe on highway 71, the first cafe in operation on said highway in outskirts of Rich Hill, we met many people famous in the sports and political life. The most famous being HARRY S TRUMAN, then a candidate for the office of United States Senator. Mr. TRUMAN, accompanied by one of his closest friends, Thomas L. Evans, President of the Crown Drug Stores (who had been a frequent customer of ours on Sunday afternoons), were on their way to Nevada, Mo., where a banquet was to be held at the Mitchell Hotel, followed by a Democratic Rally. One of the members of Mr. TRUMAN's Battery D was Justin Ritchie, better known as Jud to his many friends. Jud had extended an invitation to his former officer to stop at his home in the northwest part of town for a short visit to rest, relax and reminisce. Mr. TRUMAN gladly accepted the invitation, so Jud, accompanied by some of his friends, Earl Wiek, Jay Thompson and, I believe, Lowell Davis, decided to drive out as far north as the drainage ditch and be an escort to Mr. TRUMAN into the City of Rich Hill. They were joined by many other cars occupied by admirers of Mr. TRUMAN, among them being Ed McQuitty, a prominent Democrat and one of Rich Hills biggest Boosters for any worthwhile projects.

When the car with Mr. TRUMAN and Mr. Evans reached the city limits, Mr. Evans suggested they stop at our cafe and meet Slim (as he called my husband) and his wife, which they proceeded to do. My husband was in the kitchen making a fresh batch of pies for the evening trade, so they came into the kitchen. We were introduced to HARRY TRUMAN, who, after shaking hands, suggested we have a coke. We were all chatting like old time friends when the occupants of the lead car, which had noticed the car containing the Honor Guest had stopped, backed their car and came into the cafe. Were they astounded when they came in and saw the four of us, cokes in hand, in the kitchen. When they were ready to leave, Mr. TRUMAN again shook hands and said, "Slim if you and the Mrs. can do me any good in the coming election, I would appreciate it very much." My husband answered in a language often used by HARRY TRUMAN, as follows. "We sure as . . . won't do you any harm."

Mr. TRUMAN with his well-known smile left, saying "Slim, you're a good guy." Mr. TRUMAN won the election for U.S. Senator and in later years was elected 33rd President of the United States.

[From the Liberal (Mo.) News, Dec. 28, 1972]

DEATH COMES TO STATE'S MOST ILLUSTRIOUS SON

Death claimed former President HARRY S TRUMAN, 88, at 7:50 a.m. Tuesday, December 26, at Research hospital in Kansas City, where he had been in critical condition for several days.

Mr. Truman was much revered the world over and was one of Missouri's most famous citizens. He was born at Lamar May 8, 1884, in a house which is now a national shrine and is visited by thousands each year. The modest house where the 33rd President was born is a two-story, six-room wood structure and is open to visitors on weekends. Jim Finley is the shrine's historical administrator. The flag has been lowered to half staff and a wreath has been placed on the front door of the birthplace dwelling.

Funeral services will be on Thursday afternoon in the 200-seat auditorium of the Truman Library in private ceremonies by the Rev. John H. Lembcke, Jr., pastor of Trinity Episcopal church, where Mr. Truman married his childhood sweetheart, Bess Wallace, on June 28, 1919. Burial will be in the library courtyard, a site chosen by the late President.

Mr. Truman is survived by his widow of the home in Independence; his daughter, Mrs. Margaret Daniel; a sister, Miss Mary Jane Truman of Independence; and four grandchildren.

A memorial service will be held at Washington's National Cathedral to accommodate American and foreign dignitaries who want to pay their last respects.

President and Mrs. Nixon were to be in Independence Wednesday to pay personal respect to the widow. Also former President Lyndon Johnson was expected in Independence. Tributes have poured into the midwestern town from all over the world.

Mr. Speaker, the first public office held by Harry Truman was Judge of the Jackson County, Missouri, Court for the Eastern District. He was elected Eastern Judge in 1922 but was later defeated for that office in 1924 by Henry Rummel.

In the Oak Grove Banner, published at Oak Grove, Mo., under date of December 28, 1972, one of the staff writers, Peggy Henkins, has assembled some personal recollections by two close friends of Mr. Truman, Frank Robinson and former Judge Leslie I. George.

In her story Miss Henkins proceeds to relate some recollections of Mr. Robinson and then some of the reminiscences of Judge George.

Then she concludes with two paragraphs of her own which show the measure of affection and the great esteem for Harry Truman found in the hearts of all eastern Jackson countians.

The article, "Eastern Jackson Remembers Mr. Truman," as it appears in the Oak Grove Banner for December 28, 1972, follows:

Eastern Jackson Remembers Mr. Truman

Frank Robinson, 82, of 506 Broadway, Oak Grove, Remembers:
"Harry and I have been friends since 1920. He gave me my first county job, and he was the best friend I ever had. When Harry was a friend to you—he really was a friend. You could count on what he said.

"The first time I ever met Harry, was when I was trading livestock around over the county about 1919 or 1920.

"His father had advertised two loads of cattle, so I called him up at Grandview and he said for me to come on out and take a look. I took the train to Independence, then transferred to another train to Grandview. He picked me up at the station in an old black buggy.

"Harry was waiting at the farm, and he showed me a white face calf he had just bought. I particularly remember because that was the day that Vivian (Truman's brother) became the father of twin boys. It was quite a surprise."

Les George, 78, who served seven terms as mayor of Oak Grove and is a former eastern judge of the Jackson County Court, has known the Truman family for many years.

"The first time Truman ran for the county court, my sister's father-in-law, Tom Parrent, was running against him. But I didn't like the guy and wanted to vote for Harry. There was a split in my family over that," said George.

"I remember when Harry was just finishing up his second term as presiding judge," George said. "I was sitting in his office one morning, and I asked him what he was going to run for next fall. He said he thought he would run for county collector.

"About that time the phone rang. It was Tom Pendergast, and he was calling to ask Harry to run for the United States Senate.

"Well, he put on the darndest campaign you ever saw," George continued. "He bought a new Plymouth and went all over the State talking to people. I bet he slept in the back of that car for a month."

"We were all in Roger Sermon's office on election night," George continued. (Sermon was then mayor of Independence.) About midnight Harry said, 'I'm going home—that's all for me.' He thought he'd lost."

Truman didn't lose, however, but was elected to the Senate. The year was 1934.

This seems to pretty much sum up the feelings of eastern Jackson Countians today. Many are remembering "the good old farm boy from Missouri who made it big in Washington," and the famous sign on his desk which read "The buck stops here."

Whether one actually knew Harry Truman personally or not, eastern Jackson Countians regard him as their own. And it is perhaps this feeling of folksiness that Truman was able to transmit to the country, as well as his determination and guts in tackling some of the most tremendous problems of our time that will make him go down in history as a truly great man—a man of the people.

Our longtime friend, Jim Wolfe, writing of Mr. Truman in his paper, the Jackson County Sentinel, under dateline of January 4, 1973, entitled his editorial, "He Was Our President," and relates a story of a lady who called his paper to say—

You know, he was the last President we had.

As Mr. Wolfe suggests—

This is a strong statement.

But he recalls the woman emphasized the word, "we," and in that kind of context her statement made sense. She meant that Mr. TRU-MAN was a man of the people. The writer suggests that even that kind of description may sound corny today, in this day when people are analyzed, polled, and even manipulated.

The editorial follows:

[Editorial from the Sentinel, Jan. 4, 1973,
Blue Springs, Mo.]

HE WAS OUR PRESIDENT

A couple of weeks ago, while President TRUMAN lay on his deathbed, a woman called the newspaper office and said:

"You know, he was the last president we had."

In cold type, that is a strange statement. But the woman had emphasized "we"—and that way, it made sense.

HARRY TRUMAN was a man of the people. Lord, that sounds corny. In this day of governmental technology and computerized campaigns, it also seems obsolete. People? What's so important about people. They just exist to be manipulated and polled and analyzed (but not heeded), don't they?

Richard Nixon, Lyndon Johnson, and Dwight Eisenhower all came from beginnings as humble as TRUMAN's. They were from the people, but not of the people. Nixon may possibly make the list of great presidents, but never a list of warm personalities; Johnson was a Texan, with all the braggadocio that implies; Eisenhower was an officer corps-type officer who finally matured into a golfer. The other post-TRUMAN president, John Kennedy, a rich man's son, made no pretense of being a "people's president"; Camelot was not for commoners.

HARRY TRUMAN was a product of hard work on the farm, heroic service in the army, a disappointing business venture, and precinct politics. Who believes the new Jackson county charter will produce a president of the United States?

Mr. Speaker, the Lee's Summit Journal has had a long and distinguished history as one of the really fine papers published in eastern Jackson County. Their comment on Mr. TRUMAN as "the not so ordinary man," follows the theme that the first citizen of Independence who looked, dressed, and sounded like an ordinary person, was capable of governing the country in its most difficult and trying period in the 20th century. If you read the editorial carefully you will find that it believes Mr. TRUMAN's success was based upon an almost innate wisdom. The writer predicts that the Truman story has yet to end because history will regard him as a great statesman, and the man from Independence will be sorely missed in the years that lie ahead.

The editorial follows:

[Editorial from Lee's Summit (Mo.) Journal,
Dec. 28, 1972]

THE NOT SO ORDINARY MAN

There was something about the humanness of HARRY TRUMAN, Mr. Citizen from Independence, that made the average citizen feel more than average. He looked, dressed and sounded like the most ordinary, conventional person in the world.

Mr. TRUMAN demonstrated that a man who came from very humble beginnings in this difficult and trying period of the 20th century was capable of governing and capable of making wise and great and yet very difficult decisions.

When FDR, worn down by war, died in office his hand-picked vice-president of little experience inherited the presidency—and the world's problems. A lot of people felt their hearts sink when he was sworn in as President, following Franklin Roosevelt with all that grandeur, that aristocratic voice and face, that Harvard background.

But what Mr. TRUMAN became was one of the most impressive Presidents we ever had. He was one of the people and he took his case to the people. He talked their language—he wasn't too complicated or too sophisticated. Mr. TRUMAN sensed the values of the people. And while many of HARRY TRUMAN's programs were ahead of the time, he, himself, identified with the times and with the great majority of the people.

HARRY TRUMAN, the man and the President, believed that there was something special in the most ordinary man and America was the place where that "special" was most likely to turn out. In Mr. TRUMAN's sight the most obscure have as much divinity in them as the most famous.

Although HARRY TRUMAN was not brilliant and not eloquent, he had something else—a prime necessity for men who would lead and govern others. He acted on world events with almost innate wisdom. He acted with decisiveness and with courage. His was the decision to drop the atomic bomb, the formation of the United Nations, the Truman Doctrine, the North Atlantic Treaty Organization, the Berlin Airlift and the Korean War.

His leadership and determination was demonstrated with his familiar sign on his executive desk, "The Buck Stops Here." And it did.

The Truman story has yet to end. We're going to remember him as a very intimate human being, a devoted father and husband and yet a great politician and statesman.

The Man from Independence will be missed.

Mr. Speaker, one of the principal cities of Lafayette County, Mo., is the city of Higginsville. It can boast to be the home of the Higginsville Advance. The paper has long been recognized not only for its fair and impartial reporting of the news but also for its overall journalistic excellence. In its edition of December 28, rather than editorializing, it simply provides a capsulized version of the important events of the life of Mr. TRUMAN.

The editorial follows:

[Editorial from the Higginsville (Mo.) Advance,
Dec. 28, 1972]

HARRY S TRUMAN, 33d PRESIDENT, 1884–1972

Former President HARRY S TRUMAN died at 7:50 a.m.,
Tuesday, December 26, at Research hospital in Kansas
City where he was admitted December 5.

Mr. TRUMAN, "The Man from Missouri", was victor
in the great political upset of recent times when he defeated the late Thomas E. Dewey of New York for the
presidency in 1948. All polls and predictions had pointed
to a Dewey victory over Mr. TRUMAN, who became president in 1945 following the death of President Franklin D.
Roosevelt.

At the conclusion of World War II, Mr. TRUMAN, as
the Nation's president, played instrumental roles in shaping future policies of the war-torn world. The Marshall
Plan for aid to stricken countries, his support of the postwar United Nations and his policies toward recovery in
Japan and other nations are now a part of the historical
record of the leadership he provided.

One of his decisions—if not the most-considered of
all—was to authorize use of the newly created atomic
bomb as a means of bringing the U.S.-Japanese war to a
halt, forcing the surrender of the Japanese nation and
bringing about the signing of the peace treaty aboard the
Battleship Missouri.

Since leaving the White House, Mr. TRUMAN, except
for visits from time to time from political leaders and
other dignitaries, had lived a quiet life in the privacy of
his family home in Independence, Mo., where his political career began when he was elected a member of the
Jackson county court. He was a Missouri Senator when
he was chosen as Roosevelt's running mate for the Democratic party in the 1944 election.

The Truman Library was built in Independence only a
few blocks from his home after he returned from Washington. It is on the grounds of the library that he will
be buried Thursday following private funeral services in
the Library.

Mr. Speaker, we are indebted to the editorial-
ist of the Odessan for an interesting story about
the drive by that paper, when it was known
as The Odessa Democrat, to nominate Mr. TRU-
MAN for Governor of Missouri in 1932. Y. D.
Adair and his late father, A. J. Adair, wrote
several articles beginning as early as 1930, pointing out that Jackson County, Mo., had not furnished the State a Governor since the time of
Governor Boggs, and that the time was now ripe
to nominate a man from such a stanch Democratic county as Jackson County. He followed
with a strongly worded review of his accomplishments as county judge, closing with the
admonition:

Let's make this man, TRUMAN, Governor of Missouri.

The editorial from the Odessan is equally good
for recalling the words of the late Roy A. Roberts who was for many years managing editor of

the Kansas City Star, and who wrote extensively
about President TRUMAN after his nomination
for Vice President in 1944. The late Mr. Roberts
knew Mr. TRUMAN very well, and his paper was
published in the same city that was dominated by
T. J. Pendergast, then the head of one of the
most effective political machines in the history
of the Middle West. Mr. Roberts notes that,
while scandal may have surrounded the machine, none of it ever reflected against Mr.
TRUMAN personally. Notwithstanding, he never
bragged about being an honest man because of
his rare modesty. He had a way of letting it be
known to all of his friends that he never regarded himself as a superman.

The article follows:

[Editorial from the Odessa (Mo.) Odessan, Jan. 4, 1973]

FOR MISSOURI GOVERNOR IN 1930: LOCAL PAPER
SUPPORTED TRUMAN FIRST

(By Doug Crews)

Since the death and burial of HARRY S TRUMAN last
week, numerous stories about the personal and political
life of the "Man from Independence" have circulated
through the news media.

Y. D. Adair added another to the list of stories about
the 33d president when he recalled this week that in
1930, The Odessa Democrat was the Missouri newspaper which began a drive to nominate TRUMAN for
governor in 1932.

Adair was associate editor and his late father, A. J.
Adair, editor, when the following article appeared November 14, 1930, in The Democrat:

"It has been nearly a century since our neighboring
county of Jackson furnished Missouri with a governor,
the last man being Governor Boggs.

"The time is now ripe for the Democrats of this state
to get behind and nominate a man from that staunch
Democratic county, and The Odessa Democrat suggests
that in 1932 our party name County Court Judge HARRY
S TRUMAN of Jackson County as its candidate for governor of Missouri. . . .

"Judge TRUMAN is a native of that county; being born
and reared on a farm and coupled with his experience
gives him a background suitable for an ideal governor.
He is popular with all and has much executive
ability. . . .

"In 1928 he sponsored a movement for a system of
paved roads in his county and six and one-half million
dollars in bonds were voted and the work has been
completed. Not a dollar was spent illegally and under
the watchful eye of Judge TRUMAN the work was exceedingly well done. . . .

". . . Judge TRUMAN has a record as a road builder
and a financier and while we would not like to deprive
Jackson County of the use of this splendid citizen, we
believe he should be made governor of Missouri and
allowed to use his fine talents to the betterment of the
state at large. He is a young man and the Democrats

should nominate a man of his type as chief executive of this commonwealth."

Editor Adair concluded the article, saying, "Let's make this man TRUMAN governor of Missouri."

The Truman for governor boom launched by The Democrat never developed. However, it is ironic that the first endorsement for TRUMAN was made in the Odessa newspaper, when it seems it would have been more logical for an endorsement to appear first in a Jackson County newspaper.

Y. D. Adair said Tuesday, "People would have thought (Tom) Pendergast was involved" if a Jackson County newspaper had endorsed TRUMAN for governor.

The Pendergast organization literally ruled Kansas City at the time, and it is known that Pendergast was directly responsible for TRUMAN's election as associate judge of the Jackson County Court in 1922 and for his election and then reelection as presiding judge in 1926 and 1930.

Adair said a group of TRUMAN backers from Jackson County, including the late William Southern, Jr., editor of the Independence Examiner, conveyed to his father their interest in starting the Truman gubernatorial movement outside Jackson County in 1930.

"TRUMAN and my father were good friends," Adair said, and so the endorsement was written.

But the drive to nominate TRUMAN for governor of Missouri failed. A Kansas City Star editorial on May 26, 1930, said: "It should be a satisfaction to the people of Jackson County that Judge HARRY S TRUMAN, presiding judge of the county court, has filed for renomination.

"Judge TRUMAN has been much more than a routine official. He has contributed leadership to an efficient county administration."

TRUMAN won a U.S. Senate seat in 1934 with the support of the Pendergast machine.

When he entered the senatorial race, another endorsement for TRUMAN was printed May 18, 1934, in The Democrat by editor Adair. The headline said: "Judge TRUMAN, Ideal Senatorial Candidate."

The article read, in part, "He has been the moving spirit in the building of ten million dollars of concrete roads in Jackson County without a taint of graft or even of graft criticism. The contracts were let to the low bidders regardless of where they came from and the inspection was rigid and the roads account for the money expended . . ."

In 1940, TRUMAN narrowly won re-election after the Pendergast machine had been destroyed.

On July 22, 1944, just hours after TRUMAN had been nominated for vice-president in Chicago, Roy A. Roberts, then managing editor of the Kansas City Star, wrote:

"No man on earth ever came to the Senate with a worse handicap. He didn't want to go to the Senate, as everyone back home knows. He was chosen by Pendergast because the political situation in Missouri demanded it from the machine standpoint and because HARRY, with his war record and out-state connections, seemed the only man in sight to make the fight for the Senate on the Pendergast ticket.

"Then came the scandals that broke the machine—none of them reflecting on TRUMAN personally. But, being loyal, he did not run from T. J. (Pendergast), but defended him. It was a miracle plus the fact that there were three candidates that let him get by with the narrowest margin . . ."

"TRUMAN . . . has a great capacity for friendship. He is essentially modest . . . TRUMAN, himself, was the first to say he was no superman. He still does . . ." Roberts wrote.

Mr. Speaker, our congressional district is blessed with so many excellent newspapers that it becomes difficult to single out any one for special praise for fear of the implication that they should be assigned some kind of grade or ranking.

However, the Daily Star-Journal of Warrensburg, Mo., is a paper which we can nearly always depend upon for excellent editorials. Its comment in the edition of December 27, 1972, on Mr. TRUMAN is most exceptional.

Headlined "The Man From Independence," the editorial proceeds to delineate a concise history of the accomplishments of Mr. TRUMAN. It deviates long enough to recall Mr. TRUMAN's imitation of the radio commentator, H. V. Kaltenborn, who predicted Mr. TRUMAN's defeat on that November evening in 1948 soon after the ballot boxes had been opened. Mr. TRUMAN enjoyed this imitation as much as the occasion when he held up the banner headlines of the Chicago-Tribune with the words "Dewey Defeats TRUMAN."

The editorial follows:

[Editorial from the Daily Star-Journal, Dec. 27, 1972, Warrenburg, Mo.]

THE MAN FROM INDEPENDENCE

Missouri has lost its number one citizen and, along with the rest of the nation, a former chief executive of the United States. HARRY S TRUMAN served with distinction as the country's thirty-third president and exerted wide and effective influence in world affairs. History continues to show the magnitude of his achievements.

When the enormous responsibilities of the office were thrust upon the little-known vice president with the death of Franklin D. Roosevelt on April 12, 1945, there were few, if any, willing to predict that his record would be a distinguished one. Most were inclined to believe he would finish Roosevelt's fourth term in a nondescript manner, then fade away into oblivion. But this was not to be.

Only four months in office brought personal involvement in international affairs to the new chief executive. He went to San Farncisco to address the United Nations, to Potsdam to confer with Stalin and made the historic decision to use the atomic bomb against Japan.

Soon the Cold War became reality and the Truman Doctrine was put into effect when he granted aid to Turkey and Greece in an all-out effort to halt the spread of communism which had already submerged Eastern Europe. A massive worldwide foreign aid program was promoted by the $12 billion Marshall Plan to rebuild Western Europe.

Perhaps best known in his presidential career was his tenacious, lonely and successful fight for reelection in 1948 against what appeared to be great odds. One of the most humorous incidents was President TRUMAN's imitation of the radio commentator, H. V. Kaltenborn, as he predicted TRUMAN's defeat on one of the election evening newscasts soon after the count of the ballots had begun.

President TRUMAN was a scrappy, hard-hitting campaigner. He was firm in his decisions, leaving no doubt as to where he stood. Mixed with all of this were humility, forthrightness and courage that brought admiration and support from the masses.

"If you can't take the heat, get out of the kitchen," is one of his sage sayings that continues as a popular quote. A long-remembered sign on his desk in the White House said, "The buck stops here." And it did.

TRUMAN's handling of the Berlin blockade in 1949 and his clash with General Douglas MacArthur in 1950 give further evidence of his willingness to take decisive action when he was convinced of the necessity for it.

Quite appropriately President Nixon has called TRUMAN "a fighter who was best when the going was toughest."

Those who followed President TRUMAN in office and other high government officials, often despite party affiliation, were frequent visitors at the Independence home of the ex-president and keen student of history. They came to pay their respects and garner words of advice and wisdom as long as his health would permit.

As the nation's commander-in-chief, HARRY S TRUMAN met the challenge and he met it extraordinarily well. He has left his personal stamp on the State of Missouri, the nation and the world. It will be an enduring one.

Mr. Speaker, Clinton, Mo., is the county seat of Henry County, Mo., which has long been known as one of the rock-ribbed Democratic counties of western Missouri.

In nearly every election it turns in large Democratic majorities. The Truman years were no exception. It may be that it is for these reasons that Mahlon N. White, affectionately known as "Puny," writes with such great warmth about the Man of Independence.

The editorial contains an excellent summary of HST's important decisions or as he puts it, "a legacy of decisions so vast and earth-shaping that it is not fully appreciated to this day." The writer goes on to make a strong point of the fact that, when Mr. TRUMAN was faced with a decision, he did not fiddle around wasting time to make up his mind; and, finally, that he was undoubtedly gratified to hear during the years of so-called retirement, which was not retirement at all because he never quit working, that when the United States was faced with tough problems of near crisis proportions, important world personalities to this day would yearn publicly that "HARRY TRUMAN was President again."

The editorial follows:

[Editorial from the Clinton (Mo.) Daily Democrat, Dec. 27, 1972]

GREAT LEGACY

HARRY S TRUMAN died as he lived, battling all the way.

He left behind a legacy of decisions so vast and earth-shaping it is not fully appreciated to this day.

But, unlike many predecessors as President of the United States of America, he lived long enough beyond his years in office to hear respected authorities say his place in history would be with the handful of great Presidents.

Yet he assumed the Presidency, and won a no-hope reelection, amid criticism which would have felled a less hardy soul. He was referred to as a "little man," and the inference was incapability of handling any big problems.

He confounded the critics by handling the biggest problems faced by any world leader decisively and well. A few of HST's decisions:

The United Nations Charter Conference would proceed as scheduled later in the month in which he became President.

Dropping the Atomic Bomb on the Japanese to end World War II within a month.

Greek-Turkish aid to prevent a Communist takeover.

Rebuilding Europe with the Marshall Plan.

Rebuilding the shattered countries which had been the enemy.

Fighting the Communist attempt to seize Berlin with a great airlift.

Stopping Communist aggression in Korea by instituting the most decisive action the UN has undertaken.

Sending a message to the burgeoning military powers of the United States that the President was the Commander in Chief by firing General of the Armies Douglas MacArthur.

*   *   *   *   *

Few Presidents, even in the hectic years which followed, had to face up to problems of such magnitude that a wrong decision could see freedom spinning off into the black night.

TRUMAN made those decisions. And he didn't fiddle around making them.

Most gratifying personally to him, in his years of retirement, must have been hearing erstwhile critics yearn publicly that "HARRY TRUMAN was President again" when the U.S. faced particularly tough problems.

Mr. Speaker, the St. Clair County Courier, published in Osceola, Mo., and the Index, published in Hermitage, Mo., have each made their own contribution to the Truman memorabilia by the use of phraseology to describe the Nation's 33d President as—

A stout Missourian who made decisions with courage.

And that—

He gave unstintingly to the duties of the presidency

while he held it, and in the years afterward he honorably supported and wisely counseled each of his successors.

The two editorials follow:

[From the St. Clair County Courier,
Dec. 28, 1972, Osceola, Mo.]

EDITORIAL

We never voted for HARRY S TRUMAN as president. But we have learned through the years that he was a man who was built to lead.

He had to take over from the most popular man who ever served as president—FDR.

But through the years of the Marshall Plan that rejuvenated Western Europe, the Cold War, and other dramatic follow-up episodes, he served completely honest and courageous.

We think he will always be recognized as a stout Missourian who made decisions with courage.

In our opinion, his most famous statement was: "If you can't stand the heat in the kitchen, get out."

Missouri mourns him. So does the nation and world. May God bless HARRY TRUMAN.

[Editorial from the Index, Dec. 29, 1972,
Hermitage, Mo.]

TRUMAN—COMMON MAN . . . UNCOMMON GREATNESS

HARRY S TRUMAN, the plain-spoken man from Missouri, who served as the nation's 33d president, has gone on to his reward. The 88-year-old Mr. TRUMAN is eulogized as a common man who rose to uncommon greatness, a man who did not seek power, but who used it wisely when it was thrust upon him.

In proclaiming Thursday as a national day of mourning, President Nixon said of Mr. TRUMAN, "His farsighted leadership in the postwar era has helped . . . to preserve peace and freedom in the world . . . He gave unstintingly to the duties of the presidency while he held it, and in the years afterward he honorably supported and wisely counseled each of his successors."

Mr. Speaker, different writers each seem to display a distinctive style or manner by which they express themselves. The editorial writer for both the Marshall, Mo., Democrat-News and the Boonville Daily News displays such style when he describes Mr. TRUMAN by one word: "topnotcher."

As we read it, the reason for that one-word description is that the man, HARRY TRUMAN, had the capacity to rise above the machine politics of Missouri during the time he was Senator and served the entire Nation with his war profits committee. He also had the capacity as Commander in Chief to meet the challenges of the cold war in the form of the Berlin blockade and North Korea's invasion of South Korea, as well as each and every event of the years of the cold war, in a manner which strengthened the entire free world.

Whoever the architect of that one-word description of Mr. TRUMAN as a "topnotcher" may have been, he did such good work that it commanded identical coverage in both the Marshall and Boonville papers.

The following editorial appeared in both the Democrat-News of Marshall, Mo., on December 27, 1972, and in the Boonville, Mo., Daily News on December 26, 1972, in identical form and language:

HARRY S TRUMAN: TOPNOTCHER

It was just over a quarter-century ago that the heavy mantle of the presidency fell unexpectedly upon the shoulders of a little-known vice-president. A nation already mourning the deaths of thousands of its young men on battlefields around the world now grieved for the commander-in-chief and wondered what the future held.

There were few on April 12, 1945, the day Franklin D. Roosevelt died, who thought that HARRY S TRUMAN, one-time captain of artillery, ex-haberdasher, former county judge and U.S. senator, would be little more than a caretaker president.

The fighting in Europe was almost over; the collapse of Japan could only be a matter of months. TRUMAN would merely preside over the conclusion of a war already won and fill out the remainder of FDR's fourth term while Americans went back, once more, to "normalcy."

Surely there was no one that day who could foresee that the crises that were to come in the next few years would be as grave and as challenging as any in our history, that HARRY S TRUMAN would be faced with some of the most difficult and far-reaching decisions any president ever had to make, that he would win a surprising election to the presidency in his own right and would again find himself leading the nation in war.

Within four months after fate thrust him into world leadership, HARRY TRUMAN addressed the first meeting of the United Nations in San Francisco, met with Stalin at Potsdam and made the historic decision to use the atomic bomb against Japan.

Within a year a new kind of war—the Cold War—was a reality. In 1947, TRUMAN announced his Truman Doctrine and sent aid to Greece and Turkey to fight and "contain" communism, which had already swallowed Eastern Europe.

The $12 billion Marshall Plan to rebuild Western Europe was but the beginning of the nation's vast, worldwide foreign aid program.

At home, inflation, strikes, influence-peddling scandals and a Republican Congress gave HARRY TRUMAN little rest in office.

Had he been retired in 1948, as everyone expected, TRUMAN would still have left an indelible mark on

American history. But against all the odds, he won another term almost singlehandedly, with his own patented brand of gutty, give-'em-hell campaigning.

Then, in 1949, came the Berlin blockade, Russia's explosion of its first atomic bomb, the Communist takeover in China. NATO, the Allied military alliance, was born.

In 1950: Communist North Korea's invasion of South Korea and TRUMAN's decision to commit American troops. Then, the Chinese intrusion into the war, the clash with MacArthur, the military stalemate that cast a shadow over his last years in office.

Looking back now from our position of economic prosperity at home and a fairly stabilized East-West power balance abroad, we can judge the decisions that were made and the actions that were taken and not taken between 1945 and 1953.

We can see mistakes, but we can also see triumphs.

Not the least triumph was the fact that HARRY TRUMAN, the most ordinary of Americans, had the capacity to rise, first, above the machine politics of Missouri to become an able senator serving the entire nation with his War Profits Committee, and later, to meet the challenge of the presidency in a manner that strengthened the entire free world.

HARRY S TRUMAN—whistle-stopping, Republican baiting, letter-writing, piano-playing, helling-and-damning, peppery HARRY S TRUMAN. There was always a little of the pugnacious ward politician in him. But where it counted, behind that lonely desk in the White House where the sign said, "The buck stops here," he ranked with the best of them.

Mr. Speaker, the Sedalia Democrat in its edition of December 26, 1972, entitled "HARRY S TRUMAN: Man of the People," reviews the years of the Presidency of Mr. TRUMAN in a brief but at the same time all inclusive maner. Really, the heading of the editorial is not completely descriptive of its content because the writer dwells mostly upon the immense burdens that fell upon the shoulders of this former haberdasher and one-time county judge following World War II.

Notwithstanding, the writer is so completely accurate and correct when he observes that most of the scribes and columnists harbored doubts that this unknown man of Independence, Mo., could rise to the challenges he would have to face when he was abruptly raised to the White House on April 12, 1945. No truer words have ever been said of Mr. TRUMAN than those which appear in the Sedalia, Mo., paper in its concluding sentences which read:

> HARRY S TRUMAN will rest secure in the company of a small handful of truly great American presidents.

The editorial follows:

[From the Sedalia (Mo.) Democrat, Dec. 26, 1972]

HARRY S TRUMAN: MAN OF THE PEOPLE

In newsrooms throughout the world, HARRY S TRUMAN's obituary was freshened up a few months ago during another severe illness when it looked like the old man was finished. But true to form, he confounded those ready to count him down and out and raillied back to health.

Now, his body fatally weakened by another long onslaught against which he fought with dogged determination, HARRY TRUMAN is dead at the age of 88. The country will miss him, and if you will allow us an old cliche, probably won't see his likes again.

Perhaps more than any chief executive since Andrew Jackson, HARRY S TRUMAN was the common man's president. Throughout his public career he never lost that folksy, rough-cut manner that marked him as a man of the people.

Yet this former haberdasher and one-time county judge took upon his shoulders immense burdens. From behind his White House desk, with its sign, "The buck stops here," President TRUMAN made momentous decisions that affected the entire world.

With the Marshall Plan and the Berlin airlift he led the United States in rebuilding Europe after World War II. He fashioned the Truman Doctrine to contain expansionist communism in Greece and Turkey. He presided at the birth of the United Nations and the North Atlantic Treaty Organization. He sent U.S. troops to stem the invasion of South Korea.

And in perhaps the loneliest decision ever made by a U.S. president, he ordered the atomic bomb dropped on Japan.

Few political observers—many Democrats among them—expected this unknown man from Independence, Mo., to rise to the challenge when he was abruptly elevated to the White House after the death of Franklin Roosevelt on April 12, 1945. But HARRY TRUMAN proved that he was made of stern stuff, and in 1948 pulled off one of the longest shot re-election bids in presidential history, with almost no one on his side except the people.

The Truman Administration was not without its failures. There was the costly military stalemate in Korea; strikes, inflation, charges of scandal and influence-peddling at home.

But in balance, the only way a chief executive can truly be judged, HARRY S TRUMAN will rest secure in the company of the handful of great American presidents.

Mr. Speaker, the period proclaimed by President Nixon as a time of mourning for our 33d President has just expired. Notwithstanding I take this occasion to remind Members that the other body of the Congress will eulogize President TRUMAN on or about February 6.

I mention the foregoing simply to remind my colleagues in the House that there will be a joint resolution introduced in both the House and the Senate which will authorize the preparation of a bound volume to contain all of the remarks on the passing of Mr. TRUMAN made on the floor and all extraneous matter, including editorials, which have been or will be made a part of the Congressional Record. All of these will be included as a part of the bound volume contemplated by the provisions of the joint resolution directed to the Joint Committee on Printing.

Now, Mr. Speaker, there are three editorials from three great newspapers which have not been included in the Record. These three deserve to be included along with the collection of eulogies and tributes paid to our great 33d President. I refer to the editorial from the Washington Post of December 27, 1972; the editorial from the Evening Star & Daily News under date of December 27, 1972, and then to the editorial in the New York Times of December 31, 1972, by Cabell Phillips, who for 20 years was the head of the Washington Bureau of the New York Times during the Truman years. You may recall Mr. Phillips was the author of the book, "The Truman Presidency," which he described as "the history of a triumphant succession."

Mr. Speaker, I would feel remiss if by my negligence these three editorials should be omitted from the record of comments on the life of President TRUMAN. They are as follows:

[From the Washington (D.C.) Post, Dec. 27, 1972]

HARRY S TRUMAN

A few minutes after HARRY S TRUMAN took the oath of office as President of the United States—when, as he put it, he "felt like the moon, the stars, and all the planets had fallen on me"—he was asked if the San Francisco Conference on the United Nations would meet, as had been planned. "I did not hesitate a second," he recalled in his memoirs. "There was no question in my mind that the conference had to take place." Within hours, he was dealing as an equal with Winston Churchill and Joseph Stalin.

There were not many who were prepared to say in that dark hour that HARRY TRUMAN was equal to the appalling burden put upon him. The members of the Roosevelt Cabinet tended to feel that they would have to take him under their tutelage; they were considerate but patronizing. He very quickly replaced them. He had no very exalted opinion of himself; but he had great self-respect. Acknowledging that no one was "big enough" to be President of the United States in the crucial years of a great world war, he nevertheless felt himself to be about as big as the next fellow. What he had to do, he would do to the best of his ability.

Diffidence and doughtiness, humility and self-confidence, vulgarity and grandeur were mingled in this solid, unpretentious man, a seemingly typical product of small-town politics in middle America. He was an able and conscientious senator, although by no means one of the towering figures of Congress. He was a man for whom—and probably to whom—the Vice Presidency seemed the very summit of legitimate aspiration. Yet when immeasurable responsibility was suddenly thrust upon him against his honest wish and will, he found within himself the resources to meet the task honorably and, indeed, greatly.

"Some scholars of American history with whom I talk from time to time are of the opinion," he wrote years later, "that it is history that makes the man. I am inclined to differ. I think that it is the man who makes history. I find that throughout our own history the greatest strides occur when courageous and gifted leaders either seize the opportunity or create it."

It may well be that both views are true. In any case, HARRY TRUMAN lacked neither opportunities nor the courage to seize them. Perhaps the greatest single decision of modern times was made by him very early in his Presidency—the decision to use the atomic bomb in the war against Japan. "The final decision of where and when to use the atomic bomb was up to me," Mr. TRUMAN recalled with characteristic simplicity. "Let there be no mistake about it. I regarded the bomb as a military weapon and never had any doubt that it should be used. The top military advisers to the President recommended its use, and when I talked to Churchill he unhesitatingly told me that he favored the use of the atomic bomb if it might aid to end the war."

For good or for evil, a new dimension was added to the world. For the salvation or the destruction of mankind, a new force was created. Years of experience with the ineradicable threat of atomic war, years of reflection on the moral implications of employing so terrible a weapon, may lead to a judgment that HARRY TRUMAN was wrong. But let those who make that judgment ponder his straightforward justification for what he did: "General Marshall told me that it might cost half a million American lives to force the enemy's surrender on his home grounds." And, conversely, let those who applaud his decision ponder what foreshadows for any future war.

HARRY TRUMAN made another decision inexpressibly more life-giving and perhaps almost as momentous in its way—the decision to commit the immense resources, strength and skill of the American people to the reconstruction of Europe at the end of the war. The Marshall Plan, formulated and implemented under his leadership, represented what may well be considered the most enlightened piece of national generosity in all history. Indeed, American aid went generously to the vanquished as well as to the victorious. In Mr. TRUMAN's own estimation, "The Marshall Plan will go down in history as one of America's greater contributions to the peace of the world. I think the world now realizes that without the Marshall Plan it would have been difficult for Western Europe to remain free from the tyranny of communisim."

To arrest "the tyranny of communism," President TRUMAN took the country into a considerable and troublesome war of his own—the war in Korea. The swift

American response to the North Korean invasion of South Korea afforded a fresh illustration of the President's decisiveness and toughness in the conduct of his office. And in the course of the war he gave a democratic demonstration that as President he was also undoubtedly Commander in Chief of the nation's armed forces when he summarily removed Gen. Douglas MacArthur from his post in the Pacific.

HARRY TRUMAN was a pragmatist and a politician. He preferred the specific gain to the idealistic goal. And he understood with unblurred realism that specific gains in American political affairs are achieved by leadership which embraces not only an imaginative appeal to the aspirations of a free people but also the crasser arts of political influence, pressure and manipulation. He was in constant conflict with Congress. "When a President does not have a fight or two with Congress, you know there is something wrong," he wrote. "A man with thin skin has no business being President."

His fiercest political controversy centered in the cult of loyalty that developed in the late 1940's and reached its culmination in obsessive attacks upon Government employees, especially in the State Department, by Senators McCarthy, McCarran and Jenner. There was a passionate commitment in HARRY TRUMAN to the principles of the Bill of Rights and to the concept of individual liberty. The tactics of what came to be called McCarthyism were abhorrent to him, and he was unreserved in his condemnation of them. Unfortunately, however, in his zeal to protect Government employees from the brutal assaults of McCarthyism, he established the Federal Employee Loyalty-Security Program—a pernicious process, still in full effect, which bases the determination of an employee's trustworthiness on accusations made by informers unknown either to the accused employee or to his judges.

Despite this grievous lapse into the fundamental error of McCarthyism, HARRY TRUMAN was otherwise a stalwart champion of principle he enunciated in simple terms: "In a free country, we punish men for the crimes they commit, but never for the opinions they have." Nothing in his official career redounded more greatly to his glory than his veto in 1950 of the Internal Security Act which established the Subversive Activities Control Board. In the hysteria of the time, the bill was passed over his veto within 24 hours. But he gave assertion, nevertheless, to a reassuring faith in his fellow Americans and in their fealty to the principles of political liberty.

His faith in the American people found reciprocation. In 1948, he sought election to the Presidency in his own right. Although it was not widely supposed that he could win, he campaigned with a verve, ebullience and indomitable determination that led him to victory. It may be that the American people saw in him an embodiment of their image of themselves—an exemplification of their own rooted virtues and values. There were qualities about HARRY TRUMAN now often referred to as old-fashioned—his rather simple morality, his devotion to his family, his uncritical loyalty to his country, to his party, to past political associates who had been loyal to him; his capacity, on occasion, for intemperate and injudicious indignation, his earthiness—qualities that stamped him a common man yet a man capable, as other common men are capable, of ascent to the heights of

heroism. HARRY TRUMAN showed his countrymen what they were made of and what they could become.

[From the Evening Star and The Washington Daily News, Dec. 27, 1972]

THE MAN FROM INDEPENDENCE

HARRY S TRUMAN may not have been much shucks as a Kansas City haberdasher but he was a mighty fine President. When he came to the presidency through the death of Franklin D. Roosevelt in 1945, the world was engulfed in World War II. Mr. TRUMAN, whose ten years in the Senate had been unremarkable, showed no signs of being a man of destiny.

But HARRY TRUMAN grew into the job, handling the big and difficult decisions with determination and tenacity. He made the decision to drop two atomic bombs on Japan, a move which he always maintained, perhaps correctly, saved many thousands of lives—American and Japanese—by making an invasion unnecessary.

He launched with his secretary of state the Marshall Plan to rebuild a prostrate Europe. He played a leading role in the formation of both the United Nations and the North Atlantic Treaty Organization. He promulgated the Truman Doctrine, which certainly saved Greece from communism and helped other nations to maintain their independence.

When the North Koreans invaded South Korea, he did not hesitate to commit American troops to the defense of that small nation. When the Russians sought to starve the Allies out of West Berlin, he ordered the airlift which resulted in a stunning diplomatic defeat for the Kremlin, reasserting the U.S. commitment to defend Europe.

HARRY TRUMAN's greatest quality, and the one which so well served his nation, was his courage in the face of adversity. Once he had decided on a course of action, he stuck to it, fighting doggedly, openly and persistently until he achieved his goal. Even his intense personal loyalty, which sometimes degenerated into cronyism, had about it an epic quality.

President TRUMAN never lost the common touch, whether he was belting out a few bars of the Missouri Waltz or writing to a music critic so indiscreet as to cast aspersions on his daughter's virtues as a vocalist. It was easy for other Americans to identify with him, to believe in him, because he always seemed to know exactly what he wanted to do and how he wanted to do it. And that wasn't just the way he acted; that was the way he was.

[From the New York Times, Dec. 31, 1972]

A MAN WHO "DONE HIS DAMNDEST" (1884–1972)

(By Cabell Phillips)

On the day after Franklin Roosevelt's death in April 1945, the shaken new President, HARRY TRUMAN, said to a group of reporters, "If you fellows know how to pray, pray for me now." The plea was typical of the plain-spoken, essentially modest man who occupied the White House during eight tumultuous years in the nation's history, and who died last week in Kansas City at the age of 88.

HARRY TRUMAN worked less to ingratiate himself with people but succeeded better at it than any important public figure I have ever known. He did it, I think, because he was so utterly honest with and about himself, so free of what we call "side" or "put on."

He wasn't above cutting a corner or trimming the truth to gain a political or policy objective. He would go to almost any lengths to save the face of a friend. But neither as a public nor a private figure did he ever pretend to be anything but what he was, and it mattered precious little to him whether anyone liked what he was or not.

What he was grated unpleasantly on some sensitive nerves—his brashness, his minor crudities of speech and manner, the fact that he did not adorn the great office of President with what they considered the requisite style and grace. He was the sort who synthesized the awesome responsibilities of his office not in resonant phrases that would look good in bronze, but with a simple homespun aphorism: Tapping his desk and looking solemn as a preacher he would say, "The buck stops here."

There was eloquence and deep sincerity in the way he said it that made anything you might add redundant.

I once wrote a book about Mr. TRUMAN, and something I said then is relevant in this context: "HARRY TRUMAN was and remains an ordinary man . . . who must make do without any special endowments of genius, intellect or charm. His strength lay in his ability to do the best he could with what he had and not despair over what he did not have. . . . He never suffered the illusion that he was another Roosevelt or Churchill, neither did he agonize over whether he was their inferior. Destiny linked his life to theirs in an apocalyptic enterprise and each rode it out to greatness according to his own fashion."

The most cynical and skeptical audience a President has to face is the Washington press corps. There is a congenital distrust between them, a built-in competitiveness that more often than not degenerates into mutual hostility.

No President of the last 50 years was so widely and warmly liked by the reporters as Mr. TRUMAN. He "used" the press occasionally as most Presidents have done to test the wind. But he never tried to "con" them with flattery and devious favoritism. He was reasonably accessible to reporters, enjoyed having them along on trips and liked to play practical jokes on them or take them for their expense accounts in after-hours poker sessions.

They felt that he leveled with them. On his frequent visits to Washington after 1952, as many reporters as politicians dropped into his suite at the Mayflower on an afternoon for a friendly chat and a toast of "bourbon and branch."

Since Mr. TRUMAN never constructed any false images of himself, he enjoyed a large dividend of self-confidence. Call it cockiness: that was its outer manifestation much of the time. Whatever it was, it gave him an immense capacity for making up his mind to do what had to be done and then putting it behind him—whether it was a bit of legislative strategy, or the dropping of the atom bomb. Many people think this was one of his strongest attributes as President.

I ran into an example of this quality in 1959, I went to Independence to write an article about him on the approach of his 75th birthday. Routinely, I asked him to recall the half dozen most difficult decisions he had had to make as President. When he finished, I remarked that he had failed to mention the dismissal of Gen. Douglas MacArthur during the Korean war. "That must have taken a bit of courage," I said.

"Courage had nothing to do with it," he snapped, his eyes flashing through the thick glasses. "He was insubordinate and I fired him, and that's all there was to it. Sure, I knew there would be a lot of stink about it. But it was the right thing to do and I did it, and I've never lost any sleep over it since."

Did those qualities add up to greatness? Was HARRY TRUMAN a "great" President? There is no firm definition of the term, but many competent scholars have given him that accolade. The late Prof. Clinton Rossiter, of Cornell, said of him some years ago: "I am ready to hazard an opinion, to which I did not come easily or lightly, that HARRY TRUMAN will eventually win a place as President, if not as a hero, alongside Jefferson and Theodore Roosevelt."

One measure of greatness, certainly, is the extent to which a President uses the great potentialities of his office to advance the natioanl interest. By this yardstick, Mr. TRUMAN must be rated among the best. True, his tenure was turbulent and bedeviled by partisan strife, he would never be certain that his own party might not desert him in a showdown. But few Presidents have fought harder, or against greater odds, than Mr. TRUMAN for the programs and the values he believed in.

His net gains on the domestic front were, in the end, relatively modest, but in the area of foreign policy they were monumental. His was the era of the Cold War and of the atom. His two terms in office were overshadowed by a danger no other President has ever had to face: the grinding rebalancing of world power between two hostile and incompatible forces, each capable of destroying the other.

President TRUMAN met that danger with bold and imaginative—albeit to some persons, controversial—countermeasures. The Truman Doctrine, the European recovery program, NATO, the Berlin airlift, the Korean intervention—these were landmarks along the road to national maturity. They have profoundly affected the destiny of the American people and of the world.

Some revisionist historians now hold these measures to have been ill-chosen and wrongly conceived; that they advanced rather than retarded the Cold War. They may be right. It is hard to argue with 20/20 hindsight. But these events ought to be judged in the context of their time; in terms of the stresses felt and the wisdom at hand when they occurred. Those years from 1947 to 1952 were full of anxiety and uncertainty. Most people at the time thought Mr. TRUMAN's decisions were the right ones. Some, myself included, still think so.

One day in April, 1952, at his 300th press conference as President (to explain his decision not to seek renomination), Mr. TRUMAN said to many of the same reporters whom he had asked eight years previously to pray for him: "I have tried my best to give the nation everything I have in me. There are a great many people—I suppose a million in this country—who could have done the job better than I did. But I had the job and I had to do it.

"I always remember an epitaph which is in the cemetery at Tombstone, Arizona. It says: 'Here lies Jack Williams. He done his damndest.' I think that is the greatest epitaph a man can have—when he gives everything that is in him to do the job he has before him. That is all you can ask of him and that is what I have tried to do."

Mr. Speaker, on January 5, the day of the memorial services for Mr. TRUMAN at the National Cathedral here in Washington, I brought some of the folks from Independence, Mo., who had journeyed here to attend this service to the Capitol after the services. We were seated in the House Restaurant for lunch where it was my privilege as their Congressman to introduce my guests to former Speaker John W. McCormack. He came to our table and for some 5 or 10 minutes, recalled some pleasant moments of his long association with Mr. TRUMAN and particularly during the years when Mr. TRUMAN was President and he served as Majority Leader in the House. Before he left, he suggested that if I had anything to do with the preparation of a memorial book to be printed as a joint House-Senate publication that he would appreciate the inclusion of some excerpts from his comments entitled "Former Speaker Salutes Great Friend" which appeared in the Herald-Traveler and the Boston Record-American for December 27 and also his comments and observations headed, "Presidency Brought Out His Greatness—McCormack," as these remarks appeared in the Boston Globe for December 27, 1972.

For my part I so clearly recall over the past 14 years, on Mr. TRUMAN's birthday, either on May 8 or the nearest day that the House was in session, John McCormack, either as Majority Leader or Speaker of the House would always make it a point to be on the floor to pay tribute to the man he admired so much—HARRY S TRUMAN. Accordingly, it came to me as no surprise that he would request his comments in the Boston papers be made a part of the Truman eulogy because, as a former member, he was not present to join with the large number who participated in the special order on the floor of the House on Tuesday, January 9.

Perhaps Mr. McCormack's affection for Mr. TRUMAN is expressed when he points out:

There is in the Office of the Presidency an influence where, if a man has a reserve of weakness, that comes out. TRUMAN had a tremendous reserve of strength and the awesomeness of the Office was such that he evidenced his strength while he was President. In TRUMAN's case, the Office certainly did bring out the greatness of the occupant.

Excerpts from the editorials follow:

[Excerpts from "Former Speaker Salutes Great Friend" by Bill Duncliffe, Herald Traveler and Boston Record American, Dec. 27, 1972 and "Presidency Brought Out His Greatness—McCormack" by Gloria Negri, the Boston Globe, Dec 27, 1972]

EXCERPTS

Retired House Speaker John W. McCormack, sorrowed by the loss of an old and cherished friend, saluted the memory of former President HARRY TRUMAN by declaring:

"He lived as he believed and he died as he lived—a fighter to the very end."

McCormack, drawing on the reminiscences of more than 40 climatic years in Congress, eulogized TRUMAN as a man with the wisdom to realize that some of his decisions must be unpopular—and the courage to make them because he knew they were right.

"He will," McCormack said, "go down in history as one of the greatest Presidents we had. He will be remembered long after others have been forgotten."

"When he became President it may have been true that the country as a whole was little aware of the great qualities he possessed, but when he left office he did so as one of the most illustrious leaders this nation ever possessed."

"He was a very direct man, very courageous, very intuitive: he had a mind for making decisions. . . ."

Summing TRUMAN up, McCormack said: "There is in the office of the Presidency, an influence where, if a man has a reserve of weakness, that comes out."

"TRUMAN had a tremendous reserve of strength, and the awesomeness of the office was such that he evidenced his strength while he was President. In TRUMAN's case, the office certainly did bring out the greatness of its occupant".

Mr. Speaker, when the sad news of the passing of Mr. TRUMAN flashed across America on that Tuesday morning, December 26, 1972. It went out to reach every segment and every strata of American life. It saddened the man on the street, the great industrial leaders, those who held the highest offices in our land; but it also brought grief to what we can describe as the intellectual community, as well as those churchmen who we collectively call the clergy of our country.

As one who has had a small measure of experience in examining some of the literature on the life and times of Mr. TRUMAN, I am indebted to Mr. Bertil L. Hanson, associate professor, Department of Political Science, Oklahoma State University, Stillwater, Okla., for a worthwhile contribution. He was good enough to furnish our office with a copy of an article by Prof. Merlin Gustafson, entitled "HARRY TRUMAN as a Man of Faith," which appeared in the magazine entitled Christian Century on January 17, 1973.

Professor Hanson points out that the article not only describes Mr. TRUMAN's character faithfully but also conveys the timely lesson that religion can be a source of great private strength without a big public display being made of one's religion.

The articles follow:

OKLAHOMA STATE UNIVERSITY,
Stillwater, Okla., January 19, 1973.
The Honorable WILLIAM J. RANDALL,
U.S. House of Representatives,
Washington, D.C.

DEAR REPRESENTATIVE RANDALL: I would like to suggest that an article by Professor Merlin Gustafson entitled "HARRY TRUMAN as a Man of Faith" appearing in this week's "Christian Century" merits inclusion in the Congressional Record.

The article not only describes Mr. TRUMAN's character faithfully, but also conveys a timely lesson. It shows how religion can be a source of great private strength without a big public display being made over it.

Sincerely,

BERTIL L. HANSON,
Associate Professor.

THE LIBRARY OF CONGRESS,
CONGRESSIONAL RESEARCH SERVICE

The attached information is forwarded in response to your recent inquiry. We hope it meets your needs in this matter.

Please do not hesitate to call on us for further assistance.

Sincerely,

LESTER S. JAYSON, *Director.*

[From the periodical Christian Century, Jan. 17, 1973]

HARRY TRUMAN AS A MAN OF FAITH

(By Merlin Gustafson)

Even after the passage of more than two decades, the decisions made by HARRY S TRUMAN during his presidency still influence international and domestic affairs. His foreign aid programs and military alliances remain in force, and a number of his recommendations for domestic legislation have now been enacted.

How did he arrive at his momentous decisions? We know that a President is often a captive of events beyond his control and that decision-making in the executive branch of our government is frequently only a bureaucratic process. Hence a simple pragmatic course of action may be the only alternative left open to the President. Sometimes, however, he has the opportunity to lead, to choose which fork in the road the nation will take. At such times he will be forced back upon his personal philosophy; it is then that his personal and religious values become important.

I

Did President TRUMAN's religious values in fact influence his decisions during his White House years? It should be remembered that TRUMAN was never an idealist with a rigid set of religious principles to be applied automatically to the important problems he faced. On the other hand, he did take some religious doctrines seriously, and they undoubtedly affected his political decision-making. When we think of his religious beliefs we should bear in mind the two roles any President has to play: that of an individual with personal preferences and that of the nation's leader.

As an individual, President TRUMAN was a sincerely religious man—in fact, one of our more "religious" Presidents. He was also a politician, and he believed that his role as politician need not conflict with his religious principles. He believed the profession of politics to be, as he said, the "highest and most important business in the world." During his years in the Senate and the presidency his political opponents often brought up his earlier Pendergast associations and the taint of Kansas City "machine" politics of that era. Careful studies of his early political career, however, have cleared him of any involvement in shady politics; no solid facts have ever been uncovered to implicate him in dishonest political acts, unless he is held guilty by association. This clean bill of health applies as well to the so-called "scandals" that occurred during his last years as President.

Throughout his life he retained his membership in the Grandview, Missouri, Baptist Church, while his wife and daughter were active Episcopalians. Although a 33rd-degree Mason, he liked his religious liturgy simple and informal; he was not attracted by the more ceremonial forms of worship. After he became President he attended church only occasionally because, as he explained, his attendance attracted so much attention that the other worshipers were distracted from the service.

TRUMAN had little interest in theological issues, although he had an almost fundamentalist reverence for the Bible. He liked to read and quote the Scriptures, often reciting verses from memory to fit political situations. On many a formal and informal occasion he quoted from the Sermon on the Mount, and he would frequently say: "Every problem in the world would be solved if only men would follow the Beatitudes." Another verse he liked to recall was Luke 6:26: "Woe unto you, when all men speak well of you, for so their fathers did to the false prophets"—which no doubt gave him comfort and reassurance when under attack during his White House years.

The nation experienced a religious revival during the TRUMAN administration, and the President's occasional religious statements to the press matched the national mood of the '50; e.g., his reference to the "Christian mission" of the United States in world affairs. However, a number of religious leaders and journals (notably The Christian Century) criticized his simple religious exhortations on complex questions.

II

On the other side, TRUMAN, as President of the United States, had become an "institution," and he could no longer act simply as an individual. He had become less TRUMAN the person and more TRUMAN the executive department. He once explained: "In the White House I never allowed myself to think that HARRY TRUMAN from Independence, Missouri, was personally deciding the fate of the world. I was deciding as President and not as an individual thinking in terms of what he would prefer as an individual."

No President can manage his complicated and enormous work load without a loyal staff to help handle the innumerable details that come with the institutional aspects of his office. TRUMAN's closest aides included members of the major U.S. religious faiths—Protestant, Roman Catholic and Jewish. Many of the President's announcements and proclamations for the commemoration of religious observances were composed by his correspondence secretary, William Hassett, a Roman Catholic.

Some of his speeches and public statements (for which he took full responsibility, even though they may have been written by staff members or department heads) exhibited distinct theological attitudes—reverence for the Holy Scriptures, belief in a Supreme Being, support for a spirit of toleration among the various religious faiths, and support for the ecumenical movement. Occasionally his thinking revealed a note of Calvinistic determinism or moralism. Most significant was his deep concern for the social implications of the Scriptures, as shown in his first major religious address after becoming President—to the Federal Council of Churches in March 1945 in Columbus, Ohio. (Interestingly, it was Jewish presidential aide Samuel Rosenman who composed most of the President's address to that Protestant organization.) His speech emphasized the need for a new moral and spiritual awakening among the people—one which would help bring solutions to such problems as poor housing, juvenile delinquency, racial and religious intolerance. He took note of "selfish interests so greedy for gold" that they sought to induce Congress to hold down minimum wages and allow the further concentration of economic power. A truly religious fervor among the people, he declared, would foster needed legislation such as national programs for health insurance, housing, education, and an improved social security system. He said he believed that the very essence of religion could be found in the United Nations Charter, and he called on the nation to aid the starving millions in Europe, Asia and Africa. All these proposals, he maintained, were supported by the precepts of the ancient prophets and the Sermon on the Mount.

When militant anticommunism and McCarthyism gained popular support during his second term in office, TRUMAN argued that the social gospel held the answer: "The menace of communism lies in the areas of American life where the promise of democracy remains unfulfilled." Referring to such problems as slums, low wages, lack of education, lack of medical care, poverty in old age, unemployment, and inflated prices, he pointed out that they all involved basic human rights which, when neglected, led to extreme movements such as communism.

III

President TRUMAN supported a spirit of religious tolerance. Perhaps because of the wide variety of friendships he had in Kansas City and because of his experience in the army, he had never been dogmatic about his religious faith. After he became President he sought to encourage toleration in a number of ways: by issuing an executive order to end racial and religious discrimination in the armed forces; by championing, against strong congressional opposition, the cause of displaced persons who sought to be admitted to the United States after World War II; and by extending diplomatic recognition to the state of Israel in 1948. He favored diplomatic recognition of the Vatican as well, and he attributed to religious bigotry the powerful opposition that that proposal aroused. Perhaps there was political motivation in his support of the interests of Catholics and Jews, but there was certainly warmth in his relationships with members of these religious groups as well.

President TRUMAN supported the ecumenical movement among the churches. During his second term he sponsored a movement to bring religious leaders of the world together in what he called "a common affirmation of faith and a common supplication to the one God that all profess," but that effort, as he later admitted, ended in failure.

Occasionally a note of Calvinist determinism was apparent in TRUMAN's public statements. In 1945, at the beginning of his presidential years, he declared: "I believe honestly that Almighty God intends now that we shall assume the leadership which he intended us to assume in 1920, and which we refused. And I believe that if we do that, our problems will almost solve themselves." Again, at the end of his second term, he expressed the same thought:

"Divine Providence has played a great part in our history. I have the feeling that God has created us and brought us to our present position of power and strength for some great purpose.

"It is not given to us now to know fully what that purpose is, but I think we may be sure of one thing. And that is that our country is intended to do all it can, in cooperating with other nations to help create peace and preserve peace in the world. It is given to us to defend the spiritual values—the moral code—against the vast forces of evil that seek to destroy them.

"This is a hard task. It is not one that we have asked for. At times we would like to lay it down. And, as we go on with it, we see it is full of uncertainties and sacrifices. But we need not be afraid, if we have faith."

Like many of his contemporaries, TRUMAN perceived a divine mission in the American historical experience. Perhaps for this reason he accepted the rhetoric of the cold war against "atheistic communism" and the turn to militarism that accompanied it. No pacifist, he favored a large peacetime military system and universal military training for all men of draft age. And, of course, it was his decision to drop the atomic bomb on Hiroshima. Peace was his goal, but he believed it could be achieved only through military strength.

Shortly after the end of World War II he gave up all hope of cooperation with the Soviet Union and advocated a program of coexistence and containment of communism. He believed a strong military force and a system of military alliances that would balance the Russian military power to be the best way to maintain peace. To John Foster Dulles he wrote in 1945: "We often hear it said that spiritual values are indestructible, but I think it should be said that they are indestructible only as long as men are ready and willing to take action to preserve them." However, he did not favor a "holy war" against the communist nations, or think that war was inevitable. Despite great pressures he kept the Korean conflict a "limited war," even though that decision meant firing a popular war hero, General Douglas MacArthur.

President TRUMAN will be remembered in history for initiating the postwar foreign aid program. Although there undoubtedly were a number of motives operating—not all of them altruistic, to say the least—TRUMAN personally found a basis in religious principles for helping the less-developed nations. His 1946 speech to the Federal Council of Churches made that stance clear.

IV

Perhaps President TRUMAN left with us the most illuminating summary of his religious philosophy in a short speech he delivered in 1951 at a cornerstone-laying ceremony:

"The essential mission of the church is to teach the moral law. Religion is not an easy thing. It is not simply a comfort to those in trouble or a means of escape from present difficulties, as some people today would have us believe. Moreover, religion is not a negative thing. It is not merely a series of prohibitions against certain actions because they are wicked. Our religion includes those elements. But it also includes more. It is a positive force that impels us to affirmative action . . . Selfishness and greed can tear this nation apart. . . . Our religious faith gives us the answer to the false beliefs of communism. We are defending freedom of worship and conscience. . . ."

These, then, were the highlights of TRUMAN's religious philosophy. As President he could not afford to be too far ahead or too far behind the thinking of his constituency. His perspective was slightly more liberal than that of his times, but he was not extreme. Leadership in the mainline Protestant churches, in Judaism and in the Roman Catholic Church generally supported his goals. His public policies reflected a compromise between the individualistic and pietistic religious attitudes of many Americans and the more socially conscious theology of many religious leaders. Public opinion surveys of the time showed that most Americans saw little relationship between theology and political matters, but President TRUMAN recognized such a relationship intuitively. Aided by his advisers, he demonstrated that recognition in his speeches, his public statements, and his public programs. Hence, like the Old Testament prophets, his concern for social justice sometimes placed him at odds with a significant section of what is now called "middle America."

TRUMAN was not simply an opportunist, a pragmatic politician or a public opinion pollwatcher who reacted to each situation as it arose. He took his religious values too seriously for such characterizations to be valid, and he relied on those values as he made the leadership decisions that so greatly influenced the United States and the entire Western world.

Mr. Speaker, I take this time for two purposes—first—to announce that within the next few days I shall introduce a concurrent resolution which will authorize the Joint Committee on Printing to collect and assemble all of those eulogies, editorials, and encomiums relating to the life and times of our very dear President, HARRY S TRUMAN, as expressed in the House of Representatives and the Senate and at the memorial services in Independence, Mo., and at the National Cathedral in Washington.

My second purpose is to read into the Record one of the finest tributes to both HARRY S TRUMAN and Lyndon B. Johnson contained in one encomium that has ever been written.

The fact that in 1 short month we have lost two great former Presidents of the United States is a loss to America of almost inestimable proportions. Lyndon Johnson had the greatest of affection for HARRY TRUMAN. This, I know to be a fact because it was my honor to ride with him from the municipal airport at Kansas City out to the Truman Library upon the occasion when President Johnson came out to sign the medicare bill in the presence of Mr. TRUMAN at the library which bears his name in Independence, Mo. President Johnson said to me on the way to the airport from the library—

History will record your friend HARRY TRUMAN as one of the great American Presidents of all time.

In turn, I know that HARRY TRUMAN loved Lyndon Johnson with an affection that was somewhat like that of a father toward a son or that of a sponsor to a protege. Mr. TRUMAN was proud when the convention in Los Angeles chose L.B.J. as the vice-presidential candidate in 1960 and I know in conversation with Mr. TRUMAN that when Mr. Johnson succeeded to the Presidency he stood ready to offer advice and counsel from one who had been President any time that Lyndon Johnson called upon him.

Mr. Speaker, in HARRY S TRUMAN and Lyndon B. Johnson we had two Chief Executives who possessed many parallels—both succeeded to the Presidency, both were the products of the heart of America, both were deeply concerned not only about the good of the people but about the will of the people. Yes, within 1 short month our Nation has suffered a great loss by the passing of two great Presidents of the United States.

The eulogy follows:

[From Babson's Reports, Washington Forecast Letter, Jan. 29, 1973]

TWO WHO STOOD TALL

Our nation is today inestimably poorer with the loss, within one short month, of 2 former Presidents of the United States—HARRY S TRUMAN and Lyndon B. Johnson.

They had much in common . . . both were products of the grassroots, had close identity with the people; were thrust suddenly—and not psychologically prepared—into responsibilities of the Presidency but stretched to its demand-reach and earned the respect of a grateful nation.

Each succeeded Chief Executives of exceptional personal magnetism—TRUMAN as World War II was nearing its climax, Johnson in the wake of an assassination that stunned the nation.

Both were lifted to world stage center from relative obscurity that had masked their unique abilities and dynamic leadership qualities.

They were men of strength, masters of the art of politics—decisive Presidents whose ideas and deeds won approval, heady plaudits. Yet both were frequently misunderstood, maligned . . . especially toward end of their terms.

For the tragedy of fame and high responsibility is that seldom are integrity, devotion to principle and duty, fully recognized—except in the light of history.

Both former Presidents cared—deeply—about the good of and the will of the people . . . they were also cognizant of the inexplicable mystique of government. And neither hesitated to discommode the immediate in face of the binding necessity of achieving the ultimate end.

As we mourn the passing of Presidents TRUMAN and Johnson, it would honor their memory if we would grant the present incumbent a broader measure of understanding, support—faith in his intent and fervent prayer for its achievement.

Never before has a President stood alone for a term of 4 years deprived of the experience, wisdom, support, of a living predecessor.

Hon. Joseph G. Minish

OF NEW JERSEY

Mr. Speaker, we have all heard many outstanding and well-deserved tributes to the memory of our recently departed Presidents, HARRY S TRUMAN and Lyndon B. Johnson.

The governing body of the township of Maplewood, N.J., which I am privileged to represent in the Congress, conducted memorial services for both President TRUMAN and President Johnson. During these services, eulogies were delivered by Maplewood Mayor Robert Grasmere for President TRUMAN and by Maplewood Commissioner Robert C. Klein for President Johnson.

I should like to share with my colleagues two of the most moving statements I have encountered on the lives and times of these great American leaders:

TRIBUTE TO PRESIDENT TRUMAN ON THE OCCASION
OF HIS DEATH

(By Mayor Grasmere)

The Presidency of the United States carries with it the most awesome responsibility of any position which the world's work has yet devised.

That HARRY TRUMAN bore this responsibility well and decisively, on occasion even jauntily, the pens of historians have, in the years since his retirement, begun to recog-

nize. They are more accurately sketching the dimensions of a greatness which, at the time of his presidency was often hidden somewhat by the modest exterior and very human qualities of the man.

This somewhat reluctant titan of deed and decisions was drawn to the world's stage by the sudden death of President Roosevelt, but went on to secure the office in his own right in a campaign which is still a classic. He disregarded the critics, the press, the overwhelming odds and took his case to the people.

The people perhaps saw in him what one writer described as "Everyman". Most people could perceive his essential likeness to them and they took heart, for, in place of the sophistication which appeared to have totally pre-empted the presidency, there was once again the plainness and simplicity of an unmistakable man of the people—a man with very human faults and rather precious flaws.

A family man who would fly to his beloved daughter's defense with energy and salty language when he felt the press was overly critical and harsh toward her concert singing career.

A man who enraged great chefs on two continents by liberally salting and peppering prior to tasting culinary creations which had long and nerve wracking hours in preparation.

A man who appreciated Bourbon and Missouri Branch water and played the piano inexpertly.

A man who replied to a famous writer who had described his father as a failure saying, "My father was not a failure, he was the father of the President of the United States".

A man of immense loyalties and deep friendships who, nevertheless, didn't fear to incur the wrath of millions by removing from command perhaps the most capable military genius of this century when it appeared that presidential orders were being grudgingly carried out in Korea.

To this very human being were given some of the most soul-wracking decisions ever necessitated: Atomic warfare to prevent the predicted slaughter of a half-million G.I.'s had we, instead, engaged the non-surrendering Japanese on their home islands. The decision to save the eastern Mediterranean countries from the post-war pattern of communist subjugation through the Marshall Plan aid. The formation of NATO in Europe, and countless other decisions. He said and meant: "The buck" (often passed) "stops here".

During a President's term of office, the criticism which surrounds him is an inescapable and healthy fact of our national political life. Equally inescapable is the respect, often grudging, which we all have for the office and the man who bears its burden, inconceivable heavy to most of us. It is no accident that there are never more than one or two ex-presidents alive.

There is now only one, and we in Maplewood join Americans everywhere regardless of political affiliation in tribute to the man and the prodigious labors he performed for his nation and mankind.

That a man of such modest background could become a distinguished President is a particularly American story. When the story was unfolding, it gave many a pleased chuckle to Mr. Average Citizen, not the least of whom was HARRY S TRUMAN of Independence, Missouri, 33rd President of these United States.

To paraphrase one of his pungent sayings which has become part of America—"He could—and did—stand the heat, and has now left us for other kitchens."

***

TRIBUTE TO PRESIDENT JOHNSON ON THE OCCASION OF HIS DEATH

(By Hon. Robert C. Klein)

Lyndon Johnson gave a lifetime of faithful and effective service to his State, his Nation and the World. As an individual, his energy and drive were sources of constant amazement to those around him, thriving on work with eighteen-hour days being the norm rather than the unusual. He developed an expertise as a political master that has seldom been equaled: Yet he remained a man who loved and needed people.

At one point he analyzed himself this way: "I am a Free man, an American, a United States Senator, and a Democrat, in that order. I am also a Liberal, Conservative, a Consumer, a Parent, a Voter and not as young as I used to be nor as old as I expect to be—and I am all those things in no fixed order."

He proposed, fostered, persuaded, and eventually signed into Law, legislation in the areas of Health Care, Aid to Education, Immigration Reform, Poverty and Pollution Control.

He was the only President from a Southern State since Zachary Taylor yet he embraced the problems of the Negro and the poor. Johnson's Presidency touched the lives of millions in need of better Health Care, better Education, and expanded Civil Rights in such a way that the promise of America was more of a reality for more of our people than ever in our History.

President Johnson put it this way: The Negro says "No". Others say "Never". The voice of responsible Americans . . . Says, "Together". There is no other way. Until justice is blind to color, until education is unaware of race, until opportunity is unconcerned with the color of men's skins, emancipation will be a proclamation and not a fact. "Unfortunately many Americans live on the outskirts of hope—some because of their poverty, some because of their color, and all too many because of both. Our task is to help replace their despair with opportunity".

He was sworn in as the Thirty-Sixth President of the United States under the most adverse conditions confronting any American President at a time when even the stability of the Republic was questioned. His domestic reforms won him the admiration of the people and he was reelected with the widest margin of vote of any prior President.

Ironically the Vietnam War, in which he played so large a roll, frustrated many of his goals and overshadowed many of his accomplishments in the latter years of his Presidency. Yet he had a yearning desire to bring the War to a conclusion and achieve Peace. Unfortunately his passing occurred just hours before peace was announced. He always did what he conceived to serve the greatest good, for the greatest number. It remains for History to judge his performance but I believe the judgment will be overwhelmingly favorable and that his great domestic legislation and strong leadership will form an unforgettable monument in the Annals of History.

Hon. John C. Kluczynski
OF ILLINOIS

Mr. Speaker, the passing of HARRY S TRUMAN, 33d President of the United States, is an occurrence saddening to everyone familiar with the extraordinary political career of that most remarkable man.

It is no exaggeration to say that HARRY TRUMAN earned for himself a place among the elite guard of our Presidential greats. In every area he was knowledgeable; in every act he was swift and sure. No more can be asked of a President of the United States, except victory—and HARRY TRUMAN provided victory, as well.

Moreover, HARRY TRUMAN was capable of learning, in the midst of political turmoil. Elevated to the Presidency in the final stages of World War II, he took to the job in the manner of a man who had been preparing for the experience all his life.

Never before a diplomat, he joined in inaugurating the United Nations, with notable success; never before in a position to implement his reform ideas on a grand scale, he quickly assumed leadership of several major reform movements; never before a farmer, in the literal sense, he took on the task of sustaining wartime agricultural prosperity in the postwar world, and confronted for the first time by the tidal wave of world communism, he met the challenge in the manner of a champion.

No person with interest either in domestic or foreign affairs can easily forget the work of HARRY TRUMAN, with respect to the rescue of postwar Western Europe. In no time at all, following the war, Poland went Communist; then Rumania, Czechoslovakia, Albania, Latvia, Estonia—meanwhile, the Communists were also winning votes in France and Italy, while England, crippled by the rigors of war, stood by helplessly, unable to intervene.

At this point, President TRUMAN, with the guidance of George C. Marshall and the heartfelt support of the American people, came forward with the famed Marshall plan. This was enough to close the floodgates in the face of the Communist wave and sustain the cause of democracy in the West.

Starving Europe became the recipient of American food and other goods; the French and German economies revived; also those of Italy, the low countries, and Scandinavia. In short time communism was checked and held fast. Never before was so monumental a victory, affecting the entire world, attributable to the iron will of one leader and the immediate response to one community. The leader, of course, was HARRY S TRUMAN; the community: the great mass of the American people. They made a great and mighty team of which America could well be proud.

I take this occasion to express my admiration for the late HARRY S TRUMAN, one of the outstanding Presidents of our national career.

Hon. John J. Rhodes
OF ARIZONA

Mr. Speaker, President HARRY S TRUMAN was absolutely unique. I think his career as President can be summed up by the observation that no man's decisions were ever more questioned or derided when he made them, or more praised and approved 20 years later.

HARRY TRUMAN was a true American in every facet of his being. His patriotism was a religion which governed his every action. Although he was intensely loyal to the Democratic Party, he found time to be kind to Republicans, as I discovered.

In 1962 while I was on a tour of duty with the Army at Fort Leavenworth, Kans., President TRUMAN came to address the graduation of the Associate Course of the Command and General Staff College. Maj. Gen. Harold K. Johnston, who later became Chief of Staff of the Army, invited me to have lunch with him and the President. Mr. TRUMAN was absolutely gracious, and we enjoyed chatting about things in Washington as they were then, compared to the situation Mr. TRUMAN had known. I was also flattered at the fact that Mr. TRUMAN remembered my father, who had been associated with him many years ago in promoting better highways for the States of Missouri and Kansas, as well as for the entire United States. These recollections will always be treasured by me, as a chance to rub elbows with one of the great Americans of our time.

To Mrs. Truman, and to Mrs. Daniel and her family, I extend my deepest sympathy.

Hon. Ella T. Grasso
OF CONNECTICUT

Mr. Speaker, the annals of history will record the accomplishments of HARRY S TRUMAN.

The people of the United States will cherish forever the memory of his indomitable spirit, and his dedication to duty and country.

HARRY TRUMAN was a man of the people. He was, above all, human: tough and gentle, humble and proud, earthy, courageous and stubborn. He used a panoply of qualities to chart a new course in the world for our Nation.

HARRY TRUMAN was a tenacious President who matched courage to challenge. His response to the Blockade of Berlin was but one example.

HARRY TRUMAN was an imaginative President who met problems with innovative solutions. The Marshall plan stands in bold relief.

And always, good common sense, and a realistic appraisal of the people and nations of the world were reflected in President TRUMAN's leadership. One need only recall the Atlantic Alliance of 1949 and the NATO Defense of Europe.

Above all, a total faith in our Nation and a vision of the role it must play in human events guided the President's way. The Truman doctrine embraced the world and shaped the future of many lands.

All the while, HARRY TRUMAN was leading us through the difficult post-war period of transition. As his Point Four program made the benefits of scientific and technical progress available to the world's hungry and needy, the President started our Nation on the too long untraveled road to equal rights for all citizens by creating the Committee on Civil Rights. Increased social security and Federal aid for housing were his achievements, too. And let us not forget that the important Federal programs of the 1960's—medicare and Federal Aid to Education—trace their origins to this remarkable man.

Now our 33d President is dead. The cogent, honest comment we came to treasure will be no more. The great figures of our Nation and the world will no longer journey to his home for special insight and counsel.

All of us miss the man from Independence. We miss him because we respected and loved him—for his courage and persistence, humaneness, spirit and will.

Hon. Joshua Eilberg
OF PENNSYLVANIA

Mr. Speaker, we were deeply saddened this past December when HARRY S TRUMAN, the thirty-third President of the United States, died. All of us in the Congress, as well as the American people, and indeed, people all over this world, remember HARRY TRUMAN—a "not so average" man of the people.

We knew of his battles in life, of how he so valiantly overcame adversity after adversity, and we admired this man who so often took the measure of the most difficult decisions with that characteristic phrase of his after the task was finished, "that's all there was to it."

But there was so much to HARRY S TRUMAN, enough courage, enough determination, enough belief in America and our people to bring him all the way from a humble beginning in Lamar, Mo., to the Presidency of the United States of America.

HARRY TRUMAN knew war—from personal experience in World War I—and the decision to use atomic bombs to shorten the course of World War II and to save lives was, as he afterward said, "the toughest one of my life." Yet, as he said, "Had we invaded Japan, millions might have died." It was a fateful decision, but HARRY TRUMAN was there to make it, and for that we can be thankful.

After the war, there was a difficult period of readjustment for the Nation—inflation, shortages, unemployment, strikes, but HARRY TRUMAN stuck to his course and helped to steer the Nation through it all.

The cold war descended upon the world, and HARRY TRUMAN met the challenge of militant communism from Greece to Korea. He saw to it that the people of Berlin would not be starved into submission, and he worked through the United Nations Organization to help build a better world for all mankind.

Mr. Speaker, all of us were so much richer for having had Mr. TRUMAN as our leader during those fateful years—and, we are so much poorer now at his loss. Now, as we pay our respects to his memory, and as our Nation emerges from the long shadow of war in Southeast Asia, we may well recall the words of HARRY TRUMAN, 33d President of the United States of America:

For it is all too obvious that if we no not abolish war on this earth, then surely, one day, war will abolish us from the earth.

Hon. John B. Breaux
OF LOUISIANA

Mr. Speaker, Abe Gladstone, who celebrated his 84th birthday last October, is now the oldest living survivor of the artillery battery commanded by "Captain HARRY" TRUMAN during World War I. I would like to share with you his comments, as recorded in the Lake Charles American Press of December 27, 1972:

OLD SOLDIER WILL MISS CAPTAIN HARRY

(by Sam Tarleton)

"He was A–1. There never was another one like him and he always had a good word and smile for everyone. He was a man's man . . . and he never did have the big head."

That's how Abe Gladstone of 1617 Fourth St. in Lake Charles summed up the life of the late President HARRY S TRUMAN after hearing the news of his former artillery battery commander's death Tuesday.

Gladstone, who celebrated his 84th birthday Oct. 7, is now the oldest living survivor of Capt. HARRY's battery, now that the former commander and 33d President of the United States is dead.

Gladstone drove a team of mules which pulled the famed 75's under the command of Capt. HARRY of Battery "D" of the 129th Field Artillery Battalion during World War I.

Gladstone, a member of that Kansas City National Guard Unit that was mustered into active service in 1917, was a mechanic. "But when we got to France, we didn't have any mechanized units to fix so they made me a wagoneer—or a utility man driving the teams, helping fire the 75's and whatever I could do," Gladstone said.

"We'll all miss him. He was a great soldier, a great man and a great president," Gladstone said.

"After the war, the men of Battery 'D' formed an association which still exists and meets twice each year. The first meeting is held on the Saturday nearest St. Patrick's Day and the second one on the Saturday nearest Armistice Day," Gladstone said.

Gladstone last saw TRUMAN three years ago when he visited Independence, Mo. during their Kansas City reunion.

"We even had a few beer busts in the back of Capt. HARRY's house in Independence, until 'Miss Bess' put a stop to it," Gladstone said with a grin.

Mrs. Truman "is a grand lady and most wonderful," he said.

In France "Capt. HARRY looked after his men but didn't have a lot to say.

"Capt. HARRY didn't tolerate soldiers who didn't do their jobs either. As though prophetic of a day in the

Korean war when, as President, he would eventually remove Gen. Douglas MacArthur as commander, TRUMAN showed a dislike for subordinates who didn't do the job he wanted done.

"He busted three or four first sergeants after he took over our battery. Capt. HARRY was the third or fourth battery commander assigned to Battery 'D' and he stayed with us to the end," Gladstone recalled.

Gladstone, still active despite retirement several years ago, will miss the late president's funeral and regrets it to the point of shedding tears.

He is the chaplain of District 5 of VFW and, never misses a meeting.

Gladstone was advised of TRUMAN's death by special messenger from Ft. Polk, Tuesday, when an officer, dispatched through channels from Department of the Army headquarters brought him a message from Mrs. Truman.

It gave him the funeral schedule and offered to have an escort meet him if he could attend the funeral Thursday at 2 p.m. in the auditorium of the famed Truman Library.

Gladstone has 170,000 miles under his belt in his 1954 Ford and "just can't make it to the funeral."

"Battery 'D' may have catapulted Capt. HARRY into successful politics when we all campaigned for him when he ran for district judge in Jackson County . . . and won.

"We worked for him and voted for him," the old National Guardsman said. "Now with the Captain gone there is a void that can never be filled.

"Capt. HARRY had a few favorites but I wasn't one of them. But he was my favorite," he said, "and always will be."

"When he said anything he meant it," Gladstone concluded.

So Abe Gladstone will silently mourn the loss of his Capt. HARRY . . . as will all other living members of old Battery "D."

"They'll never replace HARRY TRUMAN," he said with a throb in his throat.

Hon. Delbert L. Latta
OF OHIO

Mr. Speaker, much has been recorded about the life and times of our former President, HARRY S TRUMAN, and I want to join my colleagues who have expressed their sorrow and regret at his passing.

World War II, the Marshall plan, the Berlin airlift, and even the Korean war, are merely events for our younger generation to read about in history books. For many of us, however, these historic milestones evoke many personal and enduring memories. HARRY TRUMAN was a part of all of them. Whatever one may think about some of his policies and decisions on the domestic scene—and there was never a more competitive partisan than Mr. TRUMAN—his determination to preserve America's prestige and power in the world was unquestioned.

President TRUMAN was, in fact, a patriot in the old-fashioned meaning of that word. His resolute opposition to expansionist world communism of that era helped to preserve the freedom of Western Europe.

President TRUMAN enjoyed 20 years of retirement after leaving the White House, long enough for the ultimate effects of his foreign policy decisions to become more fully perceived and understood. Future historians, in retrospect, will likely be kinder to him than were his contemporaries, and in any event his place in the annals of great world decisions is secure.

Hon. William J. Randall
OF MISSOURI

Mr. Speaker, since coming to the Congress in 1959, on May 8 of that year and each succeeding year it has been our high privilege and great honor to stand in the well of the House and speak some words of eulogy for our number one constituent, fellow townsman and great President, HARRY S TRUMAN.

This year, he is not with us. During Christmas week of 1972, he was called by the Great God of the Universe to his heavenly reward. All of the events of his lifetime were reviewed and recited again before and after the memorial services which were conducted at the Truman Library in Independence, Mo. All of the things about his life and times, his personal characteristics and the greatness of his accomplishments were reported and recorded. Accordingly, this year upon the occasion of what would have been his 89th birthday were he with us today, it is not the time for further eulogy or to recount again the important happenings of his lifetime. Rather, it should be an occasion to pause and with bowed head offer up a prayer for the repose of the soul of this great American.

Almighty God, our Father from whom we come and unto whom our spirits return, thou hast been our refuge and strength in every age and our present help in every hour of need. Grant us thy blessings in this moment when we call to mind the birthday of our beloved President, HARRY S TRUMAN.

We remember his indefatigable energy, his dauntless courage, his rugged honesty and his complete devotion to the service of his country. His beliefs were firm, his faith sound and his confidence without parallel, yet, his heart over-flowed with friendliness and his spirit reached out to others for good. He stands in the foreground in the progress of our beloved land.

We thank thee for him and pray that thou will grant unto him the peace that comes for those who cease from their worthy labors upon earth.

Bless his wife and family with the strength of thy devine spirit, the peace of thy comforting companionship.

We pray for them through thou who art the resurrection and the life. Amen.

Mr. Speaker, in the April issue of Ararat Shrine News which reached our office a short time ago, there is a page entitled, "Harry Truman Memorial."

After reading in this memorial I learned that Mr. TRUMAN was one of the very few, if not the only member of the Senate ever to serve as a U.S. Senator while concurrently serving as grand master of a grand lodge—in this instance, the Grand Lodge of Missouri in the year 1941.

As a member of Ararat Temple, I wish to confess that I was not as conversant with some of the happenings in the life of our greatest Missourian as I had thought myself to be. For instance, I did not know until his passing that Mr. TRUMAN was at one time a member of the divan of Ararat Temple, serving in the office of oriental guide. Upon his election to the U.S. Senate, he was prevented from proceeding further on the divan toward the office of potentate of the temple.

In the memorial I have referred to, there appears some quotations concerning Mr. TRUMAN which are the product of some of the most brilliant minds of our time. The two, which in my judgment fit so well that they deserve repetition when they describe this great man as "earthy, plain, there was no wrinkle in his honesty," and "He wore the mantle of our trust with truth, and bore his solitary power with humility."

Mr. Speaker, I am privileged and honored to have the pleasure to read into the Record at this time the words of the Harry Truman memorial as they appeared in the Ararat Shrine News for April 1973, volume 37, No. 4, as follows:

HARRY TRUMAN MEMORIAL

Illustrious noble HARRY S TRUMAN was born in Lamar in Barton County, Missouri, on May 8, 1884, and as an infant, accompanied his parents to Belton and Harrisonville in Cass County, Missouri, where they resided for a period of less than 2 years before moving to Jackson County, Missouri, where he became a resident for the remainder of his long, active and productive life.

HARRY S TRUMAN was a Baptist, and a member of the Grandview Baptist Church. He was interested in and active in freemasonry at all levels. Among his many masonic accomplishments and memberships was his membership in Belton Lodge 450, Belton, Missouri, where he became a member in 1909 and served as senior warden in 1910. In 1911 he organized Grandview Lodge 618 and was its first worshipful master when it became a chartered lodge. He served again as master of the lodge in 1917.

While he was a Member of the U.S. Senate he served as grand master of the grand lodge of ancient free and accepted masons of Missouri in 1941 and master of the Missouri Lodge of Research in 1951. He was a member of the Scottish Rite of the Orient of Missouri and was coroneted a thirty-third degree mason on October 19, 1945. He received the Order of the Red Cross of Constantine, December 26, 1945. He belonged to Orient chapter 102, of Kansas City, Missouri, Shekinah Council 24, Kansas City, Missouri, and Palestine Commandery 17, Independence, Missouri. He was a member of Ararat Temple of Kansas City, Missouri, and Court 54, Royal Order of Jesters, Kansas City, Missouri. During his more active years in Ararat Temple, he served as a member of its divan, attaining the office of oriental guide before his election to the United States Senate in 1934 prevented his proceeding farther. Our brother also served as honorary grand master of the Order of DeMolay.

During the time of all of his participation in masonry, Noble TRUMAN was also actively engaged in political life. He was elected Eastern Judge of the County Court of Jackson County, Missouri, and served as such in 1923 and 1924. In 1927 he was elected presiding judge of that court, a position that he held until 1934. In the election in the fall of 1934, Noble TRUMAN was elected to the United States Senate where he served through 1944. History is replete with his activities and constructive works during this phase of his life. In January, 1945, he became Vice President of the United States, and in April, 1945, upon the death of President Franklin Delano Roosevelt, Noble HARRY S TRUMAN became the thirty-third President of the United States. He continued to serve as President until 1953.

Upon his retirement from active political life, he returned once more to his home in Independence, Missouri, where he remained until his death, December 26, 1972, at 88 years of age. Seldom does an organization have the privilege of including within its rank a member such as Noble HARRY S TRUMAN, and at a time such as this, the inadequacy of the spoken or written word to express our pride in his accomplishments and our sorrow in this loss is self-evident. To him we say, Noble TRUMAN, well done.

As we move in travel we note in a downtown park site in Athens a life size statue of our illustrious noble set to honor his great interests in humanity throughout the world. A similar site was noted in the islands of the Caribbean. We note a few quotes from brilliant minds of our time. "A fearless son of simple soil," "of sturdy soul and tempered true" "earthy, plain, there was no wrinkle in his honesty. When the time came he stepped to the anvil humbly but not afraid, relying always in his independent way, upon the goodness of the Lord, in whose hand is the hammer of our fate." "He wore the mantle of our trust with truth, and bore his solitary power with humility."

He was in attendance and often served as speaker at the Frank S. Land breakfast given each year during the grand masters conference at Washington, D.C. He was a great personal friend of the shrine in all its endeavors. We have all been made richer in spirit and in service by his association with us down through the years.

Mr. Speaker, although our dear friend, former President HARRY TRUMAN, has been gone from us now for some time, there comes to my attention quite regularly commentaries and memorials on the life of this great American President that should certainly be incorporated in the Record in order that these eulogies may in turn be made a part of the memorial volume which will soon be published in memory of Mr. TRUMAN.

One of the best eulogies, that I must confess I had neglected to recognize until now, was the address by Dr. Richard S. Kirkendall, professor of history, University of Missouri-Columbia. His address on Mr. TRUMAN was presented at the Truman Memorial convocation held in the Memorial Union Auditorium on January 17, 1973, at the University of Missouri-Columbia.

It has now come to my attention that, although Dr. Kirkendall was a native of the State of Washington, he has become one of the authorities on the accomplishments of Missouri's most distinguished son, the great HARRY S TRUMAN.

Dr. Kirkendall has excellent credentials as a Truman authority. He joined the faculty of the University of Missouri at Columbia early in 1958 and gained national acclaim for his research and writings on the Truman years. After nearly 10 years, in 1967, he released his first large-scale survey of literature on the Truman era, as editor of "The Truman Period as a Research Field."

This distinguished Truman authority does not come by his knowledge as a matter of hearsay because he has had access to the Truman Library at Independence and had the privilege of several personal interviews with the former President. So it could appropriately be said that Dr. Kirkendall not only had a professional knowledge of Mr. TRUMAN because he is a student of history, but also a personal knowledge because of the several personal interviews with Mr. TRUMAN.

For my part, I am glad that I have recently discovered this excellent address because I would not want it to have been omitted from Mr. TRUMAN's memorial volume. It is my privilege to read into the Record at this time the address

entitled "HARRY S TRUMAN—A Great American President" as follows:

HARRY S TRUMAN—A GREAT AMERICAN PRESIDENT

(EDITOR's NOTE.—Although he is a native of Spokane, Washington, Dr. Richard S. Kirkendall has become one of the nation's authorities on the accomplishments of one of Missouri's most distinguished native sons—the late President HARRY S TRUMAN.

(Joining the University of Missouri-Columbia history department faculty in 1958, Dr. Kirkendall advanced from assistant to full professor while gaining national acclaim for his research and writings on the Truman years.

(Dr. Kirkendall is a graduate of Gonzaga University at Spokane. After two years in the Navy, he resumed his education and earned master's and doctorate degrees in 1953 and 1958 at the University of Wisconsin.

(He taught history for a year at Wesleyan University at Middletown, Connecticut, before moving to the UMC campus. Not long after his arrival in Missouri he published *Social Scientists and Farm Politics in the Age of Roosevelt* as a hardback volume. In 1967, he made the first large-scale survey of literature on the Truman era as editor of *The Truman Period as a Research Field*.

(Access to the Truman Library at Independence and personal interviews with the former President added to Dr. Kirkendall's personal and professional knowledge of Mr. TRUMAN.)

HARRY S TRUMAN was one of America's greatest presidents. This is not to say that he was always wise and always successful. None of our presidents has been wise and successful at every point. We have not been ruled by gods. We have been forced to make do with men, and men have limits on their abilities. In appraising presidents, the historian must have realistic expectations.

HARRY S TRUMAN's achievements and proposals entitle him to recognition as a great occupant of the Executive Mansion. He failed more than once; a bolder man might have accomplished more; a wiser one would have avoided some of his moves. His accomplishments may not have been as substantial and significant as Washington's, Lincoln's or Franklin Roosevelt's. Yet, he did promote valuable changes; he developed a new and larger role for the United States in the world, affected some parts of it in very desirable ways, and encouraged social and economic improvements at home. And our experiences since he left the White House suggest that his advice should have been followed more closely.

TRUMAN was not a small man who suddenly had a very big job imposed upon him. The job was very big, but he brought to it rich and varied experiences in American life and politics. He had served for eight years as the chief administrative officer of a populous county and more than nine years as a United States senator. He had campaigned for office on local and state levels, administered and constructed court houses, welfare agencies, roads, and other public facilities in Jackson County, contributed significantly to the war effort as an investigator of the economic side of it, and learned much about the American political and economic systems. Although his brief vice presidency had not supplied specialized training for the higher assignment, his selection as a candidate had enabled him to wage a national campaign in 1944, and his responsibilities as vice president had given him a chance to exercise his political talents in new ways. If he did not shape the administration's proposals, he did obtain opportunities to build support for them. His career before the White House was not a little man's career.

TRUMAN's life before April 12, 1945 also supplied him with a philosophy on the issues that he would face, including the international affairs that would dominate his presidency. His thinking on foreign policy emphasized political considerations, especially the distribution of power, the importance of the military factor, and the need to deal forcefully with aggressive nations. This philosophy was the product of his own experiences as a soldier extending over more than thirty years and of the nation's experiences in world affairs from 1918 to 1945.

As president, TRUMAN was determined to avoid what he regarded as the errors of the past: weakness and refusal to get involved in the major international problems. He feared that the American people would retreat to the foreign and military policies of the 1920's and the 1930's that had failed disastrously. He was convinced that the nation must play a very significant role in the world in the postwar period and must possess military strength.

With TRUMAN supplying essential leadership and making the basic decisions, the United States did not retreat to the policies of the interwar period. Instead, it played a large role in the world. TRUMAN carried to completion Roosevelt's plans for the creation of an American membership in the United Nations. Of greater importance, at least in the short run, his administration developed and implemented a plan—the Marshall Plan—for European recovery. The plan and the program that followed contributed decisively to the economic recovery of Western Europe and to the development of political stability and strength in the region.

TRUMAN believed that the United States could and should play a large role in world affairs, but he did not regard American power as unlimited. He did not believe that the United States could do all that it might wish nor accomplish all that it might hope. This sense of limits affected his efforts in Eastern Europe, where he relied largely on words in a futile effort to influence political developments. He was distressed by Russian behavior there but believed that there was little he could do to change it. The sense of limits also prevented him from intervening in a large way in the Civil War in China even though he hoped that Chiang Kai-shek could avoid defeat. He and his aides did not believe that the United States could mobilize the economic and military resources needed to exert a decisive influence on that very large, very complex, and deeply troubled nation.

The sense of limits also contributed significantly to another very controversial aspect of TRUMAN's presidency: his conflict with General Douglas MacArthur in 1951. The President rejected the General's proposal to throw more force against the Chinese in Korea and to carry the war into China itself, using American air and naval power and Chiang's troops. TRUMAN regarded the suggestions as extremely dangerous. "We are trying to prevent a world war—not to start one," he explained. Furthermore, MacArthur's proposals would tie the United States down in an area of secondary importance and thereby give the Russians new opportunities in a much more important region: Europe. MacArthur's strategy would, according to TRUMAN's top military adviser,

"involve us in the wrong war, at the wrong place, at the wrong time, and with the wrong enemy." MacArthur's objectives—the reunification of Korea under non-Communist control and the weakening of China—were not unattractive, but they seemed to TRUMAN to be beyond the limits of American power. The pursuit of them would result in losses that would far outweigh those objectives in importance.

The Truman-MacArthur controversy also involved another very important consideration: the place of the military in American life. TRUMAN regarded military power as essential but also dangerous. His solution was civilian control. This was, of course, the solution of the American Constitution. MacArthur tried to use his prestige to force a change in policy and appealed publicly for support of his ideas. His actions challenged TRUMAN's authority as Commander in Chief, and the President concluded that he must remove the General from command in order to uphold and maintain the essential principle of civilian supremacy.

Foreign affairs was the most significant aspect of TRUMAN's presidency. The record of his domestic accomplishments did not contain any contribution as substantial as the Marshall Plan, to cite a major example. Nevertheless, he was not insignificant in the domestic history of the United States. He was not able to gain acceptance for new domestic proposals, but he did expand and improve already established ones, such as Social Security and public power, and he did defend them against their foes. Moreover, by publicizing various issues, such as health insurance, he paved the way for later accomplishments. Furthermore, he did more on behalf of the civil rights of black Americans than any of his predecessors in the twentieth century.

TRUMAN's civil rights record deserves more than brief mention. It was influenced by his interest in the nation's relations with other people as well as by domestic concerns and humanitarian considerations. Well aware of the international implications of American race relations, he was convinced that the country "could no longer afford the luxury of a leisurely attack upon prejudice and discrimination." In 1951, when vetoing a bill that would segregate schools on federal property, he explained.

"We have assumed a role of world leadership in seeking to unite people of great cultural and racial diversity . . . We should not impair our moral position by enacting a law that requires discrimination based on race."

TRUMAN's concern in this area was expressed by several significant actions. Late in 1946, he established a Committee on Civil Rights to investigate race relations and make recommendations for government action to protect civil rights, and less than a year later, the committee produced a bold report that influenced the administration's subsequent behavior. Soon, his Justice Department joined the NAACP in an attack before the United States Supreme Court on segregated housing. This marked the beginning of that department's significant participation in the civil rights movement. Early in the following year, the President delivered a special message attacking discrimination and segregation and calling for national legislation that would provide federal protection against lynching, protect the right to vote, prohibit discrimination in interstate transportation facilities, and establish a permanent agency concerned with job discrimination. And in July 1948,

Truman issued two executive orders on civil rights, including one calling for equality of treatment and opportunity in the armed forces and the establishment of a committee to help with the implementation of the order. The President explained that it was intended to end segregation.

Truman enjoyed some successes in this area. His Justice Department continued to function as a "friend of the court" in the major civil rights cases and helped the NAACP win its battles. His appointees to the United States Supreme Court also played important roles in these cases, which attacked segregation in housing, railroad dining cars, and higher education and prepared the way for the monumental decision in 1954 attacking segregation in all public schools. And the armed forces were desegregated. They had taken on new importance as a result of the enlargement of the nation's role in the world, and he promoted progress in race relations in this part of American life.

Truman failed, however, to obtain passage of the broad civil rights legislation that he proposed. Perhaps he might have accomplished more if he had pressed his proposals more boldly. His appraisal of political realities restrained him, however. His ability to promote change was limited by strong resistance, especially in the South. Many southerners bolted the Democratic party in 1948 and supported Governor J. Strom Thurmond of South Carolina in a presidential campaign that focused upon race relations. And after the election, a congressional coalition of conservative Democrats, mostly southerners, and conservative Republicans dominated Congress on domestic issues and frustrated Truman's appeal for a legislative attack upon problems in American race relations. Even before Truman became president this coalition had demonstrated that it could thwart a president. It was chiefly responsible for his failure in this area.

Truman did not always succeed, and he did not always make wise decisions. One unwise one was the decision to provide financial support for the French in their battle against revolution in Indochina. This marked the beginning of an involvement that led to disaster.

Truman, however, was not responsible for the disaster. His successors were. They lacked his appreciation of the limits on our power and enlarged enormously a rather small commitment that could have been terminated after the French failed or at some other point far short of massive military involvement.

Many Americans, however, could not accept Truman's belief that their power had limits. That belief was one of the sources of his unpopularity during his last years in office. By early 1952, only 25 percent of the people thought that he was doing a good job. His most prominent critics were very dissatisfied with his foreign policy, seeing it as responsible for the "loss" of China and for other undesirable developments, and they assumed that the United States could and should accomplish much more than he had accomplished. It was this attitude that led to our large-scale involvement in Vietnam. It has been an effort to "avoid another China."

Truman made mistakes, he failed to accomplish some of his objectives, but he was a much greater president than most Americans realized during his years in the White House. They should have accepted rather than resisted his advice on civil rights and made a much larger effort to solve the problems in American race relations. Instead, those problems—or many of them—were allowed to grow and become a serious threat to the nation as well as a source of suffering and sorrow for many individuals. More attention should have been paid to his suggestions about the limits on American power. Instead, we enlarged our role until bitter and destructive experiences in Vietnam provided persuasive evidence on this point.

In his area of greatest significance, international affairs, Truman's point of view and performance were complex and balanced. He believed that the United States must play a large role in world affairs, but he also maintained that there were limits on what the nation could and should do. He insisted that the United States must have a strong military establishment, but he also knew that a strong military posed a threat to the American system and must be kept in a subordinate position.

We need that complexity and balance at the present moment. Alive now to the folly of globalism, we may swing back to isolationism, forgetting its dangers. The United States once tried to play a small role in the world, but that failed. It did not keep the country out of major wars. Now the nation, or at least a very substantial part of it has become aware of the shortcomings of the global role, the limits on American power, and the need to make choices, and efforts are being made to define a role in the world that minimizes difficulties. The thought and record of one of our greatest presidents could help us define that role.

Mr. Speaker, the magazine Modern Maturity is a publication of the American Association of Retired Persons. In their February–March issue, a tribute was paid to our former President, Harry S Truman, which escaped my attention until within the last few days.

The article was written by Hubert Pryor. It is not long, but it makes some points that have been emphasized before but put in slightly different terminology, with a sidelight that had not been included in other editorials or other commentaries.

The article so appropriately starts off with the fact that there was never a more difficult time for a man to succeed to the Presidency of the United States, but above all there was never a moment left for him to reflect on the difficulties he had to face. In just a few words, this well-prepared memorial points out that within 2 months after being thrust into the world's highest office, he had presided over the end of the war in Europe and had the courage to use the awesome weapons to end the struggle in the Pacific. Finally, this very brief memorial concludes with the thought that of all of Mr. Truman's virtues, his one supreme virtue was that he was one of us—and, most of all, he demonstrated what any one of us can do when we are challenged to solve difficult problems.

The full content of the article, "Memories of HARRY TRUMAN," by Hubert Pryor, as it appeared in the February–March, 1973, issue of Modern Maturity, follows:

MEMORIES OF HARRY TRUMAN

If there was ever a more difficult time to succeed to the presidency of the United States, there wasn't even a moment to reflect on the matter. In the above picture, barely two months after being thrust into the world's highest office, HARRY S TRUMAN had presided over the end of the war in Europe and was preparing to end the struggle in the Pacific with weapons so awesome that the world would never again be the same. Between VE–day and VJ–day, he made a historic appearance in San Francisco. Chopping his hands down on the rostrum, and sticking out his jaw, he wound up the conference held for the purpose of founding the United Nations and attempting to set the human course for all time on the path of peace.

It has seemed at times since then as if the high hopes of San Francisco could not have been more short-sighted. And yet, with all the turmoil of the world, we have been spared the total nuclear conflagration so often feared.

We owe no small part of that good fortune to the acts of HARRY TRUMAN during the next almost eight years—maybe not always the wisest, maybe not always the most popular, but certainly among the most clear-cut, the most decisive of any series of acts undertaken by any American chief executive.

In the social order, too, we have much for which to be grateful to HARRY TRUMAN. It was in answer to his call that the first National Conference on Aging was held in 1950, a meeting in Washington attended by some 800 men and women from around the country to prepare, as it turned out, for the first and second White House Conferences on Aging held in 1961 and 1971.

The status of older people has risen many notches since the days HARRY TRUMAN was in office. And for all our problems, we have much else for which to be grateful in our lives since then, too.

HARRY TRUMAN'S supreme virtue was that he was one of us and that he showed what any one of us can do when challenged to do so.

We will miss him. Let us not miss the high example he set us.

HUBERT PRYOR.

Hon. John J. Rooney
OF NEW YORK

Mr. Speaker, with the passing of former President HARRY S TRUMAN on December 26th last, one of the few remaining personages from a varietal and climatic period of American and World History was taken from our midst. His vociferous critics of his Presidential activities are now slowly realizing the integrity of his decisions and actions.

The chroniclers have done an excellent job of detailing the historical events and decisions of HARRY TRUMAN and I am sure that the politicians and historians will analyze and interpret them for many, many years to come. Therefore, I do not intend to include them here. However, they will be missing the intrinsic ingredient that garnishes my recollections of the era, and that is the privilege of not only working with him but also counting him as a friend.

The late President TRUMAN faithfully followed his own advice—the buck passing stops here. During his tenure as President, he had to make many tough and painful decisions, a few of which were to use the atom bomb, to resist Communist aggression in South Korea, to fire Gen. Douglas MacArthur, and how to rebuild a world torn apart by World War II. He will also be long remembered, especially by some members of the press, for his replies to picayunish news stories about his family.

Those of us who have long been concerned over finding workable solutions to the problems confronting our efforts to provide equal rights to all our citizens remember joining the late HARRY TRUMAN in his effort to provide continued appropriations to and the establishment of a permanent Fair Employment Practices Committee. It was my privilege to respond affirmatively to President TRUMAN's requests that Congress establish such a permanent Committee.

An episode in the Truman era that I am sure is seared into the minds of not only labor but also of business is the Republican-controlled 80th Congress passing the Taft-Hartley Act and overriding his veto of it. I disagreed with the passage of that act that time and continue to do so as I am sure that HARRY TRUMAN continued to do so.

My Jewish constituency in the 14th Congressional District of New York and most of the Jewish people throughout the United States remember the prompt action in 1948 of President TRUMAN in diplomatically recognizing the new State of Israel, almost immediately after the new State was proclaimed at Tel Aviv.

No tribute to the late President HARRY S TRUMAN would be complete without praise for his lovely wife for her devotion and love that gave him great strength to be true to himself in arriving at the decisions that changed mankind. Our prayers and deepest sympathy go to her and their lovely daughter Margaret. I am sure that in this period of anguishment at our great loss the knowledge that HARRY TRUMAN accepted the challenges that life placed before him as President and met them with greatness will long remain in our memories.

Hon. Wm. J. Randall

OF MISSOURI

Mr. Speaker, within the past few days, the House has passed a resolution which authorizes the printing of President TRUMAN's memorial volume. Hopefully, the other body of Congress will also concur in our action to enable the work to be started to assemble all of the contents which should appropriately be included within that volume.

One most important entry to be included in the volume is the content of the Masonic service at the final rites on December 28, 1972, as presented by Grand Master W. Hugh McLaughlin of the Grand Lodge of Missouri. While there have been several different reprints of this service, it has been noted that in some of these there were errors of content, and for that reason I have personally requested M. W. Brother McLaughlin to indicate to me which is the true and accurate wording of the Masonic service. He has advised me that the words of the service as he delivered them appear in the spring 1973 issue of the Freemason which is the official publication of the Grand Lodge A.F. and A.M. of Missouri, at page 51 and concluded on page 52.

I was one of those seated in the small auditorium of the Truman Library in Independence who heard delivered from the stage of that auditorium the words of our Grand Master, W. Hugh McLaughlin. It is my high privilege and great honor to read into the Record at this point the words of the Masonic service as I heard them delivered on Thursday, December 28, 1972.

THE MASONIC SERVICE

(By W. Hugh McLaughlin)

The Grand Lodge of Ancient, Free and Accepted Masons of the state of Missouri shares the grief and sorrow of Mrs. Truman, Mrs. Daniel and her family, Miss Mary Jane Truman and other family members in the loss of our beloved and cherished native son. This expression comes from the Grand Lodge offices and from more than 108,000 of his Masonic brothers in Missouri.

We express our gratitude to the family, to Father Lembcke, and to all other participants for the privilege of sharing in this service. We join, humbly and reverently, in paying lasting tribute to a great American and a renowned world statesman.

Masons are taught never to engage in any solemn, great or important undertaking without first invoking the aid and blessing of Diety. Shall we pray?

We hail you, Supreme Architect of the Universe. We come to you with spirits bowed low and ask the bounty of Thy Grace and mercy in our bereavement. May our deeds be such as to prepare us for entry into Your spiritual kingdom, that house not made with hands, eternal in the heavens. Amen!

President TRUMAN distinguished himself in many Masonic services, the most laudable of which was that of Grand Master of Masons of this state in 1940 and 1941. At that time he was also a member of the United States Senate. We express our gratitude to Mrs. Truman and Mrs. Daniel for sharing a portion of his exciting, magnificent life with us. He was our brother by adoption. He was our companion by choice.

The tenets of a Mason's profession are Brotherly Love, Relief and Truth. There abide with us Faith, Hope and Charity. The greatest of these is Charity for it extends through the boundless realms of eternity. Our notable brother exemplified Charity in a universal way when he directed relief to be administered, on an unprecedented scale, to alleviate human degradation in the aftermath of World War II.

The lambskin or white leathern apron is the badge of a Mason, more ancient than the Golden Fleece or Roman Eagle. It is white to admonish us to keep our personal lives pure. Our exalted brother wore it proudly and worthily.

The evergreen symbolizes a Mason's belief in immortality of the soul. It represents that vital spark of our spiritual life which shall never be quenched. President TRUMAN expressed that belief.

The Beehive is an emblem of a Mason's industry. By it we are taught to be workers in the great hive of nature. Even in his later years our distinguished and beloved citizen practiced that teaching. No more striking example than this great edifice, named for him, in which he performed his last labors, could conceivably be demonstrated to us today.

It is, therefore, fitting that we should assemble here to pay this deserved tribute. We, as Masons, extol his many virtues, not the least of which was his recognition of the high level of individual dignity. May we emulate him in his simple, sincere, sturdy and forthright conduct. May all our good intention be crowned with success. May Brotherly Love prevail in all the earth and every moral and social virtue cement us.

Mr. Speaker, virtually the entire contents of the spring 1973 issue of the Freemason, the official publication of the Grand Lodge, A.F. & A.M., of Missouri, is devoted to articles on President TRUMAN's Masonic history.

On the flyleaf of the spring issue appears the following dedication:

DEDICATION

Missouri Freemasons are especially proud that HARRY S TRUMAN was "one of our own." We join with Freemasons everywhere, with free people throughout the world, and with those whose hopes of freedom remain a dream for fulfillment, in expressing our heartfelt sympathy to all the members of his family in their very personal loss.

We pray that his family will find strength, comfort, peace and happiness in the knowledge that his life and his work will always be an example and source of strength and encouragement to millions and millions of people of the present and future generations.

It is with brotherly love and affection that this issue of The Freemason magazine is dedicated to HARRY S TRUMAN, Past Grand Master, Grand Lodge of Missouri, A.F. & A.M. 1940–41.

Fraternally yours,

W. HUGH McLAUGHLIN,
Grand Master.

In this single issue there as so many interesting articles that it is difficult to choose which is the most interesting and informative to share with those colleagues in the House who are Freemasons, as well as those who admired and respected our late beloved President TRUMAN.

Perhaps the most significant fact about Mr. TRUMAN's Masonic history is that he became grand master of the Grand Lodge of Missouri, A.F. & A.M., for 1940–41. Because of such fact I think it is best to include in the Record, an article which may hopefully be carried into the Truman memorial volume, which begins on page 44 of the spring issue of the Freemason and concludes on page 49. The article is well-written and contains some sidelights on the life of Mr. TRUMAN as a Mason which I am almost certain had never before been published.

This particular story points out that Mr. TRUMAN made the long 12-year climb of progression to become a grand master exactly like any other individual, but, unlike those who were not in public life or a well-known political figure, Mr. TRUMAN had to endure in at least one instance the brunt of an anonymous letter which claimed that Mr. TRUMAN's election as grand master would not be in the welfare of Masonry in Missouri for political reasons.

However, it is noteworthy that Mr. TRUMAN, again and again, exercised the greatest care to be sure and certain that neither the Masonic organization nor the Eastern Star participated in any way toward the advancement of his political fortunes. Throughout his entire life as a Mason, Mr. TRUMAN carefully observed and scrupulously protected the bipartisan or nonpolitical character of the Masonic fraternity.

Mr. Speaker, it is my privilege to read into the Record the story of Mr. TRUMAN's progression to

grand master of the Grand Lodge of Missouri as follows:

TRUMAN AND GRAND LODGE: A RECORD OF ACCOMPLISHMENT

HARRY S TRUMAN was proud that he was a politician. He was even more proud and, in later years, frequently pointed out to Masons and non-Masons that he was appointed to the advancing line of the Grand Lodge of Missouri by a strong and active Republican.

Some of the correspondence from his Senatorial files at the Truman Library in Independence show how zealously he observed and protected the bi-partisanship or non-political character of the Fraternity. In April of 1940 while Deputy Grand Master, he received a letter from a St. Joseph politician and member of the Fraternity disclosing that an Eastern Star chapter was going to sponsor a dance at which candidates for political office would be introduced. The dance was a fund-raising program for the Masonic-related organization. He asked TRUMAN to participate.

TRUMAN replied: ". . . I think that the Eastern Star should under no circumstances be used in any way for political purposes, even for the purpose of raising money.

"Never in my career have I used either the Masonic organization or the Eastern Star to advance my political fortunes. You will find, I am sure, that the constitution of both organizations prohibits just such activities as you are proposing to put on. It will not only ruin the organization, but if you are not careful it will cause a split where no split should occur."

THE APPOINTMENT

TRUMAN had been one of four men considered for appointments to the Grand Lodge line in 1929 but the appointment went to Karl M. Vetsburg of St. Louis. A year later in Kansas City, Judge William R. Gentry, the incoming Grand Master, conferred with the two officers next in line on the appointment. These officers were Ray V. Denslow and Thad B. Landon. All three were staunch Republicans.

TRUMAN was concluding his fifth year as District Deputy Grand Master and District Deputy Grand Lecturer. At the time he was Presiding Judge of the Jackson County Court and as the Grand Lodge session was about to open an editorial appeared in the Kansas City Star. The editorial praised TRUMAN, the Democrat, for his outstanding accomplishments with the county court, one of the few times in his active political life the newspaper editorially spoke in his favor.

Republicans Gentry, Denslow and Landon agreed on TRUMAN and at the conclusion of the 110th annual communication, held at Kansas City's Ivanhoe Masonic Temple, he was installed as Grand Pursuivant. It was a 12-year line of progression to become Grand Master unless deaths or resignations occurred.

THE ELECTIONS

TRUMAN progressed through the advancing appointive line from 1930 to 1938 without any hint of politics. But when the tellers returned from counting the ballots for Junior Grand Warden they disclosed probably the closest vote in the history of the Grand Lodge.

TRUMAN had been elected, by a vote of 395 with a scattering of 345 for others, a victory margin of only 50 votes.

One brother, Luther E. Wilhoit, District Deputy Grand Master in the 14th Masonic District, later wrote TRUMAN:

"I attended Grand Lodge at St. Louis last week and witnessed the most disgraceful thing I ever saw done in Grand Lodge.

"In expressing myself I was informed that they didn't want Pendergast for Grand Master four years from now. In reply I told the brother that I hardly considered a man worthy of Masonry who would bring that kind of stuff into Grand Lodge. . . ."

TRUMAN gave serious thought to stepping aside to avoid the possibility that politics might be brought into Grand Lodge again as he came up for election as Senior Grand Warden, Deputy Grand Master, and Grand Master. However, older and wiser heads prevailed. His Senatorial papers at the Truman Library contain a great number of letters similar to that from Brother Wilhoit, encouraging him to continue.

In addition, a letter on August 4, 1939 from the members of his own Grandview Lodge No. 618, gave him even more reason for remaining in the line. The letter said:

"DEAR BROTHER HARRY: Knowing you personally and intimately as each of us does, and fully appreciating the honors you have brought to our little country lodge, we the undersigned members in good standing of Grandview Lodge No. 618, take this means of conveying to you, the knowledge of our unswerving loyalty and support in your progress toward the East in the Grand Lodge.

"May we all live to see you installed as Most Worshipful Grand Master, and may a part of the honor and glory of that occasion be reflected, as it surely will be, on your home lodge. We are fraternally yours. . . ."

The letter was signed by the 20 other living Past Masters of Grandview Lodge as well as the Junior and Senior Wardens for 1939 and the Secretary.

The resignation in the spring of 1939 of Elwyn S. Woods as Deputy Grand Master pushed Vetsburg and TRUMAN into the two top elective offices that fall. The vote for TRUMAN as Deputy Grand Master still gave some evidence that political opponents were at work.

THE UNSIGNED LETTER

The year 1940 was eventful for TRUMAN. Not only would he face election for Grand Master but he would be in the midst of his campaign for re-election to the U.S. Senate.

His correspondence discloses that he turned down many invitations to visit or address various lodges that year because, "I would not want the lodge or any of the brethren to become involved in a political controversy on my part. It does not belong in the lodge."

Someone was bound and determined to get TRUMAN, as a political figure, into the lodge. About two weeks before Grand Lodge an anonymous letter was mailed to the "Worshipful Master or Sec'y" of each of the nearly 600 lodges in the state. The letter read:

"KANSAS CITY, MO.,
"September 16, 1940.

"BRETHREN: If Masonry is to continue to occupy an exalted position, it might be well *To Think, Look and Listen.*

"The brother in line for Grand Master, is a position to which he can not do justice, he being a U.S. Senator.

"He was sponsored and practically put in that office, by the most unscrupulous racketeering boodler, that ever disgraced our State.

"Masonry and politics can and should not mix. Nor should the good citizens vote into a government or any other office a man that was created and through the power of crooked votes, was elected to the U.S. Senate by the champion of all racketeers, Tom Pendergast.

"The man that now seeks your vote for Grand Master and for re-election to the U.S. Senate, publicly announced, that he would stay with the sinking ship. Meaning that he would still be for Tom Pendergast, now an ex-convict and a dyed in the Wool Catholic.

"Brethren, consider the welfare of Masonry.

"Let your conscience be your guide.

"So Mote It Be."

Within days TRUMAN's Senate office in Washington was flooded with correspondence from various lodge secretaries and other officers of the lodges. Nearly all enclosed the anonymous letter and expressed serious concern over the breach of Masonic law and tradition.

One of the letters to TRUMAN came from the then superintendent of schools at Bloomfield, Missouri, Elvis A. Mooney. The letter said in part:

"While your name has been before the public and you have been an official of our government there has never come to my attention any act, or failure to act on any proposition that would in any way bring disfavor to the Fraternity or have any bearing on the question raised except to do honor and to give evidence of your fitness for the highest gift within the Grand Lodge of Missouri . . .

"I have very little influence in the Masonic Brotherhood of Missouri and have had very little opportunity to have much acquaintance with you as a man; however, I shall attend Grand Lodge and will rise to my feet and state my position on this outrage on a worthy brother and do all in my power to prevent this outrage on decency and good order among us. If I can be of assistance in furthering your cause so that you may serve us more fully throughout the coming year I am at your request.

"Sincerely and fraternally,

ELVIS A. MOONEY."

(In 1958 Elvis A. Mooney was appointed to the Grand Lodge line by Dr. Harold O. Grauel, who "tried to teach him the English language" at Southeast Missouri State College, Dr. Grauel had been appointed to the line by TRUMAN's appointee, James M. Bradford, and thus, Grauel became TRUMAN's Masonic "grandson" and Mooney, TRUMAN's Masonic "great grandson." Bradford was Grand Master in 1949–50, Grauel 1959–60, and Mooney 1968–69.)

THE ELECTION

On September 24–25 of 1940, the Scottish Rite Cathedral in St. Louis was packed with one of the largest turnouts of delegates ever in the history of the Grand Lodge for the 120th annual communication. There were 563 lodges represented out of a total of 624. TRUMAN was elected Grand Master by a vote of 2,708 with 689 scattered, a total vote of 3,397. At the conclusion of the two-day meeting, TRUMAN was installed in office by the Republican who appointed him in line, Past Grand Master William R. Gentry.

GRAND MASTER TRUMAN

True to his word, Grand Master TRUMAN did not accept any invitations for Masonic activities until after the general election in November of 1940 in which he won re-election to the U.S. Senate.

He began his official visitations on Nov. 20, 1940, with an appearance at both Belton Lodge No. 450 and Grandview Lodge No. 618 on the same evening. Before his term of office was concluded, the correspondence in his Senatorial papers at the Truman Library records that he visited more than 20 Missouri Lodges, attended at least eight district meetings and presented several 50-year pins.

Grand Master TRUMAN also visited the Grand Lodge of Texas, Equity Lodge No. 591 in Philadelphia, Pennsylvania, where he was the featured speaker; attended the semi-annual communication of the Grand Lodge of the District of Columbia; the Grand Masters' Conference of North America; the annual meeting of the George Washington Masonic National Memorial Association where he presented Missouri's contribution of $1,900 to the association; and was the speaker at the annual dinner in Alexandria for Andrew Jackson Lodge No. 120.

In addition TRUMAN made 16 official decisions as Grand Master. The jurisprudence committee upheld his rulings on all but two of the decisions.

He also directed the consolidation of four lodges into two and, after investigations by his deputies and careful consideration on his part, arrested the charters of two other lodges.

Grand Master TRUMAN also issued 24 dispensations during the year, appointed and instructed two trial commissions, requested the resignation of one District Deputy Grand Master and appointed his successor.

PUFFED UP

Dr. Arthur Mather, grand secretary, forwarded to TRUMAN all correspondence requiring the Grand Master's attention including the various checks. On one occasion, TRUMAN wrote Dr. Mather:

"I am enclosing the checks which you sent me for the payroll, and also the $40,000 check for the Masonic Home.

"The office force seems to be very much puffed up that I have the ability to sign a check for $40,000. Of course, they don't understand that I don't have anything to do with whether it is good or not." (The check was partial payment from Grand Lodge of its per capita tax from the membership.)

TRUMAN RADIO BROADCASTS

Following his re-election to the U.S. Senate, TRUMAN proposed the creation of a special committee to investigate waste, mismanagement and profiteering in the nation's war defense program. TRUMAN was named chairman of the committee, selected a chief investigator and set to work.

While TRUMAN was chairing his committee and actively participating in the investigations, traveling throughout the country, he kept on top of his homework as far as other Senate business was concerned, regularly putting in 15- to 18-hour days.

It seems almost impossible, now, in the light of his involvement, to realize that he also was serving effectively as Grand Master of Missouri Freemasons.

Because of his position as Grand Master of Missouri and U.S. Senator, TRUMAN was asked to deliver a nation-wide radio address on February 22, 1941, over the Columbia Broadcasting System on "George Washington, the Mason." The speech was well received and gave TRUMAN additional national recognition.

A few months later on July 24, Carl Claudy, executive director of the Masonic Service Association, prevailed upon TRUMAN to deliver another national radio address on "Freemasonry Serves the Armed Forces," relating the story of the MSA and various other benevolent efforts of Grand Lodges throughout the United States to assist the serviceman. The broadcast elicited a great deal of interest, praise and new support for the MSA.

The broadcast also brought at least one note of criticism. Miss Mary F.. McGoldrick, Worthy Grand Matron of the Eastern Star of Massachusetts, wrote to TRUMAN criticizing him for failing to mention the OES and Rainbow Girls contributions to the various camp programs. TRUMAN responded:

"I appreciated most highly your cordial note of July 25 in regard to my address on Masonic service.

"Of course the Eastern Star should have been included, but there isn't a man in the world who can think of everything, particularly this one. I apologize, for the Star is doing a great work."

TRUMAN CORRESPONDENCE

TRUMAN corresponded fairly regularly with a number of Missouri Masonic friends as he progressed through the Grand Lodge line and through his years in the White House. These included Ray V. Denslow, George Marquis, N. D. Jackson, Renick Jones, Frank Land, and James DeWitt. Denslow, Marquis and Land were particular favorites.

One letter to DeWitt reveals the sacrifice in time that TRUMAN made as Grand Master. TRUMAN spoke in Philadelphia on April 9, left there at 1 a.m. on an airplane for St. Louis where he was met by DeWitt and driven to Kirksville.

On April 16, 1941, TRUMAN wrote DeWitt:

"The plane came along at 5 a.m. (April 11) and I got two hours sleep on a bench. They took me all the way back to Philadelphia and then down to Washington. I got here at 12:30 p.m. instead of 9:30 a.m. Just three hours late.

I cannot express to you my appreciation for all the courtesies you showed me while in Kirksville. . . . Tell the two boys who acted as Masters that they did a good job and I appreciate it. . . ."

In letter to Denslow, TRUMAN said: "Certainly is good of you to keep me properly informed on the people in the neighborhood. If I just had somebody like that in every town I would never make an error. It certainly would have been a great error to write the widow of a bachelor, wouldn't it?"

GRAND MASTER'S ADDRESS

In his Grand Master's address of September 30, 1941, Truman said, in part: "We are facing a solemn and serious period in our history; in fact, the most serious emergency we have ever faced. As Freemasons we must continually endeavor to instill appreciation of free government and free expression; freedom of thought and freedom of worship. . . . We cannot really appreciate these privileges because we have always had them. But, our brethren in Denmark, Holland, Norway, and all those other countries which have come under the heel of totalitarian dictators, are either in concentration camps, or have forsworn their liberties and their fraternal obligations.

"It is a most difficult matter for me, as Grand Master of the Freemasons of the great state of Missouri—an honor which I believe is greater than any other which can come to me—to stand here and discuss this situation with you without getting upon political grounds. I have been exteremly careful in my Grand Lodge career as a member of this Grand Lodge line, to stay entirely clear of political actions and political utterances, where the interests of the Grand Lodge have been concerned. Brethren, we should be thankful for the privileges we enjoy. We must put forth every effort possible to maintain them with everything we have. . . .

". . . I have made a thorough investigation of the Masonic Service Association of the United States, of its personnel, and of what it proposes to do, and I have come to the conclusion that this Grand Lodge should do all it possibly can to support this Masonic Service Association for a Masonic national contact with our armed force. . . .

"I am, therefore, suggesting that the Grand Lodge of Missouri join the Masonic Service Association and cooperate fully with the other Grand Lodges of the country for service to the soldiers in this emergency.

"The Grand Chapter, Royal Arch Masons of Missouri, is contributing $1,000 to this great cause. Your Grand Master is making a contribution of one-half his salary ($500) as Grand Master for the year. I hope, brethren, that this great organization will do its duty fully and completely in this national emergency. . . ."

TRUMAN concluded his address to Grand Lodge in these words:

". . . I am sure that as long as there are three million Freemasons in the country, all good men and true, who believe in a system of morals, and the Constitution of the United States, we can safely face the future, no matter what it may bring forth.

"Fraternally submitted,

"HARRY S TRUMAN,
"Grand Master."

Arthur Krock of the New York Times wrote in 1946 that "TRUMAN has very long cherished Solomon, son of David, King of Israel, as his model of a public official and believes that a wise and understanding heart is the most necessary quality in a President of the United States."

Mr. Speaker, as I have recently observed on this floor, the spring 1973 issue of the Freemason, official publication of Grand Lodge A.F. & A.M. of Missouri, contains a wealth of detailed information, not only about the longtime service of President TRUMAN to his Masonic fraternity, but also an account of the elaborate plans which had been carefully and painstakingly made for the funeral of a President.

In the publication referred to, there appears an article which reveals the fact that Mr. TRUMAN had personally requested a Masonic service as well as a religious service at his funeral.

Of the six close friends who resided in the Kansas City area previously named to assist in overseeing the plans for the funeral, only Brother H. Roe Bartle, former mayor of Kansas City, survived.

It was my high honor, accompanied by Mrs. Randall, to be admitted to the small but beautiful Truman auditorium on the afternoon of December 28, 1972, for the final rites.

At the conclusion of the TRUMAN masonic service, consisting of a funeral oration presented by most worshipful brother W. Hugh McLaughlin, the grand master of the Grand Lodge of Missouri. I distinctly recall Mayor Bartle, the only survivor of the group of six, leaning forward and whispering to Governor—and brother—Warren E. Hearnes, saying:

It makes you proud that you are a mason and can really share in this moment.

I read into the Record at this time an account of those final rites as it appears at page 50 of the Freemason for spring 1973 as follows:

THE FINAL RITES OF HARRY S TRUMAN: A BROTHER BY ADOPTION—COMPANION BY CHOICE

The details of President TRUMAN's funeral had been planned many years in advance. He had requested a Masonic service as well as religious. Six close friends in the Kansas City area had been named to assist in overseeing the plans. Only Bro. H. Roe Bartle, former mayor of Kansas City, survived. While not in the best of health, Brother Bartle shared and worked closely with the Truman family and the military in carrying out the former President's requests.

The Grand Lodge of Missouri was officially represented by Grand Master W. Hugh McLaughlin. He was accompanied by Deputy Grand Master Walter L. Walker and Past Grand Master Martin B. Dickinson.

The Masonic portion of the service on December 28, 1972 was presented by M. W. Brother McLaughlin and was delivered from the stage of the small auditorium in the beautiful Truman Library and Museum in Independence. The services were broadcast and telecast nationally and internationally reaching millions and millions of people throughout the world. Many of them had been touched and uplifted by the spirit of brotherly love exemplified in both the public and private life of Missouri's most distinguished native son and lifelong resident.

BARTLE COMMENT

Brother Bartle, Grand Orator of Missouri in 1954–55 and an intimate friend of TRUMAN's for nearly 40 years, joined with thousands and perhaps millions of other Freemasons in expressing unstinting praise of the presentation made by M. W. Brother McLaughlin.

"It was superb, eloquent in its simplicity, dignified. He captured the true spirit and meaning of the fraternity. I have never felt as proud of being a member of the masonic fraternity as I did at the conclusion of the grand master's remarks," said Bartle. "I leaned forward and tapped Gov. (and Bro. Warren E.) Hearnes on the shoulder and I told him 'that was a magnificent presentation. It makes you proud that you are a mason and can really share in the moment.' "

M'LAUGHLIN

M. W. Brother McLaughlin prepared the masonic service under a great deal of pressure. The masonic portion of the service was first "off" and then "on," and "off and on" again before it was finally confirmed the day before the service. Finally, the grand master was told he would have only five minutes and that the limitation on time must be strictly observed. The grand master tailored the service for the time allotted, writing and rewriting. His work speaks for itself.

Mr. Speaker, President TRUMAN had a great love for his Masonic fraternity. That love was frequently expressed during his years in the White House. It is estimated that he raised more than 30 candidates during the nearly 8 years he was in the White House. He insisted upon the strict injunction that no publicity was to come from his participation. Of course, that was not always possible, but it certainly was his firm intention.

In the spring of 1973 issue of the Freemason there are recited several instances of Mr. TRUMAN's participation in lodge ceremonies. One can read with great interest how he journeyed from the White House over to the Alexandria-Washington Lodge No. 22 to participate in the initiation of Lt. Neville J. McMillan, son of A. T. McMillan, master of the Grandview, Mo., Lodge No. 618 back in 1916.

Then the President later went out to Grandview, Mo., to assist in conferring the second degree in the Blue Lodge on Harry A. Truman, son of his brother Vivian and nephew of the President, at the Grandview, Mo., Masonic Lodge.

In this same article, there appears a story of the incident when Mr. TRUMAN walked from the White House to the Washington Lodge in November 1947 to assist in conferring the lodge's third degree on Capt. Thomas J. Burns, assistant White House physician. It was noted that after a 12-year lapse former Grand Master TRUMAN of the Missouri Grand Lodge recited his lines without missing a syllable.

Finally, one of the most famous Masonic incidents involving President TRUMAN occurred in 1948. It was at Kokomo, Ind., on October 15. While Mr. TRUMAN was talking from the rear platform of his train, he noticed a young man in U.S. Navy uniform. He motioned for the young man to come up and shake hands. Mr. TRUMAN had recognized the young man as one of the crew from the Presidential yacht, *Williamsburg.* The young man was Donald E. Bauermeister. He immediately invited him and his father to board the train to ride on into Indianapolis.

En route he discovered that the young man was to receive his third degree that night at Beech Grove Lodge No. 649, about 8 miles from Indianapolis. The President was invited to attend and at first declined.

But, that was not the way things turned out. Following Mr. TRUMAN's evening speech at the Indiana War Memorial in Indianapolis, the President ordered his car to proceed to the little town where the President indicated he wished to be present at the initiation of the boy from the Presidential yacht, *Williamsburg.*

Mr. Speaker, once again it is my privilege to read into the Record the article from the spring issue of the Freemason entitled, "TRUMAN the Ritualist":

TRUMAN THE RITUALIST

President TRUMAN's great love of Masonic fellowship and the ritualistic work in the tiled Lodge room was frequently evidenced during his years in the White House. Some sources indicate that he Raised more than 30 candidates during those nearly eight years, always with the strict injunction that no publicity was to come from his participation. That was easier said than done!

LT. NEVILLE J. M'MILLAN

A petition presented to Alexandria-Washington Lodge No. 22, early in 1945 bore the name of Lt. Neville J. McMillan, the son of A. T. McMillan, Master of Grandview Lodge No. 618 in 1916.

The young officer's father and TRUMAN had worked together in Grandview Lodge and TRUMAN had presided as Master at the Raising of the elder McMillan. TRUMAN offered Alexandria-Washington Lodge a highly favorable recommendation of Lt. McMillan and planned to be in attendance on the evening of April 12, 1945, when his petition was voted on. In fact, TRUMAN and Rep. William C. Cole from St. Joseph signed his petition.

President Franklin D. Roosevelt died April 12 and TRUMAN was sworn into office as President within a few short hours. He could not go to Lodge, but he sent three Masonic members of Congress to speak for him, and McMillan was elected to receive the degrees.

Bro. and Rep. Cole wrote TRUMAN on April 16 that McMillan "is scheduled to receive his Entered Apprentice Degree on Wednesday, April 19. I will keep in touch with his progress and inform you of the date that he is to be raised if you so desire."

Cole did keep the President advised of McMillan's progress and again wrote TRUMAN on September 27, 1945, that "I am happy to inform you that he has successfully completed his Entered Apprentice and Fellowcraft degrees and will be raised at the Lodge room of the National Masonic Shrine at Alexandria, Virginia, on Thursday, October 11, or at any other date that suits your convenience."

TRUMAN appended a note to the bottom of the letter addressed to his appointments secretary, Matthew Connelly.

"Matt: I'd like to go. This boy's father is my good friend. In fact I took him through and he served as Master of my little Lodge. The boy's brother was killed in the Pacific. HST."

TRUMAN ATTENDS

Thanks to the *Virginia Masonic Herald* we are able to tell the rest of the story of the Lieutenant's initiation.

Early on the day of the communication, Secret Service men swarmed into the George Washington Masonic National Memorial and carefully scrutinized every square inch of it and set up guards throughout the building.

The Alexandria-Washington Lodge was opened at 7:30 p.m. by W. M. Marvin L. Wilson. Although no notice had been given to the members through the press or otherwise the grapevine apparently had carried the news far and wide that the President was expected. An overflow gathering filled the large Lodge room and there was not even standing room left.

President and Past Grand Master TRUMAN, accompanied by Secret Service men who were members of the Fraternity, was escorted to the Altar and introduced. He was conducted to the East and accorded the honors due his rank as a Past Grand Master.

After Brother McMillan was Raised, TRUMAN spoke briefly.

When the Lodge was closed, TRUMAN remained in the room to greet the members personally and autographed the dues cards of all who asked. He remained until a late hour before his Secret Service team insisted that he must return to the White House.

President TRUMAN later wrote the Master of the Lodge that "I enjoyed the visit and wish it were possible for me to make more of them.

"Neville McMillan is a good young man—just as his father was before him."

NEPHEW OF THE PRESIDENT

The Kansas City *Times* of Nov. 2, 1946, took note of another unusual incident in the life and activities of President TRUMAN.

"After leaving his mother's home last night, President TRUMAN paid a visit to the Grandview Masonic Lodge No. 618. While Engle Wray, the Master of the fraternal organization, was supposed to be the only one apprised of the visit, somehow a rumor had spread around among the Masons of Washington Township and a good crowd was on hand.

"The meeting was called for the purpose of conferring the second degree in the Blue Lodge on Harry A. Truman, son of his brother Vivian Truman and a nephew of the President.

"In the ceremony, the President took the role of Worshipful Master and his brother performed the duties of Senior Warden.

Following the ceremony, a social period was held "in which Mr. TRUMAN visited with his fellow Masons" before starting the journey home to Independence.

CAPTAIN BURNS

Newsweek magazine of November 1947 carried this account of President TRUMAN.

"By a companion's count, not one in 20 strollers recognized the blackhatted figure walking briskly up Pennsylvania Avenue in Washington last Thursday evening, November 6. As his Secret Service guard trailed him discreetly, President TRUMAN walked the three blocks from the White House to the Masonic Temple and, once inside, donned the traditional white apron. Reason: Capt. Thomas J. Burns, assistant White House physician, was taking the Lodge's third degree. Though some of the officiating Masons flubbed their lines during the initiation ceremonies, all noticed that Former Grand Master TRUMAN of the Missouri Grand Lodge recited his, after a 12-year lapse (what *Newsweek* didn't know wouldn't hurt them), without missing a syllable. Later the President chuckled: 'I thought Burns' eyes would pop out. Wish I could get out this way more often.'"

A SAILOR

One of the most famous Masonic incidents involving TRUMAN as President occurred in 1948 during his campaign for re-election to the White House.

It was at Kokomo, Indiana, on October 15, that TRUMAN noticed a young man in a U.S. Navy uniform. After TRUMAN finished his talk from the rear platform of the train, he motioned for the sailor, Donald Earl Bauermeister, to come up and shake hands. TRUMAN had recognized the young man as one of the crew from the Presidential Yacht, *Williamsburg*.

Young Bauermeister and his father were invited to ride the train into Indianapolis and during the trip, TRUMAN discovered that the sailor was to receive his third degree that night at Beech Grove Lodge No. 649, about eight miles from Indianapolis. The President was invited to attend but expressed doubt that he could because of a tight schedule.

TRUMAN later changed his mind. William J. Bray, special assistant to the President, in an Oral History Interview for the Truman Library, recalled that "when the train arrived in Noblesville, Indiana, for another platform speech, several of the Secret Service men left the train to put into adoption a plan which had been drawn whereby the President could participate in these ceremonies. . . .

"Following the speech (at the Indiana War Memorial at 8:30 that evening in Indianapolis) the party returned in cars to the train. The car that the President was supposed to ride in at the head of the procession, however, was occupied by two members of his party and his personal secret service bodyguard, Henry Nicholson. The car containing the President and several Secret Service people proceeded to this little town where the President had indicated that he wished to be at the installation of the boy from the *Williamsburg*. . . . About an hour later the President returned to his railroad car, very much pleased that maybe he had made several people happy. Of course, he had made many, many people happy, especially the boy and his father. It was not until two days later that word 'leaked out' about the President's detour and it did not make the press feel very happy that they had missed quite a scoop."

The young sailor's mother, Mrs. John Bauermeister, wrote TRUMAN on Dec. 18, to thank him for "the time you spared, on Oct. 15, 1948, to be present at the raising to a Master Mason of our son, Don." And she said, "I also wish to thank your daughter for the beautiful orchid she sent to me. I still have it, and hope to keep it always."

Mr. Speaker, the title of this entry into the Congressional Record, "This, Too, Is for the Record," would seem to indicate that it might have been authored by a Member of Congress.

However, such is not the case. Instead, the above title is the heading of an article which appeared in the spring 1973 issue of the Freemason, which was dedicated to HARRY S TRUMAN, past grand master, Grand Lodge of Missouri AF & AM 1940-41. The article, "This, Too, Is for the Record," appeared at page 55. The central theme of the story emphasizes that HARRY S TRUMAN could easily have retired from participation in Masonic affairs at the conclusion of his term as grand master in 1941. The national spotlight was already centering on him as the head of the "Truman committee." But Mr. TRUMAN was a practicing Freemason. Accordingly, his interest and support remained constant.

Mr. Speaker, it is my considered judgment that those of us who are Members of Congress are deeply indebted to the author of the article in the Missouri Freemason for his résumé of the activities of Past Grand Master TRUMAN while he served as grand master in 1940 and 1941. Hopefully, some of this material may be included in a memorial volume now being prepared. It is my pleasure to read into the Congressional Record the article as it appears on page 55 of the Freemason, spring issue 1973:

THIS, TOO, IS FOR THE RECORD

HARRY S TRUMAN could easily have retired from active support and participation in Masonic affairs at the conclusion of his term as Grand Master on October 1, 1941. The national spotlight was centering on him more and more as the "Truman Committee" investigating waste and mismanagement in the war program gained for him unstinting praise and admiration by the populace.

But TRUMAN was a practicing Freemason. His interest and support remained constant. The following is a brief list of some of his activities as a Past Grand Master.

December 1, 1941, delivered the dedication address for Masonic Welfare Center, first Masonic Center primarily for Navy personnel, at Newport, Rhode Island.

December 17, 1941, TRUMAN wrote Ray Denslow: "I was supposed to go to a Masonic meeting last night where two gentlemen were made Masons at sight. I got to thinking about the matter and couldn't bring myself to go, because I don't approve of such a matter, however great the recipients. I suppose the high-hats here will be somewhat put out with me because they had consulted me about the qualifications of the two men. Their qualifications were one hundred percent, but as you and I know, that just isn't the way to do it."

January 8, 1942, TRUMAN responded to a West Coast publisher of a Masonic history and took exception to material on Andrew Jackson. TRUMAN wrote: "I notice where you say that Andrew Jackson received his degrees at Greenville Lodge, Greenville, Tennessee, in 1851. Andrew Jackson was Grand Master of Tennessee long before that, and it is not known exactly where he received his degrees, but it is recorded that he received them in North Carolina.

"He was born in 1767. You gave the date of his birth in 1808, and the place Raleigh, North Carolina. He was born in Wax Haws, and it is doubtful whether he was born north or south of the State line. There has always been a controversy between North and South Carolina about the location of the State line at the time of his birth. I don't know where you got those figures, but you certainly ought to make a correction on them.

"For your further information, if my dates are correct, Andrew Jackson died in 1845, so he couldn't possibly have received his degrees in 1851" (Truman Library, Senatorial file).

February 1942, attended Grand Masters Conference and George Washington Masonic Memorial Association meetings.

June 1942, addressed the Annual Convention of the National League of Masonic Clubs in Atlantic City. The Chairman, Arvid V. Swaningson, wrote that "To have had you present at the Gold Card Dinner was a pleasure, indeed, and your attendance at the Inspirational Hour on Friday evening was also a real mark of Masonry, and many of the Brothers there made mention of that fact."

September 28-29, 1942, attended Grand Lodge in St. Louis, TRUMAN served in the traditional role of chairman of the Committee on the Grand Master's address. He also had secured the featured speaker for a Masonic patriotic meeting on Monday night before Grand Lodge, Lt. Gen. Brehon B. Somervell, Commanding General Services of Supply.

Gov. Forrest C. Donnell, a Republican, was elected and installed as Grand Master at the conclusion of the communication, Donnell appointed TRUMAN as a member of the special Committee on Social Service at the training camps.

October 5, 1942, on the floor of the U.S. Senate, TRUMAN made the following remarks: "Mr. President, I ask unanimous consent to print in the Appendix of the (Congressional) Record a very timely address by Lt. Gen. Brehon B. Somervell, Chief of the Services of Supply of the War Department. The address was delivered in St. Louis on September 28, at a patriotic meeting sponsored by the Grand Lodge of Ancient Free and Accepted Masons of Missouri, and it is well worth reading by every Senator and Member of the House." The address was ordered to be printed.

Somervell's remarks included the following reference to TRUMAN:

"You may not know it but the Senator has twice volunteered to don the uniform he wore with such distinction in the last war and is serving on the Capitol front only at the express request of the Secretary of War and Chief of Staff who felt the need of his assistance there."

January 27, 1943, addressed Grand Lodge of Tennessee and made Honorary Past Grand Master.

September 27-28, 1943, attended Grand Lodge and again had secured the speaker for the Masonic Patriotic night on Monday before Grand Lodge. TRUMAN introduced the speaker, Rear Admiral George D. Murray. TRUMAN helped prepare and signed the report of the Committee on Social Service at the Training Camps.

Grand Master Donnell, at one point during the communication, said, "I think it would be very discourteous and not at all proper if I did not at this time call to the microphone a gentleman who has come from Washington, D.C., leaving his official duties, which means simply that he has to take care of them when he returns, as they have piled up, and he has come here to pay us a fraternal visit. I take great pleasure in presenting at this time our distinguished junior United States Senator from Missouri, former Grand Master of Masons of Missouri, Honorable HARRY S TRUMAN."

TRUMAN responded: "Most Worshipful Grand Master, Your Excellency: It certainly is a very, very great courtesy for you to invite me to the microphone. I am just an ordinary member of this Grand Lodge, and it is the greatest place in the world to come, I think. I do want to take this opportunity, Governor, to again thank you for delegating me last night to introduce the principal speaker . . . I appreciate most highly your courtesy, and while we differ politically, our friendship is just as strong as it ever was."

November 24, 1943, TRUMAN attended Harmony Lodge No. 17 in the District of Columbia, which met that night to honor its own member, Grand Master Carl Claudy of the Grand Lodge of the District of Columbia and executive director of the Masonic Service Association.

April 19, 1944, TRUMAN addressed the Grand Lodge of New Jersey. Sometime later he received a letter from Grand Secretary Issac Cherry expressing the Grand Lodge's appreciation and enclosing a $50 honorarium. TRUMAN responded, "I did not expect any such donation, although I do appreciate it most highly. I am endorsing the check and returning it to you with the suggestion that it go into the Masonic Home charity fund."

September 25-26, 1944, attended Grand Lodge in Kansas City. TRUMAN again had made arrangements for two of the speakers. A Masonic patriotic meeting was held Monday night in the Music Hall. The featured speaker, introduced by TRUMAN, was Senator Owen Brewster of Maine. Tuesday evening in Ivanhoe Temple, there was a program of music, the motion picture produced for the Masonic Service Association, "Your Son Is My Brother," and Carl Claudy of the MSA delivered an address. TRUMAN also served on the Committee on Social Service at the Training Camps.

At this time, TRUMAN was the Democratic party's Vice Presidential candidate.

January 20, 1945, took the oath of office as Vice President of the United States.

April 12, 1945, less than four hours after the death of Brother and President Franklin D. Roosevelt, HARRY S TRUMAN took the oath of office as President.

On May 8, 1945, Victory in Europe! Within a few weeks, Carl Claudy of the Masonic Service Association visited with the President and called his attention to the need for providing assistance to Masonic brethren and Grand Lodges in Europe that had been overrun by the Axis powers. It was suggested that a Masonic Commission be sent to Europe to make a systematic, detailed study of the needs, TRUMAN agreed to help.

The State Department was opposed to the Masonic Commission making the trip, suggesting to the President that it might unleash a flood of similar requests from other Masonic groups and other organizations.

In a White House memorandum TRUMAN advised his Special Counsel, Judge Samuel I. Rosenman: "Mr. Grew (of the State Department) is very much mistaken about the Masonic program. The situation that I had in mind would take in every section of that fraternity, and would represent all of the Masonic bodies. Under no other condition would the matter be considered.

"I think it can be worked out on that basis, and I am of the opinion that it would be an asset both to the State Department and to me."

The four-man Masonic Commission, headed by Missouri Past Grand Master Ray V. Denslow, departed for Europe August 12, 1945. The other members of the Commission were Past Grand Masters Claude J. McAllister of Montana and Charles H. Johnson of New York, and W. Bro. Justice George E. Bushnell of Michigan.

The commission returned home September 29. The President had sent a cablegram to Denslow, returning aboard the Queen Mary, and asked that he come to the White House immediately on his return. Denslow did and provided TRUMAN with a concise summary of the commission's findings.

October 19, 1945, Frank Land, founder of the Order of DeMolay, met TRUMAN at the White House and accompanied him to the Scottish Rite House of the Temple for a dinner. Following the banquet the President received the Honorary 33d degree along with 349 other designates including Gen. H. H. (Hap) Arnold, Lt. Gen. Ben. Lear, Lt. Gen. James P. Doolittle, and Secretary of Agriculture Clinton P. Anderson.

December 26, 1945, Home for the Christmas holidays at the "Little" White House in Independence, TRUMAN walked across the street to the home of Nathaniel D. Jackson, a life-long friend, for breakfast and was installed as a member of Kansas City's Mary Conclave, Red Cross of Constantine. Others present were Harris C. Johnston, George C. Marquis, Milton F. Hill, Sam A. Gilliland, Perry N. Lindgren and George M. Saunders.

OTHERS ACTIVITIES

During his years in the White House, Past Grand Master TRUMAN, with only one exception, returned home to install the officers of his home lodge.

The President also met annually except for 1948 with the Conference of Grand Masters of North America. In 1946, 1947 and 1949, TRUMAN was host to the Grand Masters for a brief visit in the White House. In 1948 he was out of the city but sent a letter of greetings.

Beginning in 1950, Frank Land sponsored a Presidential breakfast for the Grand Masters and in 1950–51 and 1952, the Masonic dignitaries were not only greeted by TRUMAN but he brought along members of his cabinet and Congress.

The Grand Masters were received in the East Room in 1947 at 12:30 p.m. and at 3:35 p.m. Frank Land, Ray V. Denslow and William R. Denslow were received for a private visit with the President.

TRUMAN's remarks to the Grand Masters were broadcast nationwide on Feb. 22, 1952, and won a host of favorable comments. One letter came from a Roman Catholic Priest, Rev. Francis G. McNulty of Sacred Heart Church in Plains, Pa. Father McNulty wrote:

"Hearty congratulations on that homey, off-the-record speech which you made at the gathering of members of the Masonic Lodge at the Hotel Statler in Washington last Friday morning!

". . . Your calm, sincere and friendly manner acted like a magnet to hold the attention of your listeners, and I am sure all who heard you could not help being convinced of the truth of your message."

November 6, 1947, President TRUMAN visited Hiran Lodge No. 10 in Washington where he Raised two Fellowcrafts from Missouri lodges who were receiving "courtesy" work.

November 1, 1948, TRUMAN attended a breakfast given by Mary Conclave, Red Cross of Constantine in Kansas City. TRUMAN made a few remarks including the comment: "Boys, I'm not a betting man myself, but if any of you want to make a little easy money just bet on me to win tomorrow!"

Later that day TRUMAN was honored by Ararat Shrine with a ceremonial named in his honor and a dinner that evening.

July 19, 1949, President TRUMAN addressed the Imperial Council session of the Shrine at Soldier Field in Chicago. It was a major address in which TRUMAN discussed past foreign policy decisions and discussed the future and prospects for "creation of a world in which we, and all people, can live and prosper in peace."

February 22, 1950, President TRUMAN spoke at the dedication of the statue of George Washington in the entrance hall at the George Washington National Masonic Memorial in Alexandria. The statue was made possible through contributions from the Order of DeMolay. It was another major Presidential speech and went through seven drafts before it was completed.

November 7, 1950, President TRUMAN visited the Jackson County Library in Independence and viewed the special Masonic collection for the Missouri Lodge of Research.

STONES

During the restoration work in the White House workman discovered a great many stones bearing the original Mason's mark. President TRUMAN found there was a sufficient number so that one each could be properly prepared and presented to each Grand Lodge in the United States.

The stones were presented through the cooperation of the Grand Lodge of the District of Columbia, which TRUMAN noted, "is Masonically supreme in the Capitol of the Nation." He further said in a letter to each Grand Lodge that "These evidences of the number of members of the Craft who built the President's official residence

so intimately aligns Freemasonry with the formation and the founding of our government that I believe your Grand Lodge will cherish this link between the Fraternity and the Government of the Nation, of which the White House is a symbol.

Mr. Speaker, once again as we attempt to assemble the most important entries for the memorial volume of President TRUMAN, I resurveyed the spring, 1973, issue of the Freemason, being the official publication of the Grand Lodge of the A.F. & A.M. of Missouri.

On page 40 of that issue appears what could be regarded as a sort of Masonic autobiography. It consists of an article, "My Masonic History," by HARRY S TRUMAN. The article is preceded by an editor's note that points out that this material was written by former President TRUMAN for and at the request of Bro. and Gen. Harry H. Vaughan. It was discovered at the library among the papers Vaughan presented to the library to assist researchers in the study of the life of the 33d President of the United States.

While the title of this article would seem to indicate that it was concerned only with Masonic history, in truth and in fact the account contains a wealth of personal history which, so far as I know, had never before been published; for example, the date of 1906 is shown to be the year Mr. TRUMAN quit his job at the Union National Bank in Kansas City to move to the farm at Grandview. Then there is the interesting account of how on the day when a man came to his cousin's farm to look at some livestock he noted the visitor was wearing a pin with a square and compass with a big "G" in the center. The young TRUMAN immediately expressed interest in the pin and forthwith expressed a desire to join the fraternity. This was back in January of 1909.

Mr. Speaker, there is a wealth of Masonic history in the article I have referred to. There are two or three quotations which deserve emphasis. One is the statement by Mr. TRUMAN when he said that as an active Mason who had served in various offices of the lodge including deputy grand lecturer, he found that being a ritualist, as he put it, "inspired me to read a great deal of history."

The other statement which revealed not only how much he loved his fraternity but also how much he valued the lessons he had learned from Masonic ritual was his conclusion that his Masonic work was, as he put it, "helpful in teaching me to get along with people."

Mr. Speaker, I read into the Record at this time the article written by the former President of the United States, HARRY S TRUMAN, as follows:

MY MASONIC HISTORY

(By Harry S Truman)

(EDITOR'S NOTE.—Former President TRUMAN wrote the following for his friend and aide, Bro. and Gen. Harry H. Vaughan. It was discovered at the Truman Library among the papers Vaughan presented to the library to assist researchers in the study of the life of the 33rd President of the United States.)

THE PETITION

In 1906 I quit my job in the Union National Bank in Kansas City and moved to the farm at Grandview. It consisted of 600 acres and belonged to my grandmother, Harriett Louise Young. She was a wonderful woman.

My uncle, Harrison Young, an old bachelor, had been running the farm since 1893, when my grandfather died. He wanted to go back to town and so arrangements were made for our family to take over.

My father, brother, and I ran the place for ten or 12 years.

I had always been interested in becoming a member of the Masonic lodge. One day a cousin of my mother's who lived on a farm east of us came over to look at some livestock. He was wearing a square and compass with a big G in the center. I told him of my interest and desire to join.

This incident happened in January, 1909 or December. 1908. Mamma's cousin came back in a few days with an application for membership in Belton Lodge No. 450 at Belton, Missouri. The imitation fee was $20.00, half of which went with the application. I signed up and gave my second cousin a check for $10.00.

INITIATED

On February 9, 1909 I was initiated, passed in two weeks and on March 9, 1909 received the third degree and after passing all examinations became a full-fledged member of Belton Lodge No. 450, A.F. & A.M. of Missouri.

About a month after, the Grand Lecturer, James R. McLachlan came to Belton for a three-day lodge of instruction. I attended all three days and accompanied the Grand Lecturer to Holden and St. Joseph becoming almost letter perfect in the ritual in all the stations.

In the fall of 1909 I was appointed a Deacon and in the fall for 1910 elected Junior Warden. I decided to organize a lodge at Grandview about this time.

The Masonic law required 20 signatures to a petition for dispensation to be presented to the Grand Master.

MASTER GRANDVIEW U.D.

The Grand Lodge met in St. Louis in September, 1910 and I presented the petition, to the Grand Master in the spring of 1910.

It was favorably acted upon and a dispensation was issued by the Grand Master with me as Master of Grandview Lodge, U.D. When the Grand Lodge met in the fall I was present and a charter was issued to Grandview Lodge No. 618.

The Deputy Grand Master Leon Thalman organized and put the lodge to work in 1911. I was elected its first Master and then its Secretary. I was again elected Master in 1916 and was Master when the war came along in 1917. While I was overseas the lodge hall burned with all the records and the charter.

DDGM—DDGL

When I came home from the war I kept up my interest in Masonic affairs becoming known as a ritualist and in 1924 I was appointed Deputy Grand Master and Deputy Grand Lecturer for the 59th District which was Jackson County outside Kansas City.

I held instruction courses in every lodge in the district in each year and held a general course of instruction for all lodges in the district with the Grand Lecturer present.

These meetings were most helpful and instructive and gave the members a chance to become better acquainted. It was also an opportunity to impress upon the membership the great lessons taught in the Old and New Testaments.

GRAND LODGE LINE

In 1930 William R. Gentry was Grand Master. He was a prominent lawyer in St. Louis and a working Republican in politics. I was Presiding Judge of the County Court of Jackson County and an organization Democrat. Mr. Gentry appointed me to the first step in the Grand Lodge line. This meant that eventually with no mishaps I'd be Grand Master.

Some partisan Republicans in St. Louis tried to head me off when I came to the first elective office but they failed as they did every year after that until I became the Grand Master of Missouri in September 1940.

In the meantime I had been elected to the United States Senate in 1934. I was having the fight of my life for reelection in 1940. My political friends were in trouble and the Governor of the state who held his office because I had been for him was trying to unseat me. So the same old St. Louis clique that tried to head me off in the Grand Lodge at the first elective office, tried again when I came up for Grand Master. They failed and I'm sure they are now sorry they tried to discredit me, because there are very few Grand Lodges that have had a President of the Greatest Republic in the history of the world as a Past Grand Master.

HONORS

When I became President in 1945, the Scottish Rite wanted me, of course, for the 33rd degree. I had been entitled to it for five years but the old man who was Sovereign Grand Commander was from Kentucky and a violent anti-new dealer. So I wasn't asked. But I didn't act the snob and tell the old man where to go when he did come around because I wanted to top off my Masonic career with the 33rd degree.

WHAT IT MEANT

My Masonic career has been helpful in teaching me to get along with people, has caused me to become more familiar with the Bible and inspired me to read a great deal of history.

FOR THE RECORD

—Petitioned Belton Lodge No. 450, December 21, 1908. Elected to receive the degrees by initiation February 9, 1909 and received first degree same date; Passed to degree of Fellowcraft March 9, and Raised to Sublime degree of Master Mason, March 18, 1909.

—June 6 and June 13, 1911, TRUMAN signed minutes of Belton Lodge as acting Secretary and on the 13th also was listed as acting Master with his brother J. Vivian Truman as acting Junior Deacon.

—In 1911, TRUMAN and several other brethren withdrew from Belton Lodge to establish Grandview Lodge No. 618 at Grandview. He was Master under dispensation and charter Master. He later served Grandview Lodge as Secretary and frequently was Organist. He was serving again as Master when he left for military service in 1917.

—Petitioned Scottish Rite bodies, Valley of Kansas City, November 11, 1911 and received 4–14 degrees January 24, 1912. Completed the 15–32 degree March 27, 30, 31 of 1917.

—Charter member with sister Mary Jane Truman of Grandview Chapter No. 365, Order of Eastern Star, and was first Worthy Patron of the chapter. He also served several years as the chapter organist.

—Petitioned Kansas City's Orient Chapter No. 102. Royal Arch Masons, and received the degrees November 11 and 15, 1919.

—Petitioned and received degrees of Shekinah Council No. 24, Royal and Select Masters, Kansas City, December 8, 1919.

—Petitioned and received the orders in Palestine Commandery No. 17, Knights Templar of Independence, June 7 and 15, 1923. This was the Commandery of his father-in-law, David W. Wallace, who was Grand Commander of the Grand Commandery, K.T. of Missouri in 1891–92.

—Became a member of Ararat Shrine Temple, Kansas City, April 2, 1917. Served as Orator, Marshal and Second Ceremonial Master before resigning from the line in 1934 following election to U.S. Senate.

—Appointed District Deputy Grand Master and District Deputy Grand Lecturer of the ten lodges in the 59th Masonic District in 1925 and served both offices until September of 1930.

—Appointed Grand Pursuivant in the advancing Grand Lodge line at the 110th annual communication of Grand Lodge held in Kansas City's Ivanhoe Temple, September 30–October 2, 1930.

—Made a Royal Jester, Kansas City Court No. 54, Royal Order of Jesters, December 18, 1931.

—Elected and installed Grand Master, September 24–25, 1940, during the 120th annual communication of Grand Lodge, held in St. Louis.

—Initiated Kallipolis Grotto, Mystic Order, Veiled Prophets of Enchanted Realm, Washington, D.C., May 27, 1943.

—First President of United States Coroneted honorary 33° of Scottish Rite, Southern Jurisdiction, October 19, 1945.

—Installed as member of Mary Conclave No. 5, Red Cross of Constantine, Kansas City, December 26, 1945, at next door home of lifelong friend and neighbor, Nathanial D. Jackson in Independence.

—September, 1947, made an emeritus member, Northern Supreme Council, Scottish Rite.

Past Grand Master TRUMAN received his 50-year pin from the Grand Lodge of Missouri in ceremonies at Kansas City's Ivanhoe Temple on March 18, 1959. It

was a tiled meeting in the auditorium and a capacity audience of more than 2,000 Masons was in attendance.

He also was a 50-year, plus, member of the Scottish Rite, the York Rite's Chapter of Royal Arch Masons, the Council of Royal and Select Masters. Ararat Shrine, and would have been eligible this June 15 for the same honor in the Knights Templar.

A member of the National Sojourners, TRUMAN for a number of years was a member of the Committee on Co-operation with the various Grand Lodges.

TRUMAN also was the Grand Representative of South Carolina to Missouri for a number of years and later the Grand Representative of Scotland and Israel.

While President he was Honorary Grand Master of the Order of DeMolay and Chairman of the Welfare Advisory Committee of the Masonic Service Association.

He was an Honorary Past Grand Master of Tennessee and Honorary Member of the Grand Lodge of Kentucky.

While in the White House and afterward in retirement, TRUMAN received numerous Masonic awards and commissions from throughout the world. Space does not allow a complete listing.

A Washington correspondent wrote in a book called *The Missouri Compromise,* that the White House under President TRUMAN "settled down to the pleasant atmosphere of a small town hotel. Many of the boys in the press room were won over to this friendly democratic man. He treated the correspondents like fellow Masons."

Hon. Wayne L. Hays
OF OHIO

Mr. Speaker, today we mourn the passing of one of the greatest patriots ever to lead this Nation. I always consider my service in this House as one of proud privilege, especially as I recall that it had its beginning under such a distinguished President—HARRY S TRUMAN. My fondest memories of him are highlighted by his tremendous qualities in taking our great country from its years of victory during World War II through the years of reconstruction in the trying historical postwar period.

Ever a bold and daring man, he was always in advance of public opinion. As a matter of fact, he never hesitated to antagonize sectors of public opinion, and always with a valor and vigor unequaled. Usually political leaders ascertain the current and drift of public sentiment and accommodate themselves accordingly. Not so with this noble Missourian. He formed his own opinions and acted on his own convictions.

Opposition, so far from weakening his resolves, only nerved him for whatever effort was necessary to the accomplishment of his purpose. His greatness came from his ability to mold public sentiment. Always ready to defend his views, no one ever witnessed him avoiding any service required by his fidelity to duty. The victims overthrown by his power and logic are legion. Many of them who were impaled by his wit, irony, and sarcasm, like himself, have gone to their reward. Others remain, retaining a lively recollection of "Give 'em Hell, HARRY." While he was at times severe, and the intensity of political excitement wounded the feelings of friends; nonetheless he was, at heart, an eminently kind, generous, and forgiving man.

The history of his public life is before the world; his name and fame are part of the possession of the people. While free government endures, HARRY TRUMAN will be remembered with honor, and his services in the maintenance of free government will be recalled with gratitude forever. In a long career of devoted political leadership, this illustrious and discerning statesman has advanced the interests of our country and all friendly countries with faithfulness and distinction.

Mr. Speaker, I came to Congress on Mr. TRUMAN's coattails. As I came to know him I came to admire him. One of my proudest memories will always be that I could call him friend.

Hon. Fred B. Rooney
OF PENNSYLVANIA

Mr. Speaker, no greater tribute can be paid to the late President HARRY S TRUMAN than to acknowledge that he was a man of the people and that he did all he could for them. Knowing that he was serving the people to the best of his ability was his greatest source of strength and pride.

We can all certainly agree that while he was among us he was a man of action who sought peace with his own conscience rather than with the popularity polls. How refreshing is the memory of the sign on his White House desk, "The Buck Stops Here."

Besides his very individual style, which will always be an important part of the folklore of the politics of this country, the substance of his public career has also left an important mark.

He rose swiftly up the political ladder to the Senate where he achieved national prominence as chairman of a special committee investigating waste in military spending. Although he fought to stay off the Democratic ticket in 1944 he finally agreed to leave the Senate for the Vice Presidency, although he felt he could no longer be a man of action in that office. As fate would have it, however, HARRY S TRUMAN was to be President within 3 months of Inauguration Day.

Although he was always a controversial figure, there was never any question that he had the courage to make some monumental decisions. During the years of his Presidency were formulated the foreign policy programs which have shaped the whole postwar world—the Truman doctrine, massive foreign aid in the form of the Marshall plan, the ratification of the United Nations Charter, and the signing of the NATO and other mutual security treaties.

On the domestic front, although Congress was not as responsive to his initiatives as it was to those on the foreign scene, he laid the groundwork for later legislation in the field of civil rights, housing, health, education, and social welfare. In fact, his forthright stand on civil rights was one of the factors which led to the confident predictions of the pollsters that Dewey would defeat him in a landslide in 1948. Although he left the Presidency in the shadow of a much more popular successor, historians have already ranked him as a near-great President—honest, courageous, and effective.

President TRUMAN had a full and rewarding life. May his wife and daughter be sustained by the knowledge that he served his country with exceptional effectiveness at a time of great crisis.

Hon. Wm. J. Randall
OF MISSOURI

Mr. Speaker, as our work in preparation for the publication of the Truman memorial volume nears its conclusion, some well deserved acknowledgments are in order. May I suggest words of some gratitude are long overdue.

My attention has recently been directed to the fact that in all of the entries preserved in the Congressional Record for publication in the memorial volume, there has been until now a neglect and an omission to take note of and commend those who planned and put into execution what is known as Oplan Missouri, being the funeral operation to conduct the state funeral of former President HARRY S TRUMAN.

Because I was privileged to be present during the days immediately preceding the funeral and also honored to be included as one present for the funeral service in the auditorium of the Truman Library, it is my good fortune to report that the entire funeral plan was executed to perfection. Substantial numbers of military personnel were involved.

The major ceremonial and support elements of Oplan Missouri came from Fort Leavenworth, Kans., Fort Riley, Kans., Fort Leonard Wood, Mo., and Missouri National Guard and from the other services including the Navy, Air Force, Marine Corps, and the Coast Guard.

Fort Leavenworth furnished a total of 450 men including 210 officers, 236 enlisted men, and 4 civilians. All of the escort officers were from the Command and General Staff School of Fort Leavenworth, Kans. In the total were included 39 officers and 164 enlisted men who manned the funeral operations center. The remainder of those from Fort Leavenworth were drivers, military police, and members of the floral detail.

Fort Riley furnished 2,132 personnel including 92 officers, 2,022 enlisted men, and 18 civilians. The great bulk of this personnel were support troops that were used as ushers, military police, drivers, medical, and mess personnel. There were 204 ceremonial troops in the band.

Fort Leonard Wood furnished 156 enlisted men that worked in the facility control and served as drivers. The Missouri National Guard furnished 289 men serving in a security cordon at the funeral home and who also served as state liaison personnel.

The U.S. Navy furnished 203 men, mostly reserves. The U.S. Air Force sent 371 men. The U.S. Marine Corps provided 341 men and the U.S. Coast Guard detailed 79 men.

While the general direction of Oplan Missouri was under headquarters 5th U.S. Army of Fort Sam Houston, Tex., it should be pointed out that some key personnel came from headquarters U.S. Army, Military District of Washington—MDW—including Maj. Gen. James B. Adamson, who is responsible for planning and arranging of state funerals through the continental United States. Also participating was Lt. Col. Paul C. Miller, the director of ceremonial and support events of the Military District of Washington who could properly be described as the original planner and executor of the entire Truman plan which later assumed the code name, Oplan Missouri.

Information furnished by the 5th Army revealed that the commanding general of Oplan

Missouri, also in command of the funeral operations center and in addition serving as commander of all escorts was Lt. Gen. Patrick F. Cassidy.

In my judgment the record would not be complete without noting the commander of all Army troops who was Col. Gustau J. Gillert, Jr., USA. The commanding officer of the Marine Corps element was 1st Lt. William V. Fello, USMC. The commanding officer of the Navy element was Lt. Michael E. Munjak, USNR. The commanding officer of the U.S. Air Force element was Maj. Clarence R. Smith, USAF, and the commanding officer of the U.S. Coast Guard element was Lt. Comdr. E. R. Williams, USCG.

All of the personnel working under Oplan Missouri deserve high commendation for a job well done. The entire operation moved ahead, perfectly timed, with a smooth precision that revealed much thoughtful planning and an equally excellent execution of the plan.

Mr. Speaker, as we continue to assemble the complete record of the order of service and participants in the state funeral of former President Harry S Truman at Independence, Mo., it seems fitting and proper there should be a listing in the Congressional Record as a matter of history and then to be included in the Truman Memorial volume, the names of all the military personnel who served as escort officers.

Headquarters of the 5th Army at Fort Sam Houston, Tex., has furnished our office with a list of all of the escort officers. All of these were in attendance at the Command and General Staff School of Fort Leavenworth, Kans. Mrs. Truman was escorted by Col. Royal S. Brown and Mrs. Margaret Truman Daniel's escort was Maj. J. L. Buckner.

It is my privilege to include the names of all of the escort officers utilized under Oplan Missouri listed alphabetically and followed by the names of the guests they were assigned to escort either in the days preceeding the funeral or during the day of the funeral service. The escorts are listed herewith:

ESCORT OFFICERS—OPLAN MISSOURI

Captain Ralph L. Allen escort for Corpsman Scott Boehm; Corpsman Jerry Crunk; Corpsman Charles Rowe; Corpsman William Wagner, Captain Raymond R. Andrae escort for Mr. Lucian L. Lucas. Major William R. Andrews, Jr. escort for Mr. Charles Murphy. Major Wesley B. Avery escort for Hon. Floyd L. Snyder. Captain Leo J. Asselin escort for Mrs. Bessie Taylor. Major Joseph W.

Bagnerise escort for Mr. Joseph L. Lavery, Major Wardell G. Baker escort for Mr. Frank G. Hoffman, Major Robert A. Bates escort for Mrs. D. A. Luckey; Mrs. Kestin. Major Ralph A. Barkman, Jr. escort for Hon. David A. Stowe. Captain Richard E. Beale, Jr. escort for Mr. Frederick J. Bowman; Mr. Floyd T. Ricketts. Major Clarence G. Berk escort for Mrs. Arletta Brown; Mrs. Geraldine Peterson; Rev. Edward E. Hobby, Major Burton G. Rice escort for Hon. and Mrs. Thomas H. Benton. Major Garland G. Bishop escort for Ambassador Averill Harriman. Major Garland G. Bishop escort for Hon. Clark Clifford. Major Lowell D. Bittrich escort for Mr. Sam Hipsh. Lt. Colonel Robert G. Black escort for Mr. John L. Gordon. Major James H. Bledsoe escort for Mr. C. J. Sampson. Major Kenneth H. Boyer escort for Hon. and Mrs. Robert P. Weatherford. Major Carter H. Brantner escort for Mrs. Harold Balfour; Mrs. Oscar King; Miss Eleanor Minor; Miss Grace Minor; Miss Margaret Woodson.

Captain Victor A. Brown escort for Mr. and Mrs. Robert Sanders, Major Richard A. Buckner escort for Mr. Frank Yeager. Major E. J. Burke escort for State Rep Wall (Rep Gov of LA). Major James E. Burns escort for Mr. F. L. Howard. Major Kenneth R. Buyle escort for Prof. Francis H. Heller. Major Ruben A. Candia escort for Mr. William Coleman Branton. Major Jeff E. Chancey escort for Mr. and Mrs. John T. Southern. Major Hilbert H. Chole escort for Mrs. John H. Lembcke. Lt. Colonel Allan R. Coates, Jr. escort for Dr. and Mrs. Benedict K. Zobrist, Major George G. Collins escort for Hon. and Mrs. Richard M. Duncan. Major David C. Conners escort for Mr. M. R. Evans. Major Joseph C. Conrad escort for Mrs. William Pesek, Major Nelson J. Cooper escort for Hon. John Snyder. Major Joseph W. Corder, Jr. escort for Miss Mary Jo Nick. Major James H. Cowles escort for Mr. Harry Groff. Major Carl L. Cramer escort for Mr. Lorain Cunningham. Major Arthur N. Crowell escort for Mrs. Harry Clarke, Jr. Major Dennis J. Crowley escort for Mrs. Guri Lie Zeckendorf; and Miss Rita Gam. Major W. F. Daly escort for Mrs. James Costin. Major John W. Dargle escort for Miss Molly Sullivan. Major James R. Daughtery escort for Senator Thomas Eagleton. Major Max A. Davison escort for Miss Solveig Simonsen. Major Richard P. Diehl escort for Mr. David E. Bell. Major Edmund J. Dolan, Jr., escort for Mr. Edgar A. Hindle, Sr. and Mr. and Mrs. Edgar A. Hindle, Jr. LCdr Philip F. Duffy, USN escort for RADM Draper Kauffman, USN. Major Douglas E. Emery escort for Hon. Henry A. Bundschu. Major Richard Erickson escort for Mr. Kenneth V. Bostian.

Major Joe B. Foster escort for Hon. Edwin Locke, Jr. Major Dwight H. Fuller escort for Mr. Wallace Smith. Major Jan P. Gardiner escort for Mr. Thomas Gavin. Major Darrold D. Garrison escort for Mr. Milton Perry. Major Emroy M. Gehlsen escort for Mr. Dennis Bilger. Captain James D. George escort for Mr. Henry Talge. Major Walter R. Good escort for Mr. Thomas J. Fleming. Major John F. Grecco escort for Mr. F. G. McGowan. Major Robert P. Greene escort for Sen. and Mrs. Hubert H. Humphrey. Major Thermon R. Greene escort for Mr. N. T. Veatch. Major James H. Griffin escort for Mr. and Mrs. John Spottswood. Major Terry J. Guess, USAF escort for Maj. Gen. Clare T. Ireland, Jr. Major Argie E. Haddock escort for Mr. Warren Ohrvall. Major Henry

H. Hair, III escort for Dr. and Mrs. Wilson Miller. Major James J. Hallihan, Jr. escort for Mr. Fred L. Younker. Major Michael Hansen escort for Mr. Robert Cress. Major Thomas M. Hanson escort for Mr. Erwin J. Mueller. Major Richard W. Haulser escort for Hon. Christopher Bond. Captain Lee L. Hayden, III escort for Mr. Charles L. Frederick. Major Ashton M. Haynes, Jr. escort for Miss Susan C. Staley. Lt. Col. John P. Heilman escort for Col. and Mrs. Corbie Truman. Major Charles W. Hendrickson escort for Mr. David D. Bridges. Major Charles R. Henry escort for Mr. Michael Flynn. Major Wayne L. Herr escort for Mrs. Keith Dancy. Major Maurice G. Hilliard escort for Mr. and Mrs. Louis Compton. Major James L. Hill escort for Dr. Elmer Ellis. Major Ashley R. Hodge escort for Mr. Joseph McGee, Jr. Major Warren F. Hodge escort for Hon. Roe Bartle. Major Harold E. Hoitt escort for Mr. James Fuchs. Major Jerry V. Holcombe escort for Mr. Edward Ingram. Major William R. Holmes escort for Dr. Bert Maybee. Major George A. Hooker escort for Dr. Javier Baz. Major Henry R. Hosman escort for Mrs. Gates Wells.

Major Martin R. Hurwitz escort for Mrs. Andrew Grey. Major A. T. Jennette escort for Sg. Wm. Story (Ret.). Major Dean C. Jones escort for Mr. and Mrs. Roy T. Romine. Major Jesse F. Jones, III escort for Mr. and Mrs. Randall Jessee. Major Wm. W. Jones, Jr., escort for Hon. and Mrs. Robert B. Docking. Major Josef C. Jordan, Jr. escort for Mr. and Mrs. Mike Westwood and Mr. Michael Manners. Major Robert J. Kee escort for Mr. F. Weidenman. Major Donald R. Kelsey escort for Mr. and Mrs. John K. Barrow, Jr. Captain Arnold E. Kendall escort for Mr. John H. Martino. Major John L. Kendall escort for Miss Rita Gam. Major John L. Kennedy escort for Mr. Archie Renadll. Major Thomas R. King escort for Hon. and Mrs. Samuel I. Rosenham. Major Wm. K. Kuhn, Jr. escort for Mr. Joyce P. Hall and Mr. Arthur Mag. Major Richard R. Kurtz escort for Miss Patrice Carter. Major Ralph H. Lauder and Major Lynn F. Coleman escorts for Mr. and Mrs. J. C. Truman; Mr. and Mrs. Fred Truman; Mr. and Mrs. Harry A. Truman; Mr. and Mrs. Gilbert Truman and Mr. and Mrs. James Swoyer, Jr.

Lt. Col. John H. Leach, Jr. escort for Mrs. Albert Ridge. Major Robert Letchwroth escort for Dr. and Mrs. Robert E. Bruner. Major Frank V. Lindstrom escort for Mrs. Louis Schlichenmaier. Major John Little escort for Hon. Clark Clifford. Major J. C. Lucas escort for Mr. Edgar Hinde, Sr. Major Wm. A. Luther, Jr. escort for Mrs. Edgar Carroll. Major Dell V. McDonald, USAF escort for Maj. Gen. Robert B. Landry. Major Robert E. McGough escort for Former President Lyndon B. Johnson. Major Thomas I. McKinstry escort for Gen. Donal Dawson (Ret.) Major Joseph R. Maio escort for Mrs. C. H. Allen and Mrs. Anne Smith. Captain Donald L. Meek escort for Mrs. Eddie Jacobson. Major John Mentor escort for RADM Walter Dedrick. Major Donald G. Mitchell escort for Mrs. Frances Nicks. LCDR Richard Montana, USN escort for RADM Owen Siler. Major Billy F. Moore escort for Mr. W. Hugh McLaughlin. Major H. J. Moot escort for Mr. Edward Stuart. Major James W. Morgart escort for Mr. James W. Porter. Major James O. Morton escort for Hon. Harry E. Whitney. Major Wm. B. Murray escort for Mr. Edward Condon. Major Pedro Najer escort for Hon. Ilus Davis.

Major George L. Nipper escort for Mrs. Benjamin Sosland. Captain Robert M. O'Donnell escort for Maj. Gen. Wallace Graham. Major William G. Pagonis escort for Hon. and Mrs. Wm. J. Randall. Major Howard S. Paris escort for Mr. Eugene P. Donnelly. Major William O. Perry, Jr. escort for Mrs. Tom Twyman. Major Humphrey L. Peterson, Jr. escort for Mr. Raymond J. Smith. Major David R. Porch escort for Mr. & Mrs. Howard Greene. Major Yancy S. Ramsey escort for Mrs. H. H. Haukenberry, Major Harry G. Rennagel escort for Hon. and Mrs. Phillip D. Lagerquist, Major Carlton F. Roberson escort for Mr. and Mrs. Edwin Pauley. Major Walter G. Robertson escort for Mr. Charles Hipsh. Major Charles D. Robinson escort for Mr. Robert E. Adams. Major John R. Robinson, Jr. escort for Mrs. Alex Sachs. Major Rovert B. Rosenkranz escort for Hon. Joseph Bolger, Jr. Major Richard H. Ross escort for Mrs. Sam E. Roberts. Major Terry N. Rosser escort for Miss Sue Gentry. Major Tarey B. Schell escort for Mrs. Ralph E. Truman. Major William J. Silvey escort for Mrs. Paul Burns. Major Robert L. Sloane escort for Mrs. Lyndon B. Johnson. Major Keith Sovine escort for Mr. McKinley Wooden. Major Harold D. Stanford escort for Mrs. Jess Donaldson. Major Charles D. Stephens escort for Mr. Edward Meisburger. Major John D. Sterrett, III escort for Mr. Jacob M. Arvey. Major Gary N. Stiles escort for Ambassador Stanley Woodward. Major Wilbert Stitt, Jr. escort for Mr. Arthur Mag and Mr. Joyce Hall. Major Donald A. Tapscott escort for Lt. Gen. Louis W. Truman (Ret.). Major Benjamin D. Taylor escort for Hon. John Snyder and Mr. and Mrs. John Horton. Captain R. H. Terrell escort for Mrs. Roy Hornbuckle. Major Richard H. Timpf escort for Mr. and Mrs. George Miller. Major Lawrence L. Tracy escort for Hon. Thomas R. Finlatter. Major Ronald A. Tumelson escort for Maj. Gen. Harry Vaughn (Ret.). Major Robert W. Turner escort for Mr. Gordon B. Jordan. Major Douglas E. Wade escort for Agent Hutch (Secret Service). Major Arlen B. Wahlberg escort for Hon. Warren Hearnes. Major Vaden K. Watson escort for Mrs. E. C. Crow. Major Ralph P. Weber escort for Hon. and Mrs. Darby. Major Robert A. White escort for Mrs. Vieta Garr.

Major Travis W. White escort for Miss Rose Conway and Mrs. Margaret Kurt. Major Gerald P. Williams escort for Mr. W. E. Tierny. Major Robert M. Wolfe escort for Mr. Frank E. McKinney. Major Andrew D. Woods, Jr. escort for Mr. Ralph Taylor. Major Danny A. Young escort for Mr. Ralph Thacker. Major William T. Zaldo, III escort for Former President Lyndon B. Johnson.

The commander of all escorts was Lt. Gen. Patrick F. Cassidy, U.S. Army, who also had the general direction of all major ceremonial and support elements of Oplan Missouri. Under General Cassidy's command was the National Color Guard; Presidential Color Guard; a firing party; the Casket Team; the Joint Guard of Honor, death watch; the Joint Honor Cordon, library steps; and the Joint Body Bearers.

Everyone of those who participated deserve to be cited for a perfectly executed plan, first at the funeral home, then on the line of march and finally at the Truman Library. All military personnel who participated earned the high homage and the compliments of all observers. They all deserve our praise and acclaim for a well-prepared plan of operation carried out with perfect precision.

Memorial Tributes

IN THE

Senate of the United States

IN EULOGY OF

Harry S Truman

In the Senate of the United States

JANUARY 4, 1973

The Chaplain, the Reverend Edward L. R. Elson, D.D., offered the following prayer:

Eternal Father, as we undertake the tasks of this day, gratefully we remember before Thee Thy servant, HARRY S TRUMAN. We thank Thee for his long and distinguished service as a Member of this body, for his high leadership as President of the Republic, for his wisdom and courage in difficult decisions, for his efforts to make and conserve the peace of the world, for his devotion to freedom and justice for all, and for his manly qualities which endeared him to so many. May some portion of the dedication which was his come upon us.

As we offer a memorial for a past President, we pray also for the present President that he may be given grace, wisdom, and strength for the burdens of this age.

We lift up to Thee the Members of this body into whose lives sorrow has so recently come. Grant to them the assurance of our brotherly sympathy and the grace, comfort, and strength of Thy pervading presence.

In the name of Him who is the resurrection and the life. Amen.

Mr. Mansfield. Mr. President, on behalf of the distinguished Republican leader and myself, I wish to make the following announcement:

The memorial service in honor of the late President HARRY S TRUMAN will be held Friday, January 5, 1973, at 11 a.m. in the Washington National Cathedral.

Buses will depart, under escort, from the Senate steps of the Capitol at 10:15 a.m. and return to the Capitol immediately after the services. Those using private transportation are advised to enter the Cathedral grounds from Woodley Road and proceed to the south transept entrance.

Members and their wives are invited. Contact the Office of the Sergeant at Arms for tickets and transportation arrangements.

Members of the Senate delegation are scheduled to be seated in the Cathedral at 10:45 a.m.

Hon. Hugh Scott
OF PENNSYLVANIA

Mr. President, as we pay tribute to former President HARRY S TRUMAN, with whom many of us served, we recall that this was a very strong man. He made difficult decisions. He served in time of war and in time of peace. As the leader of our Nation, he did not hesitate to be strong when strength was necessary. He did what had to be done in the national interest. He did it strongly. He did it notwithstanding the criticism offered against him. He moved sturdily and steadily ahead with his purposes.

He brought about a situation which enabled the succeeding President to end a difficult war. He used the most powerful weapon available in the history of mankind, with what reluctance no one will ever know. But he did it.

The Nation honors that kind of strength, as in time they will honor the strength of every President who dares to do what he thinks is right against the second guessing of the clamorous critics.

Elizabeth Barrett Browning once wrote:

> Happy are all free peoples,
>   Too strong to be dispossessed.
> But blessed are they among nations,
>   Who dare to be strong for the rest.

Mr. President, that has been the role of the United States—sometimes, we think, too much.

93

It has been the role of the United States, at times, as in the Marshall plan, to dare to be strong for the rest.

As TRUMAN, in using the Marshall plan, held great sectors of the world free from tyranny and aggression, as Eisenhower, in the landings at Lebanon, effected the same results in maintaining the stability of the Middle East, so must each President in the loneliness of his responsibilities make these strong and difficult decisions.

I believe that Congress, concerned as it is now with its prerogatives, will need to remember that there is something more important than prerogative, something more important than protocol, something more important than headlines—and that is the security of the United States.

We customarily extend broad trust to a President in the course of the protection of the Nation. It tries our souls and stretches our patience at times when we feel that we do not know all we would like to know. It raises the question more than once that the Senate may have obligations as well.

Mr. President, in the long run, the country has found that the actions of strong Presidents, courageously taken, are apt to be ratified not only by the public through the expression of its opinion, but also that such actions may well be writ large on the history books.

So that I hope, as we enter this session and extend our mutual benisons or blessings one to another, we will at least temper our language to the point where reason may prevail and we may be able to reason together as Isaiah commands us, and as would be the course of wisdom.

So, Mr. President, I pay my tribute to HARRY S TRUMAN—strong man, brave man, zealous man. earthy man—and a good man.

We will all miss him.

Hon. Jacob K. Javits
OF NEW YORK

Mr. President, I knew President TRUMAN very well. I join Senator Scott in his tribute, and I also add the following:

I have rarely seen a President who was better briefed than was President TRUMAN and who had a deeper perception of the ultimate interests of the United States and the world in terms of peace. I saw him with particularity deal with the affairs

of Germany at a time when it was possible to take a very limited view, such as the one described as the Morgenthau plan, which would have made Germany pastoral, or a very broad view which simply would have forgotten the past and might again have led Germany into some ultra nationalistic fervor.

President TRUMAN did neither, but approached the problems of Germany with the idea of integrating Germany into a new, united Europe, the whole thrust of the Marshall plan, and it turned out to be one of the most statesmanlike acts of the career of any President.

Also, Mr. President, I have had the honor and pleasure of knowing intimately Mrs. Daniel, his daughter, and her husband; and I have reflected with them many times upon the statesmanship, the humanity, the common decency, the sense of justice, and the enormous reservoirs of information of this man, who had a limited formal education, but became one of the truly outstanding Presidents of the United States and one of the outstanding statesmen of the world.

I join my colleagues in expressing my tribute and memorial to this distinguished man and distinguished President.

Hon. Clifford P. Hansen
OF WYOMING

Mr. President, from the sorrow of the passing of President TRUMAN and the command of events to examine his life and contributions, there should also come a greater willingness to question our own judgments and conclusions.

No one likely soon will know how history will evaluate the wisdom of President Nixon's courageous determination to do what he believes is right.

But as one Member of this body whose age exceeds the average and who can recall the anguish World War II visited upon millions of Americans and whose memory is still fresh with the resolve of those who gave birth to the United Nations hoping that a better way could be found than to fight yet another world war, I believe history will vindicate the actions and applaud the judgment of President Nixon.

In looking back over the long sweep of history, Vermont Royster may give us the perspective we so desperately need now as we earnestly search our consciences and experiences in trying to choose the right course ahead.

I ask unanimous consent that Mr. Royster's column from the Wall Street Journal, "Presidents and History," be printed in the Record.

PRESIDENTS AND HISTORY

(By Vermont Royster)

As President Nixon ends one term and begins another, it's interesting to reflect on the difference between how we judge Presidents while they are in office and how history judges them. For, as HARRY TRUMAN has just reminded us, history often alters the judgment.

Warren Harding would have to be put down as one of our most popular Presidents, even though then there were no Gallup Polls to take the public pulse. Harding was handsome, of commanding presence. He had been elected by a landslide, and when he died crowds lined the route of his funeral train as sorrowingly as they later did for Franklin Roosevelt. Then came all those scandals, and in history his name is tarnished.

On the other hand HARRY TRUMAN's reputation has been enhanced by time. He barely got elected to his second term—he was perennially in political hot water. You'd have to put him down among the less popular Presidents of the century while he was in office.

Yet by the time he died even his political foes recognized him as a President who had led his country through some parlous times, who had come at least near to greatness. This was not because history had erased any of his record; it was because time had altered the relative importance of things.

Some of the things that made HARRY TRUMAN controversial seem trivial in retrospect; his irate letters to music critics, for example, or his verbal tempers and blunders. From other mistakes that could have counted heavily against him he was rescued by circumstance. His attempt to draft railroad workers into the Army failed (with the help, ironically, of Senator Taft); his high-handed seizure of the steel industry was overruled by the Supreme Court. Bad they might have been, but in the end they sit on the record only as might-have-beens.

What are remembered now are the Marshall Plan which resuscitated a war-torn Europe, the Truman Doctrine which checked the easy postwar Communist expansion, the creation of NATO, the decision to stand at Berlin and the decision to fight in Korea. All these too were controversial in their day, but history has decided that in these instances President TRUMAN was right.

An awareness of this effect of time must haunt every President who has a regard for something more than the popularity of the moment. HARRY TRUMAN would surely have been more popular in his day if he had not decided one Sunday evening to send American soldiers to fight in Korea, and he could not have known then which way the verdict of history would go. So whatever you think of his judgment, you can't fault HARRY TRUMAN's courage.

Anyway, the alterations of time on the reputation of Presidents must haunt Richard Nixon. Although he was reelected by a landslide, popular has never been quite the word for Mr. Nixon, and he has never been far from controversy. Many of those controversies will fade with time; who a generation hence will care about the Checkers

speech or even the Watergate affair? The things that will count in history will be the one or two things that count most for the country.

Foremost among them will be Vietnam. Mr. Nixon is the third President to have to deal with that particular war. Beyond that, the fifth President since World War I to have to answer that agonizing question, What is worth fighting for? TRUMAN faced it in Berlin and Korea; Eisenhower in the Middle East; Kennedy in Cuba; Kennedy, Johnson and now Nixon in Vietnam. Each time it has been posed in such a way that there is no easy answer for the man who must answer.

For of course it is quite simple to avoid war or end a war, if that is all that matters. The Vietnam war could have been avoided entirely by letting South Vietnam be conquered. It could have been ended at any time these past ten years by accepting North Vietnamese terms; Mr. Nixon's critics are quite correct that he could have had peace this Christmas by signing the October cease-fire draft.

Unhappily, though, the real question is: Is that all that matters? Would the world be a better place if HARRY TRUMAN had not stood at Berlin, fought in Korea? If John Kennedy had not risked a nuclear holocaust to face down the Russians in Cuba? If Richard Nixon had given the country peace by Christmas?

Even those who would answer that last question differently from President Nixon, who truly believe nothing is worth the price of that terrible bombing, must note one thing. With Lyndon Johnson's political experience before him as an example, Mr. Nixon knew the political price he would have to pay when he first adopted his tough stance, when he counterattacked in Cambodia, when he mined Haiphong, when he began bombing North Vietnam proper.

He must have been even more acutely aware of world reaction when, after the election, the peace that seemed at hand receded and he resumed the bombing. Mr. Nixon, whatever else he is, is not politically naive. Yet he did those things anyway because, for his own reason, he thought them the right thing to do. So you have to give him credit for political courage.

For the rest, as Mr. Nixon well knows, we will have to await the judgment of time. There is little doubt any longer that his earlier policy of mixing a willingness to negotiate with a military toughness succeeded; it was this that brought the North Vietnamese to their first serious negotiations. There is not much doubt, either, that what disrupted that negotiation when peace was tantalizingly near was the willingness of Hanoi to test again the President's resolve.

The resumption of the bombing answered that test. What is left unresolved is the wisdom of the judgment. His judgment is that peace alone is not enough if it's a spurious peace, that toughness now—as in the past—will bring Hanoi back to the negotiating table, that the gamble is worth the prize. The gamble won means a more durable peace, the gamble lost means an enduring war.

What makes it all so terrible is that neither he nor you nor I can know now whether his course has been right, yet he, like other Presidents before him, has the burden of deciding without knowing. The rest of us can only be cautious in our judgments.

If his course was wrong, as President Lincoln said on another occasion, ten angels swearing it right will make no difference. If the end brings President Nixon out right, then what is said against him now won't amount to anything. And history alone will show which is which.

Hon. Edmund S. Muskie

OF MAINE

Mr. President, I know I speak with Senators on both sides of the aisle in expressing deep sadness over the death last week of President TRUMAN, one of the truly great statesmen of our time and a man revered and liked by all Americans.

HARRY S TRUMAN was an uncomplicated man—a plain-talking, unaffected man faced with some of the most complex problems of 20th century America. He met the problems head on, developing in the process a foreign policy which still shapes America's thinking abroad, and offering a domestic program which formed the basis for progressive legislation in the postwar era.

TRUMAN served ably and effectively in this body for 10 years—gaining stature as a watchdog over wastefulness in military spending. He did not seek the Vice Presidency, and when he was nominated and then elected, he mourned:

I was getting along fine until I stuck my neck out too far and got too famous—and then they made me V.P. and now I can't do anything.

Eighty-three days later, with the death of Franklin Roosevelt, HARRY TRUMAN was President of the United States. He said:

I felt like the moon, the stars and all the planets had fallen on me.

But although he assumed the Presidency with the barest of preparation, President TRUMAN immediately established a pattern of courage, directness of judgment, decisiveness, and self-confidence that became hallmarks of the Truman Presidency.

When Russia, our ally, became our adversary in the cold war, TRUMAN found a simple solution—to make our World War II enemies our allies. In those tense, sometimes terrifying postwar days, TRUMAN made the decision to develop the hydrogen bomb, broke the Soviet blockade of Berlin, laid out the Truman doctrine to meet a Soviet threat in the Middle East, formed the North Atlantic Treaty Organization to present a solid front in Europe, and through the Marshall plan helped avoid an economic collapse in Europe.

His tough, no-nonsense approach to foreign affairs has had many critics, but the economic strength of Europe in the 1970's and the rapprochement with Soviet Russia may have proved TRUMAN right.

TRUMAN is better known for his foreign policy decisions, but in domestic affairs he proposed major civil rights, labor and social welfare legislation, began desegregating the Armed Forces by Executive order, and committed the Federal Government to a policy of high employment and a strong economy. And while he lost most of his legislative battles, the theme he sounded was picked up again in the 1960's.

What do these ideas and accomplishments tell us about the man? He was a man of conviction, and he was willing to stand by his convictions, whatever the pressures to change them.

He demonstrated an understanding of the uses and limitations of military and political power which has scarcely been equaled since his administration. He knew the effectiveness of military strength to prevent aggression. And, more importantly, he knew the limitations of military strength over conquered peoples.

In addition to his major accomplishments, HARRY TRUMAN possessed qualities which commanded the admiration of his supporters and the respect of his opponents. A fairminded, straightforward, honest man, HARRY TRUMAN acted with conviction and accepted full responsibility for his actions. He added a phrase to our language—"If you can't stand the heat, get out of the kitchen." And because of this same directness and strong sense of purpose, he was "Give-'em-hell HARRY" to millions of fond Americans. Here was a man who never quibbled and never stood on the sidelines waiting for events to determine his decisions or actions.

He gave me good counsel when I became a candidate for the Vice Presidency in 1968. When I asked for his advice during a visit in Independence, he said, "Tell the truth." When I replied that my way of telling the truth was not the same as his, he gave me a second piece of advice. "Be yourself," he said. Since then I have always tried to follow that advice.

America and he world owe much to HARRY TRUMAN—the man who never lost touch with the man on the street and never forgot his Missouri roots. He was a great President and a strong, but compassionate man who directed America's energies into creative and constructive channels. In times of stress and anxiety he never faltered, never failed the American people. He served her well and brought honor to the office of the Presidency. He bravely led America into her new role of responsibility within the world community.

We shall all miss his quick wit, his disarming humility, and his deep and abiding faith in the intelligence of the American people. We must never forget what he stood for and loved: honesty, integrity, strength, and freedom.

When it was over, TRUMAN himself summed it up better than we can, and provided history with a most fitting epitaph. He said:

> I have tried my best to give the Nation everything I had in me. There are probably a million people who could have done the job better than I did it, but I had the job, and I always quote an epitaph in a cemetery in Tombstone, Ariz.: "Here lies Jack Williams. He done his damndest."

Mr. President, I request at this time that the full text of my remarks at the Harry S Truman Institute April 7, 1970, be included in the Record.

PRESIDENT TRUMAN—25 YEARS AFTER

When Dean Heller invited me to speak, today, he asked that I "talk from the viewpoint . . . of a public figure active today." I accept the compliment, because I hope those who doubt my public existence and question my activity will experience the same sense of wonder which came to Mr. Kaltenborn in 1948.

It is always an honor to be invited to pay tribute to one's heroes. I confess to my admiration for President TRUMAN, but I would not want you to think that I am wholly uncritical of his record. I think he set a bad precedent when he made presidential piano playing respectable.

Years ago, an out-of-stater struck up a conversation with an elderly native—an octogenarian—in one of our lovely little Maine towns. "I suppose you have lived in this town all your life?" he inquired. The old man replied, "Not yet!"

In the same spirit this group gathers here in Independence each year—

To pay tribute;

To draw inspiration; and

To give continuity to those values, and qualities, and principles which are the mark of greatness in a man, and his community, and his country.

I remember that one of my first political acts after becoming a Democratic National Committeeman from the State of Maine in 1952 was to defend President TRUMAN. The President had just visited the state, and had been subjected to an unwarranted and inhospitable attack by a Portland newspaper. I wrote a letter to the editor. The newspaper featured the letter and conceded, in an editorial, that it had been intemperate. I was pleased; the

newspaper editor felt virtuous and I am sure the President—if he was aware of the exchange—smiled with the knowledge that his history would be the final judge. Incidentally, it was also timely reassurance that a Democratic point of view, vigorously asserted, could be influential in Republican Maine

President TRUMAN is one of those fortunate public men who has lived to hear the vindication of history. And if he takes some pleasure in the knowledge that he confounded the doubters, we can rejoice with him.

Each of us comes to this occasion with his or her own memories of April 12, 1945, and the years which have followed. And each of us, I suspect, must confess to a change in perspective toward HARRY S TRUMAN and the Presidency since that date.

Today's observance affords a singular opportunity to use that perspective, as President TRUMAN would, to learn more about ourselves, our country, and the qualities the times require of us.

The world of that dark Thursday afternoon in 1945 was once caught between hope and chaos. The President to whom the nation and the world had looked for twelve years for leadership, was dead. A terrible world war was approaching its end, and in its wake we could see a world order far different from that we had known before. No longer were there several major powers in Europe. Both the victors and the vanquished had been decimated by the war. In Asia, Japan was defeated and China splintered. In the world there were now only two major powers—the United States and the Soviet Union—about to confront each other in a new type of war—a cold war, generated by Soviet dreams of expansion.

What would this mean—for man—and his hopes and dreams for a better world and a better life?

At home, a nation weary of war desired a speedy return to peace and the comforts war had denied us. A few saw the difficult problems of reconversion from a war economy to peace, but most were oblivious to the backlog of crisis the President would face at home.

What sort of man was this who would now preside over our effort to influence the shape of an uncertain and perilous future?

Much of his background was humble. He had been reared in a small town in middle America. He had no formal education beyond high school. He had worked as a timekeeper for a railroad, in the mail room of a newspaper, as a bank clerk, as a farmer. He had been a small businessman. a soldier and a county judge. He had experienced the rough and tumble of local and state politics, and risen through the ranks. At one phase of his development he might have been classed—if I may coin a phrase—as a member of the "Silent Majority."

And so there were questions about the quality of the new leadership in the White House.

Walter Lippmann comforted himself by writing that "The genius of a good leader is to leave behind him a situation which common sense, without the grace of genius, can deal with successfully." He was wrong, both with respect to the situation and the quality of the new President.

HARRY TRUMAN did have an average American background, but he was not an ordinary man. He had zest, vitality and energy that were the marvel of those with whom he worked. He had a rare capacity for decision and administration. He had the judgment to realize what principles in American life were worth preserving and the courage to fight for those principles.

His capacity for decision may be the most fabled of his attributes.

He made it clear—in a way which was never fully understood before by grassroots Americans—that the White House was primarily a place where decisions are made—tough, potentially final decisions which cannot be avoided and which carry awesome implications for life in our country and on our planet.

And our people understood—more clearly than before—that such decisions should be made by men of capacity, understanding, and courage—who understand that a President must lead his people in the direction indicated by their best instincts and traditions.

And they came to the realization that HARRY TRUMAN was such a President—and they have given him his place in history.

There followed the many bold—often spectacularly successful decisions of the Truman Era. Dean Acheson has described them:

"The 1947 assumption of responsibility in the Eastern Mediterranean, the 1948 Grandeur of the Marshall Plan, the response to the Blockade of Berlin, the NATO defense of Europe in 1949, and the intervention in Korea in 1950—all those constituted expanded action in truly heroic mold. All of them were dangerous. All of them required rare capacity to decide and act."

This was the leadership of a man who saw the world as it was—the need for new and unprecedented action—ranging far beyond any earlier concept of American responsibility in the world.

This man of ordinary background stepped out into the unknown—leading his people—unhesitatingly—clear-eyed—and wisely.

There have been a number of analyses of the TRUMAN decision-making process, Dean Acheson, for example, in his latest book, "Present at the Creation," credits much of the President's capacity for leadership and decision to two qualities. First of all, the President had, Mr. Acheson tells us, a magnificent vitality and energy that allowed him to assimilate and understand a prodigious amount of material. Secondly, he had a passion for orderly procedure and a superb administrative ability which had been nurtured by his experience in local government.

Acheson reports that the President employed a brand of the adversary process, adapted from the law, and that, in keeping with another venerable legal tradition, he reduced all major decisions to writing.

One of the most delightful accounts of TRUMAN's decision making process, however, came from Mr. TRUMAN himself, reportedly in a question and answer session at the University of Virginia in 1960.

The question from the floor was: "Mr. TRUMAN, how did you go about making a decision?"

Mr. TRUMAN's answer was reported as follows: "I asked the members of my staff concerned to submit their recommendations to me in writing. In the evening, I read the staff proposals. Then I went to bed and slept on it. In the morning I made a decision."

The next question was: "What happened if you made a mistake?"

The answer: "I made another decision."

Decisiveness is a TRUMAN characteristic. It is an important characteristic of leadership. As a quality, it can inspire confidence and trust in a people—impel them to risk change, to consider new values, to assume new responsibilities. But there must be more. The decision-maker must also be guided by historic principles and dedicated to their implementation. If the Declaration of Independence and the Constitution mean anything, it is that the goals of a democratic society are important, that they should be remembered and that our leaders should lead us toward them. Nowhere is this more important than in the case of civil rights.

From the vantage point of the Seventies, many of us tend to think of the 1954 decision in *Brown v. The Board of Education* as the watershed for civil rights in the nation. It was a tremendously important decision in the evolution of our country, but it followed by some years HARRY TRUMAN's drive to promote equality of opportunity. As President TRUMAN put it in his characteristically blunt language: "The top-dog in a world which is over half colored ought to clean his own house."

I doubt that this man from Missouri gave a moment's thought to a Southern strategy.

He saw the United States as a divided country—divided by barriers that were unhealthy, unwholesome, and un-American, it was his responsibility to try to make it whole.

He supported his sentiments by action. He insisted, over considerable objection, that the armed services be integrated. He established a committee on Civil Rights to investigate the need for Civil Rights legislation and upon the recommendation of the committee, he asked the Congress:

To establish a permanent commission on Civil Rights, a Joint Congressional Committee on Civil Rights and a Civil Rights Division in the Department of Justice.

To strengthen existing Civil Rights laws and laws protecting the right to vote.

To provide for Federal protection against lynching.

To establish a Fair Employment Practices Commission.

To provide for Home Rule and suffrage in Presidential elections for the District of Columbia.

At his insistence—with a full appreciation of the political risks involved—these proposals were also contained in the Democratic Party's Platform in the 1948 elections. He preferred to take risks that could lead to a united country to the risk of an increasingly divided country.

The result is well known. The Dixiecrats left the Democratic Party. In the perilously close election that followed, their defection cost the President four states from the supposedly "Solid South" that otherwise would have been in his camp. Mr. TRUMAN knew he could have avoided this result. But he refused to compromise on principle. As he wrote in his memoirs:

"I believed in the principles these platforms advanced . . . I was perfectly willing to risk defeat in 1948 by sticking to the Civil-Rights plank in my platform."

Devotion to principle means a willingness to risk such defeat. It is also the only way to appeal to the best in men. It is a quality we need now—at a time when the country is even more divided than it was in 1948. It is a quality we must produce in our leaders, if we are to provide it in our people.

There is another example of that TRUMAN blend of decisiveness, judgment and dedication to principle which has relevance today.

A principle in which Mr. TRUMAN believed deeply—that the civilian government must at all times exercise ultimate control over the military.

It was one thing to state the principle. It was another to relieve General MacArthur of his command. The General enjoyed immense popularity at home. It was clear that MacArthur's removal could precipitate the biggest fight of his administration. And it did.

But Mr. TRUMAN believed he had no other choice. As he wrote in his memoirs:

"If there is one basic element in our Constitution, it is civilian control of the military. Politics are to be made by the elected political officials, not by Generals or Admirals."

This was a deep-seated instinct, rooted in the experience of mankind. If any society is to climb toward the goals which are humanity's highest aspirations, the military response must be subordinated to non-military values.

Whenever man feels insecure—whenever he feels beleaguered by the hostile manifestations of frustrated hopes and dreams—he seeks security.

What may constitute security at a given time—in given circumstances can be a terrible judgment to make—requiring a sensitive and balanced appreciation of the nature of the threat and of the consequenecs of the available courses of action.

The principle of civilian domination over the military must be regarded as something more than a transient response to the experience of the American revolution.

It is a fundamental principle—enshrined in our Constitution—related intimately to the survival of freedom and the kind of lives our children will live.

It is a principle in which Mr. TRUMAN believed—and for which he fought at great political cost to himself and to other causes he would have liked to advance.

It is a principle which has application to several difficult national decisions with which we are confronted today:

Our policies in Southeast Asia;

The dangers of the Nuclear Arms Race and the initiatives we should take to avoid them;

Our budgetary priorities;

The "Voluntary" Army.

In each case, which course offers the real security?

What values—military or nonmilitary—should predominate in shaping our answer?

Mr. TRUMAN was a man of his time—keenly aware that his was the responsibility for dealing with problems in the "here and now."

He was enabled to do so by the personal qualities which we all know so well—and because American experience—and the principles and values which must be projected into the future, if the American experience is to survive.

All who observed the Truman years in the White House were often frustrated by the political "mistakes" he made.

The man in the White House is always the "Master Politician"—shrewd in the use of maneuver and expediency to reduce the political cost of his policies and to stretch out his political bankroll.

The perspective of time tells us that President TRUMAN believed his political bankroll to be a resource—to be spent without stint in the country's best interests.

Time also tells us that the judgment of history is more likely to vindicate such a view of the Presidency than any other. Political sagacity is not enough to make a wise President. Energy is not enough to give him a forceful Administration. Mastery of the arts of communication is not enough to win the hearts of his people. Knowledge of the principles of public Administration is not enough to command the loyalty of public servants.

Leadership consists in appealing to the best that is in a people, not in exploiting their differences and weaknesses. And that leadership can come only from a man who insists on the best from himself, by knowing what history has to tell us, by understanding what is in the hearts of his people, and by exercising judgment, courage and dedication to principle in the office of the Presidency.

Undoubtedly Dean Acheson had these qualities in mind in dedicating his book to President TRUMAN, saluting him as "The Captain with the Mighty heart."

And so he was and is.

Hon. Harrison A. Williams, Jr.
OF NEW JERSEY

Mr. President, when the Nation lost HARRY S TRUMAN, we lost a giant. The United States and the world will surely miss the stateman from Missouri and will long remember his success and accomplishments.

I have had the honor of knowing and admiring HARRY TRUMAN throughout the years and will always treasure the personal moments of our acquaintance.

HARRY TRUMAN was not only a man capable of effectively dealing with the enormous responsibilities of the Presidency, he was a man of great strength and courage and mastered every task before him with undiminished understanding and knowledge. His zest for life and his compassion for people continually prevailed in his handling of many difficult national and world affairs.

His work as President was eloquently described by The Very Reverend Francis Sayre, Dean of Washington Cathedral, when he stated at the Memorial Services for President TRUMAN on January 5:

Sometimes it must seem to every President as if the path ahead is blocked by an impenetrable wall, a river impassable, the mendaciousness of man in all his affairs makes prisoner of that leader who must see beyond; who may not allow the world to quench the spark of truth God has given to his keeping.

HARRY TRUMAN faced his decisions with truth and courage. As Dean Sayre also reflected in his eulogy:

> Many of us remember still the dark days that HARRY TRUMAN faced, the loneliness of his responsibility and the generous impulse he ever brought to it.

We are reminded of this vast loneliness as we remember that during his Presidency, HARRY TRUMAN was faced with a decision unequaled to that of any other world leader. Choosing to prevent the loss of thousands of American soldiers who would have been killed in the attack on Japan in 1945, President TRUMAN, alone, ordered the dropping of the bomb that has since shaped the world.

President TRUMAN, however, should not only be remembered for this one grave but vital act. We should appropriately reflect on his concern for all citizens of this Nation and the world. The Marshall plan executed under his administration helped to provide for war-torn Europe the salvation of lives and homes. And lost amidst the historical notations on his decisions and judgments in foreign affairs, are the works and achievements of HARRY TRUMAN in domestic matters. His undaunted endeavors in major civil rights and social welfare reform were remarkably effective, and serve to further demonstrate his understanding of the misfortunate and his compassion for the poor.

Again, in the words of Dean Sayre:

> In the eyes of his countrymen, HARRY TRUMAN was found to be such a man. Earthy plain, there were no wrinkles in his honesty; when the time came, he stepped to the anvil humble but not afraid, relying always in his independent way upon the goodness of the Lord, in whose hand is the hammer of our fate.

In addition to the courage, vitality, and self-confidence commonly noted in the character of Mr. TRUMAN, this man possessed immeasurable wit and charm. His warmth and humor is evident in a personal notation he made at the bottom of a cordial note to me following my election to the Senate in 1958. He reflected on a story he remembered from when he first entered the Senate, by writing:

> When I went to the Senate January 3, 1935, Ham Lewis was whip. He came and sat by me a day or two later after I was sworn in and said to me, "Harry, don't you get an inferiority complex. You'll sit here about six months and wonder how you arrived and after that you'll wonder how the hell the rest of us got here."

Mr. President, to a great extent, Mr. TRUMAN was what America is all about—a humble man rising to the highest office in this land. He was a man who at first glance appeared to be ordinary, but in the final analysis turned out to be a most extraordinary man and a great President. In remarks written to his daughter, Margaret, he partially summed up himself when he wrote:

> Your Dad will never be reckoned among the great but you can be sure he did his level best and gave all he had to his country.

However, HARRY S TRUMAN not only "did his level best and gave all he had to his country," but he achieved a greatness that will long be admired and respected by people throughout the world. He will be missed.

Hon. Henry M. Jackson
OF WASHINGTON

Mr. President, HARRY TRUMAN had the responsibilities of the Presidency thrust upon him overnight. He was confronted with a series of tough, unprecedented decisions—with nothing less than the future security of the free world at stake. He never shrank from those decisions, despite the hostile environment of those postwar years. It can be said that his greatest decisions were made when the public polls gave him the lowest ratings. His courage, his wisdom, and his decisiveness in that period shaped the future course of the Western World.

I am proud to have served in the House of Representatives during the Presidency of HARRY TRUMAN and proud to have supported him in his efforts to maintain the security of the free world. With the passing of the years, his place in history—and in the hearts of his countrymen—is ever more assured. He will be known as he is already—as one of our country's greatest Presidents.

Hon. Marlow W. Cook
OF KENTUCKY

Mr. President, it is with deep regret that I note the passing of the late President from Missouri, HARRY S TRUMAN. In the brief but abundant history of our great Nation, there are few who have served with such dedication, tenacity, and consistency. During his life, Mr. TRUMAN served his country in many pursuits; as a soldier during the First World War, as a judge, as a U.S. Senator, as Vice President, and President of the United States. Throughout all these endeavors, the skill, judgment, candidness, and conscious dedication which he displayed were qualities of a fine individual and a great leader, which this Nation will sorely miss.

Hon. Edward J. Gurney
OF FLORIDA

Mr. President, in this time of tough decisions, it is most fitting to honor the memory of a man who, as the 33d President of the United States, had to make some of the toughest decisions any man has had to make.

President HARRY S TRUMAN became a symbol for many Americans—a symbol of America's emergence as a full fledged world power. He rose from humble beginnings to the highest office in the land—in the finest American tradition. Prior to becoming President he served his country with distinction—as an Army officer, a judge, a Senator, and, for a brief time, as Vice President. After assuming the Presidency, he served with even greater distinction in a period beset by crises.

It took a man of courage to make the decision to use the atomic bomb; it took a man of vision to implement the Marshall plan; it took a man of wisdom to check Communist aggression in Greece and Turkey and to formulate the Truman doctrine, and it took a man of strength to deal with the conflicting pressures of the Korean war—the first war ever fought under the nuclear shadow. Indeed, President TRUMAN was a man of ample courage, vision, wisdom, and strength—and the record he compiled during 7 years in the White House is testimony to that.

Historians are already writing up President TRUMAN as one of our best Presidents. Certainly, his contributions are manifold and he became recognized around the world as a stalwart in the struggle for freedom. Some may question his judgment on this or that issue, but no one can deny that President TRUMAN was a dedicated man who loved his country and who served it well. At age 60, he did not have to accept the Vice Presidency, knowing as he did that he was likely to become President under the most dif-

ficult of circumstances, but when duty called he responded. That is the mark of statesmanship, and from the day he took office to the day he died, President TRUMAN was every inch a statesman. His presence will be sorely missed, but his record should shine brightly in the annals of history. We can all learn from what he did.

Hon. Gale W. McGee
OF WYOMING

Mr. President, I wish to express my sadness over the recent death of President TRUMAN, a man of great strength and courage.

HARRY S TRUMAN was a very uncomplicated man who demonstrated a remarkable capacity and ability to deal with complex problems facing the world and this Nation in the post-war era. He served his Nation in war, but was the architect of peace. Considerable controversy still centers around his decision to go into Korea with American troops. Yet, one can hardly disagree that it was his vigorous leadership and decisive action which has resulted in unheralded economic prosperity in Europe and rapprochement with Soviet Russia.

The aftermath of World War II left the old balance of power completely destroyed. The war had ruined several great powers, and left a vast political vacuum. In addition, two of the victorious nations—England and France—were so weakened by the conflict that they could no longer continue their historic roles in the balance of power. Perhaps never before in history had so much violence been done to the infrastructure of world stability.

It was within this chaotic setting that the United States was forced to assume a world leadership position, a decision that HARRY TRUMAN never hesitated to make. For, as President TRUMAN realized, unless the world's power balance is restored following a war, few—if any—meaningful strides can be taken toward an improved world community. The realization of the need for a power balance led President TRUMAN to accept the commitments necessary to counteract the enormous power of the Soviet Union. This he did quickly and decisively. He broke the Soviet blockade of Berlin. He laid out the Truman doctrine to confront the Soviet threat in the Middle East. He formed NATO to block Soviet expansion into Western Europe. And through the Marshall plan, he prevented the economic collapse of Europe. Under his administration, the United Nations was born.

On the domestic front, HARRY TRUMAN demonstrated an intense compassion for the people of this country. His domestic program included major civil rights, labor, and social welfare legislation. Yet, President TRUMAN remained ahead of his time. It was not until the 1960's that this Nation enacted legislation to meet these human needs.

HARRY S TRUMAN acted with strong conviction and accepted full responsibility for his actions. Throughout his life of public service he exhibited honesty, compassion, and fairmindedness. But, above all, HARRY S TRUMAN was a man of the people who never forgot the people. We will surely miss this great man.

Mr. President, I would like to add my personal experiences with our 33d Chief Executive.

I first met President TRUMAN when I was a young professor of history at the University of Wyoming. It was during the month of May 1950, on the very eve of the Korean war, and the President addressed a capacity house convocation for university students and faculty.

I remember on that occasion, President TRUMAN talked to me about launching on a political career. At that time he urged me to consider running for the House of Representatives, pointing out that times were changing and that academicians could dare to venture into the political arena.

From that moment on, until I arrived in Washington as a U.S. Senator, HARRY S TRUMAN grew in stature on the pages of history even though at the time of our first conversation he was being castigated and demeaned by his critics.

Upon my election to a first term in the U.S. Senate, I had barely arrived in Washington, D.C., when I was summoned to the Mayflower Hotel by President TRUMAN. I have never forgotten the warm, fatherly counsel he gave me on that occasion.

Thus, in a very real way he played a very meaningful part at significant moments of my life. And for that, I will be forever grateful and appreciative.

Hon. Robert C. Byrd
OF WEST VIRGINIA

Mr. Robert C. Byrd. Mr. President, at the request of the distinguished senior Senator from Missouri (Mr. Symington), and with the approval of the distinguished majority leader, I ask unanimous consent that on next Tuesday, February 6, following the recognition of Senators under any special orders previously entered, and the transaction of any routine morning business, there be a period of not to exceed 2 hours set aside for the delivery of eulogies with regard to the late former President HARRY S TRUMAN, that the Record remain open for 15 days thereafter for the insertion of additional eulogies, and that such eulogies then be collected and printed as a Senate document.

The Presiding Officer. Without objection, it is so ordered.

Mr. Robert C. Byrd. Mr. President, I ask unanimous consent that the time for eulogies to the late former President HARRY S TRUMAN on Tuesday, February 6, be under the control of the distinguished senior Senator from Missouri (Mr. Symington), or his designee.

The Presiding Officer. Without objection, it is so ordered.

Hon. William Proxmire
OF WISCONSIN

Mr. President, one is tempted to treat the man from Independence whom we honor as an ordinary American. We all know his story. From rural beginnings he worked his way up, sometimes failing but never giving up, to a place in life he revered—membership in the U.S. Senate.

Then, a position few have sought was forced upon him. President Roosevelt all but ordered him to join him on the ticket. As we like to think of the ordinary man. Senator TRUMAN accepted out of a spirit of duty. And he became Vice President.

When the responsibility of leading the world through the closings days of World War II was cast upon him that April day in 1945, there were those who were ready to despair over that "ordinary" man.

We all know what happened. The man from the "Show Me" State showed what he was made of. He made decisions many of us would pale before. He made those decisions with careful consideration, but without flinching. He made them courageously.

In addition to courage, he showed his commitment to morality and common decency. He ordered an end to segregation of the Armed Forces.

He was able to display a sense of humor. He could give the press a big "I told you so" after his reelection in 1948.

Those were wild sport shirts he wore. And his daily walks on city sidewalks astonished passersby.

All these things—his courage, his morality, his common touch—endeared him to the "little guy."

Above all, he was himself at all times. He was what he was. And proud of it. That was his dignity. He raised the common values of decency, of caring for others, of knowing oneself—he raised those to something more esteemed.

Everyone knows that Mr. TRUMAN's middle initial stood for nothing. Maybe that "S" really should have stood for many things: Sagacity, Sangfroid, Savant, Selflessness, Sincerity. He had keen judgment of men and events. He was cool under pressure, knowing where the buck stopped. He was an expert in the workings of politics. He did care for the little people of this great country. He did his job well. And above all, he believed in what he was doing; he was honest with himself and others; he was devoid of hypocrisy.

President HARRY S TRUMAN was an uncommon man. I believe historians will see him that way.

Hon. Stuart Symington
OF MISSOURI

Mr. President, it is a privilege indeed to pay tribute today to the memory of one of the most outstanding public servants in the history of America, a superb U.S. Senator and a great President—HARRY S TRUMAN.

This patriot brought dignity and credit to his many and varied accomplishments: his World War I battery, his county, the State of Missouri, the U.S. Senate, as well as his Nation which called upon him to lead this country in grave times.

For nearly 8 challenging but rewarding years, 1945–52 inclusive, he guided America in its new role of leadership of the Free World; and that leadership will long be remembered for its character, its courage, and its commonsense.

At the time President TRUMAN left the position of presiding judge of the Jackson County Court, he summed up as follows his experience as the leader of that administrative body with characteristic lack of pretension as to his own future:

"I'll go out of here poorer in every way than when I came into office . . . I hope that there are no bond issues and no more troubles, until I'm gone, and then maybe I can run a filling station or something until I've run up my three score and ten and go to a quiet grave."

The future, however, would hold neither a filling station, nor lack of trouble, for Judge TRUMAN. Some 12 years later he would become the leader of the most powerful of all nations; and he brought to the presidency in 1945 the same qualities of leadership and regard for the public trust that had been the hallmark of his entire previous career.

Most Americans, who knew relatively little about their Vice President of but 97 days, worried about the future of the country as the thread of constitutional succession passed from Franklin Roosevelt to HARRY TRUMAN on that fateful day, April 12, 1945. For some 12 years Americans had first lived through its most serious depression and then 4 years of tragic war. They had strong faith in the President who told the Nation in 1933 that "the only thing we have to fear is fear itself."

We now know that the new President we commemorate today carried out that thinking in practical fashion. A man of middle America, of farm-oriented origin, President TRUMAN would inspire the Nation with his vigor and determination to carry on the program of his famous predecessor. As a former White House assistant, the North Carolina editor, Jonathan Daniels, commented:

Americans felt leaderless when Roosevelt died. TRUMAN taught them, as one of them, that their greatness lay in themselves.

Dr. Richard Kirkendall of the University of Missouri, who has studied the Truman record for 15 years, concluded his extensive research on this President as follows:

Truman was not a small man who suddenly had a very big job imposed upon him. The job was very big, but he brought to it rich and varied experiences in American life and politics. He had served for eight years as the chief administrative officer of a populous county and more than nine years as a United States Senator. He had campaigned for office on local and state levels, administered and constructed court houses, welfare agencies, roads, and other public facilities in Jackson County, contributed significantly to the war effort as an investigator of the economic side of it, and learned much about the American political and economic systems . . . If he did not shape the Administration's proposals, he did obtain opportunities to build support for them. His career before the White House was not a little man's career.

Although reluctant to accept the Vice Presidency because, as his beloved daughter later recounted, he did not want to enter the Presidency "through the back door," Harry Truman never shrank from tackling the great problems which faced him shortly after he took the oath as our 33d President. His instinct for decisive action promptly moved his administration forward to implement plans for the United Nations at the same time he gathered the facts prior to that fateful decision which he alone could make—the first use of a nuclear weapon.

President Truman also proceeded to create a governmental structure which reflected his personal discipline and passion for orderly administration. He did this through an administration which displayed the personality of a man who believed that those in government owe their allegiance and loyalty to the people; that is to the citizens who put them in office.

In the field of foreign policy, his famous Secretary of State, Dean Acheson, described vividly some of the more momentous decisions it was necessary for him to make in the interest of America, when he said:

The 1947 assumption of responsibility in the Eastern Mediterranean, the 1948 grandeur of the Marshall Plan, the response to the blockage of Berlin, the NATO defense of Europe in 1949, and the intervention in Korea in 1950—all these constituted expanded action in truly heroic mold. All of them were dangerous. All of them required rare capacity to decide and act.

Neither the unpopularity, nor the political explosiveness of any decision would deter this firm Missourian once he had decided on the course of action he believed in the best interests of his country.

As but one example, the impressive strides made on behalf of equal rights for all Americans during later years were first advanced in the party platform and legislative proposals of the Truman administration.

Mr. Truman was conscious of the role the United States should play in guaranteeing equal rights for all Americans if this Nation were to advance that concept in other parts of the world. Accordingly, early in his administration he established a Committee on Civil Rights to recommend Government action; and out of that committee grew the first U.S. Civil Rights Commission. He thereupon sought national legislation to provide Federal protection against lynching, as well as a law to protect the voting rights of every citizen.

Always fearless about what he believed to be right, President Truman was characteristically courageous when he took his record to the people for reelection in the 1948 campaign. He felt that the constructive work of his administration had not yet been achieved; and he was always confident, despite the almost universally unfavorable polls, that the people would respond to the goals he had set for America.

Perhaps his legal counsel, Clark Clifford, later Secretary of Defense, summed up best the logic behind Mr. Truman's reelection, when he said:

Here was President Truman the underdog out appealing to the people in thousands of meetings, literally, from the back platform of his train. With his simplicity, his sincerity, they understood him. If he had a style they weren't conscious of it but they understood the man and they understood what he was saying and his ideals became their goals and their ideals.

Despite his being President of the most powerful Nation on earth, Harry Truman was always a man of the people. He followed in the tradition laid down to that end by such Presidents as Andrew Jackson and Abraham Lincoln. His stature in history grows steadily. He was truly a great President, with a humility in his efforts that was matched by both pride and faith in the United States of America.

Mr. President, in recent days, Members of the House of Representatives, led by Congressman William J. Randall, of Missouri, have already paid their respects to President Truman. During thier eulogies, Congressman Randall and others inserted outstanding editorials from Missouri and other papers across the country.

In addition to the tributes which they placed in the Record, I ask unanimous consent that editorials from newspapers throughout the Nation, reprinted in the Kansas City Star on December 28, under the heading, "Legacy of HARRY S TRUMAN," be inserted at this point in the record.

[From the Kansas City Star, Dec. 28, 1972]

THE LEGACY OF HARRY S TRUMAN

NEW YORK TIMES

HARRY S TRUMAN waged the last fight of his long life with the same courage and stamina that never failed him during eight taxing years as President of the United States. Thrust into the highest office by the death of Franklin D. Roosevelt, this unassuming, small-town politican drew on hidden reserves of those qualities, along with decisiveness and rocklike integrity, to meet with credit the staggering challenges of a momentous era in history and vindicate democracy's faith in the common man.

In a world that was just emerging from a devastating war, Mr. TRUMAN presided over one of the most constructive and innovative periods of American foreign policy. Isolation had been sunk along with the battleship Arizona at Pearl Harbor in 1941. Mr. Roosevelt had directed the mightiest armed forces ever assembled and forged the greatest coalition in history to crush the Axis powers.

In educating the nation to meet the vast new responsibilities it could not safely evade in the aftermath of the war and the rapid dissolution of the alliance with Soviet Russia, the former artillery captain of World War I demonstrated an uncommon ability to seize upon the grand strategic concepts that were developed by the extraordinary group of able men from the Roosevelt administration who surrounded him.

The Truman Doctrine of 1947, never called that by the man himself and never intended to be the globe-embracing policy that both champions and critics claimed; the Marshall Plan which restored much of a devastated continent and laid the foundation for European integration and unity; the Atlantic Alliance of 1949, recognizing the enduring identity of vital interests between North America and Western Europe; Point Four, making benefits of scientific and technical progress available to the world's hungry and needy—all these innovative manifestations of a foreign policy designed to meet the conditions of a new world took form in HARRY TRUMAN's administration.

Mr. TRUMAN's bold decision to check aggression in Korea in 1950 despite the enfeebled state of American armed forces in the area probably saved the United Nations from collapse and more or less stabilized for 20 years a highly volatile situation. It was during the Korean War that Mr. TRUMAN, in one of his most courageous and most important actions, fired an unquestionably insubordinate General MacArthur, thereby preserving civilian control over the military and over the conduct of foreign policy.

One of the most difficult decisions any President has ever had to face was the question presented to Mr. TRUMAN in his very first days in office: Whether to drop, without warning, two atomic bombs on Japan. With hindsight, it seems a terrible failure of the hu-

man spirit to have used nuclear weapons on densely populated cities without at least having given the Japanese and the world a demonstration of their unique horror by dropping a bomb on an uninhabited island.

Mr. TRUMAN knew some moments of greatness in domestic affairs. He recognized the twin evils of McCarthyism and McCarranism from the first and stood firmly against them. He championed the civil rights of the Negro in his 1948 message to Congress, and he defied the subsequent Dixiecrat revolt.

Yet he could speak and act impetuously, even recklessly, and play the pettiest kind of politics, reflecting his early training in a corrupt big-city machine.

Some of his appointments were deplorable, including some to extremely high posts in government. He was fiercely loyal to old friends, some of whom certainly did not deserve his loyalty.

He could be carried away by bad advice or by an impatience for quick results, as when he proposed to seize the steel mills.

He never cast himself in a role of a man of destiny, always retaining his sense of humor and humility. His fellow citizens trusted him, however much some may have disagreed with him, because they could be confident that the "image" of the President reflected the true character of the man.

TULSA DAILY WORLD

It will be years before historians can fully evaluate Mr. TRUMAN's presidential service and place it in perspective with the events that followed. But it's safe to guess that his stature and place in history will grow as time goes by.

In any event, in this age of yearning for "charisma" and political image-making divorced from reality, we are not likely to see another HARRY TRUMAN.

ST. LOUIS POST-DISPATCH

Looking back on the Truman years, some of our younger writers are inclined to fault the President for policies that in perspective appear to have been misguided.

It should be remembered that when Mr. TRUMAN entered the White House the world was falling apart. Colonialism was on its last legs; big powers and little powers alike were scrambling to fill vacuums. The aims and capabilities of the Communists were not fully understood.

A generation has passed since the Truman years and some of the problems the Missourian faced have not yet been solved: Germany remains divided. Korea is divided, the U.S. is engaged in paracolonialism in Vietnam. One can well afford to look back with a measure of charity.

Mr. TRUMAN was overwhelmingly a man of the people—earthy, gregarious, stubborn, courageous, honest, a mixture of pride and humility. He had small preparation for high office, but he gave the day's responsibilities the best he had and slept at night in the comfort of knowing that no man can do more. He was not only a native of this state, in many ways he was typical of its citizenry. We can be thankful that Mr. TRUMAN walked among us.

DES MOINES REGISTER

HARRY S TRUMAN never lost his flat Missouri twang nor acquired the slightest trace of cultural gloss. He remained a home-town boy who loved his home town and his family.

The American public regarded Mr. TRUMAN as a scrappy fighter who dared long odds. The greatest of these fights was his battle for re-election in 1948 when polls and political experts pronounced him doomed.

Though some of his administration's agencies were riddled with scandal, and "the mess in Washington" became a household phrase, historians polled near the close of his administration ranked Mr. TRUMAN among the great U.S. Presidents.

Historical revisionists are disagreeing with this estimate now. They see the Cold War as a serious mistake for which Mr. TRUMAN was partly to blame.

These reassessments overlook the fact that Mr. TRUMAN acted at a time when hot voices in this country were calling for more dangerous warlike responses than Mr. TRUMAN permitted.

TOPEKA DAILY CAPITAL

When he assumed the presidency President TRUMAN had been kept on the outside of all of the Rooseveltian strategies, and it was Mr. TRUMAN's task to pick up the threads of policy, action and intrigue as they were being woven by F.D.R.

For example, Mr. TRUMAN did not know the United States had developed the A-bomb although the Russians were privy to this information. But he did not hesitate to order it dropped on Hiroshima and Nagasaki.

Mr. TRUMAN had no regrets over the loss of Japanese lives. He easily translated this into the saving of a million American lives.

WALL STREET JOURNAL

His contemporaries judged him harshly, at one time his approval rating in the Gallup Poll sank to 23 percent, a record low for any President. Yet now, these 20 years later, it grows increasingly hard to remember what HARRY TRUMAN did wrong, and increasingly hard to dispute that he did most of the big things right.

Today many would deprecate some or all of these decisions, as they would deprecate the gutsy quality that went into them. But Josef Stalin was not the figment of anyone's imagination. The containment policy has achieved its purpose of moderating the ambitions of the Soviet leaders. The reason the second-guessers question whether the dam was needed is that there has been no flood since it was built.

Merely glancing through the photographs in Miss Truman's book you can guess the experiences that forged HARRY TRUMAN. Here is a child standing with relatives in a wooden-wheeled wagon, scarcely removed from the frontier. Here are slices of the Americana now mocked in fashionable movies. From this Mr. TRUMAN drew the earthy sense, the directness, the sense of self-worth by which both his contemporaries and history judge him.

WICHITA EAGLE

His honesty was never questioned, though he had the active support of the corrupt Pendergast political machine of Kansas City. He said Tom Pendergast never asked him to do a single dishonest act. And, though his connections with the machine were criticized in political campaigns, he never abandoned his friend, Pendergast.

He had his enemies. He was the object of an assassination attempt, in which two of the attackers were killed. The third was sentenced to death, but his sentence was changed to life imprisonment by Mr. TRUMAN just before he left the presidency.

DAILY OKLAHOMAN

He was uncharacteristically subdued and humble when he took the oath of office. He asked for the nation's prayers, and a great many of his apprehensive countrymen may have agreed that prayers were needed. But the office of the presidency has a recognized capacity for bringing out unsuspected qualities of greatness in its occupants and Mr. TRUMAN soon showed in what ways he was destined to become great.

OMAHA WORLD-HERALD

As an administrator and decision-maker, he proved to be both tough and wise. He could see that Soviet expansion had to be stopped in the late '40s and early '50s, and he committed the resources of this country to do it. He saw the development of the hydrogen bomb was a military necessity and our country developed it.

ATLANTA JOURNAL

His detractors wouldn't leave him alone. They said he was little, he was vulgar. He did not have the graces. What they really were saying was he was a plain, unvarnished citizen of the United States, typical of millions of us except that he had more character, more determination, more gumption and more political shrewdness than his detractors combined.

After the White House, Mr. TRUMAN lived a full life. He enjoyed his family and his neighbors. He stayed active. He was accessible. And what must have been sweetest of all was the decline of his detractors and the growth of his admirers. Now, on his death, he is praised as one of the great American presidents.

Mr. President, I also ask unanimous consent that the observations of two students of the Truman era, Dr. Richard Kirkendall, to whom I referred earlier in these remarks, and D. W. Brogan, a British historian and commentator on American life for some 30 years, be inserted at this point in the Record.

HARRY S TRUMAN—A GREAT AMERICAN PRESIDENT

(Memorial Address by Dr. Richard S. Kirkendall at University of Missouri-Columbia, January 17, 1973)

HARRY S TRUMAN was one of America's greatest presidents. This is not to say that he was always wise and always successful at every point. We have not been ruled by gods. We have been forced to make do with men, and men have limits on their abilities. In appraisng presidents, the historian must have realistic expectations. HARRY S TRUMAN's achievements and proposals entitle him to recognition as a great occupant of the Executive Mansion. He failed more than once; a bolder man might have accomplished more; a wiser one would have avoided some of his moves. His accomplishments may not have been as substantial and significant as Washington's, Lincoln's or Franklin Roosevelt's. Yet, he did promote valuable changes; he developed a new and larger role for the United States in the world, affected some parts of it in very desirable ways, and encouraged social and economic improvements at home. And our experiences since he left the White House suggest that his advice should have been followed more closely.

TRUMAN was not a small man who suddenly had a very big job imposed upon him. The job was very big, but he brought to it rich and varied experiences in American life and politics. He had served for eight years as the chief administrative officer of a populous county and more than nine years as a United States Senator.

He had campaigned for office on local and state levels, administered and constructed court houses, welfare agencies, roads, and other public facilities in Jackson County, contributed significantly to the war effort as an investigator of the economic side of it, and learned much about the American political and economic systems. Although his brief vice presidency had not supplied specialized training for the higher assignment, his selection as a candidate had enabled him to wage a national campaign in 1944, and his responsibilities as vice president had given him a chance to exercise his political talents in new ways. If he did not shape the administration's proposals, he did obtain opportunities to build support for them. His career before the White House was not a little man's career.

TRUMAN's life before April 12, 1945 also supplied him with a philosophy on the issues that he would face, including the international affairs that would dominate his presidency. His thinking on foreign policy emphasized political considerations, especially the distribution of power, the importance of the military factor, and the need to deal forcefully with aggressive nations. This philosophy was the product of his own experiences as a soldier extending over more than thirty years and of the nation's experiences in world affairs from 1918 to 1945.

As president, TRUMAN was determined to avoid what he regarded as the errors of the past: weakness and refusal to get involved in the major international problems. He feared that the American people would retreat to the foreign and military policies of the 1920's and 1930's that had failed disastrously. He was convinced that the nation must play a very significant role in the world in the postwar period and must possess military strength.

With TRUMAN supplying essential leadership and making the basic decisions, the United States did not retreat to the policies of the interwar period. Instead, it played a large role in the world. TRUMAN carried to completion Roosevelt's plans for the creation of and American membership in the United Nations. Of greater importance, at least in the short run, his administration developed and implemented a plan—the Marshall Plan—for European recovery. The plan and the program that followed contributed decisively to the economic recovery of Western Europe and to the development of political stability and strength in the region.

TRUMAN believed that the United States could and shoud play a large role in world affairs, but he did not regard American power as unlimited. He did not believe that the United States could do all that it might wish nor accomplish all that it might hope. This sense of limits affected his efforts in Eastern Europe, where he relied largely on words in a futile effort to influence political

developments. He was distressed by Russian behavior there but believed that there was little he could do to change it. The sense of limits also prevented him from intervening in a large way in the Civil War in China even though he hoped that Chiang Kai-shek could avoid defeat. He and his aides did not believe that the United States could mobilize the economic and military resources needed to exert a decisive influence on that very large, very complex, and deeply troubled nation.

The sense of limits also contributed signficantly to another very controversial aspect of TRUMAN's presidency: his conflict with General Douglas MacArthur in 1951. The President rejected the General's proposal to throw more force against the Chinese in Korea and to carry the war into China itself, using American air and naval power and Chiang's troops. TRUMAN regarded the suggestions as extremely dangerous. "We are trying to prevent a world war—not to start one," he explained. Furthermore, MacArthur's proposals would tie the United States down in an area of secondary importance and thereby give the Russians new opportunities in a much more important region: Europe, MacArthur's strategy would, according to TRUMAN's top military adviser, "involve us in the wrong war, at the wrong place, at the wrong time, and with the wrong enemy." MacArthur's objectives—the reunification of Korea under non-Communist control and the weakening of China—were not unattractive, but they seemed to TRUMAN to be beyond the limits of American power. The pursuit of them would result in losses that would far outweight those objectives in importance.

The TRUMAN-MacArthur controversy also involved another very important consideration: the place of the military in American life. TRUMAN regarded military power as essential but also dangerous. His solution was civilian control. This was, of course, the solution of the American Constitution. MacArthur tried to use his prestige to force a change in policy and appealed publicly for support of his ideas. His actions challenged TRUMAN's authority as commander in chief, and the President concluded that he must remove the General from command in order to uphold and maintain the essential principle of civilian supremacy.

Foreign affairs was the most significant aspect of TRUMAN's presidency. The record of his domestic accomplishments did not contain any contribution as substantial as the Marshall Plan, to cite a major example. Nevertheless, he was not insignificant in the domestic history of the United States. He was not able to gain acceptance for new domestic proposals, but he did expand and improve already established ones, such as Social Security and public power, and he did defend them against their foes. Moreover, by publicizing various issues, such as health insurance, he paved the way for later accomplishments. Furthermore, he did more on behalf of the civil rights of black Americans than any of his predecessors in the twentieth century.

TRUMAN's civil rights record deserves more than brief mention. It was influenced by his interest in the nation's relations with other people as well as by domestic concerns and humanitarian considerations. Well aware of the international implications of American race relations, he was convinced that the country "could no longer afford the luxury of a leisurely attack upon prejudice and discrimination." In 1951, when vetoing a bill that would segregate schools on federal property, he explained:

"We have assumed a role of world leadership in seeking to unite people of great cultural and racial diversity. . . . We should not impair our moral position by enacting a law that requires discrimination based on race."

TRUMAN's concern in this area was expressed by several significant actions. Late in 1946, he established a Committee on Civil Rights to investigate race relations and make recommendations for government action to protect civil rights, and less than a year later, the committee produced a bold report that influenced the administration's subsequent behavior. Soon, his Justice Department joined the NAACP in an attack before the United States Supreme Court on segregated housing. This marked the beginning of that department's significant participation in the civil rights movement. Early in the following year, the President delivered a special message attacking discrimination and segregation and calling for national legislation that would provide federal protection against lynching, protect the right to vote, prohibit discrimination in interstate transportation facilities, and establish a permanent agency concerned with job discrimination. And in July, 1948, TRUMAN issued two executive orders on civil rights, including one calling for equality of treatment and opportunity in the armed forces and the establishment of a committee to help with the implementation of the order. The President explained that it was intended to end segregation.

TRUMAN enjoyed some successes in this area. His Justice Department continued to function as a "friend of the court" in the major civil rights cases and helped the NAACP win its battles. His appointees to the United States Supreme Court also played important roles in these cases, which attacked segregation in housing, railroad dining cars, and higher education and prepared the way for the monumental decision in 1954 attacking segregation in all public schools. And the armed forces were desegregated. They had taken on new importance as a result of the enlargement of the nation's role in the world, and he promoted progress in race relations in this part of American life.

TRUMAN failed, however, to obtain passage of the broad civil rights legislation that he proposed. Perhaps he might have accomplished more if he had pressed his proposals more boldly. His appraisal of political realities restrained him, however. His ability to promote change was limited by strong resistance, especially in the South. Many southerners bolted the Democratic party in 1948 and supported Governor J. Strom Thurmond of South Carolina in a presidential campaign that focused upon race relations. And after the election, a congressional coalition of conservative Democrats, mostly southerners, and conservative Republicans dominated Congress on domestic issues and frustrated TRUMAN's appeal for a legislative attack upon problems in American race relations. Even before TRUMAN became president this coalition had demonstrated that it could thwart a president. It was chiefly responsible for his failure in this area.

TRUMAN did not always succeed, and he did not always make wise decisions. One unwise one was the decision to provide financial support for the French in their battle against revolution in Indochina This marked the beginning of an involvement that led to disaster.

TRUMAN, however, was not responsible for the disaster. His successors were. They lacked his appreciation of the limits on our power and enlarged enormously a rather small commitment that could have been terminated after the French failed or at some other point far short of massive military involvement.

Many Americans, however, could not accept TRUMAN's belief that their power had limits. That belief was one of the sources of his unpopularity during his last years in office. By early 1952, only 25 percent of the people thought that he was doing a good job. His most prominent critics were very dissatisfied with his foreign policy, seeing it as responsible for the "loss" of China and for other undesirable developments, and they assumed that the United States could and should accomplish much more than he had accomplished. It was this attitude that led to our large-scale involvement in Vietnam. It has been an effort to "avoid another China."

TRUMAN made mistakes; he failed to accomplish some of his objectives, but he was a much greater president than most Americans realized during his years in the White House. They should have accepted rather than resisted his advice on civil rights and made a much larger effort to solve the problems in American race relations. Instead, those problems—or many of them—were allowed to grow and become a serious threat to the nation as well as a source of suffering and sorrow for many individuals. More attention should have been paid to his suggestions about the limits on American power. Instead, we enlarged our role until bitter and destructive experiences in Vietnam provided persuasive evidence on this point.

In his area of greatest significance, international affairs, TRUMAN's point of view and performance were complex and balanced. He believed that the United States must play a large role in world affairs, but he also maintained that there were limits on what the nation could and should do. He insisted that the United States must have a strong military establishment, but he also knew that a strong military posed a threat to the American system and must be kept in a subordinate position.

We need that complexity and balance at the present moment. Alive now to the folly of globalism, we may swing back to isolationism, forgetting its dangers. The United States once tried to play a small role in the world, but that failed. It did not keep the country out of major wars. Now the nation, or at least a very substantial part of it, has become aware of the short-comings of the global role, the limits on American power, and the need to make choices, and efforts are being made to define a role in the world that minimizes difficulties. The thought and record of one of our greatest presidents could help us define that role.

ॐ

A HISTORIAN's VIEW OF HARRY TRUMAN's PRESIDENCY

(By D. W. Brogan)

From the beginning, the office of Vice President of the United States has seemed to nearly all its incumbents futile and to most of them disillusioning. The only real attraction of the office (except for a naturally lazy man) is the possibility of succeeding to the Presidency on the death of the President. This has happened eight times. Lyndon B. Johnson is too much part of current history for his role to be assessed even tentatively, but of other Vice Presidents who have succeeded, only two can have any claims to be considered great Presidents. One of them was Theodore Roosevelt; the other was HARRY S TRUMAN.

From the moment that the sudden death of Franklin D. Roosevelt made HARRY TRUMAN the center of American power, the new President was involved in issues of the highest importance. Not all of his decisions can be justified, and some have been severely criticized. But from the first Mr. TRUMAN showed the essential qualities of a President; the willingness to take responsibility and to decide rapidly. His motto, "the buck stops here," is the essential aspect of the Presidential office.

In the light of history, perhaps the most important act performed by the new President was the decision to drop the atomic bomb, a weapon of whose existence he knew nothing when he became President. That decision has been much debated, especially the resolve to drop the bomb on densely populated cities like Hiroshima and Nagasaki; but it was made. For good or ill, TRUMAN was the President who opened Pandora's box by deciding to bomb Hiroshima. Both TRUMAN and Churchill looked on the bomb as a providential weapon to end the war with Japan; without the bomb, their military advisers calculated that Japan would have to be invaded, with the possible loss of a million Allied lives. TRUMAN solicited the counsel of his top scientific, military and cvilian advisers, but he has clearly stated that the final decsion and responsibility were his. For as an enthusiastic student of American history, Mr. TRUMAN knew that on him, and on him alone, lay the ultimate responsibility of any great decision of the President and Commander-in-Chief of the United States.

TRUMAN did not look back. Having determined to drop the atomic bomb on Japan, he did not stay awake nights. Whether the decision was justifiable, whether the demonstration of the new power of destruction could have been made in another way, are still matters of bitter dispute. But Mr. TRUMAN accepted responsibility for what he did, apparently without regrets or pangs of conscience.

For the nearly eight years that Mr. TRUMAN was in office, this power of decision was the most important power to have. For it was essential that the United States should be, and should seem to be, under firm command, even if not all the examples of the command were encouraging or successful. For this reason Mr. TRUMAN will go down in history as one who maintained the power as well as the dignity of the Presidential office. He is in the line of Chief Executives who used Presidential power sometimes outside, if not quite against, the letter of the Constitution—the line of Jefferson buying Louisiana, Jackson facing down the revolt of South Carolina, Lincoln deciding, as finally he alone decided, to open the Civil War by replying in arms to the firing on Fort Sumter. TRUMAN repeatedly demonstrated his readiness to use his power, perhaps most notably by moving quickly and decisively when South Korea was invaded, without waiting for full Congressional debate and declaration of war.

At the time he took office this power of decision was not immediately visible. Mr. TRUMAN was thought of as a very accidental President—indeed, as having been an accidental Vice President (F.D.R. passed over several more impressive candidates for that office in 1944). He even showed in his early days some regard for the old hierarchy by nominating a Senate leader whom he admired, James F. Byrnes, as Secretary of State. He asked for advice from elder statesmen like Henry Stimson; he took advice. But it soon became apparent that he was fully conscious that he was President and that the buck stopped with him.

In part, this was the result of the educational impact of the office he had inherited. When Winston Churchill was asked why his successor, the very undramatic figure Clement Attlee, had shown himself so authoritative a Prime Minister, Churchill replied that he had fed "on the Royal Jelly." But of course both TRUMAN and Attlee were men whose basic qualities had been hidden in minor offices and were revealed only when each man was stretched to his fullness. That each had been a successful fighting officer commanding men in the field is perhaps significant in assessing their later roles.

There were other aspects in the new President's career that were perhaps more useful to him than his experience as a captain of field artillery on the Western Front in 1918, although that was an experience he liked to dwell on. He had been put into the Senate by the Pendergast machine in Kansas City, as he had been given his first political job by that machine, a job in which he combined executive efficiency with rigid honesty, a rare combination in the Kansas City of that age. It was these qualities of thoroughness and honesty that enabled TRUMAN to live down, both at home and among his colleagues in the Senate, his first reputation of being merely a Pendergast stooge. Yet TRUMAN preserved some of the habits of the Kansas City political world—particularly a deep loyalty to old friends that involved him indirectly in scandals, especially toward the end of his administration. But by that time more people concentrated more on the loyalty he showed than on the indiscretion he displayed. He had by then earned on a national scale the trust he had earned long before in Kansas City.

TRUMAN had not merely to live down the Pendergast machine, he had to live in the shadow of a great name, that of F.D.R. He inherited a great deal of unfinished business, and he inherited a Cabinet and other personnel chosen by a President who had been in office so long that many young Americans could not remember any other. It was natural for TRUMAN to get rid of the Roosevelt Cabinet, but it was bitterly resented by many loyal New Dealers, especially those on the radical side like Henry A. Wallace.

The Roosevelt Cabinet and F.D.R.'s great administrative chiefs had been prima donnas. The TRUMAN appointees, for the most part, were not. Yet at the end of his administration there could be no doubt that the TRUMAN Cabinet was a more effective instrument of government and contained more useful public servants than the Roosevelt Cabinet had; more than that, the devotion of the Cabinet (containing figures like Dean Acheson and Robert Lovett) to their chief was more manifest than the devotion of the Roosevelt Cabinet to F.D.R. And the relationship between President TRUMAN and General George C. Marshall was far closer and mutually far more trusting than that between Roosevelt and Marshall. In this sense TRUMAN was out of F.D.R.'s shadow long before he left the White House.

In another way, as well, TRUMAN was out of the Roosevelt shadow. He was a great maker of the modern Presidency as a department of the nation's government in its own right.

The most that F.D.R. did was to improve, to some degree, the organization of the White House. But what

TRUMAN did was to improve very markedly, and impose discipline on, the whole organization of the executive branch of the United States government. In administrative history, despite the scandals and despite the errors, Mr. TRUMAN will go down as a great innovator and reformer. There were few of the tense personal rivalries that had marked Roosevelt's Cabinets—with Roosevelt's approval, since F.D.R. believed that in the clash of personalities fresher ideas might be born. Instead TRUMAN used his Cabinet to sift carefully ideas and approaches to problems. He also met frequently with the various committees and boards that operated within the executive branch, soliciting expert opinion before making his own decisions. He often asked that memoranda and position papers be formulated for his careful scrutiny. He brought into the White House such men as Clark Clifford and encouraged them to impose organizational efficiency on what had tended to be independent chaos. (Clifford, important as an adviser and strategist for TRUMAN, remained a part-time adviser of Presidents John F. Kennedy and Lyndon B. Johnson, and became Secretary of Defense in Johnson's Cabinet.)

When Eisenhower succeeded to the Presidency, he inherited a much more effective instrument of command than had TRUMAN.

PROGRESS IN FOREIGN AFFAIRS, SERIOUS FRUSTRATIONS AT HOME

But what did TRUMAN do with this instrument of command? His accomplishments in the foreign field were substantial, but he was less lucky in domestic affairs. As always happens after a great war, the public was in the mood, consciously or unconsciously, to revenge itself on the government that had imposed such burdens on it. In addition, TRUMAN found himself confronted with serious and disruptive postwar problems—strikes, rising prices, food and housing shortages—that were bound to antagonize the electorate. He dealt firmly with these problems, sending message after message to Congress asking for needed legislation. But Congress did not always give him the laws he felt he needed to meet the onrushing crises. The people, only imperfectly aware of TRUMAN's efforts, decided on change, and the climate of the country turned against the Democrats. In 1946 the party lost control of Congress for the first time since 1930. The subsequent Republican-dominated Congress, the 80th was even less inclined to enact the domestic legislation that TRUMAN asked of it.

But if TRUMAN was often frustrated in his domestic policies, it was a different story in foreign affairs. A careful student of U.S. history, TRUMAN had learned an important lesson: not to quarrel unnecessarily with the Senate. He would not imitate Woodrow Wilson who had fought so bitterly with Senator Henry Cabot Lodge over U.S. membership in the League of Nations in 1919. Instead TRUMAN frequently invited Senate leaders to the White House for consultations, carefully and diligently asking their opinions. He won over eminent Republicans like Senator Arthur Vandenberg and was able to gain support for what could be called a national foreign policy. As a result, the Senate voted enormous appropriations and backed the bold policies that bulwarked war-ravaged Europe and started the "Free World" on its road to recovery.

Despite these accomplishments, TRUMAN was on the defensive as the 1948 election approached. It was almost universally assumed that he would be beaten.

The assumption led to very open conspiracies within the Democratic Party to deny him the nomination, a kind of mutiny that Captain TRUMAN had no intention of tolerating. He had his drawbacks as a politician. He was often indiscreet at press conferences, and he sometimes contradicted himself, relying too much on his memory, good as it was. He may be suspected of having succumbed to some political temptations: the very rapid U.S. recognition of the government of Israel was connected by some critics with vote-getting in the Bronx rather than with TRUMAN's concern to bolster the new Jewish state. TRUMAN's confidence that he could get elected never wavered, however. He coolly got the nomination in Chicago and then set out on his famous and arduous "give 'em hell" campaign. To the confusion of pundits and pollsters, he won.

By 1950 the United States had recovered from the brief postwar depression and from the brief and trivial shortages that followed the war. The fruits of TRUMAN's decisiveness and successful moves in what was the most important part of his office, foreign affairs, soon became apparent. The Marshall Plan, a brilliantly conceived blueprint for the revitalization of European industry instead of a vengeful stripping of the conquered countries' resources, was one of the key achievements of his foreign policy. Although the makers of the Marshall Plan were such men as Dean Acheson and, above all, George Marshall, the final responsibility resided in the White House. The decision to concentrate American aid and military resources in Europe was the President's. So was the "Truman Doctrine," which probably saved Greece and Turkey from a Russian-inspired Communist upheaval. The resolve to use the "airlift" to defy Stalin's attempt to isolate Berlin was a Presidential decision. Thus Western Europe was saved from the danger of collapsing in economic chaos and misery out of which a Communist controlled Europe might well have emerged.

Meanwhile TRUMAN was ever-more-vigorously taking hold of the job of Chief Executive. He would not brook sloppy work or any form of insubordination in his official family. When Secretary of State Byrnes overstepped his role by presuming to negotiate with the Russians without keeping TRUMAN fully informed of his steps (he issued independent press statements and generally acted as if *he* were the country's leader), he soon found himself replaced by Marshall. The same fate befell the irascible, powerful Harold Ickes, long Roosevelt's Secretary of the Interior, when he crossed TRUMAN.

Hindsight suggests that the President did not sufficiently allow for the fact that his bold foreign policy required more military strength than his economical administration permitted. It is often forgotten that it was Mr. TRUMAN who, for a brief period, first balanced the budget after many years of built-in deficits. Perhaps he took this part of his job too seriously. The outbreak of the Korean War put a tremendous strain on the nation's military establishment, weakened by the cutbacks TRUMAN had made in the interests of economy. The Korean War was a turning point in his administration, casting a shadow over its later years and over his miraculous election in 1948.

BOLD AND SPEEDY INTERVENTION IN KOREA

The War had three results for Mr. TRUMAN's immediate popularity and perhaps for his permanent reputation. It showed, first of all, his power of decision at its highest. Instead of giving South Korea "all kinds of aid except help," as the Washington wags predicted, President TRUMAN immediately ordered General Douglas MacArthur to dispatch troops to support South Korea's faltering forces. He did not, as we have noted, ask for a Congressional declaration of war or, indeed, for Congressional approval. It was a pure exercise of Presidential prerogative, of a sort much criticized today because of Vietnam. But there is no doubt that President TRUMAN was within his rights as Commander-in-Chief, although he was exercising those rights to the full.

A second result of the Korean War for Mr. TRUMAN was his much publicized and hotly debated dismissal of General MacArthur. MacArthur openly challenged TRUMAN's direct orders to confine the war to Korean soil and refrain from violating China's borders. TRUMAN asserted his authority without hesitation and relieved the general of his command. There can be little or no doubt that he was constitutionally right. No general can be allowed to openly criticize and oppose the policy of the Commander-in-Chief. Lincoln, as TRUMAN knew from his reading, had not stood for this from General George B. McClellan, and TRUMAN did not stand for it from a much greater soldier, Douglas MacArthur. Captain TRUMAN knew the spirit and the letter of the American Constitution better than his five-star General of the Army.

But all of TRUMAN's decisiveness could not bring an end to the Korean War. The fifth bloodiest conflict in American history, it dragged on and on, deeply disillusioning a country brought up to believe that all its wars ended in complete victories signalized by Yorktown, Appomattox or Tokyo Bay. It cast a pall over Mr. TRUMAN's last years in the Presidency and doubtless influenced the 1952 election, which put a Republican in the White House. It could and should be argued that the Korean War offered America a valuable lesson in the perils and perplexities that lurk in Asia. But it was an expensive lesson, and it was only imperfectly digested. It served to confirm in their beliefs those who clung to the legend that the U.S. somehow "lost China," that only some form of negligence (or possibly treason) allowed the Communists to take over. And it has been pointed to by those who believe that every form of aggression in Asia must be met with military counterforce.

If TRUMAN had a leading fault as Chief Executive it was that he almost invariably met problems head on—which sometimes meant that he ran his head against a Congressional stone wall. This fault, of course, is but the mirror image of his overweening virtue, his bold decisiveness. His legacy to the office, to the nation and to the world was great and on the whole beneficent.

He held the front of the "Free World" against Communism when many people believed that the front was collapsing. He defended the prerogatives of the President against an overweening general. He made the Presidency for the first time in its history an effectively organized instrument of government. He opened the Pandora's box of the atomic bomb. Perhaps it had to be opened; perhaps it had to be opened that way. Perhaps because it was opened that way it need never be opened again. No one knows.

An outstanding quality of TRUMAN himself was his ironical acceptance of his own limitations, his humor and his dislike of pomposity. He is reported to have offered an important job to a man he much admired who demurred, saying, "I don't really feel qualified for it." TRUMAN replied, "Maybe you're not. There are probably hundreds of people better qualified than you, but I don't know any of them. There are probably hundreds of people better qualified than I am to be President, but they weren't elected." Whether TRUMAN really believed the second half of this famous statement is doubtful. What is certain is that he never acted as if the task of being President was an easy one, that it demanded anything less than his never-flagging zeal and constant watchfulness. It was this quality perhaps more than any other that made him the very remarkable and possibly great President that he was.

And—a point very hard to demonstrate, but which is necessary to make—he showed in his brisk, man-in-the-street, man-from-the-farm way that the promise of American life for the average citizen had not been withdrawn. It has been an age of Presidents whose backgrounds have been very different from that of HARRY TRUMAN: a great engineer, Hoover; a country gentleman full of the social arts, F.D.R.; a great soldier, Eisenhower; a great millionaire with charm, high culture, dazzling personal appearance, Kennedy. The American public, as it rejoiced in his upset victory of 1948, took and kept to its heart the brusque little man from Independence, Missouri.

Hon. Thomas F. Eagleton
OF MISSOURI

Mr. President, we pay tribute today to a man who, during a lifetime of outstanding service to his country, was characteristically uncomfortable while being praised for his many accomplishments. HARRY TRUMAN once described a statesman as "a politician who has been dead for 15 years."

But HARRY TRUMAN was a great politician who was recognized by historians as a great statesman long before his death.

Much has been said about HARRY S TRUMAN the President. The great decisions that he made and the social programs that bear his imprint will stand as the only tribute he would enthusiastically endorse for himself.

It was a painful irony that President Lyndon Baines Johnson, a close friend and ally of HARRY TRUMAN during the years of his Presidency, would die within a month after attending President TRUMAN's funeral. Last week on network television Americans saw the last interview with President Johnson before his death.

During that interview he discussed the many social programs that were enacted during his administration and—in a fashion characteristic of Lyndon Johnson—he gave credit to HARRY TRUMAN for the most significant of those programs.

President TRUMAN fought for medicare and civil rights legislation long before it was popular to do so because, in his words, "it was the right thing to do."

Two men of humble beginnings, HARRY TRUMAN and Lyndon Johnson, shared a dream and now, in death, they share a place in history for their respective roles in bringing health care to America's elderly and equality under the law to Americans of all races.

President HARRY TRUMAN also achieved greatness through his work in foreign affairs. His initiation of the Marshall plan—his program of aid to underdeveloped countries—his courageous early recognition of Israel's nationhood—and his steadfastness in meeting aggression—have contributed to thrust upon him the title of "statesman."

But HARRY TRUMAN would not want us to remember him only for his service in the great office of the Presidency. He also was proud of the record he built as a U.S. Senator.

HARRY TRUMAN was elected to this body in 1934. And it was not an easy first term. He was unfairly labeled as a "machine" politician and when he defied the machine—as was his custom, since he voted his conscience—he was charged with disloyalty. It was the type of situation that inspires most men to pull up stakes and quit.

At the end of his first term, the effect of these attacks had taken their toll. HARRY TRUMAN was prime for defeat. It would have been easy to back out quietly and not run. But if there is one characteristic that looms larger than any other in HARRY TRUMAN's life, it is that he is not a quitter. In 1940 he said:

I'm going to run for reelection, if the only vote I get is my own.

HARRY TRUMAN ran for his second term in the U.S. Senate and defied all odds by winning reelection. It would not be the last time that he would confound the political pundits by ignoring their predictions and going directly to the people for his victory.

Returning to Washington, Senator TRUMAN took an interest in what he considered to be the alarming amount of waste and mismanagement in the defense establishment. In typical fashion he left Washington immediately on a rigorous month-long inspection tour of military installations around the country.

When he returned he told the Senate of the waste he had seen and requested that a special committee be created to oversee the Defense Establishment. This was the beginning of the TRUMAN committee that was to save the Nation billions of dollars during a period when we badly needed to build our military strength while, at the same time, maintaining a careful watch over a shaky economy.

Senator TRUMAN knew that the war effort could be damaged just as much by mismanagement as by faulty leadership.

His work in the defense area earned him a degree of notoriety in Washington that he had not known before. But he was not looking for publicity, he was simply trying to do a job. Early in 1942 he wrote to a close friend concerning the new-found prestige of the TRUMAN committee:

My committee has had so much publicity in the last 60 days that its work is not nearly as efficient as it was before that time. We are in a situation where the slightest mistake will cause us serious difficulty . . . One bad tactical error, political or otherwise, can ruin the whole structure much more easily than it could have done when we were first starting.

Senator TRUMAN was intent on doing his job and doing it well. He understood the significance of that work and he never attempted to use his new-found prominence to advance himself at the expense of his country. He was, in short, an outstanding Senator.

Mr. President, I have spoken today of HARRY S TRUMAN, Senator from the State of Missouri and President of the United States. History will recognize HARRY TRUMAN as a great President but the record will show that he was also a great Senator.

In a letter to his daughter Margaret, Senator TRUMAN, with his usual humility, showed that he knew the significance of being a United States Senator:

It's awful what it means to some people to meet a Senator. You'd think I was Cicero or Cato. But I'm not. Just a country jake who works at the job . . .

Whether serving his country as judge, Senator, or President, HARRY TRUMAN was always proud to be "just a country jake." And, whatever job he held he never failed to make an impact on his State and on his country.

Mr. President, I ask unanimous consent that articles on President TRUMAN's life that appeared in the Washington Post, the New York Times, Time, and Newsweek be printed in the Record at this point.

SAYING "WE'RE GOING TO GIVE 'EM HELL," HE DID

(By David S. Broder)

For the Washington Post's veteran political reporter, Edward T. Folliard, it was a very puzzling phenomenon.

A week earlier, on September 9, public opinion analyst Elmo Roper had announced he was suspending his polling on the 1948 election. "Thomas E. Dewey is almost as good as elected," Roper had said, "That being so, I can think of nothing duller or more intellectually barren than acting like a sports announcer who feels he must pretend he is witnessing a neck-and-neck race."

Yet, here, on September 16, was the anointed loser, President HARRY S TRUMAN, starting off on a 16-day train tour, and acting, as Folliard wrote, "not at all like a man who . . . is destined to be an also-ran on election day. He seemed gay and confident as he was boarding his 17-car campaign special and told the crowd: "We're going to give 'em hell.""

It was the start of the showdown phase of one of the most remarkable campaigns in American political history—a struggle against seemingly insuperable odds that was to result in perhaps the greatest upset in our presidential history. That campaign of 1948 remains today one of the imperishable memories left behind by Mr. TRUMAN.

Before the Democratic convention that July, Joseph and Stewart Alsop had written that "if Mr. TRUMAN is nominated, he will be forced to wage the loneliest campaign in recent history."

The "if" was needed, because there were powerful elements in the party who felt that their own political survival dictated dumping the man who had inherited the presidency from Franklin D. Roosevelt three years earlier. Their favorite was none other than Dwight D. Eisenhower and, as Irwin Ross noted in his book on the 1948 race, "The Loneliest Campaign," the coalition behind the draft-Eisenhower movement was indeed "bizarre." Two days before the convention opened, 19 prominent Democrats invited their fellow delegates to a caucus to select "the ablest and strongest man available."

Among the signers: Mayor Hubert H. Humphrey of Minneapolis, Minn., Chester Bowles, Gov. William Tuck of Virginia and Gov. J. Strom Thurmond of South Carolina.

Mr. Eisenhower chilled the fever by issuing a statement that he "could not accept nomination for any public office or participate in partisan political contest." Although such men as Connecticut's boss, John M. Bailey, persisted in their efforts to draft Ike, the desperate coalition splintered, some turning to Justice William O. Douglas, some to Senator Claude Pepper of Florida.

None of these movements got off the ground and the Democrats settled back, glumly, to renominate their "loser."

Why were they so sure he was a loser? Well, the Republicans had won a massive victory in the midterm election of 1946, capturing both houses of Congress for the first time in 16 years.

The old Democratic coalition appeared shattered. The start of the Cold War had split both labor and the liberals, with Henry A. Wallace quitting the Truman Cabinet to form a left-wing Progressive Party that threatened Mr. TRUMAN's chances in New York, California and other industrial states.

The South, traditionally Democratic, was restive over the civil rights program Mr. TRUMAN had sent to Congress.

SOUTHERNER'S WALKOUT

Before the convention was over, a tough civil-rights plank, sponsored by Humphrey, was to cause a walkout by some Southern delegations and provoke a "States Rights" Party campaign with Thurmond as its nominee.

Like George McGovern, 24 years later, Mr. TRUMAN did not reach the platform to make his acceptance speech until the small hours of the morning. "Senator Barkley (Alben Barkley of Kentucky, his running mate) and I will win this election," he said, "and make the Republicans like it—don't you forget it." But few Democrats believed either the first or second clause of that sentence, and most acted as if they would like to forget the whole thing.

Yet, as Folliard noted on the day the Truman campaign train left Washington in Mid-September, "Mr. TRUMAN's buoyancy, his refusal to believe that he is whipped, is not merely a campaign attitude, according to those who know him well . . .

"On his last barnstorming trip, the one that took him to Michigan, he said something that he has often said in private conversation: 'In 1940, I had the bitterest campaign for reelection to the United States Senate that I think any man had in the history of this country. I had every newspaper in the state against me, the governor of the state and his organization was against me, and at 11 o'clock that night all the radio broadcasters and the papers said that I was defeated by 11,000 votes. I went to bed and got up the next morning and found out I had been nominated . . .'"

TYPICAL OF CAMPAIGN

The first major speech of the trip was at the National Plowing Contest in Dexter, Iowa, and one of its lines is sufficient to recall both the rhetorical style and the substance of Mr. TRUMAN's campaign. "The good-for-nothing, do-nothing Republican 80th Congress," he said, "has stuck a pitchfork in the farmer's back."

With suitable variations for the audience, this was the Truman message—that the Republican Congress which had been elected in 1946 had hurt the farmers (by cutting grain-storage facility funds), had hurt labor (by passing the Taft-Hartley bill), and hurt consumers (by ending price controls), had helped the privileged and hurt the common man (by voting tax cuts, cutting housing programs). (It was also refusing to pass most of Mr. TRUMAN's domestic program.)

It was a broadside attack, in exaggerated language, ending with a warning that the "catastrophes" of the past two years were only a sampling of what would happen if Dewey were elected and the Republicans had the government to themselves.

"If you let the Republican reactionaries get complete control of this government," Mr. TRUMAN said on Labor Day in Detroit, "I would fear not only for the wages and living standards of the American working man, but even for our democratic institution of free labor and free enterprise."

Often, TRUMAN would chide his audiences to remember that it was their interests, even more than his own, that were at stake in the election. "How many times do you have to be hit over the head before you find out what's hitting you?" he demanded. "If you let those Republicans get in again, you deserve what will happen."

SPELLED OUT BY CLIFFORD

The strategy underlying the campaign had been spelled out back in November, 1947, in a 43-page memo to the President from Clark Clifford, then a youthful member of the White House staff. Correctly anticipating both the Dewey nomination and the Wallace third-party candidacy (but not the Southern defection and the Thurmond challenge), Clifford argued that Mr. TRUMAN could win the election by cementing the allegiance of farmers, laborers, blacks and Catholics.

His prescription for forming this alliance: Staunch anti-communism abroad and a liberal domestic program at home, designed to force Dewey to say "me, too" to the Truman foreign policy and to defend a conservative Republican congressional record on domestic affairs.

The congressional Republicans were more conservative than the likely GOP nominee, Clifford wrote the President: "The administration should select the issues upon which there will be conflict with the majority in Congress. It can assume it will get no major part of its program approved."

Mr. TRUMAN did just that in 1948, heightening the drama by concluding his acceptance speech with the announcement that he would call Congress back for a special "Turnip Day" session to let the country determine "if there is any reality behind that Republican platform," which, tailored to Dewey's desires, was more progressive than the Republican record. Predictably, nothing came out of the special session, and Mr. TRUMAN had his issue.

Both the reporters covering him could not determine if it was a real issue or not. Folliard noted that there was rarely much response to the rough rhetoric of Mr. TRUMAN's prepared speeches. Although 72,000 people turned out for him at the Plowing Contest "not a single handclap or cheer was heard."

Richard H. Rovere, writing of that September tour in The New Yorker, said, "Nobody stomps, shouts or whistles for TRUMAN . . . I should say that the decibel count would be about the same as it would be for a missionary who had just delivered a mildly encouraging report on the inroads being made against heathenism in Northern Rhodesia."

BETTER OFF THE CUFF

But it was also clear to the reporters that Mr. TRUMAN was drawing big crowds and that the response to his off-the-cuff remarks, much more homely and less strident than his prepared speeches, was overwhelmingly friendly.

On Sept. 25, Folliard wrote: "Hardly a reporter aboard the 17-car special believes that Mr. TRUMAN can reach his goal of a full, four-year term in the White House. The Republican tide is running strong after 16 New Deal years, and it looks at this time as if Gov. Thomas E. Dewey . . . can afford to drift to victory with it.

"If the decision were left to those who turn out for Mr.

TRUMAN at the whistle-stops, however—well, the outcome might be different.

"They like 'HARRY,' those people who have been gathering along the railroad tracks all across the continent and down the Pacific coast. They like him a lot. You can see it in their faces as they look up at him there on the rear platform of the Ferdinand Magellan, smiling and waiting for the high school band to finish 'Hail to the Chief' and the 'Missouri Waltz' . . ."

Whatever the faces showed, the polls showed defeat. The late September Gallup Poll put Dewey ahead, 46.5 to 39—virtually unchanged from the previous month.

DEWEY CONFIDENT

The Republican nominee, accompanied on his campaign train by a press corps twice the size of the incumbent President's, was serenely confident. In his first speech, he said his was "a campaign to unite America." He ignored most of Mr. TRUMAN's thrusts and avoided any pledges of his own more specific than "the biggest unraveling, unsnarling, untangling operation" Washington's bureaucracy had ever seen.

October was more of the same—for both the main rivals. Mr. TRUMAN toured the Eastern cities, drawing what The Post's Robert C. Albright called "huge crowds, running well into the hundreds of thousands."

Having established his domestic indictment, Mr. TRUMAN turned to the other half of the Clifford formula: anti-communism. He had been stung by Republican charges of Red infiltration of his administration. In Boston, with its heavily Catholic population, he sought to turn the tables by arguing, "You can fight communism with a clear-cut vote to defeat Republican reaction. Reactionary Republican policies invited communism in 1932. We were saved then, but we cannot afford to take the risk again."

Time and again, he ridiculed his rival, taunting him as "the man whose name rhymes with hooey." In Minneapolis, he charged, "The Republican Party either corrupts its liberals or it expels them." The crowds continued large, and Frank McHale, the Indiana Democratic National Committeeman, told reporters Oct. 15, "this election could be the biggest upset in political history."

Newsmen traveling with Dewey noted a slight ripple of apprehension and a brief sharpening of the Republican nominee's rhetoric. But an informal poll of the reporters accompanying him found a unanimous belief that he would be victorious, and he settled back into his accustomed pleas for unity.

On Oct. 26, in Cleveland, Mr. TRUMAN charged that the Republicans were using the pre-election polls to insure a light vote. "These polls are like sleeping pills . . . You might call them sleeping polls."

The next day, Dr. George Gallup said loftily that the President's comments were "all part of politics. Mr. TRUMAN would love us if we could show him out in front . . . Either he is wrong, or we are. The people will know in another week."

On the final weekend of the campaign, with Mr. TRUMAN heading for St. Louis and the 275th and last speech of his 22,000-mile campaign, The Post's Marshall Andrews wrote:

"There can be little doubt that Mr. TRUMAN has picked up votes in the last week of his campaign . . . There is a general feeling among unbiased observers that Mr. TRUMAN will poll a much larger vote next Tuesday than has been credited to him . . . He is a new man . . . a platform fighter who has been counting his own points and sees the decision in the bag."

Yet, when all was said and done, Andrews said those same "impartial observers are not willing to concede that Mr. TRUMAN's confidence is justified."

They would admit, he said, "he has put up a masterful fight against what seemed to be insuperable odds" and "if the campaign could have gone on just a few weeks longer, it might have become one of the most exciting in history . . ."

Weeks earlier, however, on Oct. 13, Mr. TRUMAN had given campaign aide George Elsey a state-by-state rundown on his election prospects in which he predicted he would win 340 electoral votes.

NO DOUBT VOICED

Clark Clifford later said that "from the beginning of the campaign until election day, I never heard him express a doubt about winning."

He was virtually alone in that faith, however. The final pre-election Gallup gave Dewey 49.5 per cent and TRUMAN 44.5 per cent. All 50 political reporters in the Newsweek survey picked Mr. Dewey. The pre-election issue of Life carried a picture of the Republican nominee captioned: "The next President of the United States travels by ferry boat over the broad water of San Francisco Bay." Drew Pearson, the Alsop brothers and others wrote advance columns for the editions of Nov. 3, discussing Dewey's Cabinet selections and the problems of the transition to a new President.

As for Mr. TRUMAN, he went home to Independence, Mo., cast a straight Democratic ballot and handed it to the Democratic receiving judge, who happened to be his brother-in-law. His name: George Wallace. Mr. TRUMAN told reporters: "It can't be anything but a victory."

Then he slipped off to Excelsior Springs, had a mineral hot-water bath, came home for a supper of ham-and-cheese sandwiches and buttermilk, and, at 7 p.m. went to bed!

He awoke about midnight and, as he later recalled in one of his most humorous and famous speeches, turned on the radio to hear H. V. Kaltenborn saying he was 1,200,000 votes ahead but was sure to lose when the country vote came in. "So I went back to sleep," Mr. TRUMAN said.

VICTORY CONFIRMED

He was up before dawn, and heard the first newscast of the day confirm the victory he had confidently expected. He went down to the Muehlbach Hotel in Kansas City to join his staff and the newsmen accompanying him.

The sequence was startlingly like that in the earlier senatorial primary, which Mr. TRUMAN had told his audience about back on Labor Day. It was also exactly the kind of "neck-and-neck race" which pollster Elmo Roper had said could not develop.

He won 303 electoral votes (37 fewer than he had predicted), compared to 180 for Dewey and 39 for Thurmond. But a shift of less than 30,000 votes to Dewey in California, Illinois and Ohio would have swung those three states to the Republican and given him an electoral-college majority.

The analyses of the upset were as numerous as the pre-election predictions of a Dewey victory. But as the Alsop brothers wrote, "There is only one question on which professional politicians, poll takers, political reporters and other wiseacres and prognosticators can any longer speak with much authority. That is how they want their crow cooked."

Mr. TRUMAN himself seemed totally nonchalant. He rode his train back to Washington and went to work.

NIXON SETS DAY OF MOURNING

Text of a proclamation by President Nixon announcing the death of HARRY S TRUMAN:

To the people of the United States:

It is my sad duty to announce officially the death of HARRY S TRUMAN, 33d President of the United States, on Dec. 26, 1972.

Throughout his long career in public service, HARRY S TRUMAN was known as a man of forthrightness and integrity. He served with distinction in the United States Senate; and when the death of President Franklin Delano Roosevelt thrust him suddenly into the presidency in April of 1945 at one of the most critical moments of our history, he met that moment with courage and vision. His far-sighted leadership in the postwar era has helped ever since to preserve peace and freedom in the world.

Confronted during his presidency with a momentous series of challenges, his strength and spirit proved equal to them all. His fortitude never wavered, and his faith in American never flagged.

President TRUMAN had a deep respect for the office he held and for the people he served. He gave himself unstintingly to the duties of the presidency while he held it, and in the years afterwards he honorably supported and wisely counseled each of his successors.

The nation to which he gave so much will honor his memory in admiration and respect, and the other countries for which he helped keep freedom alive will remember his name with gratitude.

Now, therefore, I, Richard Nixon, President of the United States of America, in tribute to the memory of President TRUMAN, and as an expression of public sorrow, do hereby direct that the flag of the United States be displayed at half-staff at the White House and on all buildings, grounds, and naval vessels of the United States for a period of 30 days from the day of his death. I also direct that for the same length of time the representatives of the United States in foreign countries shall make similar arrangements for the display of the flag at half-staff over their embassies, legations, and other facilities abroad, including all military facilities and stations.

I hereby order that suitable honors be rendered by units of the armed forces under orders of the Secretary of Defense on the day of the funeral.

I do further appoint Thursday, Dec. 28, 1972, to be a national day of mourning throughout the United States. I recommend that the people assemble on that day in their respective places of worship, there to pay homage to the memory of President TRUMAN and to seek God's continued blessing on our land and on this his servant. I invite the people of the world who share our grief to join us in this solemn observance.

In witness whereof, I have hereunto set my hand this 26th day of December, in the year of our Lord 1972 and of the independence of the United States the 197th.

[From the Washington Post, Dec. 27, 1972]

FORMER PRESIDENT TRUMAN DIES AT 88

(By David S. Broder)

Former President HARRY S TRUMAN, the man from Independence who set an example of personal courage in making the critical decisions that shaped the post-World War II world, died yesterday at the age of 88.

The 33d President of the United States, eulogized by President Nixon as "a fighter who was best when the going was toughest," succumbed at 8:50 a.m. (EST) to a combination of infirmities that had hospitalized him in Kansas City, Mo., 22 days ago.

His widow, Bess Wallace Truman, and his only daughter, Margaret Truman Daniel, who had been at his bedside until last Christmas night, were notified of his death moments later at the family home in Independence, Mo. by his personal physician since White House days, Dr. Wallace Graham.

Mr. Nixon, one of many past political antagonists whose respect for the former President grew with the years, proclaimed Thursday a day of national mourning and ordered flags on federal buildings flown at half-staff for 30 days—past his own inaugural date.

Mr. TRUMAN's state funeral will be held at 3 p.m. Thursday (EST) in the auditorium of the Harry S Truman Library in Independence. Burial will be an hour later in the courtyard of the library, in accordance with plans approved by Mr. TRUMAN several years ago. He had rejected proposals that his body lie in state in Washington.

Attendance at both events will be by invitation only, according to an announcement from Army officials handling the funeral arrangements.

President and Mrs. Nixon will fly to Independence today to lay a wreath at the Truman library and to pay their respects to the Truman family. The Nixons will return to Washington tonight. They will not attend Thursday's funeral, which will be a simple, private ceremony.

Former President Lyndon B. Johnson and Mrs. Johnson will also fly to Independence today to pay their respects.

From 2 p.m. today, when the body is moved from the Carson Funeral Home in Independence, until noon Thursday, Mr. TRUMAN's remains will lie in the lobby of his library, where the public may pay its final respects.

The ceremony in the 200-seat auditorium is expected to be devoid of pomp and pageantry. A more formal memorial service will be held in Washington's National Cathedral at a date within the next two weeks.

Mr. TRUMAN, a World War I artilleryman and unsuccessful haberdasher, who succeeded Franklin D. Roosevelt in the presidency on April 12, 1945, died in a sixth-floor room at Kansas City's Research Hospital.

He had entered the hospital on Dec. 5, suffering from lung congestion. His heart, his kidneys and other organs were also impaired and for the last four days he had been in a coma.

The official medical bulletin said: "The Honorable HARRY S TRUMAN, 33d President of the United States, died at 8:50 a.m. (EST). The cause of death was a complexity of organic failures causing a collapse of the cardio-vascular system."

In addition to his wife and daughter, he is survived by a sister, Miss Mary Jane Truman, 83, who is recovering from injuries suffered in a fall and has been a patient at the hospital where Mr. TRUMAN died. He is also survived by the four children of Margaret Truman Daniel and her husband, E. Clifton Daniel, an associate editor of The New York Times.

Mr. TRUMAN began his political career at the age of 38 with election as judge of the Jackson County court, an administrative post. He served 10 years in the Senate before being selected by Mr. Roosevelt as his fourth-term running-mate in 1944.

The almost eight years he spent in the presidency—from Mr. Roosevelt's death only 82 days into the new term until the succession of Dwight D. Eisenhower on Jan. 20, 1953—was a time of momentous change for this country and the world.

Mr. TRUMAN was barely in the White House when he was called upon to decide whether the atomic bomb—a weapon whose existence had been unknown to him until he succeeded Mr. Roosevelt—should be used against Japan.

Although the decision to drop the nuclear bombs on Hiroshima and Nagasaki remains one of the most controversial of his tenure, Mr. TRUMAN said, "It was a military decision. No other course was conceivable."

More difficult, he said, was the decision to send U.S. troops into South Korea to battle a Communist invasion from North Korea in June, 1950.

But the decision was consistent with the first anti-communism that came to dominate American foreign policy as Mr. TRUMAN guided the nation from the final months of World War II into the Cold War.

In response to earlier challenges, he had sent massive U.S. economic and military assistance to counter Communist threats to Greece and Turkey and mounted the Berlin airlift to defeat a Soviet blockade of the former German capital.

In all these crises, the blunt, plain-talking Missourian won the respect not only of his fellow citizens but of the international leaders—Churchill, Stalin, Adenauer and the rest—who had at first been skeptical of his mettle.

While Mr. TRUMAN will probably be best remembered for the series of decisions Mr. Nixon said yesterday were "crucial to the defense of liberty . . . in the world," he took equal pride in what he called his "acts for peace and human dignity."

Among these he numbered his support of the fledgling United Nations, the Marshall Plan for economic recovery of Europe, his "Point IV" program of technical aid to underdeveloped countries and his quick recognition and strong backing of the state of Israel.

Uniquely among modern Presidents, Mr. TRUMAN combined simplicity of manner with a strong assertion of the authority of his office.

"I'm a meat and potatoes man," Mr. TRUMAN said, disarming his critics, But he was also one who understood and fully exercised the powers of his office. His White House desk carried a small sign reading, "The Buck Stops Here," and he did not hesitate to dismiss a national hero, Gen. Douglas MacArthur, in a bitter dispute over management of the Korean War that Mr. TRUMAN made a classic demonstration of the superiority of civilian authority in the American government.

A strong partisan who achieved one of the great upsets of American political history in winning re-election in

1948, Mr. TRUMAN was engaged in controversy with Congress during much of his time in office.

Although few of his recommendations became law, during his own presidency, included in his "Fair Deal" program were the seeds of many of today's civil rights, housing and social welfare programs.

Those proposals—like his decisions in the international arena—were matters of great controversy at the time, but today the antagonists of the past joined in tribute to Mr. TRUMAN's memory.

House Republican Leader Gerald R. Ford of Michigan called him "one of the most courageous men ever to lead the American people." House Speaker Carl Albert said he was "a people's President, a man who always was himself and with whom every citizen could identify."

Mr. TRUMAN supplied his own appraisal in 1953 after leaving the White House, and it bespeaks the man. "There are a great many people—I suppose a million in this country—who could have done the job better than I did," he said. "But I had the job and I did it."

*

[From Time magazine, Jan. 8, 1973]

THE WORLD OF HARRY TRUMAN

While visiting HARRY TRUMAN in the closing months of his presidency, Winston Churchill spoke with blunt generosity: "The last time you and I sat across a conference table was at Potsdam. I must confess, sir, I held you in very low regard. I lothed your taking the place of Franklin Roosevelt. I misjudged you badly. Since that time, you, more than any other man, have saved Western civilization."

If Churchill was deceived at first, so were most of his contemporaries. Sir Winston, in fact, was some years ahead of other historians in his re-evaluation. TRUMAN was one of those public men whose reputations flourish only after years of retirement. His nondescript appearance, this shoot-from-the-hip partisanship, his taste for mediocre cronies who tainted the record with scandal—all the things that made him seem too small for the office—dwindled in importance with the passing decades. What loomed larger was a sense of the man's courage, a realization that he faced and made more great decisions than most other American Presidents. It was HARRY TRUMAN who decided to drop the atomic bomb. It was the Truman Doctrine that shattered the long U.S. tradition of peacetime isolation by supporting Greece and Turkey against Communist threats. It was TRUMAN's Marshall Plan that committed U.S. resources to the rebuilding of Europe. Later TRUMAN defied the Soviet blockade of Berlin and risked war by authorizing the airlift. Still later he met the Communist invasion of South Korea by ordering U.S. forces into the field.

If those accomplishments were long past, the Truman-esque spunk and will that produced them were evident right up to the end. After a tenacious 22-day struggle in Kansas City's Research Hospital and Medical Center, the nation's 33rd President died, at 88, from what doctors officially termed "organic failures causing a collapse of the cardiovascular system." TRUMAN had detested Richard Nixon for years after the 1952 campaign, when Nixon implied that TRUMAN might be treasonously soft on Communism, but the feud was since mended. Now Nixon proclaimed a 30-day period of national mourning

and praised TRUMAN as "one of the most courageous Presidents in our history" and "a man with guts." Warm tributes from world leaders flowed into Independence, Mo. France's President Georges Pompidou and Great Britain's Queen Elizabeth II both cited TRUMAN's aid in rebuilding Europe after the war. Noting TRUMAN's early recognition and support of Israel, Foreign Minister Abba Eban said the U.S. President had "helped a tormented humanity to stand on its feet and to raise its head high once again."

TRUMAN had personally approved elaborate military plans for a five-day state funeral ("A damn fine show. I just hate that I'm not going to be around to see it," he had said), including attendance by heads of state. But a shorter, simpler schedule was ordered by his wife Bess, 87, whom he had often referred to fondly as "the boss." Instead of the planned procession with muffled drums, a casket-bearing caisson and the symbolic riderless horse, a caravan of 21 cars and a hearse briskly transferred the body from a funeral home to the Truman Library in Independence. There some 75,000 people queued patiently through the night, some carrying sleeping children in their arms, to file past the mahogany coffin. Explained one mourner from Independence: "This whole town was a friend of HARRY's." A wreath of red, white and blue carnations (TRUMAN's favorite flowers) was placed at the casket by President Nixon, who, with Pat, also visited the plain white frame Truman house on Delaware Street. Nixon told Mrs. Truman that the simple ceremonies befitted her husband—"He didn't put on airs." A similar visit was made by Lyndon Johnson, now the only living former President, and Lady Bird. Johnson called TRUMAN "a 20th century giant" and "one of the greatest men to lead freedom's cause."

The funeral itself, held at the library, was basically an Episcopal service, although a Baptist minister and a Masonic leader also participated (TRUMAN, past Masonic Grand Master, was baptized in the Baptist church at age 18; Bess is an Episcopalian). At TRUMAN's request, no hymns were sung and there was no eulogy. Bess and her daughter Margaret watched the ceremony from behind a green curtain that screened them from the 242 invited mourners, all relatives or close friends of the family. At the burials site in the library courtyard—a spot TRUMAN had selected 15 years ago—a frail but composed Bess accepted the folded flag that had covered the coffin, after a trio of traditional military touches: three musket volleys, a final 21-gun salute from howitzers of TRUMAN's beloved World War I Battery D and the blowing of taps.

LIGHTFOOT

HARRY TRUMAN was the country boy of legend who comes to the big city and outwits all the slickers. His parents and grandparents were people of the Middle Border, the odd blend of Midwesterner and Southerner that enriches Missouri with all the paradoxes of that mid-continental mixture. He was innately religious and believed in daily prayer, but like his mother, he was a lightfoot Baptist; he looked on dancing, cardplaying and bourbon drinking with a tolerant eye. He wore his provincialism as proudly as he did his loud sport shirts, which, to much of the world, represent the American tourist.

And what, HARRY TRUMAN would have asked, is wrong with the American tourist? He never pretended;

better than most men, TRUMAN knew himself. He possessed some hard inner kernel of conviction—partly moral, partly intellectual, partly folk wisdom—that was neither proud nor ashamed. It made him secure.

Though he was born provincial, he was not born poor. The family farms ran to hundreds of acres. But wheat futures went bad just when young HARRY graduated from high school in 1901, and college was out of the question.

A congenital eye defect condemned him to thick lenses and excluded him from the wide fraternity of athleticism. Reserved, almost withdrawn as a boy, he read every book in the local library. Later, because he was essentially lonely, he became a joiner. In 1918, his field artillery regiment was sent to France, where Captain TRUMAN for the first time on record displayed the cockerel courage that was to characterize his career. Later he recalled his greeting to the battery: "I told them I knew they had been making trouble for the previous commanders. I said, "I didn't come over here to get along with you. You've got to get along with me. And if there are any of you who can't, speak up right now and I'll bust you right back now!"" Added TRUMAN: "We got along."

Back in civilian life, TRUMAN married his childhood sweetheart, Bess Wallace, and invested his life savings of $15,000 in a haberdashery shop in Kansas City, Mo. He prospered briefly, then went broke during the depression of 1922, but proudly paid back all his creditors although it took years to do so. His political career began when the brother of Kansas City's Boss Thomas Pendergast walked into the failing store, leaned an elbow on the counter, and asked whether TRUMAN would be interested in running for county judge in Jackson County—which includes Kansas City. The offer was apparently made because Boss Pendergast's nephew Jim had served in TRUMAN's regiment. Having no better prospects at the time, TRUMAN said, "Yes, why not?"

In Jackson County, the county judges are the chief elected executives and are concerned with roads, hospitals and political patronage. TRUMAN held the job of judge and later presiding judge for ten of the next twelve years. In 1934, at the age of 50, with the help of Pendergast's machine, he was elected to the U.S. Senate. They called him "the Senator from Pendergast."

The snide remark was unfair. TRUMAN frequently got advice from Pendergast, all right, but just as frequently he disregarded it. Even F.D.R. thought TRUMAN was in Pendergast's pocket; he asked the Missouri boss to get TRUMAN's vote for Alben Barkley as Senate Majority leader. TRUMAN voted for Pat Harrison, observing: "They better learn downtown right now that no Tom Pendergast or anybody else tells Senator TRUMAN how to vote." Reelected to the Senate in 1940, he soon launched the Special Committee Investigating the National Defense Program—the Truman Committee—which was to help carry him to the White House.

LOAD OF HAY

TRUMAN's investigation saved the nation billions of dollars during the huge hurry and grab of wartime procurement. By 1944, his personal stature had grown so impressive that some Democrats saw him as a way out for F.D.R., who was looking for a new running mate to replace the controversial Henry Wallace. James Byrnes was proposed and TRUMAN even agreed to nominate him. But the final choice was an astonished HARRY TRUMAN.

TRUMAN's tenure as Vice President was brief. In less than three months, Eleanor Roosevelt was to tell him: "HARRY, the President is dead." The new President spoke to reporters next day: "I don't know whether you fellows ever had a load of hay or a bull fall on you. But last night the moon, the stars and all the planets fell on me. If you fellows ever pray, pray for me."

He was ill-prepared because Roosevelt had not taken him into his inner councils, had not even let him in on the secret of the atom bomb. For a while, TRUMAN floundered, and he never did acquire any sense of personal grandeur. But he did come to understand his office. On his desk, he placed a sign: "The Buck Stops Here." So did pretension.

Neither status nor success made any significant change. TRUMAN's idea of a holiday was to spend a week in the VIP quarters at the Key West naval base and do a little fishing. He still took his early-morning walks (at the military quick-time pace of 120 steps a minute), to the distress of Secret Service men and reporters trying to stay awake and keep up with him. When a Washington critic said some unpleasant things about the singing talent of his daughter Margaret ("my baby"), he dashed off a letter which said, in part: I have just finished reading your lousy review. I never met you, but if I do you'll need a new nose and plenty of beefsteak and perhaps a supporter below."

MANURE

Always an earthy talker, TRUMAN once offended a friend of his wife's by referring repeatedly to "the good manure" that must have been used to nurture the fine blossoms at a Washington horticulture show. "Bess, couldn't you get the President to say 'fertilizer'?" the woman complained. Replied Mrs. Truman: "Heavens, no. It took me 25 years to get him to say 'manure.'" When confronted by a press conference question he did not care to answer, TRUMAN did not hesitate to say "no comment" or, more pointedly, "That's none of your business."

When confronted by the great issues HARRY TRUMAN never flinched. The one that has brought him the heaviest criticism was the decision to drop the atomic bomb. As was his practice, TRUMAN listened to both sides of the argument, thought, and then decided. Later he recalled: "We faced half a million casualties trying to take Japan by land. It was either that or the atom bomb, and I didn't hesitate a minute, and I've never lost any sleep over it since."

In the wake of World War II, TRUMAN enjoyed a brief honeymoon with the public. Then trouble came. Abroad, the Communists were pressing hard, backing an armed insurrection in Greece and threatening Turkey. In 1947, the hard-pressed British declared that they could no longer defend the borders of freedom in the eastern Mediterranean. Remote as such places then seemed to U.S. interests, the President proclaimed the Truman Doctrine: the U.S. would aid free countries threatened by Communist aggression.

Only months later, TRUMAN initiated Secretary of State George Marshall's plan for the economic revival of Europe. Along with the largely military Truman Doctrine, the Marshall Plan probably staved off imminent revolution in some countries and provided Western Europe with the means to rebuild its cities and industries.

At home, TRUMAN was less successful. He was heavily beset by postwar shortages, inflation, strikes and the mink-coat, deep-freezer hanky-panky of a few subordinates. In responding, TRUMAN characteristically attacked rather than turned defensive. When the railroad workers struck, he threatened to seize the railroads. In early 1948, his popularity was at a low ebb. Panicky party strategists declared that if the Democrats did not appease the South, the party would vanish. Some seriously suggested that TRUMAN should resign. TRUMAN responded by proposing an elaborate series of civil rights measures that only further antagonized the South.

The Democratic Convention in Philadelphia kept him waiting until nearly 2 a.m. on a sweltering night in July 1948 before reluctantly nominating him for a full term. HARRY TRUMAN walked in, wearing an ice-cream suit that only a haberdasher from Missouri would choose for the occasion—and brought the dispirited convention cheering to its feet. He announced that he was calling a "Turnip Day" session of what he had labeled the "do-nothing" 80th Congress to give it a chance to enact its own Republican program.

The Congress predictably did nothing, and HARRY TRUMAN, without major money or major support, set out on a whistle-stop campaign across the country. He lambasted Congress for the higher cost of living, for blocking low-rent housing, for failing to vote grain-storage bins. "Give 'em hell, HARRY!" the crowds cried. The Democratic left had deserted to the third-party candidate, Henry Wallace, the South to Strom Thurmond's States' Rights party, Republican Candidate Thomas E. Dewey was calm, self-confident, and spent much of his time discussing his future Cabinet. Not until midmorning on the day after election did an amazed nation learn that TRUMAN had scored the greatest upset in U.S. electoral history.

UPROAR

His second term soon turned frustrating. Scarcely a month went by without some congressional committee grilling one of his friends for some peccadillo or outright misfeasance. China had been taken over by Communists, contributing to the charge that the State Department was "soft on Communism." When the invasion of South Korea started, TRUMAN reacted with typical dispatch. In a space of 60 hours, he ordered U.S. forces into battle and got U.N. endorsement. When General Douglas MacArthur tried to bully him from abroad and issued battlefront ukases challenging U.S. policy, TRUMAN did not hesitate. He recalled the hero of World War II despite public and political uproar. TRUMAN's reaction was characteristic: "General MacArthur was insubordinate and I fired him. That's all there was to it."

By 1952, the Korean War was bogged down in a seemingly endless stalemate. Senator Joe McCarthy was in full cry, charging that the State Department was infested with Communists. Nervous because of the discovery of some real spies, concerned that the Russians had developed an atom bomb of their own, dismayed by the course of events in Asia, the nation was all too ready to listen. Though he could have run for another term, HARRY TRUMAN decided that he had had enough. It was another sound decision.

In retirement, TRUMAN willingly faded from public life. In Independence, he built a library for his papers of which he was inordinately proud. He still ate at lunch counters, stopped at roadside restaurants on his rare trips, and offered no punditry to later Presidents. He was discontented with the intellectual style of the 1952 candidate, Adlai Stevenson, but could not convey to him what he felt was wrong. TRUMAN was a man of action, and deprived of the power to act, he receded into near anonymity.

When he died, HARRY TRUMAN was under no illusion that he was a giant of intellect or even a "great" man. He was, as has been said, perhaps the greatest little man the U.S. has known. In a nation founded on the principle that ultimate wisdom lodges in its citizens, that is no mean accolade.

A LITTLE TOUCH OF HARRY

Margaret Truman was not only very close to her father, she also attentively followed his career. In an affectionate biography published by William Morrow & Co., she provides insights and asides to the official record.

TRUMAN's relations with Franklin Roosevelt was always ambivalent. Though F.D.R. would later select TRUMAN as his Vice President, in 1940, Margaret reveals, he tried to dump TRUMAN from the U.S. Senate. HARRY resisted and defended his relationship to Kansas City's Pendergast machine.

"It was the White House calling. It was an offer from the President. If Senator TRUMAN would withdraw from the race, he could have a seat on the Interstate Commerce Commission, a life appointment at a salary that was a lot more than Senators were paid. 'Tell them to go to hell.' Dad said. 'For my own self-respect, if nothing else, I must run.' "

Though he chaired the most important wartime committee in Congress—the Truman committee acted as a watchdog over defense—HARRY tried to enlist in the Army. He went to see Army Chief of Staff George Marshall.

" 'I would like very much to have a chance to work in this war as a field artillery Colonel,' he said.

"General Marshall pulled down his spectacles, eyed my gray-haired father, and said, 'Senator, how old are you?'

" 'Well,' said Dad, 'I'm fifty-six.'

" 'You're too damned old. You'd better stay home and work in the Senate.'

"Tartly, Dad replied: 'You're three years older than I am.'

" 'I know, but I'm already a general.' "

TRUMAN was never torn by ambition. He did not particularly want to be Vice President in 1944 when word went out that F.D.R. was interested. Margaret shows how Roosevelt maneuvered him into the job against his will. First, F.D.R. had to get rid of two contenders, Vice President Henry Wallace and James Byrnes.

"The story has long been told that F.D.R finally yielded to the hostility of the city bosses who assured him that they could not deliver their heavily Catholic constituencies for Byrnes because he had abandoned Catholicism in his youth and became a Protestant. James Farley recently told me that the true story is the exact reverse—it was the President who ordered the bosses to spread the story to eliminate Mr. Byrnes. As for Vice President Wallace, F.D.R. sent him off on a trip to China."

As the convention opened, TRUMAN was balking. Finally, Roosevelt was called by the party's chairman, Bob Hannegan, while TRUMAN listened.

" 'Bob, have you got that fellow lined up yet?'

" 'No,' said Mr. Hannegan. 'He is the contrariest Missouri mule I have ever dealt with.'

" 'Well, tell him if he wants to break up the Democratic Party in the middle of a war, that's his responsibility.'

"There was a click and the phone was dead. My father got up, walked back and forth for a moment, and then said, 'Well, if that is the situation. I'll have to say yes. But why the hell didn't he tell me in the first place?'

"In politics, and in every kind of relationship, Dad believed in dealing straight from the shoulder whenever possible. Mr. Roosevelt obviously enjoyed juggling friends and potential enemies to keep them all within the charmed political circle on which he rested his power."

While he served as President, HARRY remarked more than once that he thought the White House might be haunted. He wrote Margaret in 1946:

"I told your mother a 'hant' story which you'd better have her read to you. This old place cracks and pops all night long and you can imagine that old Jackson or Andy Johnson or some other ghost is walking. Why they'd want to come back I could never understand. It's a nice prison but a prison nevertheless. No man in his right mind would want to come here of his own accord.

'Now about those ghosts. I'm sure they're here and I'm not half so alarmed at meeting up with any of them as I am at having to meet the live nuts I have to see every day. I am sure old Andy could give me some good advice and probably teach me some good swear words to use on Molotov and De Gaulle. And I am sure old Grover Cleveland could tell me some choice remarks to make to some political leaders. So I won't lock my doors or bar them either if any of the old coots in the pictures out in the hall wants to come out of their frames for a friendly chat."

When TRUMAN gave up the haunted house he never really liked and retired to private life, he had a chilly meeting with his successor, Dwight Eisenhower. Margaret describes their drive together to Ike's inauguration.

"There was very little conversation during the one-mile ride to the Capitol. Ike remarked that he had not come to the 1948 inauguration because he did not want to attract attention from the President.

" 'You were not here in 1948 because I did not send for you,' Dad said. 'But if I had sent for you, you would have come.'

"When they reached the Capitol, they went to the sergeant-at-arms' office to wait for the summons to the platform. Ike suddenly turned to Dad and said: 'I wonder who is responsible for my son John being ordered to Washington from Korea? I wonder who is trying to embarrass me?'

" 'The President of the U.S. ordered your son to attend your inauguration,' Dad said. 'If you think somebody was trying to embarrass you, then the President assumes full responsibility.'

"My father had ordered John Eisenhower home as a gesture of thoughtfulness. He was not serving in the front lines or in any vital role in the Army, so there was no reason to accuse either his father or Dad of favoritism, or of endangering the public interest. It astonished Dad that Ike resented his gesture. It still astonishes me."

[From Newsweek, Jan. 8, 1973]

FAREWELL TO MR. CITIZEN

There is by now an established ritual for the funerals of American ex-Presidents—lying in state at the Capitol, a congregation of the mighty and the media, a horse-drawn caisson and troop-lined streets, rolling drums and a riderless black horse bearing polished boots stuck backward in the stirrups. But HARRY S TRUMAN had decided that he didn't want most of that, and when his long and exhilarating life finally ended last week at the age of 88, he went out in his own way—in Independence, Mo., his home since boyhood, in a simple funeral ceremony attended by his family and perhaps 250 neighbors and old friends, with burial following immediately, near a stand of pin oaks, flowering cherry and hawthorn trees, in the courtyard of his treasured Truman Library.

History would not be stayed entirely, however—nor would the sentiments of those millions who had come to feel an unabashed and curiously personal affection for the plain-spoken, straight-headed, good hearted Missourian who became the nation's 33rd President. The generation of postwar leaders who knew him as one of their own—Churchill, Stalin, de Gaulle, Adenauer, Marshall, Eisenhower, Attlee—is now dead, but their successors found words to remember him by. France's President Georges Pompidou spoke of the "restoration" of Europe under TRUMAN, and South Korea's President Park Chung Hee of the "heroic leadership and decisions" of the 1950's. U.N. Secretary-General Kurt Waldheim recalled that HST had been present at the creation of the U.N., and NAACP chief Roy Wilkins remembered that it was TRUMAN who first ordered the desegregation of the armed forces. President Nixon, in a measured statement from Key Biscayne, hailed his old foe's "exceptional vision and determination" and offered "a description he himself might have appreciated the most—as a man with 'guts'."

But as apt as these assessments were, TRUMAN's farewell took its real tone from his friends. A few old comrades (Clark Clifford, Averell Harriman, HST's Treasury Secretary John W. Snyder) and present-day politicians (Sen. Hubert Humphrey, Kansas Gov. Robert Docking, Missouri Gov. Warren Hearnes) were on hand for the hour-and-a-half funeral services at the Truman Library. But the mass of mourners were home folks—Bess Truman's bridge club, house painter Robert E. Sanders, several retired guards from the Truman Library, housekeeper Mrs. Vietta Garr, and about fifteen survivors, almost all in their 80's, of Battery D, 129th Field Artillery, 35th Infantry Division, the unit that Capt. HARRY TRUMAN had commanded in France in World War I. Only four pool reporters and one TV camera crew were allowed into the Library auditorium and the nearby courtyard for the services, and they were given minimal shrift. In the auditorium, the Truman family—Mrs. Truman, Margaret Truman Daniel, her husband Clifton Daniel and their four sons—sat concealed behind a green gauze curtain. Outside, at the burial, Mrs. Daniel and her mother stood silent and hatless in the 30-degree chill, flinching at the first boom of a 21-howitzer salute, dabbing occasionally at their eyes, but otherwise defending the privacy of their grief.

HST's death, when it came at 7:50 a.m. on the day after Christmas, ended a 22-day vigil for his family and the nation. The old man, increasingly frail the past two years, had been taken to Research Hospital in Kansas City, Mo., on Dec. 4, suffering from congestion in the lungs. But other complications—kidney malfunction, digestive disorders, the strain on a weakened heart, the over-all burden of his 88 years—quickly set in. The old man doggedly pulled through one crisis and then another—both times reviving enough at least to speak a few words to Bess and Margaret—before slipping into unconsciousness for the last time on Christmas Day.

After his death the next day, his body was taken to the Carson Funeral Home in Independence, where TRUMAN's long-time friend and barber, George Miller, gave him his final trim. The body was dressed in black suit, white shirt and black tie and laid to rest with HST's horn-rimmed glasses and Masonic ring in a flag-draped mahogany casket. Despite the preparations of the U.S. Army—which had spent four years rehearsing a full state funeral, complete with airlifted horses for the caisson—the Truman family settled on a simple black hearse to carry the former President's casket to the Truman Library, where it would be displayed in the main lobby for the next 24 hours.

What pomp there was to HARRY TRUMAN's departure occurred in the brief public interlude. An Army band played "Hail to the Chief" and "Ruffles and Flourishes" as the casket was borne inside the Library, and a flight of 21 A–7 attack bombers cracked over the treetops at 380 mph. President and Mrs. Nixon flew in from Key Biscayne to make a stop at the Truman Library and spend some time paying their respects to the family before heading South again. Lyndon Johnson and Lady Bird also passed through. Then the Library was thrown open to the quiet throngs lined up in the street outside, and for the next 22 hours, through the night and into the next morning, the people filed by—perhaps 75,000 in all.

There was a deeper poignance elsewhere. At the gabled Victorian house on North Delaware Street, Mrs. Truman, thin and exhausted, was supposed to be resting for the funeral—and it was perhaps the best measure of HST's final standing with the public that she got no chance to. Neighbors began phoning, Missouri style, with offers of casseroles and pies to tide the family over the long ordeal. Often, when they called, they found the 87-year-old Mrs. Truman herself on the line. She met with the Nixons, met with the Johnsons, met with the Humphreys—and sent Hubert away bearing one of HARRY's favorite black canes as a last memento. Then after the guards had cleared the last of the visitors from the Truman Library, she went off to bury her husband. When President Nixon disclosed that a formal memorial service, with full honors, would be held in Washington on Jan. 5, after Congress returns, a Truman family friend said that Mrs. Truman was not prepared to say if she would attend.

✦

HARRY S TRUMAN

To most Americans, HARRY S TRUMAN in recent years had become a ghostly figure out of a different, distant past. As his public appearances grew fewer, as frailty and age finally confined him to his large old white frame house in Independence, Mo., it became easier to forget that this quaint and elderly gentleman had been the single most powerful leader in the world through nearly eight tumultuous years—and that Winston Churchill, at dinner on the Presidential yacht Williamsburg in 1952, had roused himself from a postprandial snooze and said to him: "I must confess, sir . . . I loathed your taking the place of Franklin Roosevelt." The old tory paused, then continued: "I misjudged you badly. Since that time, you, more than any other man, have saved Western civilization."

"Saved" may be too strong a word, but the perception behind it was accurate enough. From April of 1945, when he succeeded Franklin D. Roosevelt in the White House, until he retired to his beloved Independence in January of 1953, HARRY TRUMAN made all the important decisions not only for the U.S. but for the whole of the non-Communist world. The policies he laid down in those germinal years are still, for better or worse and whatever the latter-day variations, the bedrock of the U.S. position in the world.

It was TRUMAN who ordered atomic bombs dropped on Hiroshima and Nagasaki in 1945 and then refused to use them against any other foe. It was he who presided over the victorious end of World War II and the perhaps inevitable onset of the cold war, and he who decreed that enlightened self-interest demanded that the U.S. share its incredible resources and wealth with the poor nations. It was he who pushed the once and future schism on the Democratic Party by running on a strong civil-rights platform in 1948. And most poignantly, it was TRUMAN who fixed the nation's determination—in Greece, Korea and a dozen other places—to use military force against all forms of Communist expansion everywhere, defining the dogma that led eventually, in decisions by his successors, to the U.S.'s commitment to Vietnam.

The appealing irony about HARRY TRUMAN was that all his forcefulness—all this initiative and certainty and Jovelike grace to a crushed and frightened world—came pouring out of one of the folksiest and most out-at-elbow Presidents since Andrew Jackson. At the age of 50, eleven years before taking over the Presidency, TRUMAN was a failed farmer and businessman, a lame-duck county judge and a minor pawn in the Kansas City, Mo., machine of boss Tom Pendergast. Even after his accession to the Senate, the Vice Presidency and the Presidency—even after his upset victory over Thomas E. Dewey in the 1948 Presidential campaign—he was constantly demeaned and condescended to.

Robert Taft called him "that roughneck ward politician" and Virginia-born Lady Astor made fun of his twang. (Said HARRY: "At least my accent is natural.") Everybody heehawed at his colorful sport shirts and blanched when he excoriated Washington Music critic Paul Hume for panning his daughter Margaret's singing. TRUMAN was 5 feet 9 inches tall, but the adjective for him was always "little." Even Dwight Eisenhower, riding up Pennsylvania Avenue on his own Inauguration Day in 1953, turned to TRUMAN and explained patronizingly that the reason he hadn't attended TRUMAN's Inauguration four years earlier was that "if I had been present I would have drawn attention away from you. TRUMAN replied evenly: "You were not here in 1949 because I did not send for you. But if I had sent for you, you would have come."

TRUMAN's unsurpassed sureness came partly from Missouri mulishness, partly from his almost magical belief in the power and dignity and rightness of the office of President. In the beginning, he needed all of this faith just to survive. TRUMAN himself told of being summoned to the White House from Capitol Hill on the night of April 12, 1945, and being told by Eleanor Roosevelt: "HARRY, the President is dead." TRUMAN finally stammered, "Is there anything I can do for you?" Mrs. Roosevelt replied immediately: "Is there any way we can help you? For you are the one who is in trouble now."

The new President's deepest trouble came not from the stunning news of Roosevelt's death—TRUMAN and most of the Democratic hierarchy had known that FDR could not live out his fourth term—but from his own innocence of statecraft. FDR had run the Presidency out of his hat for thirteen years, with no executive chain of command, no clear division of responsibilities and no contingencies whatever for his dying. TRUMAN was now responsible for a final decision about using the atomic bomb but he didn't know that such a thing existed. He was about to debate the course of the postwar world with Stalin and Clement Attlee at Potsdam but he had never met either of them nor been to Europe since 1918. He was a Commander in Chief who knew none of his generals, a President who barely knew his Cabinet.

Yet he got the hang of things extraordinarily fast. Stalin fooled him for about two days (he told an aide that Stalin was as nice a fellow as his old patron Tom Pendergast), but by the end of the Postdam conference he was writing home to his mother: "You never saw such pigheaded people as are the Russians. I hope I never have to hold another conference with them." TRUMAN could be pretty stubborn himself. In Iran, Trieste, Berlin and finally Korea, to the howls of Western leftists, he countered Stalin's expansionism with enough American force to do the job, at the same time holding off those who wanted a nuclear attack launched against the Russians before they got their own A-bomb. The touchiest test came when the Russians sealed off the Allied corridor into Berlin in June of 1948. Some advisers wanted to fight their way through, others to launch preventive war on Russia. TRUMAN decided (over the objections of Gen. Hoyt Vandenberg, his Air Force Chief of Staff) to fly over the blockade, and the U.S. fed, fueled and supplied a city of 2.4 million by airlift for nearly a year.

The Missourian was equally decisive about the atomic bomb, though history will probably never make up its mind whether he decided rightly. TRUMAN learned about the atomic project from Secretary of War Henry Stimson half an hour after he took the oath of office, and was assured the next day by Adm. William D. Leahy that it wouldn't work. "This is the biggest fool thing we have ever done," said the Chief of Naval Operations. "The bomb will never go off, and I speak as an expert in explosives." Three months later the first atomic device did go off at Alamogordo, N.M. Told by his advisers (now including Leahy) that use of the bomb would save 500,000 American lives—and just as many Japanese—by obviating an invasion of the Japanese mainland. TRUMAN ordered the first bomb dropped in early August of 1945 on one

of four cities: Hiroshima, Kokura, Nagasaki, or Niigata. On Aug. 6, the Enola Gay destroyed Hiroshima. When the Japanese hesitated, TRUMAN ordered the other one dropped on Nagasaki, and five days later the war end d. There had been no real thought given to showing the Japanese the awesome power of the bomb on uninhabited terrain because the U.S. had only two atomic bombs. "I never lost any sleep over my decision," TRUMAN said later.

For a man with his instant military reflexes, TRUMAN was extraordinarily receptive to the more humanitarian tools of policy. In May of 1947, he sent the late Dean Acheson (then his Under Secretary of State, later the Secretary) to deliver a speech in his stead at an obscure teachers college in Cleveland, Miss. The U.S., said Acheson, speaking the President's words, must "push ahead with the reconstruction of the great workshops of Europe." The U.S. press paid little attention, but The Times of London and other European journals saw what was coming and cheered. Ten months later the U.S. Senate passed the so-called Marshall plan, appropriating the first $5.3 billion of the roughly $29 billion in economic aid that the U.S. would send to Europe in the next twenty years. The Point Four program, introduced in TRUMAN's Inaugural Address in 1949, did much the same thing for undeveloped countries. Historian Arnold Toynbee has since written that these mammoth projects of economic assistance, both of them without any real precedent in world history, "will be remembered as the signal achievement of the age."

The substitution of Acheson for the President in Cleveland had a touch of the prophetic. In 1949 the unschooled Missourian appointed the Connecticut Brahmin to the top job at the State Department, and the two of them together laid most of the cornerstones of American cold-war foreign policy—NATO, military assistance to the "free world," a determination to contain Communism wherever an aneurysm appeared. The two men had a curiously deep symbiotic relationship. TRUMAN valued and relied on his Secretary, and defended him to the ditches when the GOP came howling for his scalp; Acheson for his part heaped his chief with praise that stopped just short of fulsome. Acheson called him "the greatest little man" he had ever known and in later years paid lengthy written tribute to TRUMAN's decisiveness, integrity, wisdom, modesty, selflessness and humanity—usually making his point with an anecdote in which TRUMAN would demonstrate the virtue in question by deferring to his Secretary of State. If TRUMAN detected a whiff of condescension, he never let on.

TRUMAN's domestic programs were frequently as bold as the foreign ones, but most of them were summarily beaten back by Congress whether or not the Democrats were in charge. In the first blaze of his triumphant Inauguration in 1949, with overwhelming Democratic control of both houses. TRUMAN sent up an ambitious 24-point "Fair Deal" program that would take up where FDR's New Deal left off. Of the 24 programs—covering medical insurance, immigration policy, farm supports, civil rights, the whole liberal range—only his public-housing bill got through Congress, and that only through the last-minute cooperation of conservative GOP Sen. Robert A. Taft.

For most of the last years of his Presidency, in fact, it seemed that everything TRUMAN touched turned to controversy and vituperation. Corruption flowered in half a dozen places, never involving TRUMAN but now and then touching old friends whom the President characteristically would not disavow—leading to widespread talk of a "mess in Washington." The Washington Times-Herald called him a dishonest nincompoop and Sen. Joseph McCarthy, waving his fictitious list of 205 "Communists in the State Department, implied that the President was a traitor. TRUMAN snapped back tartly. "We are not going to turn the United States into a right-wing totalitarian country," he said, "in order to deal with a left-wing totalitarian threat." On the other hand, he often got too tart for his own good. Acheson once remarked that the State Department "kept on hand, as a sort of first-aid kit, a boxful of 'clarifications' " for use after the boss had harpooned everyone at a news conference.

The national uproar reached its loudest over the President's instigation and conduct of the Korean War. When the U.N. Security Council—taking advantage of Russia's absence—branded North Korea an aggressor in June of 1950, TRUMAN immediately committed the full weight of U.S. forces to the defense of South Korea, at the same time avoiding a declaration of war by labeling the conflict a "police action." His middle-road policy was clear enough—he wished to hold the line in Korea without touching off World War III—but he was pummeled by criticism from both sides. If this was war, the liberals asked, why not have Congress declare it? If this was war, conservatives demanded, why not fight it all-out—not excluding the use of atomic weapons, and not excluding the bombing of Red China after the nation entered the war from the north in 1950? The President demurred; his object, he reiterated, was to preserve the integrity of South Korea, the U.S. and the U.N., not to risk global war.

TRUMAN's policy led him into a running debate—private at first but finally open and bitter—with Gen. Douglas MacArthur, the flamboyant and imperious commander of allied forces in Korea. As the war ossified into a bloody stalemate between two unbudgeable armies, MacArthur called more insistently for the right to bomb Chinese bases, atomically or otherwise. TRUMAN warned his commander to keep his arguments private. When MacArthur persisted in publicly second-guessing his Commander in Chief, TRUMAN sacked him in April 1951, then watched in apprehension as MacArthur came home to a gigantic hero's welcome in the streets and before a joint session of Congress. TRUMAN's fears that MacArthur would foment some kind of reactionary movement were unfounded. But the general's dismissal did fortify the suspicions of those right-wingers who thought they detected a "softness" in U.S. policy, and also gave new impetus to the China lobby, which held the Democrats responsible for Mao Tse-tung's defeat of Chiang Kai-shek in 1945-1949. Though the Korean intervention ended in 1953 with South Korea territorially and politically intact, it left as bad an after-taste of any U.S. war up to Vietnam.

TRUMAN's supposed unpopularity—and just about everybody who was anybody agreed that he was unpopular—led to the most flamboyant success of his Presidency: his own re-election in 1948. In May of that year, Time was calling him "awkward, uninspired and above all mediocre," and Gallup reported that only 36 percent of the nation thought he was doing well in his job. Half a dozen top Democratic politicians—including Jake Arvey in Chicago, Richard Russell in Georgia, and Mayors Frank Hague and William O'Dwyer of Jersey City and New York—tried to get Eisenhower to declare himself receptive to a Democratic draft for President. When Eisenhower finally declined, the Democrats nominated TRUMAN in a spirit of helpless gloom, "We're Just Mild About HARRY," read the signs at the Democratic convention, and The New York Post concluded: "The party might as well immediately concede the election to Dewey and save the wear and tear of campaigning."

Things got worse before they got better. Henry Wallace, FDR's Vice President from 1941 to 1945, had already formed his own Progressive Party to chip away at the Democratic left. South Carolina's Gov. J. Strom Thurmond, then a Democrat, led a massive Southern walkout over civil rights and formed his own Dixiecrat ticket to box off the Democrats' so-called Solid South. A reporter asked Thurmond why he was so angry, since TRUMAN's civil-rights platform was no different from FDR's. "I agree," said Thurmond, "but TRUMAN really means it."

Just about the only man who believed that TRUMAN had a chance was TRUMAN himself—and he knew something the others didn't. In June of 1948, before the campaign began, HST accepted an honorary degree from the University of California at Berkeley and used the cross-country train trip to deliver a score of fiery, crowd-rousing partisan speeches. They were slangy, combative, extemporaneous talks and they brought the crowds to life in a way that TRUMAN had never managed in all his Presidential years of earnest, droning statesmanlike dullness. When the campaign began, the brand-new "Give-'em-Hell" HARRY just stepped up the volume and the tempo, jeering and slashing at the Republicans and the "do-nothing 80th Congress" for 22,000 miles and reaching some 10 million to 15 million citizens in person.

Give-'em-Hell HARRY drew some phenomenal crowds—50,000 on a cold night in Indianapolis, 300,000 in Chicago, 5,000 in a driving rainstorm at 8 a.m. in Albany, N.Y. In Ohio, Democratic gubernatorial candidate Frank Lausche, fearing defeat-by-association, made plans to ride the train for only a few miles. But he peered unbelievingly at a mob in the Columbus station, murmured that it was "the biggest crowd I ever saw in Ohio," and stayed on the train all the way to Cleveland. Reporters and pundits saw it all but would not believe that it meant anything. "Could we be wrong?" asked a Washington Post reporter after TRUMAN outdrew Dewey by 2½ to 1 in St. Paul. The polls insisted that Dewey would win easily, and the papers, the pundits and politicians agreed—including TRUMAN's own staff and all the Democratic fat cats. The President's campaign was so underfinanced that he was regularly cut off the radio in mid-speech for nonpayment, and once in Oklahoma his staff took up a collection to get his train out of the station.

And in the end he won it anyway—in a way that still doesn't seem quite credible. The Wallace vote gave New York to Dewey, and Thurmond carried four Southern states for the Dixiecrats. But TRUMAN swept California, Ohio and Illinois, all supposedly safe for Dewey, and took most of the Republican Farm Belt; he woke up the next morning with 304 electoral votes, 38 more than he had to have. "You've got to give the little man credit," said Republican Sen. Arthur Vandenburg of Michigan, damning him with the adjective again, but Ohio's Taft could not manage even a backhanded graciousness. "I don't care how the thing is explained," he said, "it defies all common sense to send that roughneck ward politician back to the White House."

It defied Taft's sort of common sense for TRUMAN to have got to the White House in the first place. HARRY S (for nothing) TRUMAN was born on May 8, 1884, the eldest of three children of John Truman, a western Missouri mule trader and farmer, and his wife, Martha. His mother was the major force in the boy's life, a proud, vigorous, lemony Baptist and Southerner who lived to be 94 and who said, before her first visit to the White House in 1945, "You tell HARRY that if he puts me in the room with Lincoln's bed in it I'll sleep on the floor." She fell down an East Wing stairway on that stay—she was 92 years old—but didn't tell anyone about it until after she had gone home to Independence.

Young HARRY was bright, diligent and retentive—60 years later he was winning scripture-quoting contests from visiting clergymen—but his father's financial collapse ruled out college. For ten years in his 20s and early 30s, HARRY farmed 900 acres belonging to his mother's family, and he might never have left but for the Great War. HARRY went over as an eager first lieutenant of artillery and came back as the seasoned Capt. HARRY TRUMAN of D Battery, a good drinker and poker player and confident leader of men. "So far as its effect on HARRY TRUMAN was concerned," wrote his biographer Alfred Steinberg, "World War I released the genie from the bottle."

Flush and fired up with his own modest sense of destiny, the 35-year-old TRUMAN went back to Independence to acquire a bride—Bess Wallace, whom he had been courting since high school—and a mother-in-law, the imperious and disapproving Madge Gates Wallace, who made her home with the Trumans for the next 30 years and assured reporters in 1948 that her son-in-law was going to be thrashed by Dewey. The Trumans' only child, Margaret, was born in 1924.

By this time, TRUMAN had already taken his first political plunge and came up as county judge under the aegis of the Pendergast machine in Kansas City. (TRUMAN's one business venture—a haberdashery store that got caught in the recession of 1921—had already gone under, a failure that some Republicans were still gratuitously sneering about in 1948.) TRUMAN was beaten in 1924 by someone named Rummell, the only man ever to win an election from him, then was elected presiding judge in 1926 and again in 1930. But in 1934, not allowed to succeed himself again, TRUMAN wrote that "retirement in some minor county office was all that was in store for me."

Instead, he got lucky and stayed lucky for the rest of his life. Pendergast's three top choices for U.S. Senator in 1934 declined to run, and TRUMAN got the chance to stand as Pendergast's man in a three-way Democratic primary. The whole campaign, said The St. Louis Post-Dispatch, was "the pot, kettle and stewpan calling each other black." On election night, the bosses in St. Louis reported that TRUMAN's principal opponent, a local boy named John J. Cochran, had run up 104,265 votes to 3,742 for TRUMAN. Just hours later Pendergast announced the Kansas City vote: TRUMAN 137,529, Cochran 1,525. TRUMAN was in and he won handily in the main election against a worn-out Republican, but FDR was so offended by the logistics of his fellow Democrat's victory that he wouldn't receive TRUMAN in the White House for months after he was sworn in.

TRUMAN's connection with Pendergast was curious but probably not venal. The machine delivered plenty of votes,

and HST always declared himself grateful; on the other hand, TRUMAN always did his job independently and honestly, and even when Boss Tom was put away for taking a $750,000 bribe from a group of insurance firms. TRUMAN's name never turned up even on the fringes. The public and the press remained suspicious of the Pendergast connection clear through his nomination for Vice President in 1944. But politicians understood the niceties of the situation far better, and TRUMAN was a popular Senate club man almost from the beginning. He was trustworthy, hard-working and fanatically loyal, all of which virtues were balanced nicely by his fondness for bourbon, stud poker and courthouse camaraderie. (Unlike many of his colleagues, HST was never a womanizer; he wrote primly in his diary: "In reading the lives of great men, I found that the first victory they won was over themselves and their carnal urges.")

TRUMAN voted a straight New Deal line for six years— and his reward was that Roosevelt backed Missouri Gov. Lloyd Stark in the 1940 Senatorial primary. TRUMAN's response presaged 1948. With few allies, no money and no prospects, "Tom Pendergast's stooge" toured 75 rural counties by car, swapping insults with his opponents in what he later called "the bitterest and dirtiest fight I ever witnessed." TRUMAN put together a rough alliance of a few labor, Negro and urban leaders to strengthen his hand in the cities, and it was just enough. He won the primary by 8,000 votes, the main election against Republican Manvelle Davis by 44,000; FDR gave up and wrote congratulations.

FDR and HST were destined to come far closer together than that. World War II gave TRUMAN his first taste of national celebrity, when he was appointed to head a committee looking into chicanery and waste in defense programs. In less than three years, the Truman committee turned out 32 major reports on inefficiency and corruption in war production and claimed to have saved taxpayers $15 billion. By 1942, Tom Pendergast's stooge was a major campaign asset for the Democrats; by the spring of 1944, he was being touted to run with the ailing FDR, who was under strong pressure from labor unions and party bosses to dump his current Vice President, the excessively Russophilic Wallace. When FDR tapped him for the nomination, TRUMAN knew clearly enough what it meant, "I had a hollow feeling within me," he said after seeing FDR in early 1945. "He seemed a spent man."

TRUMAN was 60 when he took over the Presidency and 68 when he left Washington for the last time to retire to Independence. A few months after he left the White House, a reporter asked him if he wasn't getting a little less militant. "Not in the slightest degree," said HARRY. "They are trying to make a statesman out of me but they will never succeed."

One of his regular targets in those first days as a private citizen was the new President. TRUMAN's wartime friendship with Dwight Eisenhower had deteriorated in 1952 when, said TRUMAN, Ike "permitted a campaign of distortion and vilification that he could not possibly have believed was true." TRUMAN subsequently referred to Eisenhower as the "most inept" President since Millard Fillmore. In both 1952 and 1956, TRUMAN campaigned for Adlai Stevenson (although the independence and vacillation of the Illinois governor offended

HST's sense of party solidarity), as he did for John Kennedy in 1960.

TRUMAN liked to tour the nation's schools and colleges, talking about government and history. Reporters were forever seeking him out in airport lounges and hotel lobbies—or trotting behind him on one of his habitual morning walks—to ask his opinion on the latest developments at home and abroad. TRUMAN would not generally comment on foreign affairs—"no one but the President has enough information," he would say—but he went pretty much all the way with LBJ on the Vietnam war.

In between public appearances there was a happy, busy life among his neighbors in Independence. Bess took up housework again and HARRY got used to dialing a phone and driving a car. He wrote about the years of his Presidency and those that followed, later turning some of the material into a TV series. He also had more time for his daughter and her husband, New York Times associate editor E. Clifton Daniel, and their four sons. "Leaving the White House involves no problem of adjustment if you were a common citizen before," he remarked.

His favorite project was raising funds for—then presiding over—the $1,659,000 Harry S Truman Library in Independence, now run by the National Archives. The library features 9.5 million documents of TRUMAN's Administration, a replica of his old Executive Office and a White House piano—not to mention an informal talk about "The Greatest Government in the World," given periodically to visiting schoolchildren by an ebullient HARRY himself.

In the last two years, the old engine quietly ran down, confining him more and more to the frame house on North Delaware Street. One final accolade remained—a proud, thorough and loving memoir by Margaret Truman Daniel called "HARRY S TRUMAN," advance copies of which were just reaching the bookstores in the week when TRUMAN was taken to Research Hospital with lung congestion.

Through all the years of power and the accolades that came to him in retirement, TRUMAN never dropped the modest bearing that tied him to the common man. Before the sprightliness went out of his step near the end, he made a point of attending the annual birthday party thrown for him at a Kansas City hotel. At one such celebration, an unexpected phone call came through from then President Lyndon Johnson. "We've had thirteen years to see the wisdom of your policies," Johnson remarked. "I have always thought you'd rather have your friends cussing you than praising you, but you'll have to go right on paying the cost of greatness."

"I can't agree that it was great," beamed HARRY TRUMAN, "but I did the best I could."

RICHARD BOETH.

JUST CALL ME "CAPTAIN HARRY"

"Dear Mamma and Mary:

"I am 61 this morning and I slept in the President's room in the White House last night. They have finished the painting and have some of the furniture in place. I'm hoping it will all be ready for you by Friday. My expensive gold pen doesn't work as well as it should.

"This will be an historical day. At 9:00 o'clock this morning I must make a broadcast to the country announcing the German surrender."—Letter to his mother and sister.

May 8, 1945.

* * * * *

"I remember when I first came to Washington. For the first six months you wonder how the hell you ever got here. For the next six months you wonder how the hell the rest of them ever got here."—To Leonard Lyons. February 1950.

* * * * *

"I never ran for a political office I wanted. But I've fought for every one I ever had. Damn it! I've never had an office I didn't have to fight for, tooth and nail."—To a reporter, July 1944.

* * * * *

"Card games? The only game I know anything about is that game—let me see— I don't know what the name is, but you put one card down on the table and four face-up, and you bet."—To a reporter, October 1944.

* * * * *

". . . the President gets a lot of hot potatoes from every direction . . . and a man who can't handle them has no business in that job. That makes me think of a saying that I used to hear from my old friend and colleague on the Jackson County Court. He said, 'HARRY, if you can't stand the heat, you better get out of the kitchen.' I'll say that is absolutely true."—Remarks at the Wright Memorial (Dinner of the Aero Club of Washington. Dec. 17, 1952).

* * * * *

"The Republicans have General Motors and General Electric and General Foods and General MacArthur and General Martin and General Wedemeyer. And they have their own five-star general running for President . . . I want to say to you that every general I know is on this list except general welfare, and general welfare is in with the corporals and privates in the Democratic Party."—

Campaign speech, 1952.

* * * * *

The Buck Stops here!—Sign on HST's desk.

* * * * *

". . . a man in his right mind would never want to be President, if he knew what it entails. Aside from the impossible administrative burden, he has to take all sorts of abuse from liars and demagogues . . . All the President is, is a glorified public relations man who spends his time flattering, kissing and kicking people to get them to do what they are supposed to do anyway."—Letter to his sister, November 1947.

* * * * *

"We'll have none of that now. When I put on those striped pants and that top hat, you can call me 'Mr. President,' but here and at all such reunion occasions you can make it just 'Captain HARRY'."—Reunion breakfast with Battery D. Inauguration Day 1949.

* * * * *

"I have just read your lousy review [of Margaret Truman's recital] . . . I never met you, but if I do you'll need a new nose and plenty of beefsteak and perhaps a supporter below. Westbrook Pegler, a guttersnipe, is a gentleman compared to you."—Letter to Washington Post music critic Paul Hume, Dec. 6, 1950.

*   *   *   *

"It all seems to have been in vain. Memories are short and appetites for power and glory are insatiable. Old tyrants depart. New ones take their place. Old allies become the foe. The recent enemy becomes the friend. It is all very baffling and trying, [but] we cannot lose hope, we cannot despair. For it is all to obvious that if we do not abolish war on this earth, then surely, one day, war will abolish us from the earth."—Independence, January 1966.

*   *   *   *   *

"I always quote an epitaph on a tombstone in a cemetery in Tombstone, Arizona: 'Here lies Jack Williams. He done his damndest'."—Press conference, April 1952.

[From the New York Times, Dec. 27, 1972]

FROM MISSOURI FARM TO FAME

"My first memory is that of chasing a frog around the backyard in Cass County, Missouri. Grandmother Young watched the performance and thought it very funny that a 2-year-old could slap his knee and laugh so loudly at a jumping frog."

HARRY S TRUMAN was 68 when he wrote that recollection of his carefree farm childhood, so secure in strong, affectionate family bonds.

A product of the Middle Border and of hardy farming stock with frontier traditions, TRUMAN was born at 4 p.m., May 8, 1884, in a small frame house at Lamar, Mo. He was the first-born of John Anderson Truman and Mary Ellen Young Truman. The initial "S" was a compromise between Shippe and Solomen, both kinsmen's names.

Within the year the family moved to a farm near Harrisonville, Mo., where another son, Vivian, was born in 1886. A year later the Trumans were living on a Jackson County farm, near what was to be Grandview. There, Mary Jane, the third child, was born.

"Those were wonderful days and great adventures," TRUMAN said of his growing up on 600 stretching acres. "My father bought me a beautiful black Shetland pony and the grandest saddle to ride him with I ever saw." When HARRY was 6, the family moved once more, to Independence, a Kansas City suburb, but John Truman remained a farmer and took up the buying and selling of cattle, sheep and hogs.

THE GIRL WITH THE GOLDEN CURLS

It was in Independence that HARRY, whose mother had taught him his letters by 5, went to school. He made friends, one in particular. "She had golden curls . . . and the most beautiful blue eyes," he said of Bess Wallace, the childhood sweetheart who was to become his wife. HARRY was a shy boy with weak eyes who wore glasses from the age of 8. Shunning rough-and-tumble sports, he read fast and furiously. By 14 he "had read all the books in the Independence Public Library, and our big old Bible three times through."

Poor eyesight barred him from the United States Military Academy (to which he had an appointment) when he was graduated from high school in 1901; and, since the family lacked the money to send him to college, he turned

to a variety of jobs. He worked as a drugstore clerk, timekeeper on a railroad construction project, in a mailroom, in a bank. He speculated in zinc and oil. And he toiled on the family farm. Meantime he joined Battery B of the National Guard in 1905 and became a member of the Masonic Order in 1909.

When the United States entered World War I, TRUMAN, then 32, was a farmer. He left the soil to help organize the 129th Field Artillery, and he became commander of its Battery D. He led it into action at St. Mihiel, in the Meuse-Argonne offensive in France, and again at Verdun, gaining the respect and affection of his men. (At convivial reunions later, "Captain HARRY" used to play the piano—he had learned as a youth, at his mother's insistence—while his comrades sang.)

Mustered out in 1919, he returned to Independence and married Miss Wallace on June 28. Then 35 and without a firm station in civilian life, he opened a haberdashery shop in Kansas City in association with Edward Jacobson, an Army buddy. At the start, business was excellent, but the postwar depression changed all that, and Truman & Jacobson were obliged to close. Jacobson went through bankruptcy proceedings; TRUMAN did not, and he was still paying off his creditors (the total sum was $28,000) 10 years later when he was a Senator.

TRUMAN's entry into politics was fortuitious. It occurred in 1921, when James Pendergast, an Army friend, introduced TRUMAN to his father, Mike Pendergast, who, with his brother, Thomas J., ran Democratic politics in western Missouri. A veteran, a Baptist, a Mason, the personable TRUMAN was adjudged a likely officeholder, and in 1922 he was elected a judge of the Jackson County Court. The post, a nonjudicial one, had jurisdiction over the building and upkeep of the county roads and public buildings.

TRUMAN was conscientious, vigorous and industrious, both as a campaigner and as an administrator. He was defeated, however, in 1924. But in 1926 he was elected presiding judge and again in 1930, both times with the help of the Pendergast organization. In 1934 TRUMAN wanted to run for the House of Representatives, but the Pendergasts put him up for the Senate instead. Running on a pro-Roosevelt program in a strenuous campaign, he won with a majority of more than 250,000 votes. His record of probity as a county official and his Masonic connections helped him.

Although TRUMAN never disavowed his close friendship with Thomas Pendergast, the leader of the party machine, he made it clear in the Senate and elsewhere that he was not "Pendergast's messenger boy." There was never any tarnish on his reputation for personal integrity.

TRUMAN was nearly 51 when he took his Senate seat. But "I was as timid as a country boy arriving on the campus of a great university for the first year," he recalled, "I had a prayer in my heart for wisdom to serve the people acceptably."

"PLAIN FOLKS" IN CAPITAL

In Washington, Senator and Mrs. Truman lived simply in an apartment with their daughter and only child, Mary Margaret, who was born Feb. 17, 1924. The family was "plain folks," with TRUMAN coming home in the evening to talk to Margie, as he called his daughter, and to recount the day's happenings to his wife, whom he called "The Boss." The Trumans were little evident on the social and cocktail circuit. Mrs. Truman was popular with the Congressional wives and her husband with his colleagues. For relaxation, he liked to sip bourbon and water (but never in the presence of women, not even his wife) and to play a bit of poker. Otherwise he worked; there were documents and books and reports to read, committee duties to fulfill, constituents to see and do favors for, Senate sessions to attend.

The years TRUMAN spent in the Senate he recalled as "the happiest 10 years of my life." He found his fellow Senators "some of the finest men I have ever known," and he used the word "cherish" to describe his friendship for them. He was a member of two important committees—Appropriations and Interstate Commerce—to whose work he devoted himself with diligence. He read voluminously from the Library of Congress, but he spoke seldom on the Senate floor, and then simply, briefly, without ostentation. His voting record was New Deal, which earned him the opposition of the big Missouri papers.

TRUMAN was re-elected in 1940, but only after a hard and close Democratic primary race. Harry Vaughan, later to be a White House crony, and Robert Hannegan, later to be Postmaster General, worked hard for TRUMAN, and to them, as to other friends, he was unswervingly loyal. It was part of his creed of "doing right."

DEFENSE WASTE EXPOSED

When TRUMAN was sworn for his second term in 1941, the nation was preparing for war, and the letting of defense contracts was surrounded with rumors of favoritism and influence. Deeply concerned, TRUMAN got into his automobile for a 30,000-mile tour of major defense plants and projects.

"The trip was an eye-opener, and I came back to Washington convinced that something needed to be done fast," he said. "I had seen at first hand that grounds existed for a good many of the rumors . . . concerning the letting of contracts and the concentration of defense industries in big cities."

The result was the Special Committee to Investigate the National Defense Program, soon shortened to the Truman Committee after the name of its chairman. It saved the country many millions of dollars by curbing waste and discouraging graft. And it made TRUMAN a minor national figure, conspicuous for his firmness and his fairness.

TRUMAN prepared his investigation by making a thorough study of similar committees in the past, especially of the records of the Joint Committee on the Conduct of the War Between the States. Defining his approach, the Senator said:

"The thing to do is to dig up the stuff now and correct it. If we run the war program efficiently, there won't be an opportunity to undertake a lot of investigations after the war and cause a wave of revulsion that will start off the country on the downhill road to unpreparedness and put us in another war in 20 years."

The committee got under way slowly, with $15,000 appropriated for its tasks. TRUMAN invested $9,000 of this in the salary of Hugh Fulton, the group's investigator and counsel. The committee quickly turned up disquieting evidence of waste in military-camp construction and equipment. And once its first reports—sober, factual and damning—were issued, more money for its operations was forthcoming.

The dollar-a-year man came under its scrutiny, and the committee was able to produce evidence that between June 1, 1940 and April 30, 1941, Army and Navy contracts totaling almost $3-billion had gone to 65 companies whose officials or former officials were serving in Washington and elsewhere as unpaid advisers to Federal agencies.

TRUMAN also inquired into aluminum production, the automobile industry, the aviation program, copper, lead, zinc, and steel; into labor, plant financing, defense housing, lobbying, ordnance plants, small business and Goverment contracts. Scarcely any aspect of procurement escaped his attention. The committee's hearings were orderly, remarkably free of partisanship, but they produced news and, more important, correction of the abuses that the Senators had brought to light.

TRUMAN was as unsparing of industrialists as he was of union leaders. He criticized William S. Knudsen, director of the Office of Production Management, for "bungling"; he was just as harsh with Sidney Hillman, the union leader, who was associate director of the office.

The Senator was himself a zestful investigator and a keen questioner. He said later that the committee's watchdog role "was responsible for savings not only in dollars and precious time but in actual lives" on the battlefield.

In the course of the committee's work, TRUMAN was in touch with President Roosevelt, but there was no immediate serious thought of him as Vice-Presidential material. When early in 1944 some friends mentioned the possibility to him, TRUMAN "brushed it aside."

"I was doing the job I wanted to do; it was the one I liked, and I had no desire to interrupt my career in the Senate," he said.

Indeed, TRUMAN had so far removed himself from consideration that he had agreed in July, on the eve of the Democratic Convention in Chicago, to nominate James F. Byrnes for Vice President, after Byrnes told him that Roosevelt had given him the nod. Meantime Roosevelt had decided to drop Vice President Henry A. Wallace and also, it turned out, to pass over Byrnes.

The choice fell on TRUMAN. He was not so closely identified with labor as Wallace, although he was acceptable, nor was he a Southern conservative, as was Byrnes. He was without fierce enemies, had an excellent reputation, was moderate on civil rights and was a Midwesterner. TRUMAN, however, was almost the last to know of Roosevelt's decision.

"On Tuesday evening of convention week," he recalled, "National Chairman Bob Hannegan came to see me and told me unequivocally that President Roosevelt wanted me to run with him on the ticket. This astonished me greatly, but I was still not convinced. Even when Hannegan showed me a longhand note written on a scratch pad from the President's desk which said, 'Bob, it's TRUMAN-F.D.R., I still could not be sure that this was Roosevelt's intent."

It took a long-distance call to Roosevelt, then on the West Coast, to convince TRUMAN.

"Bob," Roosevelt said, "have you got that fellow lined up yet?"

"No," Hannegan replied. "He's the contrariest Missouri mule I've ever dealt with."

"Well, you tell him," TRUMAN heard the President say, "if he wants to break up the Democratic party in the middle of a war, that's his responsibility."

"I was completely stunned," TRUMAN remarked afterward. After walking around the hotel room, he said, 'Well, if that is the situation, I'll have to say yes, but why the hell didn't he tell me in the first place?''

Following the nomination, TRUMAN stumped the nation for Roosevelt and himself; for the President campaigned almost not at all. The Roosevelt-Truman slate won with ease over Gov. Thomas E. Dewey of New York and Senator John W. Bricker of Ohio, the Republican choices for President and Vice President. The popular vote was 25,602,555 to 22,006,278, and the Electoral College tally was 432 to 99.

On Jan. 20, 1945, a snowy Saturday, HARRY S TRUMAN stood on the South Portico of the White House and was inaugurated. The man he was about to displace, Vice President Henry A. Wallace, administered the oath.

Hon. Frank E. Moss
OF UTAH

Mr. President, as we all know, time is a relentless critic. It assesses a man's greatness as it never can be assessed while he is in the mainstream of life.

When HARRY S TRUMAN went home to Missouri—and private life—20 years ago, the Nation knew he had been a fine President, a courageous and strong President. But we did not realize how right had been his decisions, how wise his actions, how farsighted his views.

We know now. He has grown in stature with each passing year. Time has tested HARRY TRUMAN and has found him to be one of our truly great Presidents.

When he first assumed the Presidency, this onetime farmer and haberdasher stood in the towering shadow of Franklin Roosevelt. He had not wanted the job; he had wanted only to be a U.S. Senator. Yet when the burden of the Presidency fell suddenly upon his shoulders, he put a firm hand on the helm and steered the country resolutely through some of the most critical days of its history.

He made excruciating decisions without vascillating. He dropped the bomb on Hiroshima and ended the war with Japan. He enunciated the Truman doctrine—stood almost alone in his insistence that it was right—and got the money from Congress to prevent a Communist takeover of Greece and Turkey. He established the Marshall plan, and used its massive aid to help vast sections of the world stay free from tyranny and aggression.

He secured ratification of the United Nations, the North Atlantic Treaty Organization, the In-

ter-American Treaty of Reciprocal Assistance. He unified the armed services. And in so doing, he laid the foundations for the foreign and defense policies of the United States for more than 25 years.

On the domestic front, his Fair Deal was far reaching. The Hill-Burton hospital construction act, the program providing Federal funds for airport construction, the flexible price support program, were enacted. The minimum wage was raised; the social security program expanded. The Atomic Energy Commission was created, and housing and farm program established.

It was President TRUMAN who first saw the need for Federal aid to education, universal health insurance, the establishment of a Department of Health, Education, and Welfare, and greater leadership in the field of civil rights. Some of these things did not come until more than 10 years after he left Washington—some are still not law. But he gave them impetus and status.

But mostly he will be remembered as the President with the common touch—the man who could communicate his thoughts as few Presidents have to the rank and file of America. They liked his tough-minded approach, his fearlessness, his straight talk about what he was trying to do and why. His sincerity was unquestioned; he instilled confidence and trust.

HARRY TRUMAN brought an earthy commonsense practicality to the Presidency—and he left his mark vividly not only on his own times but on the times we live in today.

Both Mrs. Moss and I extend deep sympathy to his devoted widow and his able and charming daughter. Their loss is the Nation's great loss as well.

Hon. Mike Mansfield
OF MONTANA

Mr. President, I remember President HARRY S TRUMAN as a Senator and as "the Man in the White House." His simplicity, his lack of ostentation, his ability to understand, to see the other man's point of view, those are the characteristics which I recall in my memory of this outstanding President of the United States.

I recall the part he played in making it possible for the veterans of all wars to have a veterans hospital located at Miles City in the eastern part of Montana.

I recall being called to the White House, when I was a Member of the House—Elbert Thomas then a Member of this body was called at about the same time—and we both were asked the same question; what should be the decision vis-a-vis retention of the Emperor of Japan at the conclusion of the war.

I recall speaking to Senator Thomas about it, that we both made the same recommendation that the Emperor should be retained in the interests of harmony, stability, and commonsense.

Some of my colleagues will recall at that time that there was talk of forcing out the Japanese Emperor and establishing some other form of government.

I recall, also, when President TRUMAN came to Montana during the election campaign in 1948, that he visited the Hungry Horse Dam up in the Flathead country. I recall his humorous remark when he said to the people assembled that they should take a good look at the Hungry Horse Dam because if the Republicans were elected it would be the last dam they would see in a long, long, long time.

I recall being called to the White House while a Member of the House, when President TRUMAN notified various Members of Congress, both Representatives and Senators, that he had ordered General MacArthur to move to Korea to repel the aggression which had occurred across the 38th parallel and the North Korean forces which were on the way, down south into the area of the Pusan perimeter.

I recall President TRUMAN meeting with the Democrats on Jefferson Island in the Potomac. If I am not mistaken, the distinguished Senator from Arkansas (Mr. McClellan), now in the Chamber, was one of those present on that occasion.

I recall many things about this man who was both humble and great, who was, I repeat, a man of simplicity, a man who lacked ostentation, but a man who truly reflected the temper of the times in which he lived—and a man who, I think, will go down in the history of this Republic as one of the great Presidents.

So I join my colleagues today in expressing my family's deep regret and sadness at the passing of President HARRY S TRUMAN and to express to his wife, Bess, and to his daughter Margaret, our sense of loss because of it.

May his soul rest in peace.

Hon. Robert P. Griffin
OF MICHIGAN

Mr. President, a truly effective political leader, it has been written, is one who has the rare capacity to make hard decisions.

Judged by this qualification alone, HARRY S TRUMAN our 33d President, was one of the great leaders this Nation has produced.

Few men have been confronted with the necessity for having to make so many momentous decisions as he was called upon to make during his years in the White House.

He entered upon the Presidency at a climactic moment in history. A great war was drawing to a conclusion. Much of the world was in chaotic disarray and the problems confronting Mr. TRUMAN were immense.

But he never hesitated, he never wavered.

As liquidation of the war in Europe began, he made the difficult and terrible decision to drop the atomic bomb which ended Japanese resistance.

As the cold war ensued, Mr. TRUMAN met the challenge of Communist expansionism with the TRUMAN doctrine in Greece, the Berlin airlift, the Korean war and, perhaps most significant of all, the Marshall plan for rebuilding a shattered Western Europe.

These and other decisions, taken together, set the course of the Nation's foreign policy which, with remarkable consistency, has endured to the present time.

In 1965, on the 20th anniversary of his becoming President, he received the Freedom Award in recognition for setting "the pattern for America's worldwide activities in behalf of freedom." In an address on that occasion, Dean Acheson, who was Mr. TRUMAN's Secretary of State, described Mr. TRUMAN's decision as "in truly heroic mold."

No less a figure in history than Winston Churchill ungrudgingly praised Mr. TRUMAN as one who did more than any other man to save Western civilization.

With all the greatness he achieved as a leader of the free world, Mr. TRUMAN remained essentially a modest, unassuming, and even folksy individual. Once it was proposed that he should be awarded the Congressional Medal of Honor.

He dismissed the idea with characteristic directness, writing:

. . . In the first place, I do not consider that I have done anything which should be the reason for any award, Congressional or otherwise.

Next, the Congressional Medal of Honor was instituted for combat service. This is as it should be and to deviate by giving it for any other reason lessens and dilutes its true significance. Also, it would detract from those who have received the award because of their combat service.

Therefore . . . I would not accept it.

Mr. TRUMAN often said:

If you do your best, history will do the rest.

With Mr. TRUMAN, a most uncommon man, history, I am sure, will do full justice.

Hon. Jennings Randolph
OF WEST VIRGINIA

Mr. President, I believe the mantle of greatness falls easily on few men. Some are acclaimed because they achieve broad prominence and power, but the judgment of history may prove otherwise.

HARRY S TRUMAN, the 33d President of the United States, became the most powerful leader in the world, but it was under a cloud of uncertainty. As we look back, we know this was true. His enemies dismissed him at that time as a political accident. His friends and allies adopted a posture ranging from toleration to almost outright anguish. None could foresee that this man, who came from Missouri, would be equal to the task, and he certainly was more than equal to the awesome assignment which was placed before him.

HARRY TRUMAN grew in stature through the years. The hallmark of his public career was courage and loyalty and devotion to our country—most importantly, to our people.

His White House leadership was characterized by sound, mid-America judgment; yet, his profound actions encircled the very earth.

His philosophy was in many instances small town, but he developed a grasp of international affairs, and he carried our country and the free world through exceedingly difficult times.

HARRY TRUMAN was a man of tough mind and yet of tender heart. He has been acclaimed the last old-style politician by some, a description that is accurate only if it means that he held those virtues of which I have spoken—loyalty, integrity, and devotion—most dear during the years he served in the Senate and in other positions of trust in the executive branch of Government.

As a leader, he used candor rather than charisma. I am sure we could use more of that today, tomorrow, and in the years ahead. He used plain talk rather than polished press agentry to the degree we use it today. He was truly a man of the soil and a man of the people.

President TRUMAN identified himself with Americans in all walks of life. They came to know him and felt he was one of them. There was no question of his great love for America and for the heritage that has been a part of our country. He had a belief in the traditions of America that might be considered old fashioned by some in these changing times.

There was never a question about his unwavering faith in America's future and her people, as he discussed goals for a fuller life for all segments of our society.

I think history will judge him well because TRUMAN was a shining light in America's darkest hours. Our Nation, I believe, will be forever in his debt. He had a very rewarding life. It certainly was a full life by its achievements in those perilous days in which he led the country, when the civilization we knew at that time tottered on the ragged edges, and on the brink. His achievements are indelibly etched in the history of the world.

Mr. TRUMAN often visited West Virginia, as have other Senators, other Vice Presidents, and other Presidents of the United States. It was my good fortune on many of these occasions, as it was the good fortune of my esteemed colleague, Senator Robert C. Byrd of West Virginia, and others, to share with our guest the experiences of some of those visits to the Mountain State.

I remember when I asked the President and Mrs. Truman if their daughter Margaret might grace an occasion where she was to dedicate a commercial aircraft, new in flight at that time, the Constellation named the Capitaliner United States. About 2,500 persons attended the event in the late spring of 1950. So characteristic of him was the fact that he and his wife, Mrs. Truman, were old-fashioned but right in their belief that it was good for the family to talk matters over. I had asked their daughter, Margaret, to participate in this noteworthy program at Washington National Airport. They considered the matter and I remember we walked to the door. He said proudly—

I am happy that Margaret can do the job—the christening of this new bird of flight.

And he added—

I am glad because you know no one would do a better job.

That is the way he was about his family; not just boastful, but very conscious of the ability of his daughter to participate in a successful manner.

Yes, we have these closely knit friendships that touch our lives. I know my wife, Mary, would want me to say that she and Bess Truman also shared a friendship.

He will be judged in history not for what he did for individuals or even for entire groups and governments, but for the impact of his leadership in directing our society toward a goal of betterment of mankind.

Hon. Sam Nunn
OF GEORGIA

Mr. President, when HARRY S TRUMAN became President, I was an 8-year-old boy. Therefore, my impressions of this great man are based on my boyhood memory, but more importantly, on the historical analysis of his term in office.

President TRUMAN's courage and fortitude enabled him to make tough, hard decisions. Many, though unpopular at the time, were crucial decisions which set the course for this Nation for generations to come.

In this day and time when so many decisions are based on the popular whim of the moment, the leaders of our States and Nation should pause not only to pay tribute to this great American but also to learn from his courageous example.

The life of HARRY S TRUMAN is very much a representative American story—of how a man can rise from humble origins to the highest office in the land. He embodied in his personality and character the qualities shared by the vast majority of his fellow citizens.

Through all the great controversies in which he participated and which tested and proved his leadership, he retained that humility which we call "The common touch," the ability to speak directly and frankly to his fellow Americans. With good reason, General Marshall noted his curious blend of humility and boldness, nourished by faith in God and belief in America.

An eminent preacher of 19th century America, Henry Ward Beecher, once observed that "greatness lies not in being strong but in the right use of strength." Let it be said of HARRY TRUMAN that he used the powers of his office and the God-given gifts which were his inner resource to give effective leadership not only to his own country but to the free world in a time of grave crisis and disruption. His enduring legacy is the foundation of a just and lasting peace and the love of liberty in the hearts of free men and women.

Hon. Harry F. Byrd, Jr.
OF VIRGINIA

Mr. President, HARRY S TRUMAN was as stubborn as a Missouri mule—and as courageous as any President this Nation has had.

At least that is the way the senior Senator from Virginia views the man from Independence, Mo., who served his country in World War I as an artillery captain, who served his State as a U.S. Senator, and who served his Nation as the 33d President.

When President Roosevelt died in April of 1945, the former Missouri Senator had been Vice President less than 3 months. His Nation was at war on two fronts—with Germany and Italy in Europe, and Japan in the Pacific.

The most important decision, perhaps, which President TRUMAN was called upon to make was whether to drop the atomic bomb, U.S. scientists having just fathomed the secret of the atom. President TRUMAN determined that the use of the bomb on two Japanese cities would bring the war to an end and thus save an estimated 1 million American military personnel who otherwise would have been ordered to invade Japan.

While none was so far reaching as the decision to bomb Japan, President TRUMAN faced many difficult decisions during his nearly 8 years as President. I found myself at odds with some of Mr. TRUMAN's decisions. But always did I recognize him as being a man of courage and of the highest patriotism.

In has been 20 years now since HARRY TRUMAN left the White House. His stature has grown as the years have lengthened.

History, I feel, will treat President TRUMAN well. He very likely will stand near the top when

historians determine which Presidents of the
United States have best and most unselfishly
served our great country.

Hon. John O. Pastore
OF RHODE ISLAND

Mr. President, this is February, the month of
Presidents, as we observe the birthdays of Lincoln and Washington—while, within the week,
the birthday of Franklin Delano Roosevelt has
passed with little comment.

In this young year of 1973, this Capitol has
echoed to the inaugural triumph of a living President and the tribute eulogy of Lyndon Johnson.

This hour is given to another President, to
HARRY TRUMAN, who is in this Capitol today
only in our memories.

I note a symbolic incident from the Time magazine anniversary party last week at the National
Portrait Gallery. There the Time cover portrait
of President HARRY S TRUMAN hung on the wall.

Margaret Truman Daniel, his daughter, was
distressed when she saw that her father's portrait
was not hanging straight.

So she adjusted it.

And history continues to adjust the picture of
this President from Missouri who presided over
the most critical times in our Nation's history.

It is refreshing to recall his optimism and his
openness—the down-to-earth democracy that history will accord to the Truman era.

Historians will continue to weigh and value
the influence of this humble human being on the
fortunes of mankind.

Each of us will treasure a simpler thought—
perhaps a single episode—a precious contact we
enjoyed with this lively and lovable Missouri man
in the White House.

My mind goes back to an October day of
1948—at the height of a presidential campaign—
TRUMAN's contest for election.

All the prophets were forecasting disaster for
the Democrat.

They were grueling October days—the final
days of TRUMAN's personal appeal to the people.

In 35 days he made 365 speeches—covered
31,500 miles—and wound up October 30 in St.
Louis, Mo.

Two days before that—on October 28—TRU-
MAN's quest brought him to Rhode Island. As
the then Governor of the State, I had the honor

to escort him from one border of my State to
the other.

I treasure a newspaper picture of that dramatic day in 1948. It was reproduced at the December death of this great man of Independence.

The picture is that of President TRUMAN in
his automobile—surrounded by a sea of people.
The motor seat was shared by myself as Governor of Rhode Island and our U.S. Senator, Theodore Francis Green, already established as a
leader in this great body.

I might add that the other Senator from Rhode
Island was J. Howard McGrath, at the time national chairman of the Democratic Party and one
of the architects of what the newspaper world
termed "the greatest political upset of modern
times."

I had the chance that day to experience the
heart of America responding to the challenge
and charm of a great soul. I saw the individual
on his little farm wave his hat as we rode by—
another bless himself—and most of them shouting the war cry, "Give 'em hell, HARRY."

And I understood the confidence TRUMAN had
in his cause and its ultimate victory.

He had reason.

On that October day, 50,000 Americans
gathered to greet him and cheer him before the
City Hall in Providence.

Not only that great number but the spontaneous enthusiasm of the thousands reflected the
appeal and response of human nature in a democracy at a crucial hour in our Nation's existence.

In those 35 days of 10 speeches a day—in
large groups and small—15 million people had
seen and heard him. They confirmed the Truman doctrine—as he expressed it—that people
are not swayed by polls but prefer to make up
their own minds about candidates on the basis
of direct observation.

It is a salutary experience for a people to see
and hear their public servants at close range—
and the higher the office, the more important it
is that the servant should have genuine contact
with the common people so that he may know
their desperate needs—and so that their needs
shall shape the mood and mind of the leader.

I like a sentence from a Providence Journal-
Bulletin editorial at the December passing of
President TRUMAN.

It reads:

If, as some believe, history finds the right man in crisis
to lead a nation, history did magnificently well by this

country when HARRY S TRUMAN turned the last great bend on his road to the White House.

Indeed, the entire editorial from this newspaper—politically independent in its views—deserves a place in our comments today; and I ask unanimous consent that the Providence Journal-Bulletin editorial be printed in the Record.

[From the Providence Journal Bulletin, Dec. 27, 1972]

HARRY S TRUMAN

The cocky little man from Lamar, Missouri, went a long way in 88 years—from chores on a small farm to decisions that shook the world. HARRY S TRUMAN, 33rd President of the United States, was a man of deep personal honesty and integrity, a husband and father of folksy warmth, and a leader with shining courage in the tumultuous years of a troubled presidency.

Nothing ever was easy for HARRY TRUMAN. Poor vision denied him a career at West Point. A depression denied him a career in business in Kansas City. Sent to the Senate by the boss of a corrupt Missouri political machine, he seemed doomed to the humdrum existence of a hard-working back-seat member—until World War II engulfed the nation and the world.

Out of his assignment as chairman of the Truman committee in exposing war time frauds in work for the government, the senator built a reputation that stood him in good stead. He was handpicked to run for the vice presidency in 1944 with Franklin D. Roosevelt, but even in victory, he was denied access to the presidential confidences on domestic and foreign affairs.

When Mr. Roosevelt died in the spring of 1945, HARRY S TRUMAN took the oath of office, perhaps the most under-briefed vice president to succeed to power. Yet events did not wait upon him; it was fortunate for the country that he had and took good advice, had the wit to make the right decisions, and had the courage to stick by them when the going got rough.

It was HARRY S TRUMAN who authorized and later announced the destruction of Hiroshima by the first atomic bomb, not for the sake of destruction, but to speed the peace that soon came. It was HARRY S TRUMAN who announced and stood by the Truman Doctrine to keep Turkey and Greece on their feet, and who inspired the Marshall Plan to renew the strengths of a prostrate Europe.

In domestic affairs, he did less well. His efforts to write a Fair Deal fell afoul of a hostile Congress. It took all his courage and strength to win an election in 1948 that no political expert expected. Then in 1950 came Korea, and all his hopes of domestic progress had to give way to the problems of serving as leader of the key nation in the United Nations forces in Korea.

Yet for all the demands made upon him as the nation's leader, he had time always for the human touch. He declined to abjure his political relationships with Thomas J. Pendergast even when he was warned that the Pendergast machine's corruption might stain him fatally. He did not hesitate to berate a music critic who dared to criticize his beloved only daughter, Mary Margaret.

HARRY S TRUMAN survived an assassination attempt; he survived the bitterest political criticism. He was proud of the fact that his desk was where "the buck stopped," and when he did what he felt was right, he did not much care who criticized him. He made some gross political errors; sometimes, he wasted his friendship on ingrates who rode his coattails.

He became as much a symbol of his times as any single figure in the land. Who can forget the happy malice of his smile before the television cameras when he, victorious the day after Election Day in 1948, waved the front page of a newspaper which had prematurely and mistakenly identified his opponent as the winner? Who can ever forget his cocky grin and strut?

It will be for history to judge him finally as we his contemporaries today mark his passing by recalling the memories of the great events and the petty events of his career in the White House. If, as some believe, history finds the right man in crisis to lead a nation, history did magnificently well by this country when HARRY S TRUMAN turned the last great bend on his road to the White House.

Now the great of the nation will gather in his home state; the great of the world will send condolences. The caisson with its coffin will roll and the guns will thunder farewell in a winterswept midwest cemetery—and HARRY S TRUMAN, the brash little guy from Lamar, Missouri, will go to his last resting place, a man of his times and for his times, a dedicated servant of a land he loved intensely.

Hon. Hubert H. Humphrey

OF MINNESOTA

Mr. President, we observe in the Senate today our appreciation of the life of President HARRY S TRUMAN. I wish to address myself for just a few moments to the remarkable career of this unusual and remarkable man.

His work and his achievements are immortal. The life story of HARRY TRUMAN is America at its best—patriotic, self-reliant, courageous, simple and uncomplicated, forthright and loyal, a partisan and a patriot, a devoted husband and father, and a great President and statesman.

He was a builder in a world ravished by war. He was a healer in a world beset by disease, pestilence, and poverty.

He was a giant of a man who lived in troubled times and had the courage to make difficult decisions.

I have shared in his friendship and honor it second to none. I have followed and supported his leadership—a rare privilege for any man.

He has served America and all mankind with humility, dignity, and greatness.

I recall when the Humphreys first came to Washington in 1948. I was elected to be the freshman Senator from Minnesota. HARRY TRUMAN was our President.

My parents came to visit me during those first few months. Concluding that even a freshman had the right to make at least one request of the White House, I phoned the President's appointments secretary, Matt Connelly, to ask if my parents could meet the President. My father was a lifelong Democrat and a strong supporter of President TRUMAN. Not long after, my parents and I were escorted into the President's office.

My father and mother had never been in the White House before and for them and for me it was an exciting experience. The President was kind and gracious, particularly to my mother, who admitted she was "scared to death" to be in his office. TRUMAN gave her a hug and said, "Oh, we're just folks here."

The 33d President of the United States then took my parents on a personal tour of the White House. I shall never forget it. And I know that to my father in particular it was the high point of his life.

So as a human being we remember HARRY TRUMAN for his uncomplicated, direct, and friendly appeal. He truly was a man of the people, from the people, and for the people.

As President, we remember him for courage, frankness, and principle, in the face of monumental decisions which had to be made and which he did make.

The atom bomb and the peacetime uses of atomic energy.

The Potsdam Conference and the diplomatic and military followup to World War II.

The creation of the United Nations and the guarantee of U.S. participation in it.

His timely and firm response to the threat of communism in Greece and Turkey; the Marshall plan in Europe; the point 4 program;

His combat of disease, and pestilence, and poverty worldwide;

The North Atlantic Pact;

The Berlin Airlift;

Resistance to Communist aggression in Korea; and

The maintenance of civilian control over the military.

And then his pioneering in so many areas of domestic policy. We should never forget that it was HARRY TRUMAN's administration that laid before the Nation and the Congress proposals for the improvement and expansion of our health care system, including the proposal of medicare. Nor should we ever forget that it was

President TRUMAN who appointed the commission that came forth with a monumental study on race relations in America and recommended the shaping of a program for reform.

For these and so many other acts of leadership in the world, President TRUMAN won our admiration and gratitude. He established the basis for postwar peace and the survival of human dignity.

For most Americans, President TRUMAN was not a President whose greatness would be recognized only after the passage of time. He was recognized—as a great and Democratic President. If I may repeat here a portion of the remarks I made on March 31, 1952, following President TRUMAN's retirement, I think I can illustrate this point. I said then in part:

President TRUMAN is beloved by the American people because of his candor, honesty, frankness, and principle. He received the support of the American people because he represented in the minds of the American citizens the bold principles of the New Deal and the Fair Deal. The Democratic Party has a responsibility to choose for its candidates for President and Vice President of the United States candidates willing, eager, and determined to carry on in those traditions and faithful to a Democratic Party political platform committed to the foreign policy of the administration and to a domestic program of parity and progress for agriculture, full and equal civil rights for all, public power—REA, social legislation, development, and conservation of our natural resources, free collective bargaining, and defense mobilization. That is the program of the Democratic Party. This is our record. It is the record that has earned and received the support of the American people.

Mr. President, that is what I said in those days after the President had decided in 1952 not to seek reelection.

Mr. President, I wish to say before closing how much Mrs. Humphrey and I have admired the Truman family. All Americans have been appreciative of the quiet and resolute strength of Mrs. Truman—affectionately called by her beloved husband "Bess" Truman—throughout the years and during the difficult period of recent weeks.

Mrs. Humphrey and I were privileged to be with Mrs. Truman on the day of the funeral services in Independence, Mo. She is a beautiful woman, beautiful in character and in spirit. President TRUMAN was vastly proud also of his daughter, Margaret Truman Daniel. I considered it a special privilege to know her, her husband, and family as close and dear friends. Indeed, President TRUMAN should well have been proud of Margaret, because she is a remarkable woman.

The loyalty and love among the members of the Truman family and the quality of their lives have been a guide and an inspiration for us all.

Mr. President, because President TRUMAN died during the adjournment of Congress, I am concerned that much of the editorial comment following his death will not appear in the Congressional Record as is customary. For that reason I have made a limited selection of editorials from different sections of our country, editorials that relate to the life and the work of President HARRY S TRUMAN.

Mr. President, I ask unanimous consent that those editorials, insofar as they do not duplicate others that have been printed in the Record, be printed at this point in the Record.

[From the Atlanta Constitution, Dec. 27, 1972]

HARRY S TRUMAN

"I underestimated you," Winston Churchill once told HARRY S TRUMAN.

So did the rest of us.

So did TRUMAN himself.

Who would have thought that an ex haberdasher from Missouri would become one of the most decisive and effective leaders of the 20th Century?

A great man? Not in the usual sense. TRUMAN had none of the grand style of a Churchill or Roosevelt, none of the godlike presence and egoism of a De Gaulle, none of the intensity and mystique of a Hitler, none of the cold, ruthless power of a Stalin.

All TRUMAN had going for him was courage, a clear vision, common sense and a common touch, basic intelligence, and the ability to make up his mind on the tough questions, to make a decision, and then get a good night's sleep.

There are a lot of people like that, people who will never be President of the United States. They are among your neighbors, your fellow workers, your family. American democracy breeds them, always has. Quite ordinary, unpretentious people who are not born great, do not have greatness thrust upon them, don't seek greatness out, but who rise to the occasion whenever extraordinary demands are made on their character, their intelligence, and their judgment.

TRUMAN's daughter Margaret, in her recently published biography of her father, notes that he didn't want to be a vice presidential candidate with awesome possibility that he might become President. This was not false humility. It was the honest humility of a man who knows in his bones that the nation is greater than any one man, who hesitates because of a sense that his own personal ambitions and goals and values may not be those of the rest of the people, may not be worthy. Upon the death of President Roosevelt in the last months of World War II, TRUMAN took office with a halting and obviously sincere acknowledgment that he was aware of the tremendous burden he was being asked to carry.

But TRUMAN's basic humility was balanced by a healthy joy of life and action, and he very quickly acquired the ability to deal effectively with the problems and decisions

required of the President of the world's most powerful nation. Among his first major decisions, still controversial, was the decision to drop atomic bombs on Japan. That ended World War II within weeks (and prompted Churchill's remarks). TRUMAN presided over the reconstruction of Europe and Japan after the war, converting, in one of America's finest hours, former enemies into steadfast friends. He stood firm against Communist bids to take over other nations by political intrigue or military might. He took the first concrete steps to end our government's support of racial segregation. He didn't hesitate, as commander in chief to slap down the popular war hero, General MacArthur, when MacArthur was insubordinate. And he won reelection against the predictions of polls and pundits by going to the people, speaking their language, and delighting them in a rousing campaign devoted to "giving the Republicans hell."

"If you can't stand the heat," said HARRY TRUMAN, "stay out of the kitchen." He could stand the heat—and there was plenty to stand. His administration had its failures and its scandals and it may be that history will severely judge some of his basic decisions on domestic and foreign problems. Yet Churchill, who himself knew a thing or two about courage and greatness, said that HARRY TRUMAN "had done more than any other man to save Western Civilization." Pretty fancy language that—and TRUMAN's common sense probably took it with a grain of salt. Yet there was truth in Churchill's judgment. Everybody knew that TRUMAN was making the key decisions that determined the course of the post war world, that opened the nuclear age.

TRUMAN spent his last years a respected and honored elder statesman in his native Missouri, writing and publishing his memoirs, occasionally catching the notice of the newspapers and the newfangled television cameras when he took his "morning constitutional" and delivering himself of peppery and shrewd observations on life and politics. He lived to the ripe old age of 88. His lingering death, painful as it must have been for his family, his loved ones and admirers, demonstrated once again those strong qualities that made him one of our outstanding Presidents.

Will we see his like again? Let us hope so—because our nation's future depends on it. HARRY TRUMAN wasn't a great man in the sense that Caesar or Napoleon or even Churchill was, with all their air of power and genius and brilliance and arrogance. He was basically an ordinary man, honest, with courage and humanity and old-fashioned horse sense. And that was good enough for America in a time of great crisis—and good enough for civilization.

[From the Denver Post, Dec. 26, 1972]

UNCOMMON COMMON MAN, "HE DONE HIS DAMNDEST"

On a late afternoon in April 1945, a grieving Eleanor Roosevelt placed a hand on the shoulder of a bewildered little man in bifocal glasses and said to him softly, "HARRY, the President is dead."

HARRY S TRUMAN, the Missouri farm boy who had become vice president of the United States, was unable to find words for a moment. Then he asked: "Is there anything I can do for you?" Mrs. Roosevelt replied: "Is there anything we can do for you? For you are the one in trouble now."

As Truman himself later described it, he "felt like the sun, the stars, and all the planets had fallen on me." But he faced his troubles quickly without flinching in what he once called "the most terribly responsible job a man ever had."

On the occasion of his death, Harry Truman has passed into history as a plain, blunt, unspectacular man who made some of the boldest decisions ever to emerge from the White House.

His was the voice that authorized the first use of atomic bombs on cities, that launched the Truman Doctrine, the Marshall Plan and the Point Four Program of technical assistance to underdeveloped nations.

He also sent American troops to fight in Korea, ordered the development of the hydrogen bomb, promoted the North Atlantic Treaty Organization and directed a global cold war against communism.

On his desk at the White House was a sign, "The Buck Stops Here." He never tried to duck his responsibilities, and he never appeared to agonize over his decisions or lose sleep once they were made.

As much as any president since Lincoln, Truman brought to the White House the traits and language and values of the American common man.

He was direct and unpretentious in his manner, salty in his speech, and quick and impulsive in his reactions. He was spunky and full of fight in dealing with his political enemies and his newspaper critics.

When Truman sallied forth on the campaign trail, the crowds loved to shout "Give 'em hell, Harry." He commented later: "I never did give anybody hell—I just told the truth on 'em and they thought it was hell."

As an aroused father, he once wrote to a critic who had disliked his daughter's singing: "I never met you, but if I do you'll need a new nose and plenty of beefsteak and perhaps a supporter below."

His frequent letters to his mother and sister in Missouri, written in the midst of tumultuous affairs of state, are the kind many small-town Americans might have written if suddenly transplanted to the White House.

Writing to "Dear Mamma & Mary" that a general had given him the baton of German Field Marshal Hermann Goering, Truman observed: "I always get those dirty Nazis mixed up but it makes no difference. Anyway it's the fat marshal's insignia of office . . . Can you imagine a fat pig like that strutting around with a $40,000 bauble—at the poor taxpayer's expense. . . ."

If his manner did not always enhance the dignity of his office, it kept him in tune with many voters who felt and spoke as he did. They helped to return him to office in 1948 in an election almost all the experts said he would lose.

In a poll of American historians, conducted by the late Prof. Arthur Schlesinger, Sr. in 1962, Truman was rated among the "near great" presidents and ranked ninth on the list of all of them.

The later judgment of history will be influenced by future attitudes toward hot and cold war and by other values. But Harry Truman will always be recognized as a man who had a powerful influence in shaping the American future.

Whatever else may be said of him, even his critics will acknowledge that he deserves the epitaph he once admired on a grave at Tombstone, Ariz.: "He done his damndest."

[From the Los Angeles Times, Dec. 27, 1972]

Harry S Truman

More than half of the people now living in the United States had not been born when Harry S Truman of Missouri was called to the White House on April 12, 1945 and told that Franklin D. Roosevelt was dead. Only those who lived through those dramatic days can fully appreciate the grave problems he faced.

This little know Son of the Middle Border, the product of a corrupt political machine, a man with little experience in foreign relations and the affairs of state, was thrust into the shoes of a revered world leader at one of the most critical junctures in world history.

Furthermore, Harry Truman came into office without being informed about the secret work being done on the atomic bomb or the military, political and diplomatic complications involved in the great problems then facing President Roosevelt.

Yet this indomitable man from Independence went on to make some of the most momentous decisions in the history of the world—decisions that played a major role in shaping events in the crisis-ridden postwar period during the early days of the Cold War between the Soviet Union and the United States.

After he left office, Mr. Truman was asked how he thought history would deal with him, and he replied in characteristic fashion: "I don't give a damn what history thinks of me. I know what I did and that's enough for me."

This was the essence of the Truman creed—do what you think is right and never mind the critics. It was the creed of a self-confident man whom his close friend, the late Gen. George C. Marshall, said had that curious blend of humility and boldness.

And Harry Truman was bold enough to make unflinching decisions that would unsettle the most courageous of men. During his Presidency, he made decisions to:

Bring the United States and the world into the atomic age and drop nuclear bombs on two Japanese cities to hasten the end of World War II.

Proceed with development of the hydrogen bomb after Russia developed its own atomic capability.

Have the United States take the lead in creation of the United Nations during the closing of World War II.

Establish the multibillion-dollar postwar program for European recovery, the Marshall Plan.

Enunciate the Truman Doctrine to provide economic and military aid to Greece and Turkey to help those countries resist Communist moves being led by the Soviet Union.

Send American troops to Korea to push back the invasion of South Korea by Communist North Korea.

Operate a $250 million airlift to supply food and other essentials to the people of West Berlin and break the 327-day Russian blockade that was designed to force the Western powers out of the city.

Begin the Point Four program to give technical aid to undeveloped countries.

Form the North Atlantic Treaty Organization.

Fire Gen. Douglas MacArthur as the supreme commander in the Pacific for insubordination during the Korean war and reaffirm the historic American principle of civilian control over the military.

All of these decisions were controversial, and Mr. TRUMAN knew they would be. For example, on April 10, 1951, the day he announced the firing of MacArthur, he wrote a friend: "It will undoubtedly create a great furor, but under the circumstances I could do nothing else and still be President of the United States. Even the Army chief of staff came to the conclusion that civilian control was at stake. And I didn't let it stay at stake very long."

On the home front, Mr. TRUMAN's achievements appeared to suffer by comparison. He was in a constant struggle with Congress on domestic legislation, and many of his proposals were ignored or rejected—particularly in the field of civil rights, social welfare and education.

Nevertheless, his administration was responsible for the unification of the armed forces, a move that came only after the most bitter infighting among the separate branches of the services.

The Truman administration also was responsible for the Employment Act of 1946, which for the first time committed the federal government to a policy of maintaining high employment and a strong economy. The act also created the President's Council of Economic Advisers, which in recent years has played a major role in shaping U.S. economic policies.

When Mr. TRUMAN came to office most of the world had serious doubts that he could handle the awesome tasks of the Presidency. Many critics tended to leap on his personal faults of being loyal to his friends and a feisty tendency to "shoot from the hip." And he suffered for it. He was plagued by friends and subordinates who let him down or embarrassed him.

Criticism was also heaped on Mr. TRUMAN for his earthy manners and his blunt talk. His angry letter to a music critic who didn't enjoy his daughter's singing and another that took a dim view of the Marine Corps were incidents that were treated gravely at the time. But with the passage of the years they were looked upon by most persons as amusing events involving a very human President.

Even though Mr. TRUMAN was under constant attack from critics, the people sympathized with him and seemed to understand that he was doing the best he could under the most difficult circumstances.

This feeling, perhaps, was the main underlying reason for Mr. TRUMAN's surprising victory over Thomas E. Dewey in 1948—the most astounding political upset in American history.

Jonathan Daniels, the North Carolina editor who had served as a White House assistant under both Presidents Roosevelt and TRUMAN, hit on this point: "Americans felt leaderless when Roosevelt died. TRUMAN taught them, as one of them, that their greatness lies in themselves."

Of course, the other factor in that 1948 victory was HARRY TRUMAN's indomitable courage—the same courage he showed in the last days of his life in a Kansas City hospital.

HARRY TRUMAN's mark on history was made chiefly in the field of foreign policy, where he worked unceasingly to prevent the unthinkable devastation of World War III.

Early in his term, shortly after the end of World War II, he put some private thoughts down on White House stationery. He wrote that he could see some of the forces of "selfishness, greed and jealousy" at work, and he wondered if he could continue to "outface the demagogues, the chiselers and the jealousies."

"Time only will tell," he wrote. "The human animal and his emotions change not much from age to age. He must change now, or he faces absolute and complete destruction, and maybe the Insect Age or an atmosphereless planet will succeed him."

In his last address to the American people before leaving the White House, Mr. TRUMAN said: "We have averted World War III up to now, and we may have already succeeded in establishing conditions which can keep that war from happening as far ahead as man can see . . ."

This foundation—which each succeeding President has built upon—is the legacy HARRY TRUMAN left to the American people and the people of the world.

[From the New York Times, Dec. 27, 1972]

MAN OF INDEPENDENCE

HARRY S TRUMAN waged the last fight of his long life with the same courage and stamina that never failed him during eight taxing years as President of the United States. Thrust into the highest office by the death of Franklin D. Roosevelt, this unassuming, small-town politician drew on hidden reserves of those qualities, along with decisiveness and rocklike integrity, to meet with credit the staggering challenges of a momentous era in history and vindicate democracy's faith in the common man.

In a world that was just emerging from a devastating war, Mr. TRUMAN presided over one of the most constructive and innovative periods of American foreign policy. Isolation had been sunk along with the battleship Arizona at Pearl Harbor in 1941. Mr. Roosevelt had directed the mightiest armed forces ever assembled and forged the greatest coalition in history to crush the Axis powers. In educating the nation to meet the vast new responsibilities it could not safely evade in the aftermath of the war and the rapid dissolution of the alliance with Soviet Russia, the former artillery captain of World War I demonstrated an uncommon ability to seize upon the grand strategic concepts that were developed by the extraordinary group of able men from the Roosevelt Administration who surrounded him.

The Truman Doctrine of 1947, never called that by the man himself and never intended to be the globe-embracing policy that both champions and critics claimed; the Marshall Plan which restored much of a devastated continent and laid the foundations for European integration and unity; the Atlantic Alliance of 1949, recognizing the enduring identity of vital interests between North America and Western Europe; Point Four, making benefits of scientific and technical progress available to the world's hungry and needy—all these innovative manifestations of a foreign policy designed to meet the conditions of a new world took form in HARRY TRUMAN's Administration.

Mr. TRUMAN's bold decision to check aggression in Korea in 1950 despite the enfeebled state of American armed forces in the area probably saved the United Nations from collapse and more or less stabilized for twenty years a highly volatile situation. It was during the Korean War that Mr. TRUMAN, in one of his most courageous and most important actions, fired an unquestionably insubordinate General MacArthur, thereby preserving civilian control over the military and over the conduct of foreign policy.

One of the most difficult decisions any President has ever had to face was the question presented to Mr. TRUMAN in his very first days in office: whether to drop, without warning, two atomic bombs on Japan. With hindsight, it seems a terrible failure of the human spirit to have used nuclear weapons on densely populated cities without at least having given the Japanese and the world a demonstration of their unique horror by dropping a bomb on an uninhabited island. However, Mr. TRUMAN made this decision on the advice of experienced statesmen and generals, deeply concerned by the forecast of a million American casualties should an invasion of Japan be required to end the war. On this, as on other controversial decisions, Mr. TRUMAN never tried to blame others or to shirk his own responsibility before history.

Mr. TRUMAN knew some moments of greatness in domestic affairs. He recognized the twin evils of McCarthyism and McCarranism from the first and stood firmly against them. He championed the civil rights of the Negro in his 1948 message to Congress, and he defied the subsequent Dixiecrat revolt.

Yet he could speak and act impetuously, even recklessly, and play the pettiest kind of politics, reflecting his early training in a corrupt big-city machine. Some of his appointments were deplorable, including some to extremely high posts in government. He was fiercely loyal to old friends, some of whom certainly did not deserve his loyalty. He could be carried away by bad advice or by an impatience for quick results, as when he proposed to seize the steel mills.

He never cast himself in the role of a man of destiny, always retaining his sense of humor and humility. His fellow citizens trusted him, however much some may have disagreed with him, because they could be confident that the "image" of the President reflected the true character of the man. Today millions of his countrymen mourn as friend and neighbor and millions more around the world remember as protector and benefactor the 33d President of the United States, the man of Independence.

[From the Courier-Journal, Dec. 27, 1972]

MR. TRUMAN: FEW HAVE RISEN SO SPLENDIDLY TO THE OCCASION

HARRY TRUMAN has been singled out as a prime example of a man who "grew" in the presidency. It is a backhanded compliment, one that tends to exaggerate his presumed inadequacy when the mantle of Franklin Roosevelt fell upon his shoulders. After all, Mr. TRUMAN had been a pretty solid Senator. His instincts, if one examines his record in Congress, were good.

It is easy to remember the challenging circumstances in which Lyndon Johnson assumed the presidency in 1963. HARRY TRUMAN came to the presidency under even more trying circumstances. He was bound to suffer—any man would have—in comparison with his predecessor. Mr. TRUMAN was succeeding the only man who had been elected President more than twice, a man who was a father figure for a whole generation. Moreover, HARRY TRUMAN succeeded Franklin Roosevelt while the country was still fighting World War II.

HARRY TRUMAN suffered more in comparison than some other men would have. He lacked prestige. No one really knew much about him. His accession to power was viewed as a freakish political accident. He was rated as a well-meaning mediocrity at best, a cheap political hack at worst, a typical product of grubby Kansas City machine politics. He wasn't typical, however. He had shown a streak of independence, a stubborn adherence to certain principles.

TO USE THE ATOMIC BOMB

Despite the sudden shock of his elevation to unrivaled power and responsibility, somehow HARRY TRUMAN took hold. He had a deep respect for the office of the presidency and he knew, from his reading of history, a great deal more about it than most people gave him credit for knowing. He made the awesome decisions. It was his decision to use the A-bomb (he didn't even know it was being developed when he took the oath); he saw the war to a conclusion and he helped launch the United Nations.

Then he put the Marshall plan in motion, which helped raise a war-battered Europe from its knees, and announced the Truman Doctrine to protect Greece and Turkey from Soviet aggression. He proposed far-reaching social and economic programs at home. He called for a more comprehensive program of medical care than we have today; he set a goal of "full employment"; he pressed for action against racial discrimination.

Still, most people kept on underestimating the little man from Missouri. They said he didn't have a chance of being elected in his own right in 1948, but he was. They said he couldn't continue to stand up to the pressures of the office, but he did.

It is not now possible to make a final judgment on some of his policies. There are those who blame HARRY TRUMAN for starting the Cold War; yet, knowing what we now know about Joseph Stalin during those years, who can say it wasn't Stalin who started it? The results of the Truman Doctrine are still ambiguous. It may have saved Greece and Turkey from a Communist takeover, but it did not save them for democracy.

At home there are those who say the Truman administration opened the way for McCarthyism by going along with loyalty checks, by setting up some of the machinery of the witchhunt. Nevertheless, HARRY TRUMAN resisted some of the excesses of the witchhunters. His ringing veto of some of the repressive legislation of the period was later vindicated by events and the courts. If the Truman administration is to be blamed for letting the genie out of the bottle, it also must be credited with trying to put it back in.

From the time he took over at the White House, HARRY TRUMAN was accused of "cronyism." There was some truth in the charge. He had some fifth-rate people around him, and he entrusted some of them with responsibility. Some of his friends served him ill. However, they did not make the big decisions.

A LIFE TO REFLECT UPON

The popular understanding of just what's involved in using presidential power to the fullest goes back to such Trumanisms as, "The buck stops here" and "If you can't stand the heat, get out of the kitchen." At times a bitter partisan, Mr. TRUMAN believed in setting national priorities in the clearest terms, then getting down into the political arena for them, with the knowledge that history will redeem good causes—even those that seem beyond saving in the heat of the moment.

It was an approach to the presidency that he learned in the turmoil of politics, and it served him, and the nation, well.

In the shy boy with thick glasses who found his heroes in treasured history books, there developed a tenacious mind, a rockhard power of decision and—what many politicians claim, but few attain—an identification with the ideals of plain Americans. In their bereavement, his nation and his party could do worse than meditate on the life of HARRY TRUMAN.

[From the Philadelphia Inquirer, Dec. 27, 1972]

HST "DONE HIS DAMNEDEST"—AND HE DID IT VERY WELL

HARRY S TRUMAN, according to one of his biographers, Jonathan Daniels, liked the story of the small-town man who became Postmaster General and who, some time afterward, returned to his hometown on an early morning train. Only the village half-wit was on hand at the station, so the great man asked him:

"What did people say when I was appointed Postmaster General?"

The half-wit spoke for the town: "They just laughed."

No one laughed when HARRY TRUMAN became President. On the contrary. People wept at the death of Franklin Delano Roosevelt, and trembled at the fact that the little-known Vice President was assuming the august office of President of the United States, with all its awesome powers and in a time of awesome decisions.

For Mr. Roosevelt was a great man. There was no disputing that, even by those who loathed "that man in the White House." He had what later came to be known as "charisma," and he was an aristocrat, born to the purple, who had presided over the destiny of the United States for more than 12 years. He had led the country out of the Great Depression. He had been Commander-in-Chief of American forces in the war against the Nazis and the Japanese. He had conferred with kings and prime ministers and dictators. He was a world figure.

By contrast HARRY S TRUMAN was a very ordinary man. A haberdasher who had gone broke in the post-World War I depression, a product of the infamous Pendergast machine in Kansas City, an amiable nonentity as senator from Missouri. He had gained some distinction as chairman of a Senate watchdog committee investigating war profiteering, but the only thing great about him was that he was a great unknown, as he had been a few months before when Roosevelt picked him to replace Henry Wallace as Vice President. A very ordinary man. He even looked ordinary.

HARRY TRUMAN had to make some of the most extraordinary decisions in American history, and he made most of them with extraordinary sagacity. What he lacked in charisma he made up for in courage. Not every decision he made was right. You can still get up quite a controversy over whether he should or should not have dropped the atomic bomb on Hiroshima and, a few days later, on Nagasaki. To Mr. TRUMAN, the only issue was whether the war would be ended quicker and lives would be saved, and he never regretted his choice.

It was often observed of Mr. TRUMAN that he was great on great issues, small on small. Not a bad thing to have said of you, all things considered, and especially considering the opposite.

In these days of disenchantment about America's role in the world, it may be difficult to remember how the world looked in those years following the collapse of Germany and Japan. Indeed, almost half the Americans now living were not even born when Mr. TRUMAN entered the White House. Then, a nation which had existed in "splendid isolation" for most of its history had global responsibilities thrust upon it—to feed the starving, to restore the devastated economies of its allies and its enemies, to retool for peacetime production and reassimilate millions of American GIs into civilian life, and increasingly, to resist the glowering menace of the Soviet Union under Stalin.

Mr. TRUMAN rose to the challenges and, with considerable Republican assistance, notably from the late Sen. Vandenberg of Michigan, brought America along with him. The Truman Doctrine drew the line against a Soviet threat which was very real. The Marshall Plan still stands as a monument to American generosity, to defeated foes as well as allies.

He had spunk and a sense of the authority and dignity of the Presidency—qualities he demonstrated in 1951 when he fired General Douglas MacArthur as Supreme Commander in Korea and shogun of Japan—and had an abiding loyalty to the values of a free society, as he vetoed an internal security bill, knowing he would probably be overridden as he was.

In domestic affairs he was less successful. In those days "politics stopped at the water's edge," most of the time, but up to the water's edge it was, as it still is, fierce. Mr. TRUMAN played the partisan game with relish, won the big one in 1948, when no one but himself and Louis Bean thought he could, but lost most of his Fair Deal program to an increasingly cantankerous Congress.

He had the defects of his virtues. Much too loyal to friends who betrayed his friendship, too outspoken at times, confident on occasion to the point of cockiness, he will nevertheless be honored for his achievements and remembered for his own integrity and warmth and scrappiness.

His favorite epitaph was in Tombstone, Arizona:

"Here lies Jack Williams. He Done His Damnedest."

So did HARRY TRUMAN—an ordinary man who accomplished the extraordinary.

[From the Oregon Statesman, Dec. 27, 1972]

TRUMAN UNITED COMMON TOUCH WITH GREATNESS

A tough, little man who brought both the common touch and the greatness of indomitable courage to the U.S. Presidency died Tuesday at a Kansas City hospital.

HARRY S TRUMAN was not just respected or admired. He was loved—with a warmth which grew as the passing years measured him against those who followed him and the legacy he left his country and the world.

The United States seldom has had a more unlikely candidate for greatness. At age 36, by the time most men have their careers well under way, TRUMAN had given up life as a farmer and had ended a haberdashery business $28,000 in debt.

Turning to politics, he was assisted by the Pendergast Machine, the living symbol of big-city machine politics and favoritism.

By 1941 he was a U.S. Senator from Missouri, making a national reputation by ferreting out favoritism in defense plant contracts.

He shared the concern the entire nation felt when, as a newly-elected Vice President, the death of President Franklin D. Roosevelt pushed him into the Presidency.

He inherited the burden of ending a World War, and establishing the U.S. as Free World leader.

He asked his countrymen for their prayers. With humility but with determination, he began implanting his image on the course of history.

He decided "thousands of American lives" would be saved by dropping the atomic bombs on Hiroshima and Nagasaki. After an uncertain start in world diplomacy, he initiated the "Truman Doctrine" which drew the line against Communist aggression in Greece and established NATO. On the economic side, he sponsored the Marshall Plan to revitalize Europe and had Gen. MacArthur help re-establish Japan's economy.

At home, he presided at the stormy changeover from a wartime to peacetime economy, rapping the knuckles of business, labor and Congress. He gained the nickname "Give 'em Hell, HARRY," and won the public's votes as well as its hearts in the 1948 election.

He made another lonely decision in the middle of a June night in 1950 which sent American troops into Korea. It was a difficult war, but the American people understood his decision and supported him.

He spent his retirement years in the old family home in Independence, Mo., with his wife, Bess, his personal life untouched by the power he had known.

"Some are born great, some achieve greatness, and some have greatness thrust upon them," Shakespeare wrote. HARRY TRUMAN grew out of the heartland of America, out of its soil, its culture and its values, and when he was called to greatness, he was ready.

And in his readiness, he not only wrote an important chapter of American history, he confirmed the basic premises upon which this democratic nation was founded.

[From the Boston Globe, Dec. 27, 1972]

A GOOD AND COURAGEOUS MAN

There were many things that HARRY S TRUMAN proved in his 88 years on a troubled and often panicky earth. One of these is that he was by no means "only a small duck in a very large puddle," as he himself once described himself. (And watch that period after the S. No one, including his daughter, Margaret, knows to this day whether the S stands for Solomon, the first name of one of his grandfathers, or Shippe, the first name of the other one, and the Trumans never wanted anyone to know lest feelings be hurt on one side of the family or the other. But he himself used the period in his autobiography and he must have been quietly amused as the curious legend grew that it should always be omitted. Mr. Truman liked his little jokes and was as likely to break into a chuckle as he was to break into the irritated earthyisms for which his beloved Bess never failed to scold him.)

The late President has been variously described as "that pugnacious little rooster," the "bantam heavy-weight," and "the bankrupt haberdasher from Independence." He was all of these, and proud of it. His bankruptcy was in 1920–21 when business failures tripled overnight. Typically, Mr. TRUMAN charged it to "the Republican recession engineered by Old Mellon" (Andrew Mellon, Secretary of the Treasury under President Harding), and just as

typically he refused to go into bankruptcy but spent the next 15 years trying to pay off some $12,000 in debts.

News accounts say that death came quietly to the nations 33rd President. This is comforting to his family and friends. But death certainly is the final adversity, man's last great fight, at least in most circumstances, and it is difficult to imagine Mr. TRUMAN quitting without putting up his dukes.

He was one of the great scrappers of our times. He more than once laid out Missouri's "Boss Pendergast," to whom he was falsely reported to be beholden for his first political election as an administrative judge in Missouri's Jackson County after the haberdashery had failed. He had more than one good battle with President Roosevelt, whose third term he opposed while he himself was serving his first Senate term. Mr. Roosevelt returned "the favor" with icy coolness to Mr. TRUMAN's own successful campaign for a second term in the Senate, neither of them having the remotest idea that Mr. Roosevelt, in his own battle for the fourth term nomination, would insist that he had to have "that independent S.O.B. from Independence" as his running mate. "Tell the President to quit treating me like an office boy," was one of Mr. TRUMAN's messages to the White House. An office boy, he wasn't.

He fought with "that Do Nothing (80th) Congress," with arms manufacturers in World War II, with the brass in the military services which he unified in his own creation, the Defense Department, after he ascended to the Presidency upon Mr. Roosevelt's death in April, 1945. He fought with Gen. Douglas MacArthur, even fired him to the surprise of everyone except Bess because the popular General refused to follow orders in the Korean war. He fought the steel industry, the railroads, John L. Lewis.

There was no one in Washington or out whom he refused to take on, when need be, except Bess and daughter, Margaret. He even found time to do word battle with the music critic whose reviews of Margaret's tour as a concert singer were unkind. And most of all, this bespectacled and deceptively mousy-looking little man, who "felt like the moon, the stars and all the planets had fallen" on him when Mr. Roosevelt died, fought Thomas E. Dewey tooth and nail on city streets and in the nation's crossroads in the 1948 campaign which none but Mr. TRUMAN himself, and, of course, Bess and Margaret, thought he had a chance of winning.

Typically, he had a Turkish bath on election night, ate a ham sandwich, drank a glass of milk and went to bed while the nation piled up 24 million popular votes for him, 304 electoral, in what is generally regarded as the biggest political upset in the nation's history.

Mr. TRUMAN, in the controversies that swirled round his head, resolutely refused to pass on such blame as there might be, and proudly announced that "the buck stops here,"—his own desk. The bucks were many and varied—the prosecution of World War II to its conclusion, including the atomic bombing of Hiroshima and Nagasaki—the Korean War, where he preceded President Nixon in the insistence that Congress has no right to dictate how a President deploys American troops—the Truman Doctrine of "containment" of Communism, which, it is argued even now and perhaps rightly prolonged the Cold War if it did not actually precipitate it—the Marshall Plan—Civil Rights legislation—the airlift to break the Berlin blockade. Mr. TRUMAN even took on and licked the architects and the traditionalists when he insisted upon the building of the balcony, "the back porch," on the south side of the White House.

When he first went to the United States Senate, a friend counseled him, "HARRY, don't you go to the Senate with an inferiority complex. You'll sit there about six months wondering how you got there. But after that you'll wonder how the rest of them got there."

The friend need not have worried. Mr. TRUMAN had few, if any, complexes. An inferiority complex was not one of them. He was asked to fill the shoes of a great President. All observers are agreed that he filled them more than adequately. Some, perhaps many, insist that Mr. TRUMAN himself will be recorded in history as one of the great Presidents. Certainly to the degree that courage is one of the proper measures, HARRY S. (for Solomon or Shippe) TRUMAN will measure up.

❦

[From the Des Moines Register, Dec. 27, 1972]

HARRY TRUMAN

HARRY S TRUMAN, who died at 88 this week, never lost his flat Missouri twang nor acquired the slightest trace of cultural gloss. He remained a hometown boy who loved his hometown and his family. He supported his friends, even when they didn't deserve it.

TRUMAN was tapped as a candidate for U.S. Senator by Kansas City Democratic boss Tom Pendergast in 1934, because TRUMAN's reputation for honesty and efficiency as the Missouri equivalent of chairman of the county board of supervisors was hard to come by in the Pendergast machine. TRUMAN won the nomination and election with day-and-night campaigning. He won re-election the same way in 1940 when he was considered an underdog.

He became a national figure after the committee he organized to expose war profiteering began to grab headlines. He was a compromise choice for vice-president on Franklin D. Roosevelt's fourth term ticket. That term was only two months old when Roosevelt died and the figure of Olympian majesty in the White House was replaced by someone who looked, sounded, and acted like the guy next door.

Crucial decisions were thrust upon TRUMAN. He gave the word to drop the world's first atomic bomb. He shaped the Marshall Plan of economic aid to Europe. He bolstered Greece and Turkey against Russian pressure. He ordered U.S. troops to fight the North Korean invasion of South Korea.

The American public regarded TRUMAN as a scrappy fighter who dared long odds. The greatest of these fights was his battle for re-election in 1948 when polls and political experts pronounced him doomed.

He was equally combative when he fired an American hero, Douglas MacArthur, as commander in Korea in the face of certain public and congressional outrage.

Though some of his administration's agencies were riddled with scandal, and "the mess in Washington" became a household phrase, historians polled near the close of his administration ranked TRUMAN among the great U.S. Presidents.

Historical revisionists are disagreeing with this estimate now. They see the Cold War as a serious mistake for which TRUMAN was partly to blame.

These reassessments overlook the fact that TRUMAN acted at a time when hot voices in this country were calling for more dangerous, warlike responses than TRUMAN permitted.

America was fortunate to have as President in those unsettling days an uncommon man.

❦

[From the Chicago Tribune, Dec. 27, 1972]

THE MAN FROM MISSOURI

It would not have been like HARRY S TRUMAN to mar a holiday weekend by his death. For three days, he clung to life and confounded his doctors with the same tenacity that marked his career, yielding only when the holidays were over. He was 88 years old.

The perspective gained by Mr. TRUMAN's 20 quiet years of retirement has brought a mellowing of his reputation, just as 31 years of retirement did for Herbert Hoover. Yet two superficially contrasting judgments of his character and public life still stand confirmed.

More than perhaps anyone else, Mr. TRUMAN proved that any American boy may become President; the American people liked and trusted the way he talked and acted, after the event as well as before it. The man from Missouri faced grave historic challenges with gusty confidence and courage. His many political allies and his many political opponents [including The Tribune] could agree on that.

Few national figures were ever launched under less promising circumstances than Mr. TRUMAN. At the age of 50, he arrived in Washington in 1935 as junior senator from Missouri, by favor of the Kansas City machine bossed by Tom Pendergast. The only public offices he had held earlier were in Kansas City. Before that, he had been a partner in an unsuccessful men's clothing store and had worked on the family farm. TRUMAN was loyal to the end to the man who lifted him out of obscurity.

In the Senate, Mr. TRUMAN exceeded expectations as an investigator of profiteering and waste in war contracts. In 1944, lightning struck him again; he was slated as a compromise choice, in place of Henry Wallace, as second man on the ticket with President Franklin D. Roosevelt. When he succeeded to the Presidency on April 12, 1945, he felt, he said later, that "there must be a million men better qualified than I to take up the Presidential task." Many Americans agreed with this, yet respected him for saying it.

Despite a spunky performance as President between 1945 and 1948, few people in the country except Mr. TRUMAN himself believed that he could return to the White House in his own right. Neither the prevailing doubts nor the discouraging early returns kept him from defeating Thomas E. Dewey 24.1 million to 22.0 million in the popular vote.

Often and with glee, Mr. TRUMAN displayed a headline which appeared briefly on an early election night edition of The Chicago Tribune announcing boldly [and erroneously], "Dewey Defeats TRUMAN." It was not one of our proudest moments, but we didn't begrudge Mr. TRUMAN his laughs. He was entitled to them.

Tho eligible to run again in 1952, he declined to do so, instead vigorously supporting the ineffectual campaign of Adlai Stevenson.

Mr. TRUMAN's Presidency was spectacularly eventful. He was President at the time of the atomic bombing of Hiroshima and Nagasaki, the end of World War II and the beginning of the United Nations, the early stages of the cold war' with the Soviet Union and the founding of NATO, the Korean War and the dismissal of Gen. Douglas MacArthur, postwar foreign aid, the peacetime draft, the Berlin airlift, and critical strikes in the coal, steel, and railroad industries. It was a time to try any man's soul, especially any man burdened with heavy responsibility.

Tho, even as President, Mr. TRUMAN showed capacity for hot-tempered vulgarity and for too easy dismissal of corruption in political associates as mere "fly specks," his high office lifted this rather average man to unforeseen levels of principled decisiveness. After many hard decisions, he could say as he retired from the Presidency, "I hope and believe we have contributed to the welfare of this nation and to the peace of the world."

After 20 years, that hope and belief are still possible to hold. Certainly there is no doubt about the accuracy of another of HARRY TRUMAN's valedictory remarks: "I have tried to give the work everything that was in me." A grateful nation gives him a last salute, and his family its condolences.

❦

[From the Houston Chronicle, Dec. 28, 1972]

A DAY OF MOURNING

HARRY S TRUMAN shunned ostentation. Although he held for crucial years the most powerful office in the world, he remained true to his heritage, a man of the people with roots in the Missouri soil.

The funeral arrangements for TRUMAN reflect the beliefs of the former president. He wanted no riderless horse, no carriages, no pageantry. For TRUMAN, the simple traditions were sufficient. He believed that men provide their own dignity.

Only relatives and close friends could attend the private ceremony in the small auditorium at the Truman Library, three-quarters of a mile from the Truman home in Independence. TRUMAN himself selected the burial plot, the courtyard of the library, near a rose garden.

The simplicity of the ceremonies reflects the closeness of the former president and the people of this nation. He was a man with whom millions and millions felt empathy; he was a friend.

Today is a national day of mourning, proclaimed by President Nixon.

Our sympathies go out to TRUMAN's wife, Bess, and daughter, Margaret.

The nation is saddened, and grateful.

❦

[From the Miami Herald, Dec. 27, 1972]

FOR ALL TRUMAN'S EARTHINESS, HE DIGNIFIED THE PRESIDENCY

(By Peter Lisagor)

WASHINGTON.—President TRUMAN was the first President I ever met, and the encounter was so simple and straightforward that I forgot for a moment that I was in the presence of the Chief Executive.

It was early in 1950, and I had been in town for just about a month.

Paul R. Leach, then chief of The Chicago Daily News' Washington bureau, took me to a Presidential news conference in the old Indian Treaty Room across from the White House.

Mr. TRUMAN usually lingered in an anteroom after the conference to greet newcomers and guests. Leach introduced me as the newest addition to his staff.

"Howdy," the President said, smiling. "Your publisher has never had a good word to say about me."

It was a genial remark, but I was startled by its directness.

My lame rejoinder was, "Well, at least we know where we stand."

The President laughed, and said, "Don't worry; you fellows do your job all right."

It was President TRUMAN's lack of pretentiousness, a down-to-earth quality he never lost, that endeared him to Washington newsmen. He never got tangled up in fancy syntax or resorted to empty ambiguities to conceal how he felt.

And he rarely shrank from the use of the phrase, "No comment" when he wanted to evade an answer. Except on occasion, he would say, "That's none of your business."

The late Dean Acheson, his second-term secretary of state, once wrote that Mr. TRUMAN learned "from all mistakes but one—the fast answer in the nightmare of Presidents, the press conference. We kept on hand, as a sort of first-aid kit, a boxful of 'clarifications' for these events."

His distinguishing characteristic was that he never lost the common touch. The trappings of power didn't bend him out of shape.

He resisted what he called an "importance complex," and it was charmingly illustrated when someone asked him what was the first thing he would do when he moved back to his home in Independence, Mo., after leaving the White House. "I'm going to take the suitcases up to the attic," he said.

He stayed close to the people, and his early-morning walks through the streets of Washington were a cheerful manifestation of his refusal to be insulated behind the walls of the White House. They were also the sign of a quieter time in the life of the nation.

His dislike of critical publishers didn't extend to reporters; they were working stiffs trying to do a fair and objective job, in his view.

He especially liked photographers, and became an honorary member of the "One More Club," an informal group of lensmen which got its name from the familiar cry of photogs when shooting pictures, "One more, please."

Before he left the White House, the One More Club gave him a farewell party which has become a legend of the craft. He imbibed with "the boys" and played the piano until the small hours of the morning. And when the party was over, the club disbanded.

He was an earthy man, without airs. A favorite story of his admirers—was the one about his visit to a horticultural show at the D.C. Armory. With him was his wife, Bess, and a woman friend of hers.

As he walked among the plants, he would pause at a particularly lush specimen and remark, "My, you must use good manure on this." After several comments, the friend whispered to Mrs. Truman, "Bess, couldn't you get the President to say 'fertilizer'?"

"Heavens no," Mrs. Truman replied. "It took me 25 years to get him to say 'manure.'"

For all his earthliness, though, he dignified his office

and presided over some of the most momentous events of this century. Acheson dedicated his memoirs to "HARRY S TRUMAN—the captain with the mighty heart." In those memoirs, Acheson wrote:

"Today no one can come to the Presidency of the United States really qualified for it. But he can do his best to become so. Mr. TRUMAN was always doing his level best.

"He aspired to the epitaph reputed to be on an Arizona tombstone:

" 'Here lies Jack Williams. He done his damnedest.' "

[From the Washington Post, Dec. 27, 1972]

HARRY S TRUMAN

A few minutes after HARRY S TRUMAN took the oath of office as President of the United States—when, as he put it, he "felt like the moon, the stars, and all the planets had fallen on me"—he was asked if the San Francisco Conference on the United Nations would meet, as had been planned. "I did not hesitate a second," he recalled in his memoirs. "There was no question in my mind that the conference had to take place." Within hours, he was dealing as an equal with Winston Churchill and Josef Stalin.

There were not many who were prepared to say in that dark hour that HARRY TRUMAN was equal to the appalling burden put upon him. The members of the Roosevelt Cabinet tended to feel that they would have to take him under their tutelage; they were considerate but patronizing. He very quickly replaced them. He had no very exalted opinion of himself; but he had great self-respect. Acknowledging that no one was "big enough" to be President of the United States in the crucial years of a great world war, he nevertheless felt himself to be about as big as the next fellow. What he had to do, he would do to the best of his ability.

Diffidence and doughtiness, humility and self-confidence, vulgarity and grandeur were mingled in this solid, unpretentious man, a seemingly typical product of smalltown politics in middle America. He was an able and conscientious senator, although by no means one of the towering figures of Congress. He was a man for whom—and probably to whom—the Vice Presidency seemed the very summit of legitimate aspiration. Yet when immeasurable responsibility was suddenly thrust upon him against his honest wish and will, he found within himself the resources to meet the task honorably and, indeed, greatly.

"Some scholars of American history with whom I talk from time to time are of the opinion," he wrote years later, "that it is history that makes the man. I am inclined to differ. I think that it is the man who makes history. I find that throughout our own history the greatest strides occur when courageous and gifted leaders either seize the opportunity or create it."

It may well be that both views are true. In any case, HARRY TRUMAN lacked neither opportunities nor the courage to seize them. Perhaps the greatest single decision of modern times was made by him very early in his Presidency—the decision to use the atomic bomb in the war against Japan. "The final decision of where and when to use the atomic bomb was up to me," Mr. TRUMAN recalled with characteristic simplicity. "Let there be no

mistake about it. I regarded the bomb as a military weapon and never had any doubt that it should be used. The top military advisers to the President recommended its use and when I talked to Churchill he unhesitatingly told me that he favored the use of the atomic bomb if it might aid to end the war."

For good or for evil, a new dimension was added to the world. For the salvation or the destruction of mankind, a new force was created. Years of experience with the ineradicable threat of atomic war, years of reflection on the moral implications of employing so terrible a weapon, may lead to a judgment that HARRY TRUMAN was wrong. But let those who make that judgment ponder his straightforward justification for what he did: "General Marshall told me that it might cost half a million American lives to force the enemy's surrender on his home grounds." And, conversely, let those who applaud his decision ponder what it foreshadows for any future war.

HARRY TRUMAN made another decision inexpressibly more life-giving and perhaps almost as momentous in its way—the decision to commit the immense resources, strength and skill of the American people to the reconstruction of Europe at the end of the war. The Marshall Plan, formulated and implemented under his leadership, represented what may well be considered the most enlightened piece of national generosity in all history. Indeed, American aid went generously to the vanquished as well as to the victors. In Mr. TRUMAN's own estimation, "The Marshall Plan will go down in history as one of America's greatest contributions to the peace of the world. I think the world now realizes that without the Marshall Plan it would have been difficult for Western Europe to remain free from the tyranny of communism."

To arrest "the tyranny of communism," President TRUMAN took the country into a considerable and troublesome war of his own—the war in Korea. The swift American response of the North Korean invasion of South Korea afforded a fresh illustration of the President's decisiveness and toughness in the conduct of his office. And in the course of the war he gave a dramatic demonstration that as President he was also indubitably Commander in Chief of the nation's armed forces when he summarily removed Gen. Douglas MacArthur from his post in the Pacific.

HARRY TRUMAN was a pragmatist and a politician. He preferred the specific gain to the idealistic goal. And he understood with unblurred realism that specific gains in American political affairs are achieved by leadership which embraces not only an imaginative appeal to the aspirations of a free people but also the crasser arts of political influence, pressure and manipulation. He was in constant conflict with Congress. "When a President does not have a fight or two with Congress, you know there is something wrong," he wrote. "A man with thin skin has no business being President."

His fiercest political controversy centered in the cult of loyalty that developed in the late 1940's and reached its culmination in obsessive attacks upon Government employees, especially in the State Department, by Senators McCarthy, McCarran and Jenner. There was a passionate commitment in HARRY TRUMAN to the principles of the Bill of Rights and to the concept of individual liberty. The tactics of what came to be called McCarthyism were abhorrent to him, and he was unreserved in his condemnation of them. Unfortunately, however, in his zeal to protect Government employees from the brutal assaults of McCarthyism, he established the Federal Employee Loyalty-Security Program—a pernicious process, still in full effect, which bases the determination of an employee's trustworthiness on accusations made by informers unknown either to the accused employee or to his judges.

Despite this grievous lapse into the fundamental error of McCarthyism, HARRY TRUMAN was otherwise a stalwart champion of a principle he enunciated in simple terms: "In a free country, we punish men for the crimes they commit but never for the opinions they have." Nothing in his official career redounded more greatly to his glory than his veto in 1950 of the Internal Security Act which established the Subversive Activities Control Board. In the hysteria of the time, the bill was passed over his veto within 24 hours. But he gave assertion, nevertheless, to a reassuring faith in his fellow Americans and in their fealty to the princials of political liberty.

His faith in the American people found reciprocation. In 1948, he sought election to the Presidency in his own right. Although it was not widely supposed that he could win, he campaigned with a verve, ebullience and indomitable determination that led him to victory. It may be that the American people saw in him an embodiment of their image of themselves—an exemplification of their own rooted virtues and values. There were qualities about HARRY TRUMAN now often referred to as old-fashioned—his rather simple morality, his devotion to his family, his uncritical loyalty to his country, to his party, to past political associates who had been loyal to him, his capacity, on occasion, for intemperate and injudicious indignation, his earthiness—qualities that stamped him a common man yet a man capable, as other common men are capable, of ascent to the heights of heroism. HARRY TRUMAN showed his countrymen what they were made of and what they could become.

✝

[From the Arizona Republican, Dec. 27, 1972]

MAN FROM "MIDDLE AMERICA"

President Franklin D. Roosevelt was a glittering, sophisticated, worldly aristocrat from New York, a graduate of Groton and Harvard.

Vice President HARRY S TRUMAN was an ex-haberdasher from Missouri who studied law at night school.

The official paths crossed infrequently; their social paths never.

World War II was approaching its climax in 1945, and the scientists at the Argonne Laboratory were nearly ready to raise the curtain on the Atomic Age.

Communications between the President and the Vice-President had been so bad that Mr. TRUMAN required a briefing on the Manhattan Project after Mr. Roosevelt died.

The new President knew next to nothing about the military situation in Europe and Asia.

But HARRY TRUMAN took his place with the great and near-great as though he had been "to the manor born."

He exchanged toasts and barbed quips with Stalin, kidded with Churchill, was not overly impressed by De Gaulle, took the measure of Chiang.

In 1948, with the hot war ended and the cold war under way, Mr. TRUMAN sought the presidency on his own. The polls all predicted he would be defeated by Thomas Dewey, a prestigious Wall Street lawyer and a successful governor of New York state.

Mr. TRUMAN took to the hustings in a "give 'em hell" campaign that caught fire without the pundits realizing what was happening. He won handily, although the Chicago Tribune proclaimed Dewey's victory before all the votes were counted.

The history of the Truman presidency glistens with accomplishments. He used the atomic bomb at Hiroshima because he wanted to save a million American lives. He undoubtedly saved even more Japanese lives by forcing the Emperor to surrender without an invasion of Japan.

When the Communists started an overt drive for world domination by crossing the 38th Parallel in Korea, President TRUMAN ordered General MacArthur to repel the attack.

He later fired MacArthur, in an unnecessary belittlement of the general, but the action was in keeping with a grass-root recognition of his own power and his belief in himself.

(Another great military hero, Dwight Eisenhower, followed TRUMAN into the White House. "I didn't go to your inaugural because I didn't want to steal the show," Ike told the retiring President. "You didn't go because I didn't order you to," said the commander-in-chief. "If I had ordered you to, you would have gone.")

The seemingly parochial Missourian was as impressive in his peace moves as in his war moves.

He proclaimed the Truman Doctrine, which kept Greece and Turkey out of Communist hands.

He implemented the Marshall Plan, which restored Europe's shatered economy. He helped launch the United Nations, raised minimum wages, increased Social Security payments.

HARRY S TRUMAN wasn't always right. The U.S. Supreme Court rebuked him for seizing the steel companies.

But he was never lacking in courage, and he was much closer to being an average American than most of his nation's chief magistrates.

Death has removed a great citizen who represented Middle America long before the Republicans coined the phrase.

✝

[From the Montgomery Advertiser, Dec. 27, 1972]

HARRY S TRUMAN

As in life, HARRY S TRUMAN refused to give up on his deathbed.

In a sense, his last battle capsuled his life—the life of a doughty, audacious fighter against seemingly impossible odds.

This time the odds proved impossible, but had his will and determination been enough, the former President would have made it. Throughout the three weeks of his final illness, he continued to amaze doctors by rallying time and again at the point of death.

On April 12, 1945, when the country was still at war, he was elevated to the presidency by the sudden death of Franklin D. Roosevelt.

The nation was almost as stunned by the realization that this average man, this haberdasher, this political functionary (as he was generally viewed at the time) had become chief executive as by the death of FDR.

Truman had none of the "charisma" of Roosevelt, but he proved that wasn't necessary. He was a hard-worker, decisive and never fretted once he had made up his mind.

Fate handed him many hard decisions, which he made almost alone: using the atomic bomb on Japan, an act he and others believed saved millions of lives; the Truman Doctrine to halt Soviet expansionism in post-war Europe; the Marshall Plan for economic recovery of the war-ravaged continent; the Berlin airlift; Korea; the firing of Gen. MacArthur for insubordination when the General was a national hero and Truman wasn't; and, not least, the 1948 election which he was supposed to lose by a landslide, in the estimate of Democrats, Republicans, pollsters and pundits.

In that campaign, against what seemed the insurmountable victory of Thomas E. Dewey, and with the defection of the South and liberal Democrats under two splinter parties, he fought. His gutsy appeal to the people, his never-say-die spirit and the vitality of an uncommon common man upset all predictions.

Although many despised him (notably Southerners because of his civil rights stand, moderate by today's standards), hindsight and the verdict of history have revealed him to be one of our strongest presidents.

President Truman was the perfect example of maximum output from limited input.

He will be remembered, in spite of his pettiness and cronyism, as a great man and a great president.

But most of all, perhaps, he will be remembered as a fighter against apparently insuperable circumstances; even the final one when he survived far longer than anyone had believed possible.

With all his flaws, he was a superior American.

❦

[From the San Francisco Examiner, Dec. 26, 1972]

HARRY TRUMAN

The story of HARRY S TRUMAN is one of the most remarkable in the entire saga of America. It is the story of a small town Missouri politician, lacking either the desire or the background for the Presidency, who in less than eight years made as many history-changing decisions as any other man who ever occupied the White House.

Coming out of Middle America as the hand-picked senator of Kansas City boss Tom Pendergast, Mr. Truman first attracted national attention when he chaired a Senate investigation into World War II defense production. In that role he acquitted himself so well that Franklin D. Roosevelt, faced with a compromise between James Byrnes on the right and Henry Wallace on the left, selected Mr. Truman as his 1944 running mate.

Within three months of their inauguration, Roosevelt was dead and Mr. Truman was President. In the whole history of the Republic, no man has ascended to the Presidency in such a troubled time. One vast contingent of American fighting men was battling its way across Europe to Berlin while another was pushing across the Pacific to Tokyo. The United Nations was waiting to be born here in San Francisco.

Although Mr. Truman felt that the whole world had fallen in on him, he did not flinch before the challenge that confronted him. He did not agonize in the face of

decision nor did he torture himself with doubt after a decision had been made.

In his simple, direct, humane manner, Mr. Truman did what had to be done. He ordered the dropping of the first atomic bomb because he was convinced that was the only way to save hundreds of thousands of American lives and bring World War II to a speedy conclusion.

When Russian aggression in Europe destroyed the world's hopes for peace, the President sent aid to Greece and Turkey and thus prevented them from being overwhelmed by Communist insurgency.

In doing so, he set down the Truman Doctrine: "I believe that it must be the policy of the United States to support all peoples who are resisting attempted subjugation. If Greece should fall under the control of an armed minority, confusion and disorder might well spread throughout the Middle East."

During his Presidency, Mr. Truman was bitterly maligned by the right wing. He also was assailed by the left wing, which decreed that only political disaster could result if he were nominated by the Democrats in 1948.

How sweet it was for the hard-hitting Missourian when, in the face of opposition from both extremes, he pulled off the most surprising election victory this nation has ever known.

Mr. Truman's Presidency was one of almost constant controversy and conflict. When he finally retired to his Victorian home in Independence, his popularity was at a very low ebb.

In the ensuing 20 years Mr. Truman's stature has risen to the point where he is almost universally recognized as one of the great American Presidents.

Now, Mr. Truman is no longer with us. But this is no time for tears or vapid eulogies.

Indeed HARRY S TRUMAN's epitaph was written long before he departed this mortal world. It was written when imperial Japan surrendered aboard the battleship Missouri, when Greece, Turkey, Berlin and South Korea were saved from Communist subjugation, when the Marshall Plan resurrected Western Europe from the holocaust of war, when the North Atlantic Treaty Organization was created, when the state of Israel was founded with American support and when civilian control of the national defense was preserved with the firing of Gen. Douglas MacArthur.

But perhaps the most fitting epitaph for HARRY S TRUMAN is one that he himself liked to cite from a grave marker in Tombstone, Ariz., "He Done His Damnedest."

❦

[From the Wyoming State Tribune, Dec. 27, 1972]

TRUMAN THE COLD WARRIOR

It is absolutely fascinating to see the praise being heaped on President Truman by persons whose philosophy represents the very antithesis of what the man from Missouri believed in, particularly with respect to U.S. foreign policy.

It was HARRY TRUMAN who, by drawing a line and daring Joe Stalin to step over it, actually committed America to the Cold War, who also committed it to the Korean War, and in a sense set the stage for Vietnam.

What Mr. Truman ordained, largely by his own determination and courage, was that the United States of

America would stand as the leader of the Free World
athwart the purposes of the communist powers which was
that of world conquest.

Yet how ironic it is today that the 33rd President whose
niche in history will be carved on his policy to oppose
the purposes of the man in the Kremlin, Josef V. Stalin,
in gobbling up every bit of territory within the Soviets'
capability of seize and conquer, is being hailed by those
whose philosophical concepts are at total variance with
this credo.

If the Berlin airlift represented the extension of Truman's policy of 1946 in telling Stalin to hold back; if the
Marshall Plan implementation was to shore up the economic structure of Western Europe so it could not fall
easy prey to Soviet incursion; if the Korean War was designed to prevent overrunning of Eastern Asia by the
communist powers; and the Vietnam War a continuation
of that policy of simply resisting territorial seizures by
the communist powers, all this was faithful to the basic
thinking of Harry S Truman.

Yet today persons of note in this country are joining
in the eulogy of Mr. Truman as a man of great bravery
and sense of purpose. And many of these same persons
are individuals who have occupied high places in the councils of our country, especially the Senate; and who in those
places have done their very best to defeat the purposes
of Vietnam and in effect the whole scheme of this country's prosecution of the Cold War.

It is they who have made common cause with the
enemies of this country with whom our military servicemen have been engaged in mortal combat and still are;
and who would have had us throw in the towel long ago
to the discernible goals of the communists, and that is
simply extraterritorial conquest, the overrunning of neighboring countries like South Vietnam, Laos and Cambodia.

Mr. Truman has been out of office for 20 years and
these hypocrites who so sententiously prate about his great
achievements must think that people have forgotten Truman's endeavor in the cause of a Free World by opposing with force of arms, explicit or implicit, the thrusts of
this nation's most powerful enemies.

While there are those who set up a great noise about
the alleged injustice of the U.S. bombing of Hanoi, forgetting that it is the North Vietnamese who are the ones
who are absolutely intractable about acceding to a key
point of an Indochinese peace and that is getting their
troops out of South Vietnam, it must not be lost on the
people of America what the whole purpose of the Vietnam
War has been.

Especially in this day when the country and the world
mourns Mr. Truman, who more than any one person set
the stage for the effectuation of a policy which led to Vietnam and possibly beyond. He cannot be allowed to go to
his eternal rest with a cynical rejection of what he
wrought.

❦

[From the Richmond Times-Dispatch, Dec. 27, 1972]

Harry S Truman

When Harry S Truman astounded the pollsters and
the political prognosticators by winning the presidential
election of 1948, one of his aides explained the victory:

"People liked him. He spoke their language. They
called him 'Harry' and they liked the way he talked
and acted."

Harry Truman talked and acted in ways that ordinary citizens could identify with. They might not use
quite as crude language as he did in threatening a critic
of his daughter's singing ability, but they understood a
proud father's indignation over what he considered the
ridiculing of his child. They might not have used a
profane term in publicly referring to another individual,
but they could sympathize with a man who struck back
in anger at what he considered a political columnist's
unfair attack. And they liked a man who, though holding the highest office in the land, would candidly admit
that he was under the handicap of living two lives, "one
as President and one as a human being."

Harry Truman's term as a human being lasted more
than 88 years; his term as President of the United States
spanned seven years, nine months and eight days, and
it is this period, of course, that will put him in the history books for all time.

No one, in 1972, can see the Truman presidency
with the perspective that will be possible a generation
from now, but it can be assessed today with more objectivity than when it ended two decades ago.

It can be seen, in retrospect, that the actions of the
Truman administration may well have saved the Western nations from being devoured by the Russian bear.

The economic and military collapse of Western Europe and of pro-West Middle East countries in all probability was prevented by the massive assistance rendered
by the United States under the Marshall Plan and the
Truman Doctrine. The Soviet military juggernaut may
have attempted, at least, to roll westward had not free
nations bound themselves together for mutual protection under the NATO banner. And World War III could
have been the catastrophic result if the United States
and the other free countries of the United Nations had
been too timid to resist the Communists' naked aggression in South Korea.

THE COLD WAR

They were tense and dangerous years after World War
II when Russia probed for weaknesses in Western power
and resolve. The effort to force the West out of Berlin
by putting a strangling blockade around that city failed
only because Truman ordered an airlift which, against
almost insurmountable obstacles, kept 2 million Berliners
alive month after month with the staggering total of
2,343,000 tons of supplies transported by air.

Of all the decisions made by Harry Truman during
his nearly eight years in the White House, none seems
more awesome than that to drop the atomic bomb.
Truman knew the release of this terrible weapon would
devastate Hiroshima and Nagasaki, but he was convinced
it would save far more lives than it would take, by
bringing Japan to her knees and ending the war. History, we believe, will sustain his decision as the right
one.

On the domestic scene, Truman's "Fair Deal"—succeeding Franklin D. Roosevelt's "New Deal"—was an
effort to push social legislation much faster than many
Americans wished. He antagonized the South with his
antidiscrimination legislative program, yet years later he
was outspoken in his denunciation of sit-ins and other
civil rights protests and referred to Dr. Martin Luther
King Jr. as a "troublemaker." (When somebody reminded him that King had won the Nobel Peace Prize,
Truman growled: "I didn't give it to him.")

TRUMAN was out of touch with reality when he dismissed the Alger Hiss spy hearings as a "red herring," and some of his criticisms of his successor, Dwight Eisenhower, were ridiculous. He once said that Ike was a great military commander in Europe and in NATO "when he had someone to tell him what to do." He added that he was the one who told him.

ANTISTRIKE ACTIONS

Pro-labor though he was, TRUMAN took far-reaching actions in strike-preventing efforts. A rail strike ended after he seized the railroads and threatened to use troops to run the trains. But the Supreme Court ruled he went too far when he seized the steel mills in a vain attempt to halt a strike in that industry.

Master politician though he was, TRUMAN's political influence quickly waned after he left the White House. The Democratic party rejected his choice of Averell Harriman as presidential candidate in 1956 and of Stuart Symington in 1960. He resigned as a delegate to the latter convention in bitter protest.

But although the ex-President's political clout was gone, the American people as a whole came to regard HARRY TRUMAN with growing affection during the latter years of his life. They nodded in agreement when, in referring to juvenile misconduct, he declared that "Mama and Papa are more to blame than the kids; parents should stay home and raise their children and spend less time in taverns." And they liked the down-to-earth quality of a man who, upon arriving at a dinner party without his wife, passed up fancy excuses and bluntly explained: "Bess' feet hurt her, so I told her to stay home."

"NEAR GREAT"

A decade ago 75 American historians were asked to rank the presidents in order of greatness. Among the 31 presidents included in the assessment, HARRY TRUMAN was listed ninth, below five who were classified as "great" and with six who were viewed as "near great." The vast majority of Americans would not have the historical knowledge to attempt any comparative rankings of greatness among the men who have occupied the White House. But only the most shortsighted and biased citizens would deny that, on balance, the Truman administration served the nation creditably, particularly in the field of foreign affairs. And regardless of what one may think of his political philosophy, the man who headed that administration was a scrappy, courageous and dedicated leader who deeply loved his country and who was held in affection and admiration by most of his fellow-Americans.

❧

[From the Burlington Free Press, Dec. 27, 1972]

MAN FROM INDEPENDENCE

On Nov. 2, 1948, President HARRY S TRUMAN with his customary aplomb, switched off his radio and went to sleep. By then he had heard the inimitable H. V. Kaltenborn and several other radio commentators of the period pronounce his epitaph.

While he slept, the presses at the Chicago Tribune ran off their now-prized editions which screamingly proclaimed, "Dewey Defeats TRUMAN." Others in the country quietly were preparing for the transition from a Democratic to a Republican President.

By the next morning, though, the picture had changed and the perky little haberdasher from Independence, Missouri, had pulled off one of the most stunning upsets in political history.

It seemed, too, that HARRY TRUMAN was making a career of confounding his critics. After living in the awesome shadow of the magnetic and articulate President Franklin D. Roosevelt, Mr. TRUMAN was not a figure likely to stir the imagination of the American people when he became the nation's leader in April 1945 after Roosevelt's death. But it was not too long before his critics learned that he would not evade crucial decisions.

Though much has been written and said about his decision to drop the atomic bomb on Hiroshima and Nagasaki, there can be little doubt that his action headed off a disastrous invasion which could have claimed countless thousands of American and Japanese lives.

Much of the credit for resurrecting Western Europe from the ruins of World War II must go to the blunt and outspoken President. His Marshall Plan shored up teetering governments and curbed the Soviet Union's voracious appetite for more and more territory.

Mr. TRUMAN, too, was a strong backer of the United Nations and opened that international organization's conference by radio. In June 1950, he demonstrated just how much he backed the U.N. when he ordered American troops into Korea to meet the threat of a Communist takeover of that country.

On the domestic scene, Mr. TRUMAN pushed for a higher minimum wage, increased Social Security benefits and housing aid for all Americans.

Even after he left Washington, Mr. TRUMAN retained a keen interest in the nation's affairs and could be counted on from time to time to delivery a typically acerbic opinion on any political subject.

He has left an indelible imprint on the minds of many here and overseas for putting the pieces of the world together again after it had fallen apart in history's worst war.

Hon. Sam J. Ervin, Jr.
OF NORTH CAROLINA

Mr. President, if I had to describe HARRY S TRUMAN in a nutshell, I would say that he was an ordinary man who was endowed with the most extraordinary character, commonsense, and justice. He had the courage to make great decisions when the time for the making of those decisions was at hand. He was the ultimate determinator of all that he did, as is shown by the fact that he is said to have kept on his desk in the White House a statement to the effect that "The buck stops here."

He had, as I have stated, a great amount of commonsense. He was a man who came from the people, and was one of the people, and he understood their hopes and their aspirations. He was faithful to the highest degree in all that he did as President of the United States to the best interests of the people of this Nation.

In addition to these things, HARRY TRUMAN was a very humble man, as was so well exemplified in the manner of funeral he wished to have held for himself.

Although he was, as I say, an ordinary man who came from the people, he will go down in history, in my book, as one of the greatest Presidents this country has ever had, simply because he was endowed with such extraordinary character, commonsense, and courage. We shall not see his like again.

Hon. Philip A. Hart
OF MICHIGAN

Mr. President, the delivery of eulogies is rarely a pleasant experience. But I think all of us have been fortunate, in thinking about what we might say on this occasion, to find that grief—though present—is not the prevailing emotion.

It cannot be said that we were deprived of HARRY S TRUMAN unexpectedly or with total suddenness. He lived a good life, a full one and a long one.

And so when we reflect on the man and his career, it is easy to find ourselves possessed less of sorrow than in nostalgia. And the memories, in history's perspective, are pleasant ones indeed.

HARRY TRUMAN entered history's spotlight as an ordinary American, uncertain of his own talent, who found himself running the country.

And when he walked offstage, he was still an ordinary citizen but there was no longer any uncertainty about this particular American's talents for leadership, compassion and decision.

Those are truly nostalgic. He was the last President, I think, to walk freely and regularly out into the street among his fellow citizens.

He was the last President, as far as we know, to dial his own phone calls.

Probably the reason that history took a few years to really appreciate the merit of his decisions was because he embarked on them in a totally understated manner.

He occupied the office of the President without presumption, with no pomp and without self-importance.

The public in those days, I believe, held politicians in somewhat higher regard than they do now and it is my guess that it was because HARRY S TRUMAN upgraded the image of the profession.

There may have been muttering about administration mistakes in those days, but there was no talk of a credibility gap.

There was never any doubt about where he stood. And his retirement was a victory for every stuffed shirt in the Nation.

In a way, I suppose, it could be argued that he did the public a disservice by teaching the people that candor and politics, honesty and government are not incompatible items.

After President TRUMAN, the public—not unreasonably—expected complete straightforwardness and frankness from everybody elected to Federal office thereafter. The disappointment was inevitable.

He was a great man, yes, but he has given us a gift that we do not always get from great men—he gave us the gift of warm, smiling memories.

George Washington, I think, was a great man. Samuel Adams. Andrew Jackson. Woodrow Wilson. Franklin Roosevelt. The list is long.

But how many great men have really left us with warm, human memories as a wrapping to their impressive deeds? Great men are rather prone to become more and more one-dimensional with time, honored but faded and lifeless, like paintings of medieval saints.

Not Abraham Lincoln, for example. Somehow, his humanity projected itself into history without effort and so we can read about him a century later and still occasionally want to nudge a companion and relay a warm anecdote or a self-effacing remark.

HARRY TRUMAN, to the good fortune of all who come after him, will be remembered that way, too. Because his humanity, too, projected itself beyond all the barriers and insulations surrounding the Presidency.

Happily, he had a daughter with the wit and talent to record his character. But even absent her valuable book, Mr. TRUMAN's humor and humility would have become his trademarks.

Yes, we will all remember those decisions about the atom bomb and the Korean development. But is it not a delight now to remember that the wisdom to make those decisions was in the possession of a President who could get irritated because an expensive gold pen did not work?

Had he been given one more term, the consumer protection movement would doubtlessly have had an earlier birth.

Unhappily, I cannot claim to have known him well. He left this town before I came. So I am in the position of most Americans: It pleases me that I live in a nation that had the wisdom to make him President.

Hon. Bob Dole
OF KANSAS

Mr. President, Americans of every political affiliation mourned the death of former President HARRY S TRUMAN, who was a unique figure in modern history.

A strong leader, Mr. TRUMAN never shrank from the difficult decisions of his Presidency. In the closing days of World War II, when freedom was threatened and when Israel was born out of controversy and discord, he always stood firm. But he was also a wise and compassionate statesman who led the reconstruction of a war-torn Europe through the Marshall plan.

The Senate has a special fondness for Mr. TRUMAN who considered a seat in this body one of the highest and most important positions to which an individual could aspire. His reluctance to give up his Senate seat and become President Roosevelt's Vice President was well known, and throughout his Presidency he always held the Congress in high regard and maintained warm relationships with many of its leaders.

I first became interested in politics when President TRUMAN was in office; and, though we sometimes held different views, he always had my utmost respect for his integrity, decisiveness, and dedication to America's best interests.

Millions of free people—here and around the world—will long remember and be grateful for President TRUMAN's service to his country and mankind.

Hon. Joseph M. Montoya
OF NEW MEXICO

Mr. President, the man we gather here to honor today was a reluctant genius. A man who celebrated his common origins and proudly continued to live humbly throughout his whole life.

This is no small accomplishment for a person who wears the mantle of President of the United States. But then HARRY S TRUMAN was a man who made a habit of doing the unexpected—and

doing it well—during a long, distinguished career in public service.

For HARRY TRUMAN, unlike so many others, was a man dedicated to the act instead of the word. He came from Missouri, the "show me" State. That was his personal philosophy, too.

When visitors came into his office, the first thing that always caught the eye was the famous sign: "The buck stops here." He knew that someone must be responsible, and he accepted the challenge.

Although a farm boy, to his lot would fall some of the most important decisions of the 20th century. Decisions requiring subtle analysis of the most complex questions. And while we may—from the perspective of 20 years and more—criticize some of those decisions, none of us can say they were not made.

To the everlasting credit of HARRY TRUMAN, policies of his Presidency were created and molded for the needs of the times. There was no drift. The Nation did not lack for leadership.

When HARRY TRUMAN was suddenly catapulted into the Presidency, he was immediately confronted with dozens of decisions that would determine the course of peace and war in the world for the next generation.

HARRY TRUMAN made the decisions, living one day at a time. "I never look back," he used to say.

HARRY TRUMAN brought World War II to a close, settling the division of war-torn Europe and establishing a new order based on democracy and justice.

Former enemies became firm and staunch allies under the guidance and leadership of HARRY TRUMAN, and old allies remained good friends.

When war-ravaged Europe was threatened with economic catastrophe, HARRY TRUMAN worked with George C. Marshall to develop the Marshall plan to save the European democracies from totalitarianism.

When Greece, already staggered from 4 years of Nazi atrocities, was attacked by a Communist neighbor, HARRY TRUMAN propounded the Truman Doctrine and we aided in that Nation's self-defense.

To many, the policies of the Truman administration and their nearly unanimously successful outcome were miraculous. To HARRY TRUMAN, there was nothing miraculous or even strange. After all, he said, commonsense works wonders.

All his life he applied the lessons he learned on his parents' Missouri farm. Do not be afraid to ask about something you do not know. Learn from others. Get all the information you can before you decide, but once you are sure you are right, do not back down.

Honesty, straightforwardness, a sense of humor about himself, a deep and abiding faith in his fellow man and an equally deep faith that American citizens will do the right thing if they have all the facts.

These were the virtues of the American frontier, and these were the virtues that HARRY TRUMAN brought with him to his Nation's highest office. And these were the virtues that carried him through seven of the most difficult years that the office has ever seen.

When HARRY TRUMAN won a political victory that all the experts said he could not win, he was not surprised. Although the experts knew about politics, he said, but he knew about the people. And the people were the voters, not the experts.

HARRY TRUMAN had a long history of knowing the people. HARRY TRUMAN, really, was the people.

He grew up poor, he operated his own small business. He was a soldier and a member of the Reserves. Although he was an officer, he obtained his rank through an election of the battalion members. His commission only served to confirm the judgment of his fellow artillerymen.

HARRY TRUMAN was not a man to be called great. He was not heroic. He was not a ringing orator.

Instead, he was a man who looked like your next door neighbor and talked like him too.

For some the thought of that fellow in the White House was terrifying. But for millions of Americans, the thought of him in the White House was a reassurance to them that America worked. That a common man could not only become President, but could also stay President.

That reassurance in a time of turbulent change gave him a special importance. In a turbulent time, he was a symbol the world was not turned upside down.

Hon. Alan Bible

OF NEVADA

Mr. President, few Americans have served their Nation with the devotion and dedication of HARRY TRUMAN. He became President in one of the most critical periods in our country's history and faced some of the most awesome and far-reaching problems ever to confront an American President.

HARRY TRUMAN assumed the Presidency only months after his election to the office of Vice President, and at a time when the United States was engaged in one of mankind's most devastating wars. In rapid order, he faced some of history's most difficult decisions. There were the negotiations with Stalin, the decision to drop the atomic bomb, the Berlin blockade and the Korean war, to name only a few.

And through all these monumental decisions, HARRY TRUMAN was more than equal to the challenge. His courageous and decisive leadership during those troubled years stand today as a hallmark of excellence in American history. With each passing year since he left the White House, we have gained a deeper appreciation of the enormity of his contribution to his nation and to the free world.

Today there is little question that time and history have judged HARRY TRUMAN to be one of our greatest Presidents.

But HARRY TRUMAN was more than a bold and decisive leader, he was a man of great compassion and vision. He was totally committed to building a better America for all of our people. Many of the great social programs enacted during the decade of the 1960's were first suggested by President TRUMAN. He was an early leader in the struggle to provide equal treatment for all Americans regardless of race, and he advocated Government assistance in providing medical care for our senior citizens years before medicare finally became reality.

Throughout his life, HARRY TRUMAN cared deeply about the people of this great country. And in return, I think the American people cared deeply about HARRY TRUMAN. We admired his strength and wisdom, and we loved his warmth and honesty.

The magnitude of his contributions to the American people and to all the free nations of the world can never be adequately measured. Perhaps it is enough to say that we are immeasurably in his debt, just as future generations of freedom-loving people everywhere will be in his debt.

Hon. Bob Packwood
OF OREGON

Mr. President, former President HARRY S TRUMAN served his State, the Senate, and the Nation with dedication and distinction, and his death is a sad loss.

During his decade of service in the Senate, President TRUMAN compiled an impressive record. He took his duties seriously and will long be remembered as one of the hardest workers in the history of the Senate. The story is often told that as a member of the Senate Appropriations Committee, HARRY TRUMAN never missed a meeting of the committee.

But, perhaps his greatest and most lasting achievement while a Member of this body, was his service as chairman of the Special Committee To Investigate Contracts Under the National Defense Program. Realizing that billions of tax dollars were being wasted, HARRY TRUMAN drafted the resolution creating this committee, was named its chairman, and is largely responsible for saving the taxpayers countless billions of dollars by exposing much of the waste and corruption which permeated our military programs during World War II.

In 1944, because of his outstanding work in the Senate, President Roosevelt chose HARRY TRUMAN as his Vice-Presidential running mate. After serving as Roosevelt's Vice President for only 3 short months, HARRY S TRUMAN acceded to the Presidency on the death of Franklin D. Roosevelt.

As the 33d President of the United States, HARRY TRUMAN performed with the same zeal he had previously demonstrated in Missouri and in the Senate. Within his first 6 months as President, HARRY TRUMAN presented the United Nations Charter to the Senate, attended the Potsdam Conference to plan the peace in Europe, ended the war in the Pacific and sent his "Fair Deal" domestic legislation package to Congress.

He will long be remembered as the architect of the foreign policy programs and commitments which have endured for the past quarter of a century. He was largely responsible for the Senate ratification of the United Nations Charter, for the initiation of the massive foreign aid programs which rebuilt and stabilized half the world and for the conclusion of the mutual security treaties which were designed to keep the hard-won peace.

Mr. President, I ask unanimous consent that there be printed in the record, at the conclusion of my remarks, an article which appeared in the "Congressional Quarterly Weekly Report" of December 16, 1972, itemizing in great detail the dramatic foreign and domestic achievements of the TRUMAN administration.

President TRUMAN's courage and determination will never be forgotten. Nor will his boundless foresight and imagination.

Mrs. Packwood joins me in extending our deepest sympathy to his devoted wife, Mrs. Bess Truman, their daughter Margaret, and the Truman grandchildren.

HARRY TRUMAN: HIS CAREER, ACHIEVEMENTS, VIEWS

HARRY S TRUMAN, the 33rd President of the United States, has been waging yet another uphill battle. The 88-year-old former chief executive, suffering from pulmonary congestion, complicated by bronchitis, a weak heart and kidney problems, remained hospitalized in serious condition Dec. 15.

TRUMAN's condition has flluctuated from fair to critical to serious since he entered Research Hospital and Medical Center in Kansas City, Mo., Dec. 5. His heart—weakened by hardening of the arteries—was being closely monitored.

The former chief executive had been hospitalized seven previous times since he turned the presidency over to Dwight D. Eisenhower early in 1953.

Only two Presidents, John Adams and Herbert Hoover, lived longer than TRUMAN. Both died at the age of 90—the age TRUMAN pledged a few years ago to reach. Lyndon B. Johnson, 64, is the other remaining former chief executive.

Although TRUMAN went home to Missouri two decades ago, the legislation enacted during his presidency continues to shape and affect policies today. The United Nations, Marshall Plan, North Atlantic Treaty Organization and Taft-Hartley labor law are but a few of the landmarks of the Truman era.

But TRUMAN is remembered for more than his legislative triumphs and defeats. The earthy, populist style of the onetime farmer and unsuccessful haberdasher is recalled with nostalgia in an age of Madison Avnue techniques, programmed politics and alienated voters.

Reluctant Candidate.—Despite the monumental events of his post-World War II presidency, TRUMAN would have preferred to participate as a senator from Missouri rather than as President. Great pressure, from the White House on down the line, had to be applied to get him to accept the vice presidential nomination in 1944. According to *Harry S Truman,* a new book by his daughter, Margaret Truman Daniel, TRUMAN knew of President Franklin D. Roosevelt's ill health and tried his best to avoid being on the Democratic ticket.

"Do you remember your American history well enough to recall what happened to most vice presidents who succeeded to the presidency? Usually they were ridiculed in office, had their hearts broken, lost any vestige of respect they had had before. I don't want that to happen to me," he remarked to a St. Louis *Post-Dispatch* reporter during his fight to stay off the ticket.

"It is funny how some people would give a fortune to be as close as I am to it and I don't want it." TRUMAN wrote to his daughter in July 1944, shortly before the Democratic convention. "Hope I can dodge it. 1600 Pennsylvania is a nice address but I'd rather not move in through the back door—or any other door at sixty."

But party loyalty came first. After Roosevelt warned him that he would be responsible for splitting the Democratic Party if he refused the nomination, TRUMAN abandoned his first love and home for 10 years—the Senate—and agreed to be Roosevelt's running mate. Within three months of their inauguration. Roosevelt died and TRUMAN was sworn in as President on April 12, 1945.

Despite his earlier reluctance, TRUMAN did not shrink from his duties, whether it meant standing up to Soviet leader Joseph Stalin, doing battle with a Republican Congress or deciding to assist South Korea. "The buck stops here," read a sign on his White House desk—and he observed it. Within his first six months as President, TRUMAN presented the United Nations charter to the Senate, attended the Potsdam Conference, ordered the atomic bombing of Hiroshima and Nagasaki and sent his Fair Deal domestic legislation package to Congress.

TRUMAN CONGRESSES

The pace had been set, and there were few lulls, especially in the administration's early years. TRUMAN and his Congresses—the 79th, 80th, 81st and 82nd—did more than return the country to postwar normalcy. Together they launched foreign policy programs and commitments that have laid the foundation for U.S. defense and diplomatic policies for the past 25 years. During the Truman presidency, Congress ratified the UN charter, established the Atomic Energy Commission, approved and funded massive foreign aid programs and ratified mutual security treaties.

In domestic legislation, Congress passed a major housing bill, authorized federal aid grants for hospital construction and created the President's Council of Economic Advisers. But TRUMAN's domestic proposals did not fare as well as the foreign policy innovations. Conservative elements in the Truman Congresses banded together to thwart many of the administration's Fair Deal proposals.

In addition, they passed many measures of which the administration disapproved. TRUMAN vetoed 78 bills during his eight years in office. Twelve of his vetoes were overridden.

Only one Truman Congress—the 80th—was controlled by the Republicans. It came under special attack from the President, who termed it the "do-nothing Congress." He called it into special session on July 26, 1948 (Turnip Day in Missouri), to act on a number of domestic measures he considered necessary to the public interest.

The special session produced no domestic legislation, TRUMAN charged. "The Congress ran off and left everything just as I expected they would do and now they are trying to blame *me* because they did nothing," TRUMAN wrote to his sister afterward. "I just don't believe people can be fooled that easily." And he set out to tell his side of the story in the "give 'em hell" presidential campaign of 1948.

Second Term.—TRUMAN, unwilling to join the ticket in 1944, had decided it was necessary to run for another term. "I'm rather fed up on all the fol-de-rol it takes to be President," he explained to his sister. "If it were not for the world situation and my lack of confidence in the presidential candidates I'd throw the whole works out the window and go home and stay there. But I can't run from responsibility as you know."

A few days after he began his second term, someone asked him if he were going to run another term. "Have you lost your mind?" he replied. According to Margaret Truman Daniel, he had thought for some time that eight years in the White House would be enough.

By the time TRUMAN finished his second term, he did not appear to have a choice. His popularity rating was at low ebb. The opposition was shouting "communism, corruption and Korea." Estes Kefauver beat TRUMAN decisively when the President's name was entered in the New Hampshire primary of 1952.

MAJOR LEGISLATION

Labor Management Relations Act.—One of the most significant pieces of domestic legislation enacted during the Truman administration was the Taft-Hartley Labor Management Relations Act. The bill, which was bitterly opposed by organized labor, included provisions permitting 80-day injunctions against strikes imperiling national health and safety and outlawing the closed shop, secondary boycotts and jurisdictional strikes.

The 80th Congress passed the bill in 1947 over the President's veto, and the 81st Congress in 1949 successfully countered an administration attempt to have Taft-Hartley repealed.

Fair Deal.—TRUMAN appeared before Congress early in 1949 to urge a sweeping new program of social reform. The 81st Congress approved some of the "Fair Deal" measures sought by the administration, including a long-range housing bill providing for expanded federal programs in slum clearance, public housing and farm improvement.

It passed the Social Security Expansion Act of 1950 and raised the minimum wage from 40 to 75 cents an hour in 1949.

Otherwise the "Fair Deal" programs hit formidable obstacles. A religious controversy over aid to parochial schools snagged federal aid to education bills. The administration's compulsory health insurance plan—labeled "socialized medicine" by its opponents—never was enacted.

The Truman plan for the establishment of a new Department of Health, Education, and Welfare was disapproved by the Senate in 1949 and by the House in 1950.

Civil Rights.—On Oct. 29, 1947, TRUMAN's Committee on Civil Rights released a report calling for greater leadership by the federal government in the field of civil rights.

Early in 1948, the President called for a comprehensive legislative program which included the establishment of a Fair Employment Practices Commission and legislation that would halt lynching, poll taxes and segregation in transportation.

Administration leaders never were able to push TRUMAN's program through Congress in the face of opposition by Republican leaders and southern Democrats.

However, TRUMAN issued two executive orders in 1949 ending segregation in the armed forces and barring discrimination in federal employment and in work done under government contract.

Truman Doctrine.—The threat of a communist takeover in Greece and Turkey prompted TRUMAN, addressing a joint session of Congress on March 12, 1947, to declare that "it must be the policy of the United States to support free peoples who are resisting subjugation by armed minorities or by outside pressures"—the Truman Doctrine.

Nine weeks after the President made his request, Congress authorized $400-million in military as well as economic aid to Greece and Turkey.

European Recovery Program.—The concept of massive economic aid to European countries to assist them in their postwar recovery received final congressional approval in the passage of the European Recovery Program (Marshall Plan) in 1948.

In an interview shortly before he left the White House in 1953, TRUMAN cited the assistance to Greece and Turkey and the Marshall Plan for European recovery as the most significant accomplishments of his presidency.

Investigations.—The Truman Congresses began in 1948 to hold investigations on domestic communism which were to continue and to haunt the nation throughout the 1950's.

Television audiences watched a series of hearings conducted in 1951 by the Senate Special Committee to Investigate Organized Crime in Interstate Commerce. The investigation centered on testimony of reputed gangland figures.

LEGISLATIVE SUMMARY

Following is a topical summary of the most notable congressional accomplishments in the domestic area during the Truman years:

Labor—Labor Management Relations Act (Taft-Hartley Act) in 1947. Increase in the minimum wage in 1949 from 40 to 75 cents.

Agriculture—1948 enactment of the Hope-Aiken flexible farm price support bill.

Atomic Energy—Creation in 1946 of a five-man civilian Atomic Energy Commission to control all aspects of atomic energy development.

Transportation—Federal Airport Act of 1947—authorization of $500-million in federal matching grants for airport construction.

Government—Legislative Reorganization Act of 1946—streamlining of congressional procedure and regulation of lobbying activities. Unification of armed forces under a single Department of Defense and creation of the Central Intelligence Agency in 1947.

Presidential Succession Act—designating the speaker of the House and the president pro tempore of the Senate next in succession to the vice president, in 1947.

22nd Amendment—limiting Presidents to two terms—was approved by Congress in 1947 and adopted in 1951.

Health, education and welfare—Hospital Survey and Construction Act of 1946 (Hill-Burton Act).

Housing Act of 1949—expanding federal programs in slum clearance, public housing and farm improvement.

Social Security Amendments of 1950—extending coverage to 9.2 million persons and increasing some benefits, and the Social Security Act of 1951, which increased benefits further.

Most of the major congressional accomplishments were in foreign policy. Following are some of those:

Senate ratification of the UN charter in 1945.

Authorization of a $3.75-billion, 50-year loan to Great Britain in 1946.

Authorization of $400-million in U.S. assistance to Greece and Turkey in 1947—the first implementation of the "Truman Doctrine."

Inter-American Treaty of Reciprocal Assistance, signed by the United States and 18 Latin American countries, ratified by the Senate in 1947.

Funding of the European Recovery Program (Marshall Plan), started in 1948.

Senate ratification of the North Atlantic Treaty in 1949.

TRUMAN AS SENATOR

TRUMAN called his years in the Senate—1935 to 1944—"the happiest 10 years of my life."

He first won election to the Senate in 1934 with the support of the Kansas City Democratic machine led by Tom Pendergast, the organization that had sponsored TRUMAN's rise to the Jackson County Court, the county administrative body.

In the Senate, TRUMAN was a strong supporter of New Deal domestic programs. In 1935, he voted for the Wagner Act, which strengthened union bargaining power, and the Social Security Act. He also supported legislation to regulate public utilities and transportation, as well as President Roosevelt's "court-packing" plan in 1937.

In his 10 years as a senator, TRUMAN became the 11th-ranking Democrat on the Appropriations Committee and the sixth-ranking Democrat on the Interstate Commerce Committee. He gave particular attention to legislation dealing with transportation and communications.

His efforts on the Appropriations and Interstate Commerce Committees gained him a reputation for hard work and attention to detail. He never missed an appropriations meeting and frequently worked 12-hour days.

"Most of the senators who really apply themselves never get much attention in the headlines," he once said.

TRUMAN faced an uphill battle in his 1940 senatorial campaign. Despite his support for Roosevelt's legislative program, the President appeared to favor Missouri Gov. Lloyd C. Stark for the nomination. In fact, early in 1940, the President offered TRUMAN an appointment to the Interstate Commerce Commission if he would withdraw from the race. TRUMAN refused.

Military Investigations.—In his second term, TRUMAN won national attention by investigating corruption and waste in military programs. Concerned by charges that defense contracts and purchases were awarded through favoritism, he drafted a resolution creating a Special Committee to Investigate Contracts Under the National Defense Program. After approval of the resolution, TRUMAN was named chairman of the five-member committee.

TRUMAN called leading defense officials before the committee, and its investigations received much public attention.

Witnesses heard by the special committee included Gen. George C. Marshall, Secretary of War Henry L. Stimson, Under Secretary of War Robert P. Patterson and Secretary of the Navy Frank Knox.

TRUMAN also held hearings on a coal strike that threatened the nation's war effort. The strike ended after he threatened to summon mine owners before the committee.

Washington was a long way from the small Missouri town of Lamar, where TRUMAN was born on May 8, 1884, and from the farm near Independence where he was raised. He spent 11 years as a farmer after graduation from high school and brief stints as a railroad employee, mail clerk for a newspaper and bank bookkeeper.

TRUMAN received a commission in the national guard and served in France during World War I. Returning home as a major in 1919, he married Elizabeth (Bess) Wallace and opened a clothing store in Kansas City. When that venture failed during the Depression, TRUMAN at age 38 turned to politics.

Public Offices.—Taken under the wing of Pendergast, the power in the Kansas City machine, TRUMAN was first elected to public office in 1922 as judge of the Jackson County Court (a county administrative position). Defeated for re-election two years later, he came back in 1926 to win election as presiding judge, a position he held for eight years.

From there, it was the Senate and then the White House. But he never forgot his humble beginnings, nor did he drop his earthy style.

Once in 1956, Democratic nominee Adlai E. Stevenson, whose campaign was not going well, reportedly asked TRUMAN what he was doing wrong. The ex-President walked over to the window and pointed to a man standing in a doorway across the street. "The thing you have got to do is learn how to reach that man," TRUMAN advised.

"Give Em Hell."—It was something TRUMAN did with ease. President or not, he was one of the people. His 1948 whistle-stop campaign typified his common-man politics. He would come out on the observation platform of the trains sometimes twisting an imaginary Thomas E. Dewey-like mustache—and would lash out at the "do-nothing" Republicans to cries of, "Give 'em hell, HARRY." His election victory over Republican Dewey defied all predictions by pollsters and the news media.

In a 1958 television interview, TRUMAN discussed modern campaign techniques: 'Well, it's just like selling soap, and it's not right. It doesn't work. You can't sell human beings. . . . The way this last election came out in 1956 conclusively proves that. This is the first time in 140 years that a President has been elected—and that was a personal matter of popularity on his part—has been elected and has not carried a Congress with him shows Madison Avenue didn't fool the people.

"All my experiences as candidate for office I never did have money enough to run. In the campaign of 1948, the train stopped in the station on several occasions because we didn't have the money to pay the fare. When I campaigned for the Senate both times, we never did have money enough to meet the necessary expenses. We had no chance at all in those campaigns to talk over the radio or anything of the kind, and we won just the same. I'm not so sure that people have the respect for the big money that everybody thinks they have, because they like to vote for a poor man sometimes."

Hon. James O. Eastland
OF MISSISSIPPI

Mr. President, HARRY TRUMAN was a friend—a protector—a benefactor—a striver for peace—for countless millions of people around the world. He was that rare leader who did much for all mankind.

History's present verdict lists him among the great Presidents of this Republic. History's final judgment could well place him with the few who will be honored and revered through the centuries.

His gallantry was a cornerstone of freedom's victory in World War II. His compassion was a cornerstone of the unprecedented effort which—following the conflict—rehabilitated friend and foe alike.

President TRUMAN's Valley Forge was the complete destruction of Western Europe—which his Marshall plan restored. His declaration of independence was the Truman doctrine—which saved whole nations and peoples.

He steered our ship of state when a hurricane threatened all we have and all we hope to be. I speak of the storm which developed from the monumental conflict between Eastern communism and Western democracy. It was—truly—a testing time for humanity. At stake was the destiny of the race of men.

As always—through his life—HARRY TRUMAN met this ultimate test head on. In his inaugural address he said:

> Events have brought our American Democracy to new influence and new responsibilities. They will test our courage, our devotion to duty, and our concept of Liberty.

President TRUMAN's strong hand shaped vital events which brought America new influence and new responsibilities. His devotion to duty was a model for all who aspire to leadership. His concept of liberty was tested—and, like him, measured up to every test.

During the closing months of World War II—and in the aftermath of that widest of all wars—he made a lasting contribution to the protection and the preservation of Western civilization.

HARRY TRUMAN's station—a station he

earned—will be conveyed to grateful Americans of tomorrow in the pages of history.

It was here in the Senate that I first knew and came to admire him. Among our present membership—only the senior Senator from Vermont, the senior Senator from Arkansas and I were privileged to be Senator TRUMAN's colleagues in this body.

He loved the U.S. Senate. Modest—kind—unaffected—unostentatious—he was, nevertheless, highly respected and regarded on both sides of the aisle.

His dedicated service—his honesty and integrity in the discharge of his Senatorial duties—first brought him to national prominence. He moved—in a few short months—to the Vice Presidency, and—in April of 1945 he assumed the burden which brings with it the greatest power and the most crushing responsibility that any man has ever held.

I think people here—and in every corner of the earth—came to love HARRY TRUMAN because he was—in addition to being a world leader—a very human individual.

He never had an opportunity to earn a college degree but he was educated in the very best of schools—here and abroad.

On the farm in Missouri, he saw poverty at first hand—and became its enemy. On the battlefields of France, he witnessed the horror of war—and sought peace all the days of his life.

In government he earned his bachelor's degree at the county level—his master's in the U.S. Senate—and his doctorate in the Presidency itself.

Every college and every university would honor him today as a master of statecraft—and no one denies that he deserved a doctorate in the art of politics.

He was a statesman who was proud of the profession of politics—the art and science of public service—and he used his unsurpassed skill to strengthen the concept of liberty.

My most enduring memory of the man from Independence is—and will be—linked to his matchless courage.

His great valor brings to mind the words of Pericles, who said:

The secret of happiness is freedom—and—the secret of freedom is a brave heart.

All who knew HARRY TRUMAN should be comforted by the knowledge that he must have been a happy man through all of his years of service to Missouri—his beloved country—and the world.

Hon. Robert Taft, Jr.
OF OHIO

Mr. President, President TRUMAN, above all else, was a realist. He understood and appreciated the dangers of communism to a free people in the postwar period. In his inaugural address of January 20, 1949, he said:

Communism is based on the belief that man is so weak and inadequate that he is unable to govern himself and therefore requires the rule of strong masters.

Democracy is based on the conviction that man has the moral and intellectual capacity, as well as the inalienable right, to govern himself with reason and justice.

Communism subjects the individual to arrest without lawful cause, punishment without trial, and forced labor as a chattel of the State. It decrees what information he shall receive, what art he shall produce, what leaders he shall follow, and what thoughts he shall think.

Democracy maintains that government is established for the benefit of the individual, and is charged with the responsibility of protecting the rights of the individual and his freedom in the exercise of those abilities of his.

In the aftermath of World War II, President TRUMAN led a nation that was weary of war and wanted to demobilize its Armed Forces. But President TRUMAN recognized the dangers of total disarmament in the face of Soviet militarism. In his book, "Year of Decision," he wrote:

War weariness leads to easy illusions. It was natural for people everywhere, when fighting ended, to hope that peace and harmony would come at once without too much effort. But keeping the peace is a vast undertaking, and constant vigilance and effort are needed to keep conflicting interests from destroying it.

In that same volume he wrote that:

Once hostilities are over, Americans are . . . spontaneous and . . . headlong in their eagerness to return to civilian life. No people in history have been known to disengage themselves so quickly from the ways of war.

This impatience is an expression of a deeply rooted national ideal to want to live at peace. But the tragic experience following World War I taught us that this admirable trait could lead to catastrophe. We need to temper and adjust the rate of demobilization of our forces so that we would be able to meet our new obligations in the world.

Today, we are once again confronted by political forces, weary of the war in Vietnam, which would have America abdicate its military responsibilities in Western Europe and other parts of the world. President TRUMAN recognized the dangers of these forces and we should learn from his courage and his resolve. As much as he yearned for peace, he understood that in the cold war era the United States would have to undertake firm measures to shore up democracy in Western Europe and in Asia. He launched the Marshall plan, the Truman doctrine, the Berlin airlift, NATO, and our efforts in Korea.

He understood that realistic efforts toward international cooperation would have to be launched if we were to arrive at an age of peace. His first act as President had been to reaffirm the American desire for a world organization to keep the peace.

Because of his realism toward the Russians, he set the stage for the detente that only now may be possible.

In his last address to the American people before he left the White House he said that:

We have averted World War III up to now, and we may have already succeeded in establishing conditions which can keep that war from happening as far ahead as man can see.

I hope that we can be as realistic in our age as President HARRY TRUMAN was in his.

Hon. John G. Tower
OF TEXAS

Mr. President, HARRY S TRUMAN earned a significant place in the history of this country by displaying the type of leadership that was demanded of him at a crucial time. Our Nation was trying to extricate itself from a massive global hot war and survive a massive cold war imposed by the Communist world.

The Nation's highest office was thrust upon HARRY TRUMAN by the death of President Roosevelt during the closing days of World War II, but there were still some far-reaching decisions hanging over the Executive Office which only the new President could make. President TRUMAN proved to have the courage to make those decisions; and his leadership in ending the great war—the decision to employ the world's first

atomic bomb—and his steady and determined hand during the dark days of cold war diplomacy are his great marks on world history.

President TRUMAN exemplified the compassion of his great Nation through his postwar recovery programs for Europe and the Far East. His Truman doctrine blocked the spread of communism over Western Europe and prevented its domination by Soviet Russia. His determination not to yield to threats in West Berlin kept that part of the city from being engulfed, and, perhaps, forever lost to the free world. Clearly, the policies which President TRUMAN established during those dark days made it a bit easier in our own time for President Nixon to exert the strong leadership which has given us our best chance for an eventual end to the strained relationships which have separated East and West.

True to the great American tradition, HARRY S TRUMAN, rising from a humble background, found the strength and determination to face the decisions which were thrust upon him, and to prove his worth as a world leader. He was put to the test as only the Presidency can test a person, and he was found worthy of that high office.

Hon. William D. Hathaway
OF MAINE

Mr. President, HARRY TRUMAN was a man whose stature increases as the years pass. He stood as a leader unafraid of difficult decisions and confident that the American people would support him if he took the time to explain his actions to them. Not one for press agentry, HARRY TRUMAN talked commonsense and the people knew, almost by intuition, that he was telling the truth.

His career and success as a President are important to those of us in public life today because of the example he set of courage and candor in office. He proved that the public can understand complex problems and hard decisions and will respond positively if dealt with honestly and openly.

Beyond this, HARRY TRUMAN provided leadership on issues of substance which foreshadowed much of the work of succeeding administrations. Aid to education, medical care, and justice for minorities were problems addressed by HARRY TRUMAN more than two decades ago, problems which we have only recently begun to grapple with in any realistic way. Unencumbered by outworn myths and prejudices, he taught us the value of recognizing what had become "acceptable" problems and confronting them in a direct and concrete way.

But above all, it was HARRY TRUMAN's style, or lack of it, as that word has come to be used, that so endeared him to the American people. He was truly the citizen-President and our public life is infinitely the richer for it.

Hon. Claiborne Pell
OF RHODE ISLAND

Mr. President, on December 26, the American people lost not only a great former President of the United States but a man beloved by those he so valiantly led. HARRY TRUMAN has been called a man of the people. He was this, but he was much more. He had rare gifts of compassion and understanding, and the even more rare ability to translate these qualities into actions which made our Nation and our world better places for all of us.

The immense legacy of accomplishment which he left behind continues with us. It includes his leadership in civil rights, in health care, in housing and education. It includes the Marshall plan and the Truman doctrine and a foreign policy which gave Winston Churchill cause to say to President TRUMAN—

You, more than any other man, have saved Western civilization.

And it includes the abiding example of an individual of modest means, not far in those early years from the edges of poverty, who rose to our Nation's highest office and dignified it with exceptional wisdom.

It seems symbolic that he came from a town in Missouri called Independence. For he exemplified the independent spirit which is so cherished by our country and which, indeed, formed the basis for its founding.

Along with this spirit went enormous courage. He was not a man of awesome stature, but his courage filled his world, and above all it filled our hearts, and it lasted until the very end of his life. That courage gave strength to us all. That independent spirit gave us courage.

President TRUMAN was a constant and unrelenting student of history. He knew both the broad visions our history contains and the small details which are the building blocks of those visions and aspirations. He was unafraid of historic judgment. "Do your duty and history will do you justice," he said. A full sense of duty was perhaps his greatest attribute.

His sense of duty was nothing less than complete dedication. It was enhanced by an honesty and a decisiveness which served as brightest beacons for our own people and for freedom-loving people all over the world. And his dedication was enhanced by fairness. The Fair Deal, which became synonymous with his administration, epitomized his own integrity.

At this moment when we pay our tributes to President TRUMAN let me recall another historic occasion which took place in this Chamber on May 8, 1964. Previously, during the 88th Congress, I had the privilege of sponsoring Senate Resolution 78, which for the first time entitled former Presidents of the United States to address the Senate. After this resolution was approved, President TRUMAN was the first former President to speak to us here.

We welcomed him both as a beloved former President and as a beloved former Senate colleague.

He said in part on that occasion—

It is one of the greatest things that has ever happened to me in my whole life-time. It is unique. It is something that has never happened before. And between you, and me, and the gate post, since I profit by it, I think it is a good rule.

He was then celebrating his 80th birthday, and he graced this Chamber with his wit and wisdom as he did life itself, and the people he served, and such numbers of those who had the honor of knowing him.

In August of 1964 I had the honor of visiting the Truman Library in Independence under his guidance. I will always remember his kindness and hospitality—and I cherish particularly the good advice he gave me for my own endeavors.

In that library, in whose courtyard he now rests, is the draft of his message to Congress on January 5, 1949. It states in his own stalwart hand—

All I want to do is to carry out the will of the people of the United States—the greatest of all nations.

He so wonderfully fulfilled this ideal.

I am sure that our hearts reach out today to his wife, to his daughter, to his family, as they have for so many years, and with feelings of deepest sympathy since last December 26.

It has been said of President TRUMAN that as a young man and farmer he plowed the straightest furrow in Jackson County, Mo. That furrow widened as his own horizons grew broader and his responsibilities increased; but it did not deviate in its directness.

He could see beyond the horizons of today and his legacy and his life's work rise up now against our American sky.

Hon. Clifford P. Hansen
OF WYOMING

Mr. President, it is an honor for me to join my colleagues today to pay tribute to a late President of the United States, whom history will record as a great one.

HARRY TRUMAN served our Nation for many years, and most of them were troubled years. He made many of the hard decisions for this country because he knew "the buck stops here"—in the Oval Room of the White House.

President TRUMAN presided over the end of World War II, and that was a time, as all of us will recall, that the United States was the only nation in the world strong enough to preside in anything resembling a fairness to both the conqueror and the conquered. He endorsed the Marshall plan—a revolutionary concept of a single nation contributing of its wealth to aid the many nations of the world—even the nations of the vanquished enemy. Prior to that, TRUMAN made the decision to use the atomic bomb to bring a speedy end to the war in the Pacific. That was a hard decision, but President TRUMAN felt that in the long run it would save more lives by bringing the end to the war sooner.

TRUMAN was not afraid to draw the line on aggression. He made the decisions to aid Greece and Turkey in preventing a takeover by the Communists there, and this became a part of the Truman doctrine. He helped establish the North Atlantic Treaty Organization, and he sent Americans to fight in Korea in the name of freedom for all mankind. History will record the importance of those decisions.

Interestingly, HARRY TRUMAN was the first post-World War II President of the United States to send troops to Vietnam, when military advisers were sent there in June 1950. That certainly is a move that only history can judge fairly, but we know that it has been customary for the United States to have military advisers in many countries as a gesture of friendship to allies.

TRUMAN was himself a soldier in World War I, and knowing the horrors of war, he did not lightly enter this Nation into a military conflict. But he believed many things were worth fighting for and he never lacked courage when he felt the United States had to face down a threat by any nation. He knew that to maintain the world balance of power the United States could not shrink from its natural leadership role in the free world. He confronted the Soviet Union and prevented a Berlin blockade, and this came at a time when the world had only recently been through the long struggle of World War II, and it was an especially hard time for Americans to think they might have to fight again. There is a lesson here for us in the wake of the long struggle in Southeast Asia, and that is to show a firm hand now when some nations may assume, with some cause, that America does not have the stomach to stand firm against aggression.

President TRUMAN, because he was a relative unknown in the minds of many Americans when President Roosevelt's death made him President, gave great credence to the theory that the Presidency makes the man. In any event, TRUMAN proved he had the potential for greatness, and in my opinion, HARRY S TRUMAN was a great President.

Hon. John L. McClellan
OF ARKANSAS

Mr. President, freedom-loving people everywhere mourn the death of former President HARRY S TRUMAN. He was an American son. But he was liberty's apostle the world over. He was our beloved 33d President. His quest for peace reached the four corners of this earth.

I first knew HARRY TRUMAN as the distinguished junior Senator from Missouri, whose sweeping probe of the national defense program during World War II set a standard for the firmness and fairness which we strive for in our investigations today. I knew HARRY TRUMAN as a conscientious legislator who voted his convictions; a diligent advocate for the people of his State and Nation; an industrious worker who shunned spectacle and ostentation for quiet learning and more lasting pursuits. It was also my privilege to know HARRY TRUMAN when he briefly presided over this Chamber as our Vice President, a few months before he was summoned to a greater mission.

HARRY TRUMAN's answer to history's call has been etched indelibly into the chronicle of time. No man faced more momentous challenge. No man met its test more decisively. He hastened the end of civilization's bloodiest conflict. He cleared away the rubble of Europe and rebuilt the ravaged continent. He strenghtened the will of our allies to resist Communist aggression. He opposed Soviet efforts to isolate West Berlin from the free world. He brought democracy to the Middle East and to Japan. He turned back the conquering Communist horde from South Korea.

The Marshall plan, point 4, the North Atlantic Treaty Organization, the Berlin Airlift—but a few of HARRY TRUMAN's extraordinary achievements—meant more than just survival for millions during the Second World War and its aftermath. His resolute stand against tyranny and oppression ignited the torch of freedom in lands throughout the globe.

So, too, did he bring America into a new era of independent growth and prosperity. He fought for his Fair Deal at home with the same ferocity and perseverance as he battled the scourge of despotism abroad. Under his remarkable leadership, our Nation made the difficult transition from wartime controls to a stable, peacetime economy. HARRY TRUMAN believed in and practiced the kind of virtues we so critically need today—restraint and prudence. These were his fiscal bywords and he brooked no inflational deviations from them whether on the part of big business, big labor, or big government.

In his domestic vision, HARRY TRUMAN was as ahead of his time as he was in drawing the line against the forces of international terror. His proposals for bettering the life of our people were forerunners of many important services our Government provides today.

Many descriptions aptly characterize the kind of man HARRY TRUMAN was. He was at home on Main Street as he was on Pennsylvania Avenue, never hiding the basic qualities of his rural heritage—plain talk, humility, and straight dealing—which made him one of the people and raised the stature of his high office to new heights of respect. HARRY TRUMAN also was first and foremost a fighter—a man with unique forti-

tude—a man willing to stand up to adversity and conquer it, whatever the odds.

The HARRY TRUMAN I was privileged to know was once characterized as "the captain with the mighty heart." This is a most fitting and enduring tribute for HARRY TRUMAN—a true 20th century giant.

Hon. Herman E. Talmadge
OF GEORGIA

Mr. President, today I wish to join my colleagues in expressing my deep admiration for the late President HARRY S TRUMAN.

HARRY TRUMAN was a great American and a strong leader of our Nation during a most perilous time in history. He was a man of courage and conviction who called shots as he saw them. He made momentous decisions without fear or favor in accordance with what he believed to be in the best interests of the United States.

It was HARRY S TRUMAN who, virtually alone, made the agonizing decision to drop atomic bombs on Hiroshima and Nagasaki—thus unleashing the most powerful, the most potent, the deadliest weapon this world had ever known. It was he who weighed the promise of peace against the tragedy of war and chose the deadly price of peace. The bomb was dropped. The war concluded.

It was HARRY S TRUMAN who campaigned for peace in Potsdam and signed his hopes for world unity into a United Nations. It was he who attempted to insure that unity by offering the U.S. resources to a war-torn world in its attempt to rebuild.

History will no doubt record HARRY TRUMAN as one of our greatest Presidents and one of the world's greatest leaders.

But as we pay tribute to Mr. TRUMAN let us not only recall the caliber of his decisions and the importance of his terms in office—let us remember, as well, HARRY S TRUMAN, the individual.

He was a fighter, and a courageous fighter. He never forgot what was at stake during all of his battles: the future of a world recovering from the most devastating war in the world's history. He worked brilliantly toward a better tomorrow for all peoples.

Mr. TRUMAN brought to this Nation simple freshness—the flavor of the farm, the values of Midwest America. Never once did HARRY

TRUMAN, the man, forsake what he believed Americans held dear. Never once did he lose his humbleness. Never once was he afraid of being human in the seemingly inhuman world of international politics.

Many felt that President TRUMAN was too blunt a man, too earthy, to hold the position he inherited. But a man can never be too close to the earth—he can never hold too dear the lesson of the land.

Mr. TRUMAN was indeed a great President. He was indeed a great individual. We are grateful for the sincerity and understanding he employed as President and for the dedication he inspired as a man. We mourn his passing.

Hon. Strom Thurmond

OF SOUTH CAROLINA

Mr. President, on Thursday, April 12, 1945, HARRY S TRUMAN was propelled into the most important position in the world, the Presidency of the United States. It fell his lot to succeed the urbane and cosmopolitan New Yorker, Franklin Delano Roosevelt, who had served as President longer than anyone in our history. The Roosevelt name had become synonymous with national leadership, and suddenly he was gone.

It was not by choice, but by circumstance, that HARRY TRUMAN had the grave responsibility and awesome power of the Presidency thrust on his shoulders. He was a smalltown boy who had been elected to the Senate and then chosen Vice President as a compromise. He had no formal college education and little preparation for his new office, but he was determined that he could and would succeed in his efforts to lead our Nation.

Mr. President, he knew that national leadership called for perseverance and hard work. Timidity was unknown to President TRUMAN and "The Man From Independence" set out to reassure an apprehensive Nation.

The Truman trademark became swift and decisive action, and in his trait the American people discovered a characteristic which they long for in national leaders. His readiness to accept responsibility was found in the motto which he placed on his desk, "The Buck Stops Here."

Mr. President, both those who agreed and those who disagreed with him will acknowledge that President TRUMAN did not shirk his responsibility to make a decision.

We must leave it to history to judge the decisions he made, but we all recognize that his decisions were some of the most important in the 20th century. President TRUMAN was faced with the task of dropping the atomic bomb or prolonging World War II in the Pacific. He saw the necessity for swift action in the Mediterranean or the possibility of a Communist takeover. He presided over the formation of NATO and the implementation of the Marshall plan. Other crucial decisions were also his, and he always took the initiative to act.

Mr. President, he did not shun controversy and he welcomed the duties of his position. When HARRY TRUMAN relinquished the Presidency, he returned to private life but maintained his interest in national affairs.

As an elder statesman, the former President always answered when his successors in office beckoned. He used his vast experience and knowledge to counsel Presidents Eisenhower, Kennedy, Johnson, and Nixon. I am sure that his perspective was always a comfort to them, and his presence was always a reminder of decisive action.

Mr. President, even though "The Man From Independence" rose to the Presidency of his Nation, he was always proud of his place of origin. The glory and fame of national prominence did not change his manner, and this, Mr. President, was one of his most admirable traits.

From the haberdashery in Kansas City to the White House and back to his home in Independence, HARRY S TRUMAN represented the fulfillment of the American Dream. He was always willing to work and to accept responsibility, and he persevered.

Mr. President, HARRY S TRUMAN never passed the buck, and this made him a successful leader in American politics. May his life shine forth as an example to all Americans who aspire for success.

Hon. Birch Bayh

OF INDIANA

Mr. President, in recent weeks the Nation has mourned the passing of two former Presidents, both of whom served in this Chamber with distinction for a number of years before being elected Vice President. Lyndon Johnson, whom we eulogized here just 2 weeks ago, and HARRY TRUMAN, whom we pause to remember today, both assumed the Presidency under the most difficult of circumstances.

When we spoke a fortnight ago about the greatness to which Lyndon Johnson rose in his Presidency, we could not help but recall that two decades earlier HARRY TRUMAN had similarly risen to the extreme demands of our Nation's highest office.

In recent years, historians have developed a "revisionist" theory of the Truman Presidency. This theory recognizes the strength of his leadership and the foresight of the direction in which he carried the United States. Curiously, these historians are running 25 years behind the American people who, in 1948, gave HARRY TRUMAN a strong vote of confidence in the face of predicted disaster at the polls.

Back then, when just about everyone was predicting a victory for Thomas Dewey, HARRY TRUMAN had faith in the American people. And they returned that faith in a great electoral upset which stands as a lasting testament to the popularity this great American enjoyed.

Today, in an era when public cynicism has cast suspicion on the credibility of politicians, it is refreshing and instructive to reflect on the total candor of HARRY TRUMAN. Not only did it assure him success at the ballot box; that candor provided him with the necessary public support to pursue domestic and foreign initiatives of great importance in the period following World War II.

The achievements of HARRY TRUMAN's public career, from Missouri to the White House, make a long list. Certainly high on that list must be his courageous actions which helped rebuild and defend Europe in the tense years after fascism when there was the serious threat of communism. He carried out with forthrightness the policies of Franklin Roosevelt in order to end World War II; a war whose spending he admirably policed while serving earlier in the Senate.

While he fought inflation, sought to ease labor-management strife, attempted to meet a burgeoning housing demand, HARRY TRUMAN also showed a vision which went beyond the crises of his Presidency. As Lyndon Johnson was quick to point out before his death, when he was lauded for the enactment of medicare, it was HARRY TRUMAN who first proposed medicare many years earlier.

When some in the Democratic Party urged HARRY TRUMAN to ease off from the civil rights plank in the 1948 platform, he showed a valuable and remarkably clear perception of the need for racial justice. He would not renounce the platform, and took a gamble with political disaster as a consequence. That gamble paid off handsomely at the polls when HARRY TRUMAN emerged with his honor and his job.

In his retirement HARRY TRUMAN returned to the simple life he treasured. Not one to place himself beyond the reach of the American people, he lived with them, laughed with them in times of joy, and cried with them in times of sadness. To say that he never lost his common touch only suggests the humility and outspokenness which were his trademark.

The fact that he was able to live a long life with his loving wife, Bess, was a deserved reward for a man who had spent decades in public service. It is men like HARRY TRUMAN who together make this country the wonderful place it is. Pausing to honor his memory one cannot help but sense the void his death has created.

No more will there be a sudden urge to play the piano for favored guests. Sprightly walks with newsmen who found his pace a bit taxing are ended. But our respect, appreciation, and thankfulness for the life of HARRY TRUMAN will live on as an eternal part of our history.

Hon. Barry Goldwater
OF ARIZONA

Mr. President, on many occasions, particularly during America's involvement in Indochina. I have expressed my appreciation for the great service which former President TRUMAN performed for this country in standing firm in times of repeated crisis. And I noticed that more and more as the years pass the true stature of HARRY TRUMAN was becoming recognized by the people he served. Because of this I find myself regretting that President TRUMAN did not live a few years longer—until the full importance of his contributions to the world found its true expression.

It is sufficient for us today to recognize that this quiet, unassuming man proved a tower of strength in those periods when American firmness and determination was the only language understood by America's cold war adversaries. Looking back we find one instance after another where HARRY TRUMAN stood firm against the forces of aggression—in Berlin, in Korea, in Greece and Turkey, and elsewhere.

In paying tribute to this fine American it should be noted that Western Europe owes its present prosperity and its continued freedom, in very large part, to actions taken by President TRUMAN to initiate the Truman doctrine and the Marshall plan for the containment of international communism.

All of us, Republicans and Democrats alike, owe a debt of gratitude to former President TRUMAN which we will never be able to repay. In this connection I wonder how many times recently—especially during the last bombing of North Vietnam—President Nixon called to mind the advice once spoken by HARRY TRUMAN when asked if he was annoyed by public criticism of his policies. As I am sure everyone remembers, President TRUMAN replied:

> If you can't stand the heat, you ought to get the hell out of the kitchen.

Hon. James B. Allen

OF ALABAMA

Mr. President, on April 12, 1945, HARRY S TRUMAN was sworn into office as the 33d President of the United States. Incidentally, he was the first President in our Nation's history to assume office in the midst of war. From the standpoint of experience, he admittedly was unprepared to cope with problems of the magnitude which destiny had thrust upon him. In fact, he had been Vice President for only 82 days during which time he had not been privy to President Roosevelt's far-reaching plans for ending the war and securing the peace.

In truth, few Presidents in our Nation's history have ever assumed office so completely inundated by a flood tide of momentous events originating in causes and plans completely beyond their control. Consider these circumstances: Not only was our Nation at war but in less than a month after assuming office he would be compelled to cope with problems arising from the surrender of Nazi Germany. The Yalta Agreements negotiated by President Roosevelt were even then under suspicion—but worse, they were in the process of disintegration. Too, the date of the San Francisco Conference called to set up the United Nations was but 2 weeks away. The first successful explosion of the atom bomb was but 3 months off, and the decision to use the atom bomb to help end the war in the Pacific was but 4 months off. In July and August of that same fateful year, HARRY TRUMAN was to be thrust upon the international scene at the Potsdam Conference in the

role of world leader. During the conference, Winston Churchill's Conservative Party was defeated in a general election and Winston Churchill was to be replaced by Prime Minister Clement Attlee.

Mr. President, in evaluating HARRY TRUMAN on the basis of nearly 8 years as President, it is well to remember that it was not he who had been the architect of the plans leading up to momentous events with which he was confronted. Instead, it became his awesome duty to make the necessary decisions to implement the plans of the man who had preceded him in office. This he did in a manner true to his determination to protect the interests of the United States and that of the free world.

With the war in Japan successfully concluded, President TRUMAN was next confronted with a series of serious domestic problems. He was faced with the herculean task of leading the Nation through the ordeal of transformation from a war economy to a peace economy. Throughout this truly character-testing period, on both the international and national fronts, two facts became unmistakably clear. First, HARRY TRUMAN was determined to be President of the United States in his own right. Second, he had the capacity of making bold and decisive decisions.

On the domestic scene, when railroad unions called a strike in May 1946, TRUMAN seized the railroads and asked Congress for authority to draft workers into the Army so they could be made to go back to work. When coal miners called a national strike, he took over the mines by Executive order and operated them under the Department of the Interior.

In addition, despite the fact that HARRY TRUMAN had served in the U.S. Senate from January 1935 to January 1945, when he became Vice President, and had many close friends in both the House and the Senate, he did not hesitate to do battle with Congress when he deemed it in the public interest. He vetoed bill after bill when he thought the national interest demanded it.

In the area of foreign policy, he acted with equal vigor, boldness, and decisiveness. He locked horns with Communist Russia which had repeatedly reneged on terms of the Yalta and Potsdam Agreements. President TRUMAN responded with the Truman doctrine. In announcing the doctrine in March 1947, he told the people of the world:

I believe that it must be the policy of the United States to support free peoples who are resisting attempted subjugation by armed minorities or by outside pressures.

As a result of the President's determination to oppose subjugation of free peoples, Congress voted the funds necessary to save Greece and Turkey from being taken over by the Communists, and Congress supported the President's request for funds to reconstruct war-ravaged Europe as reflected in the multi-billion-dollar Marshall plan. Soon thereafter, he was confronted with the Berlin blockade. He responded to this challenge by ordering the Air Force to break the blockade with the Berlin airlift—which it did.

These examples of courageous, decisive leadership during extremely crucial years of our history are striking evidence of a potentiality for greatness that lies latent in most men. A potential that can be fully developed only under the stern discipline of adversity or under pressures of extraordinary responsibilities, President TRUMAN rose to the occasion time and time again.

Fortunately, in evaluating a political leader, and particularly our Presidents, it is of little consequence that one may or may not have agreed with some of his decisions. No man is equipped with the power of prescience. From the standpoint of ultimate consequences, we must await the verdict of history. But this we do know—in his conduct of the war and in his resistance to Communist aggressions, his motives were idealistic. At a visit to Berlin during the Potsdam Conference, he said:

We are not fighting for conquest. There is not one piece of territory or one thing of a monetary nature that we want out of this war. We want peace and prosperity for the world as a whole. We want to see the time come when we can do the things in peace that we have been able to do in war. If we can put this tremendous machine of ours, which has made this victory possible, to work for peace, we can look forward to the greatest age in the history of mankind. That is what we propose to do.

I believe most sincerely that in these words, HARRY TRUMAN expressed the sentiments of the overwhelming majority of American citizens. In doing so, he reflected a conviction which we then all shared. I am pleased to note that historians today are more kindly disposed than in earlier years in passing judgment on his tenure.

Mr. President, I salute the memory of HARRY S TRUMAN—a patriotic, courageous, and dedicated man who steadfastly faced and responded to unprecedented challenges without equivocation and in a manner true to himself and true to the tradition of great national leaders.

Hon. Howard H. Baker, Jr.
OF TENNESSEE

Mr. President, former President HARRY S TRUMAN led our Nation wisely and well through one of the most critical periods of our history. The 7 years he served in the White House were years of challenge and change. The decisions he made affected not only this country, but all the world.

Perhaps no man so suddenly elevated to the office of the Presidency was ever confronted with such a bewildering succession of difficult decisions. Yet President TRUMAN did not shrink from his responsibilities. He acted with the characteristic determination and judgment which proved to friend and foe alike the truth of his familiar maxim: "The buck stops here."

Almost immediately after taking office he was faced with the decision of how to end the Second World War. He presided over the final victory in Europe and the uneasy peace that followed. Because he desired to bring the war in the Pacific to a rapid conclusion with a minimum loss of life on all sides, he gave the order to drop the bomb which changed the stakes and the meaning of warfare from that time on.

President TRUMAN also proved to be a strong leader in the transition period from war to peace. He emphasized domestic needs, but was ever mindful of America's new international responsibilities. Faced with the threat of Soviet advances in Europe, he responded with the Marshall plan and other forms of economic and military assistance to rebuild and revitalize the war-torn nations of the continent and help them preserve their freedom.

In Asia, too, he was confronted with the challenge of open Communist aggression. He acted with firmness in using America's strength to protect a small ally. Yet he acted with control to prevent the outbreak of an even wider war.

President TRUMAN was vitally interested in achieving peace through strength and understanding. He believed the United States must always stand ready to honor treaty commitments of the North Atlantic Treaty Organization and other alliances, yet he was also one of the strongest supporters of the United Nations and the quest for peace through international agreement.

Mr. TRUMAN was a proud and fiery partisan whose courage was admired even by those who disagreed with him. No matter how far he rose, he always retained his individualism—his candid, sometimes salty manner and his folksy, smalltown neighborliness. These qualities, as well as his good judgment, incredible stamina and free spirit, endeared him to the American people. They helped explain his remarkable personal victory against the odds and the polls in 1948.

Harry Truman was a fighter for what he believed in. He was his own man. He lived in Independence, the newspapers and commentators recalled when he passed on. The reference, of course, was to his hometown in his State of Missouri. It could just as well have been to his state of mind.

Hon. Milton R. Young
OF NORTH DAKOTA

Mr. President, I would like to join my colleagues in paying tribute to the late President Harry S Truman.

Harry Truman was not only a great President, but one of the more able members of the U.S. Senate in this era. He had an earthy, frank, honest, and courageous way about him that won him the admiration and respect of everyone. He was a friend and you always knew where he stood. He did not hesitate to tell you if he thought you were wrong, and he was always very willing to help you if he thought you were right and you had a good cause.

Harry Truman was a man of the soil, and a good friend of farmers and all of rural America. He was unique in that he was one of the few Presidents whose stature continued to grow in the years following his Presidency. He had to make some of the most difficult decisions of any President.

I had a special warm feeling toward him as a friend and as Vice President of the United States. I was the last one he swore in as a Member of the Senate before he became President of the United States.

Mrs. Young and I extend our heartfelt sympathy to Mrs. Truman and all the Truman family.

Hon. Howard W. Cannon
OF NEVADA

Mr. President, it is with great honor that I rise today to speak of our late, great President, Harry S Truman.

Harry S Truman was one of the most outstanding Presidents ever to serve this Nation. Just as surely, he was one of the most outstanding leaders the world has ever known.

He guided the United States with exceptional adroitness in the difficult transition from war to peace in the late 1940's. His accomplishments throughout his time in office are many and one could spend hours enumerating them and praising them and still not do this man justice.

The milestones of the Truman era are justly celebrated. The Marshall and point 4 plans are surely two of America's greatest contributions to the peace of the world; for, by "building up rapidly the combined political, economic, and military strength of the free world," they formed the cornerstone of President Truman's foreign policy: That American generosity could enable Western Europe to repel the tyranny of communism.

The dropping of the bomb on Hiroshima to bring a swift end to World War II was, of course, a controversial decision then and now. But President Truman took sole responsibility for this momentous action—"The buck stops here" philosophy was never more apparent. History has already written that, on balance, the vast majority of his decisions were proper. They strengthened the United States and the cause of peace everywhere in the world.

They were the decisions of a human being devoted to the old-fashioned virtues of responsibility and patriotism. He knew his shortcomings and never assumed he was infallible. But he knew final decisions affecting the whole world must be made at his desk and nowhere else.

I regret that I could not have served under Harry S Truman's Presidency. He was a man who greatly respected the Office of President, yet he listened to wise counsel, developed an excellent working relationship with the Congress based on mutual respect, and equally respected the intelligence and good sense of the electorate.

He was a man of the people, not remote from them. There was no need or desire on the part of Harry Truman to be insulated or isolated from the critical eye of the press and on a broader scale, the American people.

When Harry Truman said "If you can't stand the heat, get out of the kitchen," you knew that here was a man who had the moral fiber needed to handle the toughest job in the world.

He served us faithfully and well, and future American Presidents in time of crisis will be measured against the record of his courage and determination.

Hon. Walter F. Mondale
OF MINNESOTA

Mr. President, men make history and not the other way around. In periods where there is no leadership, society stands still. Progress occurs when courageous, skilled leaders seize the opportunity to change things for the better.

So did the late Harry S Truman sum up his philosophy in 1959. And if any man of the last quarter century has helped to reshape our history and set our Nation on the path to economic and social justice, that man was Harry S Truman.

Mr. Truman assumed the Presidency at a critical moment in America's history. Throughout almost 8 difficult years in that office, he fought courageously to achieve economic and social justice for all Americans, to maintain civilian control over the military establishment, and to bring about the recovery of war-torn Europe. And at a time when fear and hysteria threatened the basic civil liberties of many Americans, President Truman never hesitated in speaking out for reason and fair play.

Above all, President Truman's long and productive life demonstrated his abiding love for this country. He was a public servant, in the best meaning of that overworked phrase. First, as a U.S. Senator, and later as President, he sought at all times to carry out his responsibilities under the Constitution, never permitting personal ambition or political expediency to interfere with his devotion to public office and to public service.

When President Franklin D. Roosevelt died, Harry Truman asked the Nation to pray for him. "Last night the moon, the stars, and all the planets fell on me," he commented. The Nation prayed for Harry Truman, and President Truman left this Nation with a legacy which shall long outlive him in the hearts of each one of us.

When the history of this century is written, future generations will look to those among our Presidents whose goals were just, whose purpose was steadfast, and whose judgment was unerring. The late Harry Truman will undoubtedly be among those held in highest regard for the service he rendered and the lasting changes on the face of our society he left. We shall all miss him greatly.

Hon. Thomas J. McIntyre
OF NEW HAMPSHIRE

Mr. President, today we honor the memory of the 33d President of the United States, the late Harry S Truman.

Each of us who speak to his memory will reveal what it was about the man from Missouri that particularly impressed us or particularly won our affection.

We will hear about his courage.

We will hear about his vision.

We will hear how he held us together and moved us ahead after the death of Franklin Roosevelt staggered the Nation and shook the free world.

We will hear about his quantum leap beyond a humble beginning and a limited education to an exalted place in history.

And everything in these eulogies will be richly deserved by the man whose memory we honor.

But for me, Mr. President, the most enduring and endearing characteristic of Harry S Truman was the humility that came with his humaneness.

He was a man. No more. No less. A man.

His humility was genuine, because he recognized his own frailties. His humaneness was genuine because he recognized himself—faults, virtues, weaknesses, strength, and needs—in every man.

In my judgment, Mr. President, it was this characteristic more than anything else that made him truly the people's President.

It was this characteristic that enabled him to say with sincerity that the only lobbyist the whole people had in Washington was the President of the United States—and to act in the Presidency as the whole people's lobby.

Sometimes the people and Mr. Truman were ahead of their times.

I was reminded of this just last week as I watched Walter Cronkite's last filmed interview with the late President Lyndon Johnson.

In that interview, Mr. Johnson graciously noted that he was not the first man to recommend medicare.

Mr. Johnson said:

Mr. Harry Truman recommended Medicare, and he was called a Socialist and a Communist and everything else.

And so he was.

But in his humaneness, Harry Truman recognized the inhumanity of letting the elderly live out their final years in terror of catastrophic illness that would wipe out their modest savings, and plunge them and their sons and daughters into debt.

The people had a need. Mr. TRUMAN related to that need. And Mr· TRUMAN recommended a means to meet that need.

But what he proposed took nearly a quarter of a century for the Congress to accept, and who can judge how much anguish and misery resulted from that long delay.

I cannot help but wonder, Mr. President, how many—if any—votes could be found on the floor today if a motion were made to repeal medicare.

A final thought, Mr. President, but a related one.

Perhaps no President in our time was able to separate the office from the man with more clarity and determination than President TRUMAN.

Of the office he demanded the highest respect. Of the man who held the office, he asked only human understanding.

In his tenure as President, he did not always get either.

But once the man was separated from the office, the man at long last got both.

Hon. Vance Hartke
OF INDIANA

Mr. President, born to English-Scotch-Irish parents in Lamar, Miss., in 1884, HARRY S TRUMAN was one who perfectly exemplified a typical average American. In reality, however, he proved he was far more than typical, far more than the average American.

At the time of World War I, HARRY TRUMAN left his pastoral home life and enlisted in the Armed Forces in service of his country. Quickly rising to the rank of captain and finally to the rank of colonel at the close of the war. A businessman in his home State in the early 1920's. TRUMAN succeeded in being elected county judge in Missouri and served with honesty and efficiency from 1922–24.

HARRY TRUMAN continued to develop politically and gained a seat in the U.S. Senate in 1934. Throughout his stay in the Senate, TRUMAN served with integrity and honesty, and never failed to pursue objectives which he felt were correct. As chairman of the Railroad Investigation Committee, TRUMAN was informed by his staff that his personal friends in Missouri were involved in questionable practices concerning railroads. He ordered the investigation to continue.

In 1944 when most did not expect President Roosevelt to complete his fourth term, HARRY S TRUMAN was nominated and became Vice President of the United States. He became President just 83 days after having been elected to office, at one of the most critical moments in the Nation's history. He took office at a time when World War II still had to be won and when the United Nations was just started. President TRUMAN, however, faced these problems with courage and steadfast strength.

In the first few weeks of his administration President TRUMAN had to make the awesome decision to drop the Atomic bomb. He made that decision which brought peace to the Allies and peace to the world. He also faced the difficult task of organizing and changing the economy from wartime to peacetime. In the face of these problems TRUMAN took his stand and acted with firm resolve.

Following peace in World War II, President TRUMAN faced the arduous task of aiding wartorn countries. Western nations contemporaneously were also confronted with Communist subversive activities and aggression at a time when the cold war divided the world. He met these challenges by creating such far-reaching programs as the Marshall plan, point 4 program, the Truman doctrine, and NATO.

In 1948, HARRY TRUMAN sought reelection to the Presidency confronted with a Democratic party that had been split by the Dixiecrats and Progressives. With the opposition feeling confident of complete victory, President TRUMAN disregarded what seemed to be insurmountable odds and began his famous "Whistlestop campaign" and engineered one of the greatest political upsets in our country's history.

President TRUMAN was destined to be plagued throughout his administration. In 1950, he encountered another grave problem when North Korea invaded South Korea. President TRUMAN had to decide whether to risk war with Russia by sending armed troops with or without U.N. action, or possibly sacrifice the free state of South Korea. If he delayed taking his course of action it might be too late. Again President TRUMAN made the decision by sending U.S. troops 2 days later and preserved South Korean independence.

President Truman's strong personality and fighting spirit won him loyal friends as well as bitter enemies. But his courage and steadfastness in grave situations when security of liberty was at stake secure him a place as one of the world's great leaders.

Often outspoken, at times blunt, he never avoided using forceful rhetoric toward his opposition if he felt justified. His opponents described him as undignified, but his friends loved him as an honest straightforward man of the people.

And President HARRY S TRUMAN should forever hold a place as a great leader, a great man of strength and firm spirit in the face of great adversities. He will always stand out as a pillar of courage and honesty and should be an example to us and to all future leaders of the United States.

Hon. J. W. Fulbright
OF ARKANSAS

Mr. President, we pay tribute today to a man who led this Nation through one of the most trying periods in our history—and who did so with vision, determination, and courage. HARRY TRUMAN took his oath of office with as little preparation for the job as perhaps any President of this century, and yet he met the responsibilities of his time forthrightly and, to a large extent, wisely.

President TRUMAN was brought up in my neighboring State of Missouri and circumstances of the time did not allow him to enjoy the benefits of much of the formal education and travel which many other Presidents had early in life to help prepare them for the office.

Fortunately, the President was candid enough with himself to realize that he was human—subject to error—and I believe this recognition of his personal limitations was an asset which inured to the benefit of our country. The President did not, as he said, acquire an "importance complex," and I think the perspective made him more receptive to constructive suggestions which were not in line with his own thinking. As his Secretary of State, Dean Acheson, later put it:

Awareness that he was not an intellectual did not result in self-distrust. The conviction that views opposing or critical of his own might be sound held his irritation in check and made dissent and criticism possible.

President TRUMAN's capacity for decision was one of his finer qualities, and while we had spirited and honest differences, I will always admire the courage he displayed in making crucial decisions, unprecedented at that time in our history.

Of his decisions, I believe one of the most courageous and correct of his Presidency was the relieving of General MacArthur of his Far East Command. A grave constitutional question was at issue, and the President's choice was not a popular one. Yet, after considering MacArthur's contradictory views on our Asian policy, he unflinchingly decided to dismiss the general, reasoning that "If there is one basic element in our Constitution, it is the civilian control of the military."

While HARRY TRUMAN is well remembered for his activity in the area of foreign affairs, it should not be forgotten that many of the important domestic legislative programs which came following his administration—notably in the sixties—were first envisioned and initiated by TRUMAN. His programs included a national health plan, increased minimum wages, aid to education, higher farm prices, and broadened rights for minorities.

A widely reported misunderstanding between the two of us occurred as a result of a suggestion I made after the 1946 elections that it might be best for the country if the President resigned in favor of a Republican, so that the responsibility of running the Government would be in one party, thereby preventing a stalemate. As I said then, my comment was in no way a personal reflection on the President. Some years after the incident, he received me cordially during a visit to Washington and indicated that he understood my suggestion as it was intended.

Mr. President, HARRY TRUMAN was courageous, dedicated, and honest. I am honored to be here today to join in paying tribute to the man who "stayed in the kitchen."

Hon. Harold E. Hughes
OF IOWA

Mr. President, to me, as to millions of other rank-and-file Americans, HARRY S TRUMAN was at once a national hero and a personal friend. I am sure he will forever hold this special place in the affections of the American people. He was the unaffected good guy from back home who met the ultimate test of leadership, but never let it change his friendliness, his forthrightness, or his decent lifestyle.

His honesty, his penchant for speaking his mind, will stand in history like a national monument. Whether he was on target with big decisions or wide of the target with minor shots from the hip, this wonderful human quality endeared him to all of us.

It was his unique humanness, as I see it, that enabled him to unite and lead the country as he did so well. His was a big world of inclusion, not a cramped world of exclusion. This is something for future generations of Americans to remember.

We remember the rich quality of his commonsense. He said:

Whenever the press quits abusing me, I know I'm in the wrong pew.

The humor of this remark should not be allowed to divert us from its essential wisdom.

This humble, plain man, who said unabashedly that he felt as if the moon and stars had fallen on him and asked the citizens of the country to pray for him when he became President, never thought of himself as a great man. He did not waste time worrying about it, though. He prided himself on trying hard and giving the best he had.

He was modest and friendly, but when the great decisions were to be made, he moved with sure-footed self-confidence and courage.

He was not famed for his eloquence, but he was eloquent because he was straightforward and right in principle. He said:

We are a moral people, Peace is our goal, with justice and freedom. We cannot, of our own free will, violate the very principles we are striving to defend. . . . Starting a war is no way to make peace.

Mr. TRUMAN said:

When Franklin Roosevelt died, I felt there must be a million men better qualified than I, to take up the presidential task. But the work was mine to do, and I had to do it. And I have tried to give it everything that was in me. . . .

We know now that the verdict of history will be that this modest, plain man from Missouri was one of the greatest Presidents.

Perhaps the affection in which they held him might blur the objectivity of his own countrymen. But the great leaders of other Nations confirm the judgment.

As Sir Winston Churchill put it:

His celerity, wisdom and courage in this crisis make him worthy, in my estimation, to be numbered among the greatest of American Presidents.

Hon. William V. Roth, Jr.
OF DELAWARE

Mr. President, when HARRY S TRUMAN was sworn in as President on April 12, 1945, his national reputation rested on his investigation of corruption and waste in military programs. As the new President of the United States, HARRY TRUMAN succeeded one of the most influential men of the 20th century. This circumstance alone would have proved exceedingly difficult for any individual, but HARRY TRUMAN was not, contrary to many popular statements, the average individual. HARRY TRUMAN was a most uncommon man. His stewardship of the Presidency of the United States encompassed some of the most crucial decisions made by this country in the past several decades.

HARRY TRUMAN never shrank from the awesome responsibility of the Office of the President. A sign on his desk read, "The buck stops here." HARRY TRUMAN fully implemented the idea contained in that sign regardless of the popularity of those decisions.

Within 6 months of taking office, President TRUMAN presented the United Nations Charter to the Senate, attended the Potsdam Conference, ordered the atomic bombing of Hiroshima and Nagasaki, and sent his Fair Deal domestic legislation package to Congress.

President TRUMAN's battles with Congress are legendary. His criticism of the 80th Congress as a "do-nothing Congress" was the central theme of Mr. TRUMAN's "give 'em hell" presidential campaign of 1948. Despite the predictions of almost all political pundits, HARRY TRUMAN was victorious in his appeal to the people.

Although Mr. TRUMAN was not always on the best of terms with the Congress, his domestic legislative proposals did meet with substantial success.

The same was true in the area of foreign affairs. World War II left Europe prostrate, and the Soviet Union promptly moved in to fill the political vacuum. President TRUMAN quickly moved to counter the attempts of Communists to take over other nations. In an address before a joint session of Congress on March 12, 1947,

Mr. TRUMAN stated what was to become known as the Truman doctrine.

He stated:

> It must be the policy of the United States to support free peoples who are resisting subjugation by armed minorities or by outside pressures.

Congress concurred with President TRUMAN and authorized $400 million in military as well as economic aid to Greece and Turkey. This aid and subsequent funds provided under the auspices of the TRUMAN doctrine have been credited with allowing Greece and Turkey to resist the efforts of Communist insurrectionists.

Likewise, the European recovery program of 1948, or the Marshall plan as it is better known, is credited with preserving European autonomy.

In an interview shortly before he left the White House in 1953, President TRUMAN cited the assistance to Greece and Turkey and the Marshall plan for European recovery as the most significant accomplishments of his Presidency.

History, of course, must make the final assessment of the effectiveness of HARRY S TRUMAN as President of the United States. In the two decades since he held that office, President TRUMAN's reputation has risen steadily among historians. Mr. TRUMAN expressed his own opinion of his efforts as President in a press conference of 1952.

In the humorous, plain-folks manner for which he was noted, President TRUMAN stated:

> I have tried my best to give the nation everything I had in me. There are probably a million people who could have done the job better than I did it, but I had the job, and I always quote an epitaph on a tombstone in a cemetery in Tombstone, Arizona: "Here lies Jack Williams. He done his damnedest."

President TRUMAN did, indeed, do his best, and it was a best which America will for all time remain proud.

Hon. Daniel K. Inouye

OF HAWAII

Mr. President, I wish to join with my colleagues today in paying my respects to one of the truly great men in the history of our Nation, HARRY S TRUMAN. As a U.S. Senator, as Vice President, and as President of our Republic, he was a living demonstration of the enduring qualities of what he referred to as mid-America. A plain-spoken, unassuming, modest man, with impeccable honesty, integrity, strength of character, and decisiveness, HARRY S TRUMAN was admired and respected by all who knew him and millions who knew of him.

President TRUMAN tried less to ingratiate himself with people and succeeded more in earning their respect and admiration than any other political leader in memory. He became not only respected and warmly liked, but deeply loved by the American people. While political analysts predicted his overwhelming defeat, HARRY TRUMAN maintained his faith in the people and the people their faith in HARRY TRUMAN to confound the expert professional image makers, poll takers, and election prognosticators among us.

HARRY TRUMAN's eloquence resided in his simplicity and in his directness. Though a coherent and forceful man he was never superfluous with words. To him those who were less than honest were "damn liars" and he wasted few moments or words on them. You knew where you stood with HARRY TRUMAN and you also knew where he stood and what he stood for. While he was a flexible man he was not one easily swayed and he firmly adhered to his creed of "doing things right."

My most outstanding recollection of HARRY TRUMAN was his courage to commit himself to a course of action and his self-confidence in his decisions. He never built any false images of himself and yet his unassuming manner lent stature to the Office of President and to the man who utilized its potentialities to advance our national interests in a most trying and turbulent period of our history.

A man of fierce partisan loyalties, he was yet to guide the free world through the closing months of worldwide war with a bipartisan spirit toward a world of stability and peace.

When that peace was threatened, whether in the East or the West, he did not hesitate to use the power of our Nation to protect the freedom of others. The man from Independence would rise to meet any test. While he did not seek confrontations, neither did he flinch from those forced upon us as a nation or a people.

During HARRY TRUMAN's Presidency, as seldom before in history, our Nation had to face great decisions of worldwide and lasting significance. With the pressures of war and recovery from conflict always present, HARRY TRUMAN never lagged in his quest for a better life for the American people, however.

A man of humble beginnings and great achievements, he gave us self-confidence as a people even as he exhibited confidence in his own judgment and capabilities. He dared to be himself and it is for himself that we loved him and admired him.

Proud of his family, we on this day share our sense of loss with them and thank them for sharing their husband and father with us. We are all so much richer for having had him among us.

Hon. Floyd K. Haskell
OF COLORADO

Mr. President, I join Senators in paying tribute to the life and service of former President HARRY S TRUMAN, who passed away in late December.

Though I did not serve with him and though I never knew him personally, I did know him as my President. During the last years of World War II and during the turmoil of the postwar years, America needed a leader; a man who would make the tough decisions that had to be made; a man who would think of people first; a man who would work to bring peace out of the holocaust of war. America was fortunate. America had HARRY TRUMAN as President.

In these times of trouble, the abilities of President TRUMAN will again be needed. May America be so fortunate once again.

Hon. Roman L. Hruska
OF NEBRASKA

Mr. President, this Senator notes the passing of HARRY TRUMAN, 33d President of the United States, with regret. He also wishes to extend his sympathy to Mrs. Bess Truman and their daughter, Margaret Truman Daniel.

President TRUMAN did not wish to be taken to Washington for the customary ceremonies nor did he wish to be buried in Arlington Cemetery. Throughout his life President TRUMAN had a special attachment to his home State and it is proper today that he rests close to his home in Independence, Mo.

President TRUMAN described himself as a "meat and potatoes man" who was a "homegrown American farm product." Those of us who knew President TRUMAN admired the qualities that the Midwest engendered in him. He

was a competent administrator and a great President.

As President, he checked Communist expansion in Greece and Turkey. The Marshall plan put Europe on her feet. President TRUMAN became the man who protected freedom in the post war world. President Nixon has said about HARRY TRUMAN:

> Our hopes today for a generation of peace rest in large measure on the firm foundations that he laid. Recognizing the new threat to peace that had emerged from the ashes of war, he stood boldly against it with his extension of aid to Greece and Turkey in 1947—and the "Truman Doctrine" thus established was crucial to the defense of liberty in Europe and the world.

A grateful nation will long remember his Presidency and his contribution toward a generation of peace.

Hon. Quentin N. Burdick
OF NORTH DAKOTA

Mr. President, America lost a great man and a great former President when HARRY S TRUMAN, our 33d Chief Executive, died this past December.

We shall surely miss him—as a former leader of our party, and as the living embodiment of those qualities that made his years in office among the finest and proudest our great Nation has ever known. We think back to those fateful years—so long ago, yet so close—and recall the agonizing decisions that fell upon the shoulders of this brave man, this man whom some called in admiration the average-man President.

Yet there was so much about HARRY S TRUMAN that was anything but average. He overcame adversity at every turn, from the childhood affliction of poor eyesight, through the business recession of 1921, and into the rough and tumble world of politics. He was the underdog so many times; with no money for campaigning, he still managed to meet the people of Missouri and convince them he was the best man for them to send to the Senate. He confounded the professional politicians and pollsters in 1948. No, HARRY S TRUMAN was not average in his determination, in his perseverance, in his profound belief in America and its people.

HARRY S TRUMAN will surely be recorded by history as one of our greatest Presidents, a man who had tremendous impact on the course of world history and on the lives of us all.

The Board of City Commissioners of Fargo, N. Dak., adopted a resolution of condolence to the family of the late President. I ask unanimous consent that this expression of sympathy and grateful appreciation for our departed leader be included in the Record at this time.

CITY OF FARGO, N. DAK.,
January 2, 1973.

RESOLUTION OF CONDOLENCES ADOPTED—FAMILY OF THE
LATE HARRY S TRUMAN

President Lashkowitz relinquished the Chair to offer the following Resolution and move its adoption: (Vice President Markey presiding.)

Whereas, It was with profound sorrow that the Board of City Commissioners of the City of Fargo learned to the untimely demise of the 33rd President of the United States, The Honorable HARRY S TRUMAN: and

Whereas, The citizens of the City of Fargo deeply mourn the passing on of the beloved HARRY S TRUMAN as a President who commanded respect and admiration for his unparalleled leadership during the difficult dark days of the Cold War; and

Whereas, HARRY S TRUMAN was the sort of President that everyone felt a close kinship with because of his humility and decisiveness; it is these qualities of humility, decisiveness, fearlessness, courageousness, and a deep concern for the well-being of his fellow man that kindled the warm affection of the people of Fargo for HARRY S TRUMAN; and

Whereas, HARRY S TRUMAN, as a public figure and as a private citizen, set an example for Americans every-where to emulate in terms of devotion to his country and service to his fellow man; the people of Fargo join with the people of the rest of the United States and even the Nations of the world in mourning our beloved HARRY S TRUMAN; and

Whereas, HARRY S TRUMAN has earned a secure place in history as one of the true giants of this or any other era. Now, therefore, be it

Resolved, That the Board of City Commissioners, in be-half of the citizens of the City of Fargo, North Dakota, takes this opportunity and means of expressing its heart-felt condolences upon the passing on of the Late Beloved HARRY S TRUMAN and wishes to express its gratitude and admiration for the lasting contribution made not only to his nation but to the freedom and dignity to mankind gen-erally, and be it further

Resolved, That this Resolution be inscribed upon the permanent records of the proceedings of the Board and that certified copies be forwarded to the family of the Late HARRY S TRUMAN, the Truman Library, and to the North Dakota Congressional Delegation.

Hon. Edmund S. Muskie

OF MAINE

Mr. President, I am honored to join my distin-guished colleagues from Missouri in paying trib-ute to President HARRY TRUMAN, one of the truly great statesmen of our time and a man revered and liked by all Americans.

HARRY S TRUMAN was an uncomplicated man—a plain-talking, unaffected man faced with some of the most complex problems of 20th cen-tury America. He met the problems head on, de-veloping in the process a foreign policy which still shapes America's thinking abroad, and offer-ing a domestic program which formed the basis for progressive legislation in the postwar era.

TRUMAN served ably and effectively in this body for 10 years—gaining stature as a watch-dog over wastefulness in military spending. He did not seek the Vice-Presidency, and when he was nominated and then elected, he mourned:

I was getting along fine until I stuck my neck out too far and got too famous—and then they made me V.P. and now I can't do anything.

Eighty-three days later, with the death of Franklin Roosevelt, HARRY TRUMAN was Presi-dent of the United States. He said:

I felt like the moon, the stars and all the planets had fallen on me.

But although he assumed the Presidency with the barest of preparation, President TRUMAN immediately established a pattern of courage, directness of judgment, decisiveness, and self-confidence that became hallmarks of the Truman Presidency.

When Russia, our ally, became our adversary in the cold war, TRUMAN found a simple solu-tion—to make our World War II enemies our allies. In those tense, sometimes terrifying post-war days, TRUMAN made the decision to develop the hydrogen bomb, broke the Soviet blockade of Berlin, laid out the Truman doctrine to meet a Soviet threat in the Middle East, formed the North Atlantic Treaty Organization to present a solid front in Europe, and through the Marshall plan helped avoid an economic collapse in Europe.

His tough, no-nonsense approach to foreign affairs has had many critics, but the economic strength of Europe in the 1970's and the rap-prochement with Soviet Russia may have proved TRUMAN right.

TRUMAN is better known for his foreign policy decisions, but in domestic affairs he proposed ma-jor civil rights, labor, and social welfare legisla-tion, began desegregating the Armed Forces by Executive order, and committed the Federal Government to a policy of high employment and a strong economy. And while he lost most of his legislative battles, the theme he sounded was picked up again in the 1960's.

What do these ideas and accomplishments tell us about the man. He was a man of conviction, and he was willing to stand by his convictions, whatever the pressures to change them.

He demonstrated an understanding of the uses and limitations of military and political power which has scarcely been equaled since his administration. He knew the effectiveness of military strength over conquered peoples.

In addition to his major accomplishments, HARRY TRUMAN possessed qualities which commanded the admiration of his supporters and the respect of his opponents. A fairminded, straightforward, honest man, HARRY TRUMAN acted with conviction and accepted full responsibility for his actions. He added a phrase to our language—"If you can't stand the heat, get out of the kitchen." And because of this same directness and strange sense of purpose, he was "Give-'em-hell HARRY" to millions of fond Americans. Here was a man who never stood on the sidelines waiting for events to determine his decisions or actions.

He gave me good counsel when I became a candidate for the Vice-Presidency in 1968. When I asked his advice during a visit in Independence, he said, "Tell the truth." When I replied that my way of telling the truth was not the same as his, he gave me a second piece of advice, "Be yourself," he said. Since then I have always tried to follow that advice.

America and the world owe much to HARRY TRUMAN—the man who never lost touch with the man on the street and never forgot his Missouri roots. He was a great President and a strong, but compassionate man who directed America's energies into creative and constructive channels. In times of stress and anxiety he never faltered, never failed the American people. He served her well and brought honor to the office of the Presidency. He bravely led America into her new role of responsibility within the world community.

We shall all miss his quick wit, his disarming humility, and his deep and abiding faith in the intelligence of the American people. We must never forget what he stood for and loved: honesty, integrity, strength, and freedom.

When it was over, TRUMAN himself summed it up better than we can, and provided history with a most fitting epitaph. He said:

I have tried my best to give the Nation everything I had in me. There are probably a million people who could have done the job better than I did it, but I had the job, and I always quote an epitaph in a cemetery in Tombstone, Ariz.: "Here lies Jack Williams. He done his damndest."

Hon. Richard S. Schweiker
OF PENNSYLVANIA

Mr. President, I wish to join my colleagues today in tribute to the 33d President of the United States, HARRY S TRUMAN.

HARRY S TRUMAN was a man thrust suddenly into a position of world leadership during a time of grave crisis who rose to meet awesome responsibilities with distinction.

He did not seek out these responsibilities, but was always equal to the challenges that faced him. As U.S. Senator from Missouri, he was dubious about running for Vice President in President Roosevelt's last election. Only 3 months later, he became Chief Executive upon the unexpected death of President Roosevelt.

In ending World War II, setting the stage for world peace, and taking up the new cold war, President TRUMAN was faced with complex international problems that no President in American history ever had to review. He has already gone down in history as a strong President who made tough decisions. History will record that the man famous for his desk plaque, "The Buck Stops Here," did not flinch from meeting difficult new international decisions head on. The development of atomic energy, the Marshall plan, the Berlin airlift, creation of the United Nations, and the Korean war were all important developments of the Truman years in the Presidency.

Although President TRUMAN will perhaps be best known for taking the United States out of its pre-World War II isolationist position and into a position of international leadership as a major power, he also was a leader in domestic affairs as well.

He will be particularly remembered as a strong advocate of civil rights, who insisted on desegregation of the armed services, who established a Commission on Civil Rights, and who initiated many pieces of civil rights legislation and ideas that eventually became law in the 1950's and 1960's.

President TRUMAN was a significant leader. He never forsook his principles for political expediency, but he actively entered into political activities in order to accomplish positive goals he believed were for the good of all Americans, and the country.

President TRUMAN will go down in history as an important President. He will be missed.

Hon. Mark O. Hatfield
OF OREGON

Mr. President, I speak today to honor the memory of a man who rose from the owner of a small store in Missouri to serve as President of the United States during some of our most "formative" years. Others in this Chamber have noted many areas where his memory will be honored by future historians. I will not repeat what they have said, but will add only a few more comments.

Today, one of the greatest problems facing government at all levels is the general mistrust by the people of any form of government. I noted, with embarrassment, that a survey of "respected" professions ranked politicians 19th out of 20— we finished only ahead of used car salesmen. This problem of growing disenchantment with government is a critical one we face, and we must act to reverse this drift.

I call attention to this because of the unique quality possessed by HARRY TRUMAN to call shots as he saw them. People recognized this, and responded to it. It was not necessary to agree with HARRY TRUMAN, but you knew he was speaking his mind, without concealing or hiding anything.

How many times have we in this body read or heard charges that as individuals or as a group, we "waffle" on an issue—we avoid it or diffuse it; we conceal a straightforward answer in a barrage of verbiage.

HARRY TRUMAN spoke plain truths. We as a Congress must return to speaking plain truths to the people of this country. If we do not speak the truth at all levels of government—from Washington to city councils across the country, continued erosion of confidence in government will occur, and problems confronting us today will be magnified manifold.

President TRUMAN's legacy to us in Congress should be that—we will level and be honest with the people of this country. Just as the people responded to TRUMAN 25 years ago, I believe they would respond today. A renaissance of confidence

in government should be a worthy goal of all of us here today who honor TRUMAN.

In closing, I wish to point out another aspect of President TRUMAN of particular interest to me. As my colleagues are aware, I am a student of former President Herbert Hoover. My master's thesis at Stanford dealt with Hoover's labor policies and it was my extremely good fortune to get to know this great American in his later years. I have studied in some depth about his life and his Presidency.

Mr. President, soon after HARRY TRUMAN became President, he invited Herbert Hoover to the White House for consultation. TRUMAN utilized the bountiful skills of Hoover during his years as President. In this way, former President Hoover was able to contribute in many ways on a number of important projects. I always believed that President Roosevelt had followed a senseless policy in not seeking the assistance and counsel of Herbert Hoover during the years of Roosevelt's Presidency.

Hon. John V. Tunney
OF CALIFORNIA

Mr. President, "The buck stops here."

Perhaps better than any other phrase, those four words sum up the Presidential character of the 33d President of the United States, HARRY S TRUMAN.

However difficult the dilemmas, however tough the decisions, HARRY TRUMAN made them. He acted. He led.

We know that he never expected to be President. When that burden fell on him suddenly with the death of Franklin D. Roosevelt, TRUMAN shouldered it without hesitation.

If he was new to the office, he understood its great fundamental requirement—decisiveness.

HARRY TRUMAN was human. Not all his decisions were wise ones. And not all of them became part of the fabric of the Nation he served so well.

But TRUMAN battled untiringly for his beliefs. He fought for public housing, for fair employment practices, for improved social security, for civil rights. He fought for the little man.

His accomplishments in the foreign policy field were truly monumental.

It was the Truman administration that developed the historic aid program to rebuild a shattered Europe after World War II. "The most unsordid act in history," it was called by Winston Churchill.

It was the Truman administration that saw to it that America participated in the United Nations, the first successful attempt in modern times to build international cooperation among all nations—large and small.

It was the Truman administration that stood up to provocative expansionist moves in Europe after the war, including the Berlin blockade. And it was the Truman administration that mounted the incredible airlift providing food and fuel for nearly 2.5 million Berliners for almost a year.

The early years of the Truman Presidency presented crisis after crisis. And TRUMAN responded to them with courage, with compassion, with determination.

His Secretary of State, Dean Acheson, paid this tribute to the Truman response in foreign affairs:

His policies showed a sweep, a breadth of concentration and boldness of action which were new in this country's history. All of them were dangerous. All required rare capacity to decide and act. All of them were decided rightly and vigorously and followed through.

Yet, despite his accomplishments, HARRY TRUMAN was all but written off in the presidential election of 1948.

Again, HARRY TRUMAN showed his characteristic courage.

He conducted one of the most extensive, exhausting, and amazing campaigns in American history.

They said the people would not respond. But HARRY TRUMAN had faith in the people. He spoke to them in plain language. He trusted their judgment. And his faith in the people was rewarded by a stunning and impressive victory.

In the next 4 years HARRY TRUMAN worked unceasingly building the foundations for what were to become the New Frontier and the Great Society at home, and preserving the peace abroad.

Our Nation and our world are better places because of HARRY S TRUMAN. He was a giant of the 20th century.

Hon. Mike Gravel
OF ALASKA

Mr. President, when I was a student at Columbia University in New York City, I drove

a taxi cab to support myself and to pay the bills for my tuition. My college education had been interrupted by enlisting in the U.S. Army, and my family had already contributed to my earlier education. I was determined to do as much as I could to pay for the rest of my education myself.

One day in the mid-1950's, I was out in my cab looking for a fare. I was driving slowly along Central Park South, a wide avenue that has the lower end of Central Park on one side and a row of fashionable hotels and apartment houses on the other. It was a good area to look for a customer, because it was almost certain I would get a big tip.

I saw a knot of people walking slowly along the sidewalk and slowed down to see what the reason for it was. It was former President HARRY TRUMAN, taking one of his famous morning walks. He was in New York City for a visit and I remembered having seen pictures in recent newspapers of him out walking. He liked to walk along Central Park South because of the park and the variety of people he would meet.

There were no cars parked along the curb. I maneuvered my cab so that I could drive slowly along the sidewalk. When I came abreast of President TRUMAN, I noticed that he was surrounded by secret servicemen and newsmen, but that he was going out of his way to greet almost everyone he passed on the sidewalk. He would tip his hat to the ladies and have a cheery hello for everyone.

I slowed down almost to a stop, and leaned across the front seat of the taxicab, until I could put my hand and head out the front window. The secret servicemen looked at me with concern.

I waved and called out:

Good morning, Mr. President. It's good to see you.

He took a few steps over to the curb and shook my extended hand. He said:

Good morning.

And added:

Young man, you look good to me; just make something of yourself.

I thanked him and drove on. I picked up a fare in the next block. I must have told every customer I had for the next week, along with all my friends, about my meeting with President TRUMAN and what he had said to me.

After I graduated from Columbia, I drove the Alaska Highway and settled in Alaska.

A year or so ago, after becoming Alaska's U.S. Senator, I was invited to speak to a group of people in Kansas City, Mo. On the speaker's platform was the honorary mayor of Kansas City, H. Roe Bartle. He was one of HARRY TRUMAN's closest friends and one of the few people who saw him regularly.

I started talking to Mr. Bartle about Mr. TRUMAN and asked if it would be possible to visit him. He explained to me that the former President's health had deteriorated and that he seldom left his home. He was not able to have many visitors. Even when visitors did come to the house, it was for a very short period of time.

But, he said he would call "Miss Bess" and see how Mr. TRUMAN was feeling that day. He did so promptly and assured Mrs. Truman that we would only stay a short time. She said to come.

Within an hour or so, Mr. Bartle and I were at the Truman home. President TRUMAN greeted us with a smile and a twinkle in his eye. He said to me:

Yep, I'll tell you, you've been a good Senator.

Then he started to tell me how I had voted on this issue and that issue. He told me when he thought I was right and when we disagreed. I was overwhelmed that a man his age would know so much about how one Senator had voted on so many issues.

Then I told him about our meeting in New York and what he had said to me. He, of course, did not remember the chance meeting but he enjoyed the story and felt that I had done well in making something of myself. After we had left the President, I told Mr. Bartle:

I will never forget this. He was just as friendly to me when I was just a cab driver. He didn't know then that I would be the Senator from Alaska.

HARRY TRUMAN was a down-to-earth, real person. A cab driver and a U.S. Senator got the same attention and respect from him. He was interested in people and took the time to talk with them, whether it was to wish them well in the future, or to talk about their votes in the Senate.

We will miss HARRY TRUMAN. He was a great President and a great leader of this country at a crucial time in its history. He was also a master politician who won an election no one thought he could win. The reason for his success is that he never let his position change him. He was always the man who liked people, who felt their problems. He was one of us.

Hon. Robert C. Byrd
OF WEST VIRGINIA

Mr. President, I thank the senior Senator from Missouri for arranging this period for eulogies to a great American. It is one of the comforts of the human condition on those occasions when our hearts are full of sorrow, that sorrow can often be alleviated by feelings of the highest pride.

So it was when HARRY S TRUMAN laid down the burden of the years. Surely no great man who ever lived had a birthplace which more typified his personal qualities in one word than did the 33d President of the United States. When HARRY TRUMAN was born in Independence, Mo., he was born into humble circumstances, relative to the riches of those things that are worldly. But while he did not enjoy the benefits of material wealth, there were born into him qualities of heart, mind, and spirit, the worth of which far transcend the values of things of the flesh.

It is beyond the comprehension of any man to whom it has not happened, that in one tragic moment, he finds himself charged with the awesome responsibility of conducting the affairs of the most powerful nation in the world; that he assumes the mantle of a predecessor who had become a legend in his lifetime; and that he is thrust by circumstance into the role of guardian of freedom, not only of his own country, but of tens of millions of human beings in all corners of the world.

If this humble American, ill-prepared as he was for the monumental task that fell upon him, had tried and failed, history could only have been charitable. But he did not fail. Those qualities that were born into him—the qualities of heart, mind, and spirit that had sustained so many of his Missouri forebears in the difficult years after this Nation's birth—triumphed over every challenge that was placed before him.

Even in the most benevolent of circumstances, the burden of the Presidency of the United States is the heaviest burden on earth. But when that burden is thrust upon a man whose country and the world are engaged in the most disastrous war in history, it might well have been unbearable. Yet, HARRY TRUMAN not only brought his country out of that war with the highest honor; he also devoted the rest of his years in office to being the architect of a charitable peace.

Historically, the Marshall plan and the North Atlantic Treaty Organization, the genesis of the United Nations and the war against aggression in Korea will be HARRY TRUMAN's monuments. But to the millions of middle Americans, of whom he was one, his monument will always be that regardless of the heights to which he rose in the service of his country, he remained at all times, a man of the people.

I will always be thankful that HARRY TRUMAN lived long enough to see his tenure as our President praised and admired even by those who were once his severe critics. I have not the slightest doubt that when the history of the middle years of this century is written, the man from Independence, Mo., will emerge as a giant among his peers.

In this Republic, we have been fortunate throughout the 200 years of our history that in times of crisis and great travail, there has emerged upon the national scene a man of destiny whose strength, courage, capability, and patriotism have steered the ship into calm waters. HARRY S TRUMAN will go down as one of our greatest Americans, one of our greatest Presidents.

If you can talk with crowds and keep your virtue,
Or walk with Kings—nor lose the common touch."

Hon. Jacob K. Javits
OF NEW YORK

Mr. President, my memorial to the departed President TRUMAN must be intensely personal, as I served in the Congress immediately after World War II and I vividly recall his succession to President Roosevelt, his 1948 surprise electoral victory, and the ensuing postwar reconstruction years of his incumbency. This period included the era of point IV, the Greek-Turkish aid program, the Marshall plan, and the occupation of Germany, as well as the Berlin blockade and the opening of the cold war. Domestically it saw signal progress in the beginnings of racial desegregation in the Armed Forces, massive new housing programs—including the landmark Taft-Ellender-Wagner bill for public housing—to recover from the war moratorium and the GI bill for higher education and veterans' housing. President TRUMAN was extraordinarily well briefed and really magnificent as a President, especially following his election in 1948.

He had an excellent feel for foreign policy and a truly balanced appraisal, both of our future role with the Soviet Union and of the dynamics of communism as an ideology in the world. He also had an excellent grasp of Germany's prior role in the world—and of Germany's potential role in an integrated and ultimately united Europe.

I have met few men who could more thoroughly absorb the facts, get to the essence of a problem, and lock into his solution more decisively than President TRUMAN.

History is already rating him as one of our great Presidents for his initiatives in postwar reconstruction; point IV technical aid, the Greek-Turkish aid program, and the Marshall plan. The latter has often been called generous, but it was far more than that; it was astute. It recognized that the more speedily the world was rehabilitated after World War II, the more sure would be American security and American prosperity—and it worked out just that way. It was an historic example of the most beneficent great-power leadership, and President TRUMAN deserves to be forever honored for it.

Hon. George McGovern
OF SOUTH DAKOTA

Mr. President, today we pay tribute to a man who was ordinary, in the best sense of that word, and who became an extraordinary President in a difficult time.

HARRY TRUMAN was thrust into the Presidency by fate—and in that place, he affirmed anew the faith of America's people in American democracy. He was blunt and plain, a son of the Midwest frontier with the uncommon gift of commonsense.

Magnanimous in victory, he worked to rebuild nations that had been enemies and to restore the lands and economies of our wartime allies.

Courageous in a time of continuing crisis abroad, he acted decisively to do what he believed was right to protect America's vital interests.

Farsighted about the problems and potential of our society, he was a pioneer in the struggle for civil rights, the father of medicare and Federal aid to education, the spokesman of working people and the poor against the special interests.

Most of all, HARRY TRUMAN taught us that in the modern age, too, government for the people can also be government by the people.

He dismissed General MacArthur and some said how dare this ex-haberdasher fire this military genius. But HARRY TRUMAN was right—and our free system is safer because he preserved civilian supremacy over the military.

He won an election the columnists and commentators were certain he was bound to lose. In the end, he lost the pollsters, but won the people. And that was the way HARRY TRUMAN wanted it.

HARRY TRUMAN was an adornment of this democracy. He left us after a full measure of years and a lifetime of service as Senator, Vice President, President, and—the title he gave himself in retirement—the title he treasured most— Mr. Citizen. We honor him today, and Americans will remember and cherish him always, for he was one of us and among the best of us.

Hon. Bill Brock
OF TENNESSEE

Mr. President, HARRY S TRUMAN will long be remembered by those with whom he served, and by all in our land who take our governmental process seriously. In particular, he will be remembered by those who were privileged to study, watch, and appreciate his dedication and integrity.

He was a rare individual, colorful and lovable, a man of great candor, but also a man who spread his irresistible humor and good fellowship everywhere he went.

His presence will be missed, yet, there is comfort. We are a better, stronger Nation for his wisdom. We not only enjoyed the years of his leadership, but know that he, too, enjoyed being a leader. It is indeed gratifying to see a deserving man live to be a legend in his own time.

Hon. Norris Cotton
OF NEW HAMPSHIRE

Mr. President, they called the late HARRY TRUMAN "a man of the people." He was just that throughout his entire private and public career, even in the White House. What better tribute can we offer today than to reflect on the fact that this "Government of the people" was, most appropriately, led through some of its most fateful hours by this "man of the people."

When the crises of our nuclear age confronted President TRUMAN, he called upon personal strength and commonsense which were still rooted in the soil of his rural Missouri birthplace.

He walked among us, we the people. He spoke our language to the extent that his more caustic critics originally derided some of his basic terminology but then lived to learn that his plain-spoken messages had been understood and heeded. Even amid the splendor of the home of our Presidents on Pennsylvania Avenue, HARRY TRUMAN was ever the unpretentious family man with a beloved wife and daughter on whom he unashamedly doted.

All the adulation and fanfare surrounding the Presidency rarely fails to have its impact on the best of men. HARRY TRUMAN was the outstanding exception. He came out of the White House thoroughly unspoiled—the same unassuming, down-to-earth, commonsense individual he was when he entered it.

He was the first President under whom I served in the Congress, and on this day of memory I have little concern at what place in history the scholars and wise men may accord him. Instead, I shall merely note that we folks from New Hampshire count ourselves among those who will never forget and always respect a man who can speak clearly and directly, a man undaunted by the heat of the kitchen, a man prepared to take the responsibility at the end of the buckpassing.

To his wife and daughter and his many personal friends who love him we extend our deepest sympathy.

Hon. Edward M. Kennedy
OF MASSACHUSETTS

Mr. President, HARRY TRUMAN came from the heartland of this Nation, from the vast and rolling plains of Missouri that he loved so well. A great American, a great leader of his party, and a great President, HARRY TRUMAN spoke for the people and acted with the independence and determination that has characterized this Nation.

For those of us who have watched the course of events over the past two decades, it is clear today how difficult and courageous were the decisions that he made after 1945—decisions to pledge the energies of America to rebuilding Europe and Japan, decisions to forge the shield of NATO, and decisions to commit the United States to the creation of a United Nations and the promise of peace.

In public and private, he was dedicated to the same principles that he urged on others:

> To do the right thing, to do the best we could, never complain, never take advantage, don't give up, don't be afraid.

The example of President TRUMAN is one which has inspired every President since, none more than President Kennedy. On his first day in the White House, Saturday, January 21, 1961, I recall President Kennedy greeting his predecessor and the two men talking together in his office. During the years John Kennedy served in the White House he and President TRUMAN developed a warm and strong regard for one another. Every year President Kennedy would call President TRUMAN on his birthday and I remember that on one birthday, his 77th, he asked him how he retained his resilience through seven long and very hard years in the White House.

And President TRUMAN's response was, quite simply:

> Well, I'll tell you how I did it. I did just what you are doing, try to make the right decision—and then sleep at night and try and forget about it.

It was good, sound, commonsense advice, typical of the man and his philosophy of life.

HARRY TRUMAN was a forthright and honest man, and in the eyes of history, I believe he will be regarded as one of our wisest leaders.

Hon. Adlai E. Stevenson III
OF ILLINOIS

Mr. President, when I think of HARRY S TRUMAN, I think first of that unforgettable photograph of 1948—surely one of the most expressive in the history of journalism. It shows the victorious President holding aloft a copy of the Chicago Tribune which bears a banner headline:

> It's Dewey by a Landslide.

That photograph, it seems to me, was great because it told us so much about HARRY TRUMAN— about his sense of humor; his unquenchable exuberance for politics, about his fighting spirit. But it also expressed a great deal about the people who elected him: about their love for the fighting underdog—and about the sheer American cussedness that loves to confound the experts, the pollsters, the know-it-alls.

Now the man who gave us that memorable picture is dead. HARRY TRUMAN, who for so many years was a part of the American political landscape, is now a part of its political memory.

But to millions of Americans, HARRY TRUMAN is also a warmly personal memory. For he was not a President who held himself above us—he was one of us. He was not a mere symbol of the uncommon virtues of the common people—he was, in his life and personality, an embodiment of those virtues.

At the very pinnacle of political power, he saw himself simply as a citizen with a big job to do. His simplicity seemed to some Americans almost eccentric: Though he lived in the White House, he washed his own socks. Though he was burdened with urgent matters of state, he wrote his mother long, chatty letters explaining events in Washington and the world as if they were bits of homey local news.

But if HARRY TRUMAN's vision of himself was small, his vision of his job—and his performance in that job—were never small.

Some of his monuments were completed during those tumultuous years of his stewardship: He made history with a stroke of his pen when he ended racial segregation in the Armed Forces. And with that act, he launched the modern era of progress in civil rights.

Other of his monuments had to wait until long after he had gone back to Independence: Federal aid to education is one. And medicare, which he proposed almost a generation before it was written into law, is another.

A few years ago President Johnson went to Independence to sign the medicare bill and to give President and Mrs. Truman the first medicare enrollment cards. He said then,

> The American people love HARRY TRUMAN, not because he gave them hell, but because he gave them hope.

And HARRY TRUMAN answered:

> I never gave them hell. I just told the truth and they thought it was hell.

He managed this Nation's foreign policy in the turbulent years after World War II with admirably clear eyes and unfailing courage. These days, the clarity of hindsight makes it easy to minimize the real threats of the cold war—to disparage the architects of the postwar policy of containment.

Let us not reopen that debate; let us only acknowledge what is undeniable: The Truman doctrine and the Berlin airlift were expressions of HARRY TRUMAN's own great courage and his determined assessment of this country's national interest. And they succeeded.

But he was no mere cold warrior. Point Four and the Marshall plan—those historic programs of postwar reconstruction and nation building—were expressions of HARRY TRUMAN's compassion and again of his view of our national interest. They were—and are—landmarks of national goodwill and generosity. They, too, succeeded.

And it was his great blessing to live long enough to see the fruits of his efforts.

The lesson of his life is a lesson about ourselves; an object lesson in the vitality of popular government; an example of the ability of this society to yield up, from the most unremarkable origins, the most remarkable men.

"Now the Trumans" Eric Hoffer wrote a few years ago:

Are a dime a dozen in this country. You can almost close your eyes, reach over to the sidewalk, and make a man President—and he'll turn out to be a Truman. Show me any society on earth or in heaven that can supply potential leaders like that. It's breathtaking.

"Such a man," Hoffer said:

Is not a hero, but one of us, saddled with the toughest job in the world and trying to do his best. If he fails, we fail; if he succeeds, we succeed.

Because he succeeded, we are the more successful as a people. For he was one of us. Let us remember now that he was not only one of us but one of the best of us.

Hon. Edward J. Gurney
OF FLORIDA

Mr. President, in this time of tough decisions, it is most fitting to honor the memory of a man, who, as the 33d President of the United States, had to make some of the toughest decisions any man has had to make.

President HARRY S TRUMAN became a symbol for many Americans—a symbol of America's emergence as a full fledged world power. He rose from humble beginnings to the highest office in the land—in the finest American tradition. Prior to becoming President he served his country with distinction—as an Army officer, a

judge, a Senator, and, for a brief time, as Vice President. After assuming the Presidency, he served with even greater distinction in a period beset by crises.

It took a man of courage to make the decision to use the atomic bomb; it took a man of vision to implement the Marshall plan; it took a man of wisdom to check Communist aggression in Greece and Turkey and to formulate the Truman doctrine, and it took a man of strength to deal with the conflicting pressures of the Korean war—the first war ever fought under the nuclear shadow. Indeed, President TRUMAN was a man of ample courage, vision, wisdom, and strength—and the record he compiled during 7 years in the White House is testimony to that.

Historians are already writing up President TRUMAN as one of our best Presidents. Certainly, his contributions are manifold and he became recognized around the world as a stalwart in the struggle for freedom.

Some may question his judgment on this or that issue, but no one can deny that President TRUMAN was a dedicated man who loved his country and who served it well. At age 60, he did not have to accept the Vice-Presidency, knowing as he did that he was likely to become President under the most difficult of circumstances, but when duty called he responded. That is the mark of statesmanship, and from the day he took office to the day he died, President TRUMAN was every inch a statesman. His presence will be sorely missed, but his record should shine brightly in the annals of history. We can all learn from what he did.

Hon. John J. Sparkman
OF ALABAMA

Mr. President, I join Senators in their tributes to the late President HARRY S TRUMAN.

HARRY TRUMAN was a Member of the U.S. Senate when I entered Congress. I recall quite well campaigning in Missouri for President Roosevelt and the national ticket in 1940 when the then Senator TRUMAN was running for reelection. Our trails crossed from time to time during that campaign. He was reelected to the Senate, and soon thereafter he was to show his independence of thought and his insistence upon the proper conduct of all those connected with our Government.

I remember, soon after we got into World War II, meeting Senator TRUMAN in the corridors of the Capitol, when he told me that he had just introduced a resolution to provide for checking war contracts. I remember so well his typical statement, saying:

> We know that all of these dealings will be checked later. I think it would be better to check them as we go along and for us, who are friendly to the Administration, to check them ourselves in order to make certain that the war contracts are handled properly.

As chairman of the Truman committee on war contracts, he did a tremendous job for the benefit of the country and made a name for himself throughout the Nation. He became known as a man who insisted upon honesty in all dealings with the Government. It was in large measure this work of the Truman committee, under his leadership, that catapulted him into the nomination and election of Vice President.

He had very little time as Vice President to ready himself for the awesome job of President of the United States. However, he took hold while the war was still going on and made his decisions clear and firm. No President was ever called upon to make more far-reaching decisions than those that fell to his lot in the Presidency. He never hesitated; when he reached a determination as to what was right, he took that action. It was due to these decisions that the world was able to reshape itself after such a disastrous war.

HARRY TRUMAN was my friend. I respected him then and I respect his memory today as one of the most outstanding Presidents that this country has ever had.

Hon. Ernest F. Hollings
OF SOUTH CAROLINA

Mr. President, today we mourn the passing of former President HARRY S TRUMAN. I believe that when the history of the tumultuous times over which he presided is written, HARRY TRUMAN will emerge as one of America's truly great Presidents. The decisions he made have charted the course of our subsequent history, and even today we still feel the imprint of the Truman years.

It is often said that HARRY TRUMAN was not well prepared for the duties suddenly thrust upon

him on that day in April 1945, when Franklin Roosevelt died. From the standpoint of TRUMAN's not being included in all the deliberations of the Roosevelt administration, this observation is undoubtedly correct. Indeed, TRUMAN had never even heard of the atomic bomb when he became President. But from the most important standpoint, HARRY TRUMAN was singularly well-equipped for the highest office in the land. He brought to his job genuine love of country, rare courage, uncommon decisiveness, and the ability to penetrate directly to the heart of a problem. He knew and felt the aspirations of the people, because he always remained close to the people. He was one of us, and he never forgot it—even in the heady atmosphere of the Presidency. He had unstinting confidence in the American people, and that confidence was returned by the voters in 1948 when TRUMAN was reelected in spite of all the projections of the pollsters and the musings of the pundits.

HARRY TRUMAN was also a Democrat—the kind of Democrat we need to emulate today. He believed in opening wide the gates of opportunity, so that each and every American would have the chance to share the abundance of the Nation. He grasped the fundamental concerns of the people to have a job, educate their young, and care for themselves. For those who were unable to care completely for themselves, he urged compassionate care. It was TRUMAN's belief that either we all progress together, or we do not progress at all.

HARRY TRUMAN was also a devout disciple of strong national defense. He knew the importance of keeping our powder dry and of maintaining a defense establishment second to none. Nor was he afraid to face down the Soviets, as he did in Iran, Western Europe, and Asia. TRUMAN understood the importance of rebuilding both Germany and Japan, and it is thanks to the wisdom of his foresight that these two countries are now rebuilt, modernized, and members in good standing of the free world. the Marshall plan, the North Atlantic Treaty Organization, and Point Four are enduring legacies of the Truman Presidency.

Today as we look back upon that earlier period, we appreciate more than ever the directness, the candor, and the simplicity of our 33d President. He preferred to be himself and let the cards fall where they may, rather than try to alter his "image" for the benefit of the media. He spoke the truth as he saw it and was always willing to abide by the consequences. "The buck stops here," he often said in accepting the responsibilities and burdens of the Office.

Now he has been taken from us. But we are consoled by the fact that his was a long and productive life in the service of his country. Of HARRY TRUMAN it will be written that he was a credit to himself, his family, his State, his country, and to those in every part of the world who cherish the freedom and nobility of man. HARRY TRUMAN—the plain-spoken son of the soil—will long be remembered for his heritage which made America great. We shall not see his likes soon again.

Hon. Joseph R. Biden, Jr.
OF DELAWARE

Mr. President, I am not in a position to discourse at great length about former President HARRY TRUMAN. However, I wish to comment on one aspect of his Presidency that stands out in my mind.

My observations do not relate so much to matters of grave public policy—the Berlin airlift or aid to Greece and Turkey or the Taft-Hartley Act or his relations with General MacArthur—but rather to his sense of the Presidency.

Mr. TRUMAN was a visible President, a fact even more notable when one considers that television was in its fledgling state during his Presidency. By being a visible President, I mean that Mr. TRUMAN could be seen—a living, breathing human being who also happened to be President. He could be seen walking the streets of Washington or the streets of the community in which he happened to be visiting. Moreover, he was accessible to the people's surrogates, the White House press corps.

Today, unfortunately, the Presidency carries with it the trappings of monarchy and, at times, the appearance of Caesarism. Presidential entourages become larger and more dense. The panoply of presidential power becomes more ornate, at times resembling a scene from a Victor Herbert operetta. And, logically, the occupant of the Presidency—the President himself—becomes less visible, less authentic, less real, if you will.

One contrasts this with HARRY TRUMAN, showing himself to Americans. Waving, smiling, talkative, a reassurance that the Presidency was somehow, despite its exhalted status, close to the people.

Somehow, this was a better way. Perhaps some day it will return. Perhaps.

Hon. James B. Pearson
OF KANSAS

Mr. President, I want to comment on the passing of our 33d President, HARRY S TRUMAN, of Missouri.

HARRY TRUMAN was a President whose highest eulogy is written in the memory of his own people. Every American has a good word for "HARRY." Perhaps, more than other men who have achieved the highest office in the land, HARRY TRUMAN stands out as a man who lived in and loved the American political process. Not that he was too much the partisan. His sense of what was good for the Nation rarely failed him.

But in a review of his period in office, there is no suggestion that the political process, those earthy, colorful, hectic methods by which the American people choose their leaders, was beneath anyone's dignity or too dirty for an honest man to become involved in. In short, people believed in their government. A lot of the reason was HARRY TRUMAN's straight-talk and the kind of man he was.

One of the qualities we always attribute to him is decisiveness. This attribute is well documented. When HARRY made a tough decision, he did not look back in doubt—at least not for the world to see.

First, there was the awesome decision to use the atomic bomb in 1945. Then, with the Soviet Union developing nuclear weapons, there was the decision to move on to build the hydrogen bomb.

The security of Europe was threatened, and the Truman doctrine came forward to meet this threat.

The war in Korea brought a reluctant America to commit ground forces in Asia, under United Nations auspices, in order to resist an expansive Communist power there.

Perhaps the most dramatic challenge of all was the decision to remove an insubordinate General MacArthur from his post as commander of our forces in Korea.

No man wants to make such decisions. Yet they came to the desk of the President, where "the buck stops"—as TRUMAN himself put it—and, once taken, they stand as markers in history for the course of later policies and for the understanding of later times. For this understanding, we owe a lot to HARRY TRUMAN.

As one who had enormous respect for the office of the Presidency, TRUMAN with all his plainspoken, Midwestern ways, did not fail to exercise the power of the office. He did this not only in the course of making war in defense of the free world, but he also took decisive and constructive steps for peace.

Under the Truman administration, the United Nations was established, and the first proposal for the control of atomic energy, the Baruch plan, was tabled for world debate. These initiatives tend, in my view, to bring to the Truman years a balance and a true sense of human struggle. While frontiers of new destructive power were being crossed yearly, or more often, this period was not one of a headlong rush toward the exercise of raw power. It was a time when men and governments awoke to the dangers, as well as the security, which is bound up in the technological revolution brought by the development of the aircraft the rocket engine, the nuclear weapon, and the computer. In short, the mind and hand of the 20th century man combined to risk new forms of self-destruction, but they also combined to steady the world on a course of survival as well. HARRY S TRUMAN is for us the man who best brings these tendencies together in that era. And we can be grateful that his commonsense prevailed to the extent that it did.

He was not the kind of political leader, however, whose career skyrocketed him to high position in Government. As President, perhaps he could best be described as a little like any other fellow who found himself promoted to a new position, before he knew he was ready to handle it. HARRY TRUMAN became President in an atmosphere of doubt about his ability to fill the responsibilities carried so long and so jauntily by Franklin Roosevelt. As the record shows, he rose to the challenge. As a result, he represents for many a solid, human way of achieving the qualities of a national leader, a way which breeds confidence and loyalty and patience among the people who follow.

He served in a period when new governments around the world were electing "men of the people" to carry out the affairs of state. This was to be the era of the common man, a period of sharing the wealth and racial equality and consumer rights. Unfortunately, this era has struggled for a foothold ever since—though great strides have occasionally been made—and the policies which would seek to realize these goals have too often been diverted by foreign conflicts or domestic strife.

A man whose career was tuned to the welfare of the average citizen, HARRY TRUMAN was forced by events to take a great many steps which delayed or diluted the good of the common man. Yet one of his great triumphs, in my judgment, was his action to desegregate our Armed Forces. This was a step required by our Constitution and impelled by the military needs of the cold war. If we look closely, we can see that the commitment of HARRY TRUMAN led to a "fair deal" for every citizen, regardless of race or background, happily came together on occasion with his responsibilities as a President and Commander in Chief during a period of hostile world conditions. Another example of this coincidence can be found in his prompt action to recognize the newly formed State of Israel. Here was another point where his compassion for the oppressed would guide a policy step taken in the Nation's interest.

HARRY TRUMAN came from the State of Missouri, and long before he died he had the vision to bring back to Independence, to the Truman Library, the valuable collection of papers from his administration. This action, which set a precedent for three successor Presidents, reveals the acute sense of history which has come to be part of the Presidency in this period of America's rapidly changing role in the world, and of severe strains upon the institutions of American democracy.

The life and times of HARRY S TRUMAN will be the subject of study for many future historians, and I believe every Member of the Senate will agree that an understanding of this man, and of his use of the presidential powers, will be fundamental to understanding the Nation in the 20th century.

Finally, I wish to compliment the Truman family on the dignified and orderly manner in which they carried out the ceremonial duties required at President TRUMAN's death. There was a quality of restraint and humility throughout which carried one's thoughts back to the origin of the country and to the simple principle of equality. This itself was a fine tribute to a great man.

Hon. Edmund S. Muskie

OF MAINE

Mr. President, in the past month, I have received many letters expressing an outpouring of sympathy to Mrs. Truman and her family, paying tribute to the great memory of President TRUMAN. HARRY TRUMAN's courage, his boldness, his simplicity, and his vision touched the lives of millions of Americans. His loss is very keenly felt.

One of the most moving and thoughtful tributes I have received is that of Rabbi David Berent of Congregation Beth Jacob in Lewistown, Maine. Rabbi Berent expresses with eloquence and warmth the great affection in which President TRUMAN was held by the Jewish people of our country and the world. I ask unanimous consent that the tribute be printed in the Record.

ADDRESS BY RABBI DAVID BERENT OF CONGREGATION BETH JACOB FOR MEMORIAL PRAYER SERVICE FOR PRESIDENT HARRY S TRUMAN, DECEMBER 31, 1972, SAINT JOSEPH'S CHURCH, LEWISTON, MAINE

Reverend clergy, distinguished citizens, and fellow Americans: It is with great diffidence that I accepted the invitation of the Arrangements Committee to be its spokesman at this Memorial Service—all sparkling ornaments in their professions, whose tongues are far more eloquent than my poor lips to speak words or tribute in memory of the 33d President of the United States.

Millions of words have been written since HARRY S TRUMAN breathed his last on Tuesday. There is little that I can add to that which has already been said.

Mourning is often little more than official. It is seldom the portion of the famous to evoke sincere grief at their passing. In all the years of my ministry, I have seldom looked upon truer sorrow than that which was evoked by the American people when the news of HARRY S TRUMAN's passing became known.

As I recall it, when Daniel Webster died, his passing was lamented in the perfect tribute: "There is no Daniel Webster left to die." Last Tuesday morning, another Homeric figure was called to death, and America plunged into mourning might well express its sense of loss in the terms: "There is no HARRY S TRUMAN left to die." Surely in all America there survives no other figures before whom detraction long was silenced and calumny transformed into praise. Best of all, he was not a martial figure, though he steered a nation towards ending World War II. He was not an exciting personality such as were two other octogenarians at the zenith of their mighty careers—Gladstone and Clemenceau. He had none of the oratorical genius or hypnotic potency of Franklin Delano Roosevelt. But HARRY S TRUMAN was a great American, as truly as Wilson or Franklin Delano Roosevelt. One does not lightly liken any American or any human to Abraham Lincoln, but HARRY S TRUMAN had something of the simplicity and of the sheer human greatness which were Lincoln's. One might also add ruggedness, except for his

fact that HARRY S TRUMAN, with all his strength in and for the right, was one of the most gentle and gracious of human beings. As was pointed out to me by our own Mr. Democrat, Louis Jalbert, who knew HARRY S TRUMAN personally, HARRY S TRUMAN's code was simplicity, even as he was a profoundly humble human being. Throughout his life, this man from Independence, Missouri, devoted all his energies to the perpetuation of the American way of life, and was a flame in the battle against the wrong and the injustice of tyranny.

HARRY S TRUMAN will live in history as one of the elemental figures which created a new political world. How great he was as Commander-in-Chief which he inherited from Franklin Delano Roosevelt as he ended World War II, when, with heavy heart, he dropped the bomb in order to avert another "D" day on Japanese soil, which would have cost a million lives and another million maimed and/or ruined—history will determine.

When in the United States Senate, he was termed "the Senator with a conscience." HARRY S TRUMAN was not only a Senator with a conscience; but pre-eminently the conscience of the Senate. He stood out as the great apostle and servant of demoracy. No American since the day of Lincoln was more truly "of the people, by the people and for the people." He recognized and acted upon the imperatives of social-economic as well as political democracy, and sought to move his country to live by them, and in obedience to their commands. Each of the mighty battles HARRY S TRUMAN fought will abide as an inspiring memory to his fellow Americans. He was Jeffersonian in his political idealism, like Lincoln in his American simplicity, and Roosevelt in his illimitable dedication to the democratic hope of his country and of mankind at its highest. He was prophetic when he declared after his request to Congress in 1950 for economic aid to Korea was denied—when he said that had the $200 million been allocated that unfortunate war would have been averted, as indeed our tragic misadventure in Viet-Nam.

HARRY S TRUMAN championed civil-rights legislation which resulted in Senator Strom Thurmond's candidacy for the Presidency as a "Dixiecrat" in 1948. History will record, I believe, that HARRY S TRUMAN more than any President in American history thus far, equal only to the lamented John F. Kennedy, vigorously challenged the morality of racial and religious discrimination.

I cherish the memory which I have refreshed by referring to the text of an address by HARRY S TRUMAN in 1948 which he made in New York's Madison Square Garden when he said: "When the word went forth that a home for the Jewish people was to be established in Palestine, it was a matter of profound interest not only to the Jewish people but to people throughout the world. It seemed in accord with a beautiful and sacred tradition. The story of a marvelous people surged upon our mind, enriching our thought. It seemed in accord with the highest and loftiest principles of justice that this should be so." He then burst into a paragraph that still haunts one's memory:

And he closed with the words: "In the faces of this vast audience I see great anxiety, great worry and great sorrow. But I also read in your faces great purpose and great determination. Let that purpose and determination be your pillar of fire by night and your pillar of cloud by day, to lead you into possession of that which belongs to you as a people." The great audience hungering for comfort, and passionately eager for light, burst into a demonstration which, HARRY S TRUMAN told his friend Judge Rosenman, he would remember to his last day.

Indeed, there is little doubt that HARRY S TRUMAN was the most important American non-Jew in Judaism's contemporary history. Eleven minutes after the State of Israel was proclaimed by David Ben Gurion, on the 14th day of May in 1948, a few months after this stirring address, HARRY S TRUMAN personally ordered de facto recognition of the new State. TRUMAN's action served immediate notice to the nations who stood with tanks on Israel's borders.

Had TRUMAN not taken the action he did, Israel could have been destroyed within hours.

On the holiest day of the year, on Yom Kippur, the Day of Atonement, the High Priest in Jerusalem's Temple, 25 centuries ago, would read a portion from the Sacred Scroll to the people. He would conclude with these words: "Much more than I have read is written herein." I, too, have read fom the life-scroll of a truly great American and human being. More, much more, is written and will be written in the pages of our nation's history about this extraordinary, outstanding, God-blessed person. History will treat him kindly. In God he has now found ultimate repose. May the Eternal send his comforting balm to the heart of his beloved Bess, his daughter Margaret, and all his loved ones, and to all who mourn the passing of HARRY S TRUMAN. America will never forget a man equal to himself, who served in the United States Senate with character, and the Presidency with dignity and dedication. "He never sold the truth to serve the hour" nor sought less than to keep his country upon the highest level of equal law and unfailing justice.

May the memory of this great American President be constant inspiration to all people who seek the better world for which he labored.

Hon. Abraham A. Ribicoff
OF CONNECTICUT

Mr. President, the many words of tribute paid to President TRUMAN upon his passing cannot do justice to this great man. His accomplishments were so numerous and his leadership so bold that it will be up to future generations to place his Presidency in proper perspective.

As I listened to my colleagues' eulogies, each seemed to dwell on yet another display of President TRUMAN's remarkable strength of character. So many courageous decisions are associated with this great man that any brief listing is necessarily incomplete.

The Truman doctrine and the Marshall plan put Western Europe back on its economic feet and saved it from the specter of foreign domina-tion. The creation of NATO and the unification of our armed services served as the basis for our foreign and defense policies up to the present day. President TRUMAN's decision in 1948 to recognize the State of Israel was an act of great statesmanship.

Domestically President TRUMAN paved the way for many of the worthwhile social programs which we take for granted today, but which were novel in their time and bitterly opposed by powerful interests. Hospital and airport construction, expanded social security benefits, higher minimum wages, aid to education and leadership in civil rights all made up President TRUMAN's Fair Deal for the American people.

In everthing he sought to do, President TRUMAN's compassion for ordinary people and his determination to do the right thing, regardless of the consequences, guided his hand.

Those of us who had the privilege of serving in the Congress during his Presidency will always treasure our own personal recollections of HARRY TRUMAN.

I recall the 1948 election campaign when I first ran for the Congress. Along with other Connecticut Democrats, I had joined the Presidential campaign train in Springfield, Mass., on its way to Hartford where a big rally was scheduled. This was at a time when President TRUMAN was at his lowest point in the polls.

I visited with the President in his private quarters and was struck by the confidence he exuded. I questioned him about this in the light of all the dire predictions of the pollsters. President TRUMAN looked me straight in the eye and said:

Young man, you're entering the big time now. Let me tell you one thing. Once you start your campaign, forget what the polls say, and what the papers say—just listen to what the people say. That's what I've always done—and the people are telling me I'm going to win.

Needless to say, the rally in Hartford was one of the greatest expressions of support in the history of the State, and the 1948 presidential election is in the history books.

HARRY S TRUMAN, more than any other man, had confidence in himself—and in the American people. Perhaps that is why, when he passed away, so many people paused to remember all the good he had done, and so many could recall how much like all of us this great man really was.

Hon. Edward W. Brooke

OF MASSACHUSETTS

Mr. President, HARRY TRUMAN was a common man with extraordinary talent. He made no pretensions to wealth, sophistication, or power. He was a country boy who went to the city to match wits with the best of the city politicians. He would live to match wits with the world's great statesmen.

Born and raised in the lovely State of Missouri, TRUMAN gained a deep appreciation for the goals and aspirations of America's common man. Like many Americans at the time, he had to forego college because there simply was not enough money. So he educated himself. His Secretary of State, Dean Acheson, used to tell of the time that the President, responding to a query on the Middle East, lectured the startled Secretary on the very complicated history of that area, leaving the knowledgeable Mr. Acheson quite breathless over the breadth of his expertise.

After serving honorably as a captain in the First World War, TRUMAN married his childhood sweetheart, Bess, who later became known as "the Boss" around the Truman household. He sunk his life earnings into a haberdashery only to suffer the agony of the depression. Although he went bankrupt, he proudly pointed out that he paid back every creditor. Honesty would be a hallmark of his rich, amazing life.

His political career was launched with his election to be a county judge and by 1934 he was serving in the U.S. Senate. As a Senator, TRUMAN distinguished himself as an independent man, always putting the interests of the people first. He never shunned the weight of difficult decisions. He never waivered from what he thought right to do. Rarely have Americans been gifted with such a courageous man, and it was this courage that would manifest itself when HARRY TRUMAN went to the White House.

Taking the reins from a giant among Presidents, TRUMAN proved indomitable. Few men have faced decisions of such magnitude and scope; few men have met them with such verve. Analysts often single out the decision to drop the atomic bomb, and indeed, who amongst us would wish to decide such an issue? Yet, he never flinched; new to the office, he never tried to shirk the responsibility.

The atomic explosions brought an end to the war and the end of the war brought to America new problems, new complexities, new roles. The decisions were as hard as they were many: reconstruction of Europe and Japan; defense of Greece and Turkey; the building of NATO; the creation of the United Nations; the Berlin airlift; the Korean war; the dismissal of General MacArthur. Many men would buckle under such weight but not Mr. TRUMAN. "Captain HARRY"—as he loved to be called—rose to each occasion, judiciously leading us through those difficult days. Many have come to regard those days as among our Nation's finest.

And let us not forget his bold initiatives in domestic policies. As President, he put before the Congress legislative ideas which took the American public 15 years to grasp and accept. He knew in his heart that health care for our citizens and civil rights of all Americans were "the right thing." I well remember those days—days of hope, days of enthusiasm. And though it would take years for his ideals to manifest themselves, the man from Independence had broken the ground.

As I look back over the dizzying succession of events in the Truman years, I am awed by the personal stamp he left both here in America and throughout the world.

He was instrumental in restoring peace to a shattered world and dignity to a doubting mankind. He fought against injustice; for freedom. Against ignorance and deceit; for truth. He was healer in wounded times. An inspiration. A leader.

Most men would relish the thought of leaving such a legacy but it would be incomplete in Mr. TRUMAN's case. I have always felt that he was more than his many magnificent achievements, greater than his incisive decisions. I think his greatness lies in his love of life itself, his joy in action, his delight in friends. These are qualities which have been recognized throughout the ages as fundamental to a good and noble life. HARRY TRUMAN was a man to whom such marvelous traits came naturally. And in a country whose system of government is based on unbridled faith in the wisdom of the individual citizen, I think no kinder words can be said, no greater tribute paid.

If HARRY TRUMAN was anything, he was "plain folk" as he once described himself to old friends visiting the White House. A haberdasher leading America into an entirely new area of international relations. A country farm boy about whom Winston Churchill said:

> You, more than any man, have saved Western civilization.

In a time when politics is increasingly frowned upon and politicians increasingly scorned, we forget that there were men like HARRY TRUMAN who possessed a truly genuine rapport with the people. A great campaigner, he naturally drew people to him with his vibrant personality. And despite all the trappings of office, all the power and the glory, HARRY TRUMAN remained true to these people and true to their values and beliefs.

No one can measure the love Americans had for this great man, just as no words can express the true measure of his contribution to our country. But in a land so dedicated to the people, I think the words of Edward Folliard captured the essence of HARRY S TRUMAN when he described the reaction of the people to Mr. TRUMAN as the President barnstormed the continent during his stunning 1948 presidential campaign. Wrote Folliard:

> They like "HARRY", those people who have been gathering along the railroad tracks all across the continent and down the Pacific coast. They like him a lot. You can see it in their faces as they look up at him there on the rear platform of the Ferdinand Magellan, smiling and waiting for the high school band to finish "Hail to the Chief" and the "Missouri Waltz."

We will miss this man. Americans have lost a gifted servant and a treasured friend. To his lovely widow and devoted daughter, my family and I express our sincere condolences, grieving at his loss, rejoicing in his life.

Hon. Frank Church

OF IDAHO

Mr. President, on Tuesday, February 6, when Members of this body rose in tribute to the late HARRY S TRUMAN, I was in Idaho and therefore, could not participate. I would like to take this opportunity to pay tribute to one of America's finest statesmen.

From the small Missouri town of Lamar, where he was born, to the highest public office in this land, Mr. TRUMAN was the kind of citizen who makes democracy work. He was a farmer, a railroad employee, a mail clerk for a

newspaper, a bank bookkeeper, and a clothing store operator. From these humble beginnings, which molded his characteristic earthy style, HARRY TRUMAN became a U.S. Senator, a Vice President, and then the President of this Republic.

During his 10 years of service in the Senate, HARRY TRUMAN won recognition as chairman of the Special Committee To Investigate Contracts Under the National Defense Program. His alacrity saved the American taxpayer millions of dollars by exposing waste and corruption in procurement contracts. The relish and zeal with which he pursued his senatorial tasks made him most reluctant to leave the Senate. But destiny had much greater things in store for this Missourian. Three months after his election as Vice President, Franklin Roosevelt died, and HARRY S TRUMAN succeeded him as President of the United States.

History will accord our 33d President a prominent place for his contribution as President. During his first term in office, he was obliged to make some of the most difficult decisions of this century. America was still at war when HARRY TRUMAN entered the White House. But momentous occasions have often produced able and distinguished leadership. HARRY TRUMAN was no exception. In fact, the direction he gave set our national course for a generation to come.

Within his first 6 months as President, Mr. TRUMAN presented to the Congress his "Fair Deal." Out of this prescription for social reform, the Nation was to adopt housing legislation to attack urban blight. The farm program was improved, social security was expanded, and the minimum wage was raised. His Presidency brought a new sensitivity toward the Federal Government's role in the field of civil rights.

His foreign policy soon established HARRY TRUMAN as a world leader. During his era, he called upon the generous instincts of the American people in creating public support for the Marshall plan. HARRY TRUMAN secured this country's participation in the United Nations, and sought to uphold its writ with the Armed Forces of the United States in Korea.

Americans will remember HARRY TRUMAN as much for his forthright and unassuming manner as for the accomplishments of his administration. They will remember him for his honesty and commonsense, which never failed him during the turbulent times he held the helm.

Thus, while historians record the momentous decisions of the Truman era, his contemporaries are more likely to recall the HARRY TRUMAN of Lamar, the man of humility and humanity, who once led them well.

Hon. Alan Cranston
OF CALIFORNIA

Mr. President, the distinguished poet laureate of the State of California, Charles B. Garrigus, has memorialized the passing of two great Americans, HARRY S TRUMAN and Lyndon B. Johnson.

Mr. Garrigus' eloquent and heartfelt words lyrically honor the spirit and passions of two of our greatest Presidents.

I know my colleagues will want to share these panegyrics with me. Mr. President, I ask unanimous consent that they be printed at this point in the Record.

IN MEMORIAM: HARRY TRUMAN

Now by Missouri's lonely hickory hills,
A noble civil servant takes his rest.
He was an unpretentious, common man;
And yet his record ranks him with the best.

Salesman, captain, clerk and politician
Are terms that designate a simple man.
He was all of these, but so much more
That history proudly marks the course he ran.

Thrust by cruel chance into an awful task,
He ne'er complained nor wavered in his course.
His duty and his conscience were his guides;
His deep religious faith in God his force.

The common people saw themselves in him,
Saw faith and fear and doubt before the fact;
Saw anger, pride, and pleasure in the game,
Saw victory in the way he dared to act.

In centuries hence across the stage of time,
The world shall see great men pass in review—
Warriors, kings, the leaders of the earth—
Our Man from Independence walks there too.

IN MEMORIAM: LYNDON BAINES JOHNSON

Beside the Pedernales cattle low
And Texas skies are filled with starlight's glow;
The winding waters have a ghostly gleam
As if the stars were floating in the stream.
This is the land where Lyndon Johnson grew.
Here live the people Lyndon Johnson knew.
This land—this people—shaped what he would do.

Friendly, proud, ambitious in this place,
He marked the course where he would run his race.
What most he sought was exercise of power,
To furnish civil rights as each man's dower.
He believed that what American must be
Would show the world how true democracy
Could guarantee all men their dignity.

This man whom strong ambition lifted high
Became conspicuous in his country's eye.
Proud, persuasive, pompous and profane,
He drove himself and others for our gain.
He knew his trust, his faith, and his desire
Would lift him to the heights where men aspire
To work for service rather than for hire.

Long hours of stress and anguish caused by war
Weakened a heart already strained too far.
He saw so well the twilight of his day,
But walked with cheerful courage all the way.
Remember Lyndon Johnson for his cause:
That each man suffers for his neighbor's flaws;
That men find freedom in respect for laws.

Hon. Russell B. Long
OF LOUISIANA

Mr. President, HARRY S TRUMAN was a great President, a great Senator, a great judge; but, above all, he was a great American.

He led our country with wisdom and dignity for nearly 8 challenging years and the leadership he provided for the free world will be remembered by history as a credit to our country.

President TRUMAN's foreign policies did much to promote peace in the world. I am thinking especially of his initiation of the Marshall plan, his program of aid to underdeveloped countries, the creation of NATO and the birth of the United Nations, both during his administration, and his steadfastness in meeting aggression. The Truman doctrine and his defiance of Stalin's attempt to isolate Berlin point up both his courage and his foresight.

I am reminded of the observation of the eminent 19th-century preacher, Henry Ward Beecher, when he said:

Greatness lies not in being strong, but in the right use of strength.

HARRY TRUMAN was President when I first came to Washington as a U.S. Senator in 1948. I can remember well not only his courage and fortitude but also his humility. He had what we call "the common touch." Although he was the President of the United States—having achieved the highest office in our Nation and the most important position in the world—he never forgot that he was a simple man from Lamar, Mo.

The spirit of his honesty and integrity are captured in this excerpt from a letter he wrote to his daughter, Margaret.

Right must always prevail. Do not let glamor get you. There are decent, honorable people among the very rich, just as there are among the very poor. Honor knows no class. . . . Remember always to keep your balance no matter how great you may become in your own time. Your Dad will never be reckoned among the great but you can be sure he did his level best and gave all he had to his country.

President TRUMAN often said:

If you do your best, history will do the rest.

Mr. President, he did his best and his best was great. History will do him justice.

Hon. Lee Metcalf

OF MONTANA

Mr. President, accolades have been paid to ex-President TRUMAN for his courage, his forth-rightness and his inherent honesty and he has been widely praised and extolled. I concur. However, Montana's claim on HARRY TRUMAN has not been completely presented.

The story of his appearance in Butte and his inspiration the "Give 'em Hell, HARRY" shouts from the audience gave to President TRUMAN's campaign have been frequently told. Likewise, his statement at the dedication of Hungry Horse Dam in Kalispell admonishing the people to go out and look at the dam because it would be the last river and power project if the Republicans were elected was prophetic and often quoted.

But to complete the record, the Montana Historical Society in February of this year summarized the odyssey of HARRY TRUMAN in Montana. This account of his early years explains why Mr. TRUMAN as Senator, Vice President and President was especially beloved by Montanans. I ask unanimous consent that the Montana Historical Society article be printed in the Record.

ODYSSEY OF HARRY TRUMAN IN MONTANA

It is nearly 60 years ago that a 29-year-old farmer named HARRY S TRUMAN, from Grandview, Missouri came out to Glasgow, in Northeastern Montana, to register for a homestead. It was the first of six known visits which this irrepressibly "common man" was to make to Montana. Except for the 1913 trip, during which he was one of thousands, most of them nameless now, Mr. TRUMAN's visits were well publicized. Indeed, his campaign of 1948, following which he triumphed so surprisingly over Thomas E. Dewey, reached a high-water mark in Montana. Until his life ended the day after Christmas, 1972, TRUMAN himself maintained there was no doubt that his famous "Give 'em hell, HARRY" style got its start when he addressed a crowd of nearly 10,000 at Butte's Naranche Stadium on June 8, 1948.

Well known, and sometimes criticized for his flat, mid-

western delivery, President TRUMAN's remarks in Butte were anything but dull. He defended his programs and blasted the 80th ("Do Nothing") Congress. His hard-hitting, no-punches-spared style was set from then on. Moreover, Butte became one of his favorite cities, and he never forgot it.

But in September, 1913, these things were far in the future for HARRY TRUMAN. World War I, a haberdashery in Kansas City, a judgeship, the U.S. Senate, the vice presidency and the shattering death of Franklin D. Roosevelt were worlds removed from the life of a young man trying to establish a livelihood to support his younger brother and sister and someday make it possible for him to marry his childhood sweetheart, Elizabeth Wallace.

In that September of 1913, some 1,600,000 acres of the Fort Peck Indian Reservation near Glasgow were thrown open to homesteaders. To avoid the land speculators and "musclemen" land grabbers who dominated many earlier land openings, a drawing was held for the Fort Peck land.

No record remains describing young TRUMAN's thoughts as he visited the small Montana town between September 1 and 21 to register for a chance for land. Over 12,000 people registered for the 8,405 homesteads of 160 acres each.

Apparently an unsuccessful registrant, TRUMAN went back home to Grandview, where, in the same year, he bought a second-hand Stafford touring car to make it easier for him to court the golden-haired Bess, who lived in Independence.

It was over three decades later, in 1944, that he made his next visit to Montana, in behalf of Franklin D. Roosevelt, whose death soon after he began his fourth term in 1945 propelled the farm boy from Kansas to the presidency.

In 1944, Vice President TRUMAN began his love affair with Butte. He donned a hard hat and descended, along with the four reporters covering his trip, into the Leonard mine. He and this group formed the "Hard Rock Club," to which he referred many times on subsequent visits to the state. The presence of only four reporters, however, suggests the lacklustre news value of the trip.

But June, 1948, was a different story. Now TRUMAN came to Montana as President of the United States and drew an estimated 40,000 people along his parade route in Butte. This time, he was accompanied by 58 newsmen.

It was in 1948 that TRUMAN lashed out at the 80th Congress and defended himself and the policies he had begun. "They have been telling you a lot of things about HARRY TRUMAN," he said, "but the country has been pretty well run in the last three years. . . ."

President TRUMAN returned to the Big Sky Country in 1950 and again spoke in Butte, before a crowd of 6,000.

He defended U.S. government involvement in business and other areas, pointing to low cost housing and un-employment insurance, on which many miners in Butte had recently been forced to depend.

Introduced by Montana's U.S. Senator Mike Mansfield as a "man of the people," TRUMAN said his 1950 trip was not political, but was to "report to my boss—the people."

In 1952 President TRUMAN was back in Montana to set off the dynamite charge that moved the first earth for the Tiber Dam Project near Chester and later to put Hungry Horse Dam at Columbia Falls into production by throwing a switch in the Kalispell gym.

In his speech, he backed Montana democratic candidates for office, and spoke warmly for the Adlai Stevenson-John Sparkman ticket. But the Eisenhower-Nixon team won in Montana by 51,181 votes.

In 1956, HARRY TRUMAN came out of his "retirement" to again travel the campaign trail, this time for Stevenson and Estes Kefauver. He made only one speech in Montana, and requested that it be given in his favorite city. It was a nostalgic visit, a remembrance of old days and old glories. To Montana's U.S. Senators Mike Mansfield and James Murray, the former President said, "It's like old times. I'd give my right eye to be back in the Senate with you."

He told his audience, "It was in Butte where I began telling people about that do-nothing Republican Congress. You know what happened after that. The people took proper care of the Republicans when election day rolled around. . . . A lot of people were surprised at the outcome of the 1948 election. I think the same people are going to be surprised this year—because I think Stevenson and Kefauver are going to win." But they lost, and in Montana, Eisenhower and Nixon won by 38,695 votes.

HARRY S TRUMAN, with whom historians are expected to deal kindly, apparently sensed, in Montana, and especially in Butte, that people knew him for what he was, a "common man" with uncommon courage. An interesting supposition, now that he is gone, is what history might have had to say about him had he drawn a good number that day in Glasgow, Montana, nearly six decades ago.

Hon. Stuart Symington
OF MISSOURI

Mr. President, today marks the 89th birthday of the No. 1 citizen of Missouri. The U.S. Postal Service has chosen to honor the memory of the late President by issuing a stamp bearing his portrait in ceremonies at the Truman Library in Independence.

The Postmaster General, E. T. Klassen, will preside today at the ceremony, and Margaret Truman Daniel will represent the Truman family.

It is appropriate that the first issue of this 8-cent commemorative stamp again focuses attention on the library to which Mr. TRUMAN dedicated so much of his time and effort in the years following his Presidency.

As the Kansas City Star noted in an editorial shortly after his death, President TRUMAN never regarded the library as a personal monument. Quoting from his memoirs, they pointed out his hope for the library's role in advancing public knowledge of the Presidency:

I encouraged the building of the library only because it was to be a center for the study of all the Presidents and the Presidency as well as the history of the United States.

Each passing year of the past quarter century has added understanding and a deepened appreciation for Mr. TRUMAN's accomplishments. He had brought to the office of President not only the experience of administering a metropolitan county government and serving as a U.S. Senator, but a deep appreciation for the history of his country, which he had studied throughout his life.

When suddenly faced with his new responsibilities, his instinct for decisive action and sense for orderly administration promptly moved his administration to a new world role of leadership for the United States.

Upon leaving office, President TRUMAN felt a strong sense of responsibility to preserve the record of his administration, and those of other Presidents, so that those who followed him would share his appreciation for the study of the decisionmakers in our Nation's past.

The Harry S Truman Library truly is a "memorial to a man and his 8 momentous years in the White House, although, in keeping with his wishes, the scope is larger. The room devoted to the American Presidency contains some of the most important documents in the history of the Republic, dating from George Washington to the present day."

In recognition of the accomplishments of this great Missourian and President, I ask unanimous consent that the editorial, "Heritage of Truman Library," from the January 14, 1973, Kansas City Star be printed in the Record.

HERITAGE OF TRUMAN LIBRARY

Although HARRY S TRUMAN, the most distinguished citizen of Mid-America, has died, his library and museum will remain a permanent legacy to the area where the 33rd President spent a large part of his life. The names of Hyde Park, Springfield and Abilene have taken on a special significance in American history because of the Presidents who were closely associated with those communities and who were finally buried there.

Independence has the same status. From the start Mr. TRUMAN presided over every detail in the planning and construction of the library that bears his name. He never regarded it as a personal monument. In his memoirs, Mr. TRUMAN wrote: "I encouraged the building of the library only because it was to be a center for the study of all the Presidents and the presidency as well as the history of the United States."

Try as he might, Mr. TRUMAN could never completely escape the inevitable. Essentially the Truman Library is a memorial to a man and his eight momentous years in the White House, although in keeping with his wishes the scope is larger. The room devoted to the American presidency contains some of the important documents in the history of the Republic, dating from George Washington to the present day.

Mr. TRUMAN wanted to create a capsule of history in the Middle West. He saw no reason why most of the nation's treasures should be concentrated along the Atlantic shoreline in libraries, museums and public shrines that were remote to most of the people. As a result visitors can read Thomas Jefferson's letter requesting funds for the Lewis and Clark expedition. Nearby is Woodrow Wilson's proclamation of war against Germany in 1917 and the final version of Franklin Roosevelt's message to Congress Dec. 8, 1941.

The people responded as Mr. TRUMAN knew they would. From 1957, when the library opened, through Jan. 1, 1973, almost 2½ million visitors passed through the heavy glass doors to inspect the rare documents on display. Hundreds of scholars have spent thousands of hours poring over the 9,804,000 manuscript pages, the 59,619 photographs and 41,687 books stored there. Since Mr. TRUMAN's death an additional 100,000 people have visited the library and the courtyard grave.

The library keeps growing. In his will Mr. TRUMAN specified that his remaining personal papers would be deposited there permanently. The late Dean Acheson, who served as secretary of state from 1949 to 1953, made a similar provision. The Acheson papers are yet to arrive. When they do, they should bring an extra dimension to the Truman files of the same period.

Based on the experience at Springfield and Hyde Park, it is reasonable to assume that the crowds will continue to arrive in Independence into the distant future. Today there are other presidential collections in the center of the nation. But HARRY S TRUMAN's was the first. His dream and his legacy of the Truman Library put Mid-America on the historical map of the United States.

Hon. Robert C. Byrd

OF WEST VIRGINIA

Mr. President, I ask unanimous consent to have printed in the Record a tribute to former President TRUMAN by the distinguished Senator from Mississippi (Mr. Stennis).

A TRIBUTE TO FORMER PRESIDENT HARRY S TRUMAN BY SENATOR STENNIS

The people throughout the nation mourned the passing of former President HARRY S TRUMAN. He was of the people, he spoke the language of the people, and he fought for the principles that can make our nation strong.

President TRUMAN was a man of high integrity who also had tremendous personal and political courage.

He served as President during turbulent times, and it became his lot to make many difficult decisions. He made them with courage and stood with the consequences. He had to decide on the use of atomic weapons to end the war with Japan. In 1946 he had to deal with vast strikes in the railroads and mines. In 1947 he had the problem of resisting communist expansion in the Eastern Mediterranean, and he propounded the Truman Doctrine. In 1948 the Marshall plan for the recovery of Europe was brought into being. Then there was the North Atlantic Alliance, and the Berlin Airlift. In 1950 he had the decision of whether to stand in Korea, and in 1951 the question of whether or not to relieve General MacArthur. These were indeed troubled times.

President TRUMAN, however, was a man who rose to the occasion in difficult times. His experiences in life had prepared him well. He lacked many advantages in his earlier years, and had experienced adversity, including a business failure wherein he ultimately paid all his debts to the last dollar. He had learned at the county level of government to understand the people and to make sound decisions that represented the wishes of the majority of the people. His life in public service had formed his abilities.

He was a man of great strength of character and dedication, and with these qualities he combined an uncommon amount of common sense. During the time he served as President it was not always possible in the time available to be sure that all of the facts had been completely obtained and analyzed and it was sometimes necessary to proceed on the basis of assumptions, but he had a fine instinct to sense the right decision. He made sound judgments and carried them out with courage.

Mr. TRUMAN's personal characteristics served him well in office. He had an unusual amount of vitality and stamina, and this helped him to devote the necessary energy toward solving the great problems that arose successively during his tenure in office. He was a man who was very human and approachable, and who had more than his share of humility for one who held his high office. This made it easy for Americans to understand him and to place themselves in his position when he arrived at national decisions. This also enabled him to understand very thoroughly the American people, as he repeatedly demonstrated over the years, and especially in his campaign for reelection in 1948.

I have read with the utmost interest the book "HARRY S TRUMAN," written by his daughter, Mrs. Margaret Truman Daniel. It makes clear some facts that have been misunderstood by a great many people, and it is a definite contribution to history. I have written Mrs. Daniel a personal note to tell her that I think she rendered the country a splendid service in writing the book.

I think that while Mr. TRUMAN was President, and making the many decisions that were so crucial for the free world, it was not evident that in time he would be readily recognized as one of the best of our Presidents. Perhaps this was because he did not recognize this himself. He thought of himself only as a hardworking man who did the best he could. Time has proven that most of his major decisions were correct. History is proving that he was one of our great Presidents.

Mrs. Stennis and I extend every expression of condolence to Mrs. Truman, Mrs. Daniel, and other members of the family.

INDEX

Memorial Tributes in the House of Representatives of the United States

Memorial Tributes in the Senate of the United States

U.S. GOVERNMENT PRINTING OFFICE : 1973—O-98-588